Structural Change and Cooperation in the Global Economy

NEW HORIZONS IN INTERNATIONAL BUSINESS

General Editor: Peter J. Buckley
Centre for International Business,
University of Leeds (CIBUL), UK

This series is aimed at the frontiers of international business research. The study of international business is important not least because it gives researchers the opportunity to innovate in theory, technique, empirical investigation and interpretation. The area is fruitful for interdisciplinary and comparative research. This series is established as a central forum for the presentation of new ideas in international business.

Titles in the series include:

Structural Change and Cooperation in the Global Economy

Edited by
Gavin Boyd

Honorary Professor in the Political Science Department, Rutgers University, USA and Research Associate at the Centre for International Business Studies (HEC), University of Montreal, Canada

John H. Dunning

Professor of International Business, Rutgers University, USA and Professor Emeritus, University of Reading, UK

NEW HORIZONS IN INTERNATIONAL BUSINESS

Edward Elgar
Cheltenham, UK • Northampton, MA, USA

Published by
Edward Elgar Publishing Limited
Glensanda House
Montpellier Parade
Cheltenham
Glos GL50 1UA
UK

Edward Elgar Publishing, Inc.
6 Market Street
Northampton
Massachusetts 01060
USA

A catalogue record for this book
is available from the British Library

Library of Congress Cataloguing in Publication Data
Structural change and cooperation in the global economy
    edited by Gavin Boyd, John H. Dunning.
        —(New horizons in international business)
        'Revised papers from a May 1997 conference sponsored by the Center
    for Global Change and Governance and the Center for International Business
    Education and Research, Rutgers University, Newark, New Jersey'—Pref.
        1. International economic relations—Congresses.
    2. International cooperation—Congresses.
    3. Structural adjustment (Economic policy)—Congresses.
    4. Competition, International—Congresses.   I. Boyd, Gavin.
    II. Dunning, John H.   III. Series.
    HF 1352.S77   1999   98–27889
    337—dc21   CIP

    ISBN 1 85898 754 7

Printed and bound in Great Britain by Biddles Ltd, Guildford and King's Lynn

Contents

List of figures

List of tables

Notes on contributors

Alice H. Amsden is Professor of Economics in the Department of Urban Studies and Planning, Massachusetts Institute of Technology, Cambridge, Massachusetts, USA.

Gavin Boyd is Honorary Professor in the Political Science Department, Rutgers University, USA and Research Associate at the Centre for International Business Studies (HEC), University of Montreal, Canada.

Peter J. Buckley is Director of the Centre for International Business, University of Leeds, UK and editor of the series *New Horizons in International Business* for Edward Elgar Publishing.

Adriana Castro is an Economist in the International Trade Division of the World Bank, Washington DC, USA.

John H. Dunning is Professor of International Business, Rutgers University, USA and Professor Emeritus, University of Reading, UK.

J. Michael Finger is a Senior Economist in the International Trade Division of the World Bank, Washington DC, USA.

John Kirton is Associate Professor of Political Science and Acting Director of the Centre for International Studies, University of Toronto, Canada.

John de la Mothe is Professor of Public Administration in the Faculty of Administration, University of Ottawa, Canada.

Rajneesh Narula is Senior Researcher in International Business at the University of Oslo, Norway.

Terutomo Ozawa is Professor of Economics at Colorado State University, USA.

Gilles Paquet is Professor of Political Science at the University of Ottawa, Canada.

Alan M. Rugman is the Thames Water Fellow of Strategic Management at Templeton College, Oxford University, UK.

Preface

This volume comprises revised papers from a May 1997 conference sponsored by the Center for Global Change and Governance and the Center for International Business Education and Research, Rutgers University, Newark, New Jersey. The contributing authors are international political economy and business scholars whose work has focused on the evolution of structural and policy interdependencies between states and on the operations of multinational corporations which are increasing the dimensions and the complexities of those interdependencies.

A major theme in the volume is the increasing significance of national economic policies and of forms of international economic cooperation for the management of corporate strategies, and of the cross-border structural consequences of those strategies for decision makers shaping fiscal, monetary, financial, trade, industrial, foreign direct investment, and competition policies. There is a changing pattern of very extensive interactions between governments, between governments and firms, and between firms, in which the scope for corporate initiatives with structural effects is much wider than the scope for structural policies. This is the case because there has been a vast expansion of transnational production by multinational corporations, and because the management of policy mixes has remained distinctly national and has been influenced by liberal economic thinking that has stressed the efficiencies of free market forces.

A concern in the planning of the volume has been to assist understanding of the multidimensional processes of global structural change, in the hope that policy communities and corporate managements will be encouraged to cooperate for the development of greater and more balanced complementarities, especially between the industrialized states. This concern has reflected awareness of the greatly increased significance of specialized divisions of labour, in deepening global integration, and, thus, of imperatives to promote broad collaboration for full use of the potentials for those specializations, in the interests of equity and efficiency. Considerations of order and growth in the global economy have thus led to reflections on ways of concerting forms of entrepreneurship, and of linking policy communities across borders.

Hence there has been some exploration of opportunities for interactive corporate learning and policy-level learning. Planning for such learning, it has seemed clear, is a highly significant challenge for international business and economic policy institutes.

Contributors to the volume have benefited from several OECD studies of globalization and public management issues, and from UNCTAD surveys with somewhat wider coverage of those issues, as well as from specialized research literature representing the work of numerous colleagues. Most of the contributors, moreover, are grateful to each other for comments during the discussions at the May 1997 Rutgers conference.

The initial decision to sponsor that conference was taken by Professor Richard Langhorne, Director of the Center for Global Change and Governance at Rutgers Newark. We and our contributors are very grateful for the hospitality which we received, and for Richard's participation in our discussions while chairing sessions at the conference.

Interactive interdisciplinary learning was possible in the friendly atmosphere of the conference, and we hope that the results in our volume will encourage more ventures by international political economy institutes and business schools for productive dialogue between planners and decision makers at the corporate and government levels. Our views on the prospective benefits of such dialogues have become stronger since the disruptions of East Asian economies in 1997/8, as these dramatized problems in administrative–corporate partnering which obscured major achievements in the concerting of entrepreneurial energies and in cooperation between policy makers and firms.

John H. Dunning
Gavin Boyd

1. Economic cooperation: summitry, institutions and structural change

John Kirton[1]

INTRODUCTION

The international political economy of the 1990s is being transformed by several major forces. The first and most fundamental change is the collapse of the USSR, cold war and communist world, and the resulting spread of open market economies and democratic polities on a substantially global scale. Contributing to this spread is the globalization of financial markets, production networks, communications, technology and corporate strategy, with attendant disruptions of national economies and societies, and their labour and resource-ecological foundations. Market globalization in turn breeds a rapid and widespread move from the shallow integration of lowered trade and investment barriers, to deeper integration embracing the international convergence and collective management of national standards in diverse fields such as environmental, labour, and competition policy. Such movement is rapid on a regional basis in Europe and, to a degree, in the Americas and across the Asia-Pacific region. And in response to globalization, deepening integration and regionalism, has come a major intergovernmental effort to reform the world's leading multilateral economic institutions so that they might better meet the needs of the post-cold war, globalizing twenty-first century world.

At the centre of the global effort to shape these transformations stands the system of global governance constructed around the institutions of the Group of Seven (G7), the club of the seven major industrial democracies, assisted by the European Union and most recently Russia, and based on their annual summit. From Mikhail Gorbachev's request to the G7 leaders at Paris in 1989, requesting the integration of the USSR into the world economy, to the Denver 'Summit of the Eight' in June 1997, at which Russia's Boris Yeltsin participated as virtually a full member throughout, the G7 of the 1990s has been preoccupied with successfully concluding the cold war, and ensuring the peaceful, stable transition of the post-communist world into productive market democracies. Since 1989, it has continued to address its seminal core issues of macroeconomic policy, trade and investment liberaliz- ation, and north–south development and debt. However it has added the microeconomic, social and environmental issues that globalization and deeper integration are thrusting on to the international agenda. Moreover, beginning in 1994, the G7 took up the task of international institutional reform, aimed at adjusting the inherited edifice of 1945 to address the new challenges of the next century.

In the face of such far-reaching global transformations and the resulting expansion of the summit agenda, many judge the G7 to have performed poorly in the 1990s, and to offer an inadequate foundation for global governance in the future. One critique comes from those who conceive the G7's central purpose as producing large package deals, embracing macroeconomic, trade and energy policy, through which governments can optimize economic performance through direct, collec- tive intervention. From this perspective the G7 appears to be a reactive rather than preventive institution, which has over the past decade failed to produce a coordinated growth strategy, dealt poorly with the Mexican currency crisis, currency misalignments and trade tensions, mishandled Russian reform, and failed to provide additional financial resources to the developing and post-communist world (Bergsten and Henning 1996).[2]

A second critique deals with the G7's alleged failure as a summit- level institution to respond to the new political and security as well as economic challenges (Smyser 1993; Ikenberry 1993; Whyman 1995). A third bases its scepticism on doubts about representativeness and legitimacy, indicting the G7 for unfairly and unwisely excluding emerging powers, such as China, Indonesia, Brazil and dynamic Asian middlepowers. Such members, it is argued, would increase the G7's collective power, its sensitivity to and thus legitimacy with developing countries, and its effectiveness in dealing with issues where non- members' interests and resources are critical. (Commission on Global Governance 1995; ul Haq 1994; Jayarwardena 1989; Labbohm 1995). In contrast, with rare exceptions (Bayne 1995; Ionescu 1995), those who defend the institution tend to do so in prescriptive rather than empirical terms and on classic security grounds – integrating a potentially men- acing Russia – rather than for its contribution to managing the international political economy at a time of major change (Lewis 1991–92; Odum 1995).[3]

This chapter offers a different view. It argues that contemporary changes in the international economy have increased the need for, and movement towards, international economic policy cooperation on a global scale and that the G7, by virtue of its particular institutional characteristics and recent performance, is serving effectively as the centre of global governance for the new generation of issues. During the 1990s, rapidly intensifying structural and policy interdependencies are increasing the classic rationales for intergovernmental cooperation, and doing so on a broadly global, transregional rather than restricted, geographically regional basis.

The G7 is developing the institutional depth, policy breadth, and authoritative reach to direct governmental and societal response to these issues. Simultaneously, its strengthening features as a modern international concert enable it to effectively deliver the ambitious collective agreements that catalyse required change in critical areas. In particular, the G7 has produced a substantially complete, non-violent, democratic and market revolution on a virtually global basis; is maintaining an international consensus and global momentum for continuing globalization; and is serving as the primary transregional connector to manage the proliferating regional economic arrangements. In the monetary and financial field it is allowing market forces to flourish in a growing G7 and global economy, while managing the political difficulties associated with financial disruptions and currency changes, and directing a comprehensive reform of international financial institutions. In the trade and investment field it has provided the critical impetus to complete the Uruguay Round and create the World Trade Organization (WTO); it is managing trade tensions between the US and its partners in Europe, Japan and Canada, and is injecting impetus and direction into the next stage of liberalization. Finally, it is now starting to confront in a major way the new generation of structural issues, dealing with employment and social policy, labour and environmental standards, and competition, information and technology policy, that more directly affect the corporate strategy of global firms.

To develop these arguments this chapter first outlines the enhanced rationales for international economic cooperation in a globalized world of deepening integration. It then examines how they reinforce the role of the G7, rather than the new regional or old multilateral institutions, as the centre of global governance, and how the G7 has responded with the institutional depth, policy breadth, and authoritative reach on critical issues in the international economy. It finally explores the record of, and forces behind, recent G7 accomplishments in the areas of money and finance, trade and investment, and microeconomic policy.

1. RATIONALES FOR INTERNATIONAL ECONOMIC COOPERATION

There is a long-standing disagreement about the value of international economic cooperation between governments.[4] Some argue that the mere attempt at and achievement of intergovernmental coordination is undesirable, in that it sends inaccurate and confusing signals that deflect market forces from desirable trajectories, delays the needed adjustments which unencumbered markets best produce, and coordinates policies on the wrong policy targets (Feldstein 1988; Frankel 1988). From this vantage point a perceived retreat of the G7 from macroeconomic policy coordination in the 1990s, as in the early 1980s, is felt to allow the forces of globalization to operate with maximum effect.[5] Opposition to any government intervention in markets is consistent with the logic of 'negative' or 'shallow' integration, in which unilateral or collective government action to reduce border barriers to the free movement of goods, services and factors is desirable, in that it allows markets to generate specializations and economies of scale (Lawrence et al. 1996: 44; Feldstein 1988).

It has, however, long been recognized that there are several rationales for collective government intervention. The most basic is the advantages in scale, and at times speed, which accrue when trade, investment and technology liberalization is accomplished on a bilateral, regional, plurilateral and, optimally, global basis. Institutions such as the G7, which can promote global liberalization and induce the outward-looking systemic perspective among members required for such action, thus have considerable value (Bergsten and Henning 1996). Moreover, there is an additional need for markets or mechanisms which ensure against risk and operate with complete and symmetric information. More recently, with the expanding recognition that costs and comparative advantage are determined not only by relative factor endowments, technology and tastes, but also by government regulations, policies and institutions, there has arisen a rationale for international cooperation to ensure that national government actions do not produce major market distortions, and that they more broadly reflect the legitimate political process of social preference aggregation within each country.

From this flows the case for 'deeper' or 'positive' integration, and the international coordination and harmonization of policies (Lawrence et al. 1996; Esty and Geradin 1997). Such collective international action is required for a broad range of purposes: to provide global public goods and manage the global geographic commons (the deep seabed, radio spectrum, atmosphere, global species diversity); to cope with macroeconomic spillovers among the world's increasingly open and market-sensitive economies; to deal with externalities such as transborder pollution; to prevent monopoly power; to maintain inalienable or basic individual rights; and to prevent gross violations by governments of the preferences and interests of their citizens.

The major theories of international political economy offer such rationales for governments to cooperate. In regime theory's rational egoist variant, Robert Keohane points to a persistent demand for international regimes, defined, in Stephen Krasner's classic formulation, as 'sets of implicit or explicit principles, norms, rules, and decision making procedures around which actor expectations converge' (Keohane 1984; Keohane 1994; Krasner 1983). The competitiveness, uncertainty and conflicting interests that pervade world politics leads rational egoist states to demand regimes as 'nests' through which specific agreements can be efficiently arrived at in ways that compensate for market failures, establish an informal substitute for formal frameworks of liability, reduce transactions and information costs, diminish the fear of being taken advantage of in the future, and provide a common reference point for moving away from mutual aversions. Regimes arise particularly in situations of dense interdependence, where there are many important issues in a single policy area, with complex linkages and possible side-payments, and a low-cost vehicle for organizing agreements is needed. Regimes form most readily where states forgo maximizing short-term interests in the expectation of long-run gains, in ongoing relationships involving transnational interactions, share otherwise internal evaluations, intentions, and preferences, and are willing to keep commitments in difficult circumstances.

This rational egoist variant of regime theory points at its conceptual core to the value of the G7 as a deliberative forum. The G7 allows leaders, ministers and others to provide frank, face-to-face, high-quality information about national priorities, and the rationales for present and prospective action, allowing each autonomously to adjust to the most beneficial degree. It may also create personal relationships that lead to more open and intense communication during the intervals between the annual summits. As an international institution which uniquely gathers the leaders of the world's major powers together at fixed annual intervals, and one reinforced by an intense preparatory and follow-up process on a functional basis among the officials of the open democracies that compose it, the G7 is institutionally well adapted to perform these deliberative functions. Such deliberation is of particular value at times of far-reaching, rapid change, such as financial crises or panics, or major transformations, such as the transition to a post-cold war world.

In such radically novel circumstances where there is a lack of historical referents to rely on, confidence in the actions of others can be eroded by a lack of communication. The participation of G7 central bankers in the G7 Finance Ministers' forum reinforces this capacity for high-quality communication, rapid reaction and resource deployment.

A more robust rationale for international economic cooperation comes from that variant of regime theory emphasizing the value-laden, shared social purpose lying at the core of regimes. John Ruggie points to the embedded liberalism at the heart of many of the post-1945 regimes and multilateral institutions, while others note how the 1945 generation of multilateral institutions responded to the collectively understood failures of the depression and war of the 1930s, and by the onset of the cold war (Ruggie 1975; Eichengreen and Kenen 1994; Ikenberry 1996; Keohane 1994).

The core commitments to liberalized trade and controls on competitive exchange rate devaluations provided a common ideological floor under the competing perspectives bred by distinctive national experiences (such as the acute inflation suffered by Germany in the 1920s, and the depression experienced disproportionately by the United States and Canada). They were reinforced by the post-World War II consensus, as the major western victors rapidly embraced (in the case of Italy) or imposed on the vanquished (Japan and Germany) a domestic commitment to a democratic welfare state, and a social market economy with full employment as the core objective. Only when such memories fade is there an awareness of the consequential differences that exist in the structure of G7 domestic economies, notably the US market economy, British socialism, German 'ordungspolitik', and Japanese corporatism (Portes 1994).

The presence of common values points to the primacy of the directional role of the G7. Its dialogue among leaders can lead to a collective process of adaptation or formation of a new consensus, particularly in the face of more recent policy failures experienced by all. Indeed, the G7 leaders have a good record in successfully responding to the second oil shock of 1979, and initiating and concluding the second round of multilateral trade liberalization from 1986 to 1994, following the failure of the GATT system at the ministerial level in 1982 and 1988 (Kirton 1989). Intense dialogue and the creation of a new policy consensus can extend to a genuine process of learning, with leaders collectively setting new policy directions on the basis of a forward-looking epistemic consensus.

The ease with which the G7 can reach and redefine consensus is enhanced by its small membership, and by its unique character among global institutions as a club that contains only major market democ-racies.[6] Because its members are all major powers, they are better able to maintain an outward-looking systemic perspective, and a shared sense of responsibility for minimum order among the society of states. Because they are all market democracies, headed by democratically elected leaders, they are well structured to engage in both adaptive and dynamic learning. Direction-setting can emerge from the G7's deliberative function, as sharing domestic experiences over various micro-economic policies and best practices can lead to policy benchmarking, or creation of a new consensus about the desired global norm. It can further ensure the reduction of systems friction, because of greater transparency and incremental unilateral policy convergence (Ostry 1990). The directional role of the G7 is of particular value in the face of transformative processes and events (such as the Chernobyl explosion or financial market globalization) for which there are few well under-stood historical precedents. Included in this directional function is the task of socializing outsiders (beginning with Russia) into the new policy consensus.

The strongest conception of the rationale for international economic cooperation, and the role of the G7, comes from the classic formulation of Charles Kindleberger, who argues that the successful functioning of the global economy requires the provision of core public goods by governments. The core functions include creating a common unit of value for international transactions, serving as a lender of last resort, and providing liquidity to ensure the clearing of markets at times of panic (Kindleberger 1973). Such functions are at times performed by a single globally dominant power such as Britain in the nineteenth century or the United States in the post-1945 period, but can be equally per-formed in a world of less concentrated power by a small set of powerful countries acting as a K-group (Snidal 1985).

These functions constitute the core of the G7 as a decisional insti-tution, taking often far-reaching collective action to address major challenges in the world economy. Here the first function of the G7 is to serve as a crisis response mechanism, and to contain financial and economic panic by providing real resources (as a lender of last resort) and psychological reassurance. As in the October 1987 stock market crash, the G7's role is to show the world and its firms and markets that there is a group with the financial capability, willingness and concerted organizational ability to mobilize the required funds in a timely and well-tailored fashion. In an era where the US lacks the capability and credibility to perform this function unilaterally, the G7 has assumed this basic task.

The political dimension of this function is to maintain G7 members as major powers, market economies and democratic polities. Indeed, the G7 was born amidst a 'crisis of governability' caused by 'stagflation', in which a beleaguered core of liberal democracies was newly threatened by weakened monetary and trade systems, the 1973 oil shock and 1994 Indian nuclear explosion, the 1975 defeat of the US in Vietnam, and the spread of Eurocommunism across southern Europe. The central function has been to provide the financial resources to protect and where possible extend the market democratic order within its members and beyond. In both realms leadership has been necessary to reinforce or replace international regimes proven ineffective by systemic shocks or transformative change, and to form new regimes in emerging areas of ungoverned interdependence. In times of relative peace, prosperity and stability, the G7 is likely to play a less dramatic role. Under such circumstances, it is free to address the expanded tasks of international economic cooperation, beyond the provision of public goods, such as the promotion of collaborative competition policies, or mechanisms to combat electronic commercial crime.

2.   SUMMITRY: TRENDS AND ISSUES

The G7 is challenged to meet the need for an effective centre of world governance, to address problems that are increasingly global, at a time when regional institutions are collectively inadequate, developing at different rates, and operating least robustly in those areas of the world where they are most needed. The fundamental advantage of the G7, relative to other centres of transregional connection and global governance, is its particular character as a modern international concert.

Despite the rapid development of regional economic arrangements in the 1990s, regionalism is likely to remain an inadequate response to the new challenges facing the international political economy. Most basically the members of the G7 remain heavily concentrated and dependent upon trade relations with one another, rather than with regional partners of emerging economies outside. Moreover as internationalization extends to behind-the-border areas, such as foreign direct investment (FDI), where domestic policy and the operation of MNCs is most engaged, the interdependence of G7 countries with one another is increasing.

As Table 1.1 indicates, from its 1975 inception until 1990, each G7 member increased the concentration of its exports on other members. In general, whereas G7 members sent about half their exports to G7 partners in 1975 (with only Japan and Britain below the norm), by 1990 they sent about three-quarters to other members of the club (with all members sending more than 50 per cent). The increase was most dramatic for the United States, which rose from 50 to 60 per cent; for Japan which jumped from 32 to 54 per cent; and for the United Kingdom, which leapt from 45 to 74 per cent. As the case of the US illustrates, these increases are accounted for not only by proximate G7 partners, but broadly by more distant ones as well.

Table 1.1   *Intra-G7 exports, 1975–95 (as percentage of members' total exports)*

From/To	US	Japan	Germany	UK	France	Canada	Italy	EEC	Total
1975									
US	0.00	0.09	0.05	0.04	0.03	0.20	0.03	0.07	0.50
Japan	0.20	0.00	0.03	0.03	0.01	0.02	0.01	0.03	0.32
Germany	0.06	0.01	0.00	0.05	0.12	0.01	0.07	0.20	0.51
UK	0.09	0.02	0.06	0.00	0.06	0.03	0.03	0.17	0.45
France	0.04	0.01	0.16	0.06	0.00	0.01	0.09	0.16	0.54
Canada	0.62	0.06	0.02	0.05	0.01	0.00	0.01	0.03	0.80
Italy	0.07	0.01	0.19	0.05	0.13	0.01	0.00	0.09	0.53
EEC	0.18	0.06	0.34	0.08	0.13	0.02	0.05	0.00	0.86
1990									
US	0.00	0.12	0.05	0.06	0.03	0.21	0.02	0.10	0.60
Japan	0.32	0.00	0.06	0.04	0.02	0.02	0.01	0.07	0.54
Germany	0.07	0.03	0.00	0.08	0.13	0.01	0.09	0.32	0.73
UK	0.13	0.03	0.13	0.00	0.11	0.02	0.07	0.27	0.74
France	0.06	0.02	0.17	0.09	0.00	0.01	0.11	0.26	0.72
Canada	0.75	0.06	0.02	0.02	0.01	0.00	0.01	0.03	0.89
Italy	0.08	0.02	0.19	0.07	0.16	0.01	0.00	0.20	0.74
EEC	0.05	0.07	0.33	0.08	0.08	0.00	0.07	0.00	0.67
1995									
US	0.00	0.11	0.04	0.05	0.02	0.22	0.02	0.08	0.54
Japan	0.28	0.00	0.05	0.03	0.01	0.01	0.01	0.06	0.45
Germany	0.07	0.02	0.00	0.08	0.12	0.01	0.07	0.30	0.68
UK	0.12	0.02	0.12	0.00	0.09	0.01	0.05	0.28	0.70
France	0.06	0.02	0.17	0.09	0.00	0.01	0.10	0.27	0.71
Canada	0.80	0.04	0.01	0.01	0.01	0.00	0.01	0.02	0.90
Italy	0.07	0.02	0.19	0.06	0.13	0.01	0.00	0.19	0.67
EEC	0.04	0.07	0.30	0.08	0.12	0.00	0.10	0.00	0.72

Source: adapted from, IMF, *Direction of Trade Statistics*, 1979, 1996.

From 1990 to 1994 there was some decline in concentration, both overall and for each member of the G7. But the G7 focus for all countries save the EC remained at levels much higher than those of 1975. More importantly, these high levels were accompanied by a continuing opening of the largest and traditionally protected economy of the US. The US share of GDP accounted for by trade rose from 10 per cent in 1970 to 15 per cent by 1980, and 23 per cent by 1996 and is projected to rise to 34 per cent in just over a decade (USTR 1997).

More strikingly, concentration among the G7 through FDI has steadily increased into the 1990s. As Table 1.2 indicates, from the early 1980s to 1994, the stock of FDI held by G7 members abroad grew most rapidly within fellow G7 members and with a particular intensity from 1990 to 1994. By 1995 all G7 members had from 62 to 83 per cent of their FDI within the club. The increase was led by Japan, Italy, the United States, and Britain. Only France and Canada experienced a slight decline. Again the increase was broadly spread. For example, the US increased its share of FDI within each G7 country save for neighbouring Canada, with whom it was joined by the 1989 bilateral Free Trade Agreement (FTA) and 1994 North America Free Trade Agreement (NAFTA). Given the high percentage of world and G7 trade accounted for by exchanges among parts of the same firm or its affiliates, this investment concentration reinforces the need for G7 engagement with trade issues.

This investment concentration has provided a strong incentive for the G7 to add to its traditional focus on macroeconomic and trade issues the microeconomic agenda relating to FDI and the operation of multinational enterprises (MNEs). As Table 1.3 indicates, the G7 has responded with a vast expansion of its microeconomic, or macroorganizational agenda during the last summit cycle from 1988 to 1996.

Accompanying the intensifying, intra-G7 economic interdependence is a similar increase in intra-G7 contact among policy elites. This is most prominent in the case of owners and managers of multinational enterprise. But it extends naturally to their service firms in law, accounting, management consulting, insurance and other business services, and into the policy community.

This concentrating transregional interdependence and transnational contact has been reinforced by other forces that limit the scope of regionalism. At a time of slowly declining US global economic predominance, and slow growth in Germany and Japan, no regional power has the economic resources or the political freedom to singularly bear the burden of crisis response and providing public goods for the entire international system, even if the demand arises in the first instance in

*Table 1.2 Intra-G7 FDI stock, 1982–94 (as percentage of members'
total FDI stock)*

From/To	US	Japan	Germany	UK	France	Canada	Italy	EU	Total
1982									
US	0.00	0.03	0.07	0.13	0.04	0.21	0.02	0.09	0.60
Japan	0.26	0.00	0.02	NA	0.01	0.02	0.00	0.04	0.35
Germany*	0.28	0.01	0.00	0.04	0.07	0.03	0.03	0.26	0.74
UK**	0.37	0.01	0.04	0.00	0.03	0.07	0.01	0.08	0.61
France***	0.24	0.01	0.07	0.08	0.00	0.02	0.04	0.39	0.85
Canada	0.67	0.00	0.01	0.08	0.01	0.00	0.00	0.03	0.80
Italy****	0.12	0.01	0.04	0.04	0.05	0.01	0.00	0.26	0.53
1990									
US	0.00	0.12	0.05	0.06	0.03	0.21	0.02	0.10	0.60
Japan	0.32	0.00	0.06	0.04	0.02	0.02	0.01	0.07	0.54
Germany	0.07	0.03	0.00	0.08	0.13	0.01	0.09	0.32	0.73
UK	0.13	0.03	0.13	0.00	0.11	0.02	0.07	0.27	0.74
France	0.06	0.02	0.17	0.09	0.00	0.01	0.11	0.26	0.72
Canada	0.75	0.06	0.02	0.02	0.01	0.00	0.01	0.03	0.89
Italy	0.08	0.02	0.19	0.07	0.16	0.01	0.00	0.20	0.74
EEC	0.05	0.07	0.33	0.08	0.08	0.00	0.07	0.00	0.67
1994									
US	0.00	0.08	0.09	0.24	0.06	0.16	0.03	0.16	0.83
Japan	0.42	0.00	0.02	0.07	0.01	0.02	0.00	0.07	0.62
Germany	0.21	0.02	0.00	0.09	0.07	0.02	0.04	0.36	0.81
UK	0.32	0.01	0.05	0.00	0.07	0.03	0.01	0.23	0.71
France	0.20	0.00	0.06	0.10	0.00	0.01	0.04	0.37	0.78
Canada	0.52	0.03	0.02	0.10	0.01	0.00	0.01	0.06	0.75
Italy	0.09	0.02	0.06	0.08	0.10	0.01	0.00	0.40	0.75

Notes
* Data for Germany is 1983 (1982 is not available).
** Data for UK is 1984 (1982–83 is not available).
*** Data for France is 1987 (1982–86 is not available).
**** Data for Italy is 1985 (1982–84 is not available).

Source: adapted from OECD, *International Direct Investment Statistics*, Yearbook,
1993–6.

its home region. Thus in the currency crises of 1994 in Mexico and 1997
in Thailand and Southeast Asia, the United States and Japan each took
the respective lead in organizing the required support fund to ensure
global stability and prevent possible systemic risk. But each needed to
look beyond national financial reserves to mobilize support from other
major countries and international institutions.

Table 1.3   The G7's microeconomic agenda, 1988–96: most common issues in economic declarations

1. Education/vocational training	8
2. Unemployment reduction	7
3. Technological innovation	6
4. Regulatory reform	5
5. Tax reform	4
6. Social system reform	4
7. Enhanced competition strengthening	4
8. Saving and investment encouragement	4
9. Labour market flexibility	3
10. Social security flexibility	3

Source: Author's analysis of G7 communiqués.

The end of the USSR and cold war had the primary effect of expanding the system to embrace the former 'east' and 'south'. It thus multiplied the demands the international political economy bred to those of a much larger array, including failed states. A model of regional hegemony was also not possible on capability and polarity grounds. Germany in the early 1990s was unable to cope alone with post-communist Europe (beyond the special case of Eastern Germany), let alone the major demands which await in the Middle East and Africa. Japan alone is unable to provide core public goods in Asia, especially in the security domain.

Collective G7 leadership across regions has been consistently required. Although the US took the lead in responding to Iraq's invasion of Kuwait in 1990, the G7 was mobilized to secure the funds and military participation for the war. Similarly, while Germany took an early lead in providing financial assistance to the USSR in the early 1990s, by 1993 the full G7, through a special ministerial meeting in Tokyo in April, assembled a package of $43 billion to provide financial assistance to Russia. More recently, G7 members have repeatedly shown their attachment to the principle of providing financial assistance on an extraregional basis as part of a G7 club, as a means of demonstrating global solidarity, and easing the burden on their respective political systems. At the 1996 Lyon Summit, the Japanese successfully insisted that the Europeans contribute to a relief fund for the Korean peninsula, just as the Japanese had previously contributed to a similar fund for the former Yugoslavia (Kirton 1997b).

The intense interconnections within the international economy mean that shocks bred in one region are rapidly transmitted throughout the globe, and thus require a response on a fully global and preferably co-ordinated basis. The Mexican peso devaluation of 20 December, 1994 rapidly affected currency markets not only in South America but in Asia, emerging economies around the world, and even in G7 member Canada (then approaching a year in which it held a referendum that could have led to the breakup of the country). While the United States moved initially to prevent a financial collapse, or a reimposition of border financial and trade barriers, it quickly secured $1.5 billion from Canada, and an induction of substantial support from Japan. Moreover, despite initial reluctance the European G7 members eventually made a contribution through the International Monetary Fund. The global character of the basic problem was evident in the ensuing collapse of Barings Bank, which involved a failure on the part of markets and supervisory authorities in three jurisdictions and two regions (Kirton 1995a).

Regional institutions capable of performing key macroeconomic and microeconomic functions are also developing at different rates, and remain least developed where they are most needed. The European Union, as it moves towards monetary union (EMU), offers the most replete array of institutions. But while it faces relatively few remaining integration challenges, it includes mature and slow-growing economies, and is reluctant to absorb the transition economies to the east, let alone those in the Middle East or in Sub-Saharan Africa.[7] Moreover it is uncertain whether the EU will be able to manage the monetary cooperation with the USA that will be needed after the establishment of monetary union in Europe (Henning 1996).

Within the Americas, the three years since NAFTA have seen the emergence of more than 50 intergovernmental institutions, covering a wide array of functional fields, and actively mounting cooperative work programmes leading to regulatory convergence (Weintraub 1997; Kirton and Fernandez de Castro 1997). Yet the discomfort within the United States over NAFTA suggests it will not soon move towards deeper integration involving financial and other fields. Moreover the difficulties the Clinton administration faced in securing fast track authority indicates that the region will be slow to meet its declared goal of hemispheric free trade by the year 2005.

In the Asia-Pacific region, the dominant forum is that for Asia-Pacific Economic Cooperation (APEC) created in 1989. Yet its longstanding approach to expanding membership demonstrates that it is rigorously wedded to maintaining its seminal character as a transregional institution, with a balanced membership from Asia and the Americas. Its commitment to 'open regionalism' in trade liberalization further shows its global orientation. Economic and political incentives provide all its major power members, and many of its lesser members, with strong incentives to maintain this transregional embrace (Kirton 1997a). Despite the emergence of several stand-alone APEC ministerial forums for functional purposes aimed at deeper integration (trade ministers in 1990, finance ministers in 1994, environment ministers in 1994, small business in 1994, and telecommunications and transport in 1994), the high degree of diversity in such an expansive regional arena, and the prevailing approach of concerted unilateralism point to slow progress in accomplishing the shallow integration to which APEC is now committed.[8] Yet it is in Asia where the high growth countries of the future, and the systemic shocks which they breed, are concentrated.

   If the inadequacies of regionalism require an effective centre of global governance to address the challenges of deeper integration, the G7 possesses a decisive advantage over the competing United Nations–Bretton Woods system in meeting this need. The G7's character as a modern international concert, and its consequent ability to effectively deliberate, set policy directions for the global community, and reach and respect ambitious, timely and well-tailored agreements, rests on four fundamental features: concerted power (as a body containing both collective predominance of the international system and an effective equality among its members within); restricted participation; common purpose; and political control by democratically and popularly elected leaders (Kirton 1989; Kirton 1993). Moreover, during the 1990s the G7 has increased its character as a concert in the aggregate and along most of these four dimensions.

   The G7's concerted power remains pronounced. On such decisive dimensions as trends in the share of world GDP, trade, foreign exchange reserves and world private transactions, international monetary reserves and IMF quotas, the G7 retains its dominance over the international system as a whole (Bergsten and Henning 1996). Despite recent short-term rises in United States GNP and currency levels (as in 1996–97), the generally diminishing share of the USA within the club generates a greater effective equality within (Bergsten and Henning 1996; Kirton 1995b). Moreover, continuing globalization, dramatized as financial market contagion (the Tequila effect), transnational crime and money laundering, or the presence of common dangers (as in the 1986 Chernobyl nuclear explosion) widens the spread of vulnerabilities. Finally, current G7 discussion of microeconomic and social policies increases the equality among members of the club, as the national experiences of each country have a commensurate value, as negative or positive models, for the others.[9]

Since 1977 the G7 has retained its limited participation despite the many efforts to expand it.[10] It has also shown a flexibility in adjusting membership according to function, by creating a trade ministers' forum of only four members, a finance ministers' forum expanded from five to seven, and several regimes (such as the London Suppliers Group on nuclear materials and Missile Technology Control Regime) with potentials for expansion. During the 1990s the G7 has continued to ward off claimants for membership, while developing new consultative mechanisms that have increased its legitimacy and effectiveness *vis-à-vis* the developing world.[11]

With regard to the Russians, it has retained its residual capacity, as shown at Halifax 1995 and Lyon 1996 respectively, to act 'at seven' on areas such as Bosnia and terrorism, where the Russians have been accorded full membership. Moreover, despite the major concessions made by its US host to transform the 1997 meeting into the 'Denver Summit of the Eight', the forum retained its capacity to meet alone 'at seven' to discuss core macroeconomic, microeconomic and trade issues, as well as political questions (such as Russia itself and Ukraine) where the seven do not want the Russians present. Thus Denver featured a brief meeting of the seven alone during the midst of the 'Summit of the Eight' and ended without the expected announcement that the G7 as an institution would become the G8. The 1996 presence of the Russians at a post-summit lunch of the G7 with the leaders of the world's four major international economic institutions (including the WTO to which the Russians do not belong), the compression of time available for economic discussions 'at seven' at Denver, and the resulting failure at Denver to address the looming Asian currency crisis, show the costs that expanded participation and legitimacy can impose on effective action in core domains.

The G7's common principles are grounded in a membership that comprises only, and all of, the countries that are simultaneously major powers, market-oriented economies and democratic polities. Excluded have been all other claimants that have not simultaneously met these three criteria. Moreover, in keeping with the principles of a concert, the timely admission of a defeated rival, under new leadership, has increased the bands of solidarity among the members of the club, and eliminated the danger of a rival state on the outside. Russia's much enhanced participation in 1997 came only after its presidential election confirmed the basic democratic character of its political system, after a major if highly imperfect marketization of its economy, and along with the emergence of strong reformers as the dominant coalition within the government.

In addition to the commonality bred by shared attributes comes that constructed through collective political dialogue. The ideological cleavages apparent across G7 governments and parties in power at the earlier stages have been substantially reduced, with the end of the pronounced left–right divides of the Reagan–Mitterrand years.[12] Throughout the 1990s there has been a deep, enduring and widespread consensus on the core macroeconomic imperatives of fiscal consolidation and non-inflationary growth, the microeconomic advantages of deregulation and structural reform, trade and investment liberalization, and, more reluctantly, the need to manage the global commons through sustainable development and support for global conventions on climate change and biodiversity.

Despite a dissent from G7 host France at the 1996 Lyon Summit, and continuing divisions over high unemployment rates (and underlying policies) in continental Europe there emerged a reaffirmed consensus on the advantages of globalization, along with a recognition of the difficulties of social exclusion and personal insecurity it was thought to bring. This commonality is thus much deeper than the 'new consensus' grounded only in a shared belief in the impossibility of government management of globalized financial markets and the value of independent central banks (Bergsten and Henning 1996). It recognizes the need to further the shallow integration of trade and investment liberalization through reduced government intervention at the border as well as manage the global commons through increased government intervention in domestic society, and the need to cooperate on investment and domestic microeconomic and social policy.

Finally, the G7 during the 1990s has increased interaction between its democratically elected leaders.[13] John Major's initiative for summit reform in 1992 began a process of increasing the real control of leaders, by giving them more time together for genuine exchange, consensus formation and decision (Hodges 1994; Kirton 1994). The 1996 addition of the ad hoc Moscow Nuclear Safety Summit expanded the occasions on which leaders met together, while preserving the time for economic discussions at the regular G7 Summit at Lyon. The proliferation of ministerial level G7 forums in the 1990s has further increased intra-elite interactions. While the personal representatives of the leaders have recently tended to be officials in the national bureaucracies, the G7 has continued to resist the creation of a permanent Secretariat. It is the distinctive character of the G7 as leaders and cabinet-level driven, rather than bureaucratically and organizationally confined, that has provided the institution with the flexibility required to achieve success amidst the major transformations of the 1990s.[14]

The 1990s have also witnessed a substantial growth in the institutional depth of the G7. As Table 1.4 indicates, prior to 1990, the summit system was managed by the annual leaders' meeting, and on-site gatherings of the internationally-oriented finance and foreign ministers responsible for the shallow integration. The 1980s brought stand-alone ministerial forums for lowering border trade barriers (through the trade ministers' 'Quadrilateral' established in 1982), addressing macroeconomic spill-overs (the finance ministers' G7 in 1986), and managing nation-to-nation disagreements (the G7 foreign ministers' annual dinner on the eve of the opening of the United Nations General Assembly in 1984).

Table 1.4   The G7 system of institutions

Leaders:
    Annual G7 Summit, 1975–
    Ad Hoc Summits, 1985 (New York), 1996 (Moscow)

On-site ministerial forums:
    Annual Finance Ministers' Summit Site Meetings, 1975–
    Annual Foreign Ministers' Summit Site Meetings, 1975–
    Trade Ministers' Meetings, 1978, 1993, 1995

Stand-alone ministerial forums:
    Trade Ministers' Quadrilateral, 1982–
    Foreign Ministers, 1984–
    Finance Ministers, 1986–
    Environment, 1992, 1994–
    Employment, March 1994 (Detroit), April 1996 (Lille), April 1998 (Britain)
    Information, February 1995 (Brussels), May 1996 (Midrand)*
    Terrorism, December 1995 (Ottawa), July 1996 (Paris)

Ad hoc ministerial meetings:
    Russian Financial Assistance, April 1993, Tokyo
    Ukraine Financial Assistance, October 1994, Winnipeg
    Energy Ministers, Spring 1998, Russia

Note: * More than G7 members present.

The 1990s have seen two major developments. The first is the flexible proactive response to the Russian challenge through ad hoc summit and foreign and finance ministerial meetings to provide the collective good of financial assistance to Russia in 1993, financial assistance to the Ukraine in 1994, and nuclear safety in 1996. The decision at the Denver Summit to hold a meeting of G7 energy ministers in Russia in the spring of 1998 continues this process. These moves have also limited the disruption which the Russian question caused for the central G7 forum and its agenda.

The second development is the proliferation of regular forums and ad hoc meetings of ministers responsible for the deeper integration embracing domestic affairs. There is some danger that such ministerials, if poorly operated and integrated, would clutter the G7's agenda, reduce the control of leaders and divert issues from more competent international institutions (Bayne 1995: 486). Yet the ministerials also increase political-level control, expand the range of issues the G7 can deal with, intensify its pace of interaction, and give the leaders valuable instruments for preparation, implementation and compliance monitoring. The process began in 1992 with environment ministers meeting to address issues of the global commons, both in a stand-alone ministerial called by the German hosts in the spring and again in a meeting of G7 ministers on-site at the Rio United Nations Conference on Environment and Development (UNCED) to maintain the consensus required to secure US support for the Climate Change convention.[15] A further functional extension came in 1994 with a conference of employment ministers at the 'Detroit jobs summit' to compare labour market practices, an initiative followed up by France at Lille in the spring of 1996. The decision at Denver, at the initiative of Britain's new Prime Minister Tony Blair, to host a G7 employment ministers' meeting in Britain in the spring of 1998 suggests that this biennial ministerial focus on the microeconomic agenda has become routine.[16] Both 1995 and 1996 have also seen the emergence of meetings of G7 'domestic' ministers dealing with the global information society, and terrorism.[17]

This political level deepening of the G7 institutional structure has been accompanied by a plethora of often invisible, official-level G7 working groups, operating on an ad hoc or continuing basis to prepare particular issues or follow up G7 leaders' decisions. Their work has led to a major increase in transgovernmental contact among G7 members, growing in intensity and spreading across a wider range of government departments and agencies.

The recent proliferation of ministerial meetings also reveals the expanding policy breadth of the G7, as the institution rapidly takes up subjects ever more deeply embedded in domestic affairs. As Table 1.5 indicates, the Toronto Summit of 1988 began the G7's strong and sustained focus on the global commons and economy–environment spillover issues of the natural environment, and on behind-the-border microeconomic issues, including such long-term social policy issues as literacy, education and the ageing society. The subsequent years have seen an expansion of the attention devoted to such subjects, and of the number of component issues. At Denver in 1997, the list extended to embrace human cloning, and electronic commerce and crime.

Table 1.5   The G7 agenda, 1989–96*

	Summit meetings							
Issues	1989	1990	1991	1992	1993	1994	1995	1996
Macro	14	11		13	7		14	12
Micro	3	2				6	9	4
Trade	7	12	8		2		6	11
Development	13	14	12		3		7	12
Int. financial institution reform		2					4	10
Environment	32		11	2	2	6	3	
Drugs	2	6	6					
Aids	1							
Central/East Europe		15	12	18	3	11	3	5
Energy			5					
Nuclear safety				8		7	3	
Transnational organized crime						4		
Middle East			2					
Migration			1					
UN reform						3		

Note: * By number of paragraphs in communiqué per issue area.

While expanding in institutional depth and policy breadth, the G7 has maintained its authoritative reach, as a regime whose collective decisions constrain and induce compliance from its members. Compliance with the economic and energy commitments encoded in the communiqué of the G7 summit from 1975 to 1989 falls in the positive range, if rather weakly, with striking variations among members and issue areas (Von Furstenberg and Daniels 1992). The variation across members provides general support for the core realist view, as the weak (Britain, Canada) comply with international commitments whereas the strong (the United States, France) do not. This is a sharp contrast with a world in which weak and strong alike are compelled to cooperate by the compounding, multidimensional sensitivities and intervulnerabilities of intensifying interdependence.

The variation across issue areas is consistent with a world, existing prior to the 1990s, in which successful government intervention was limited to producing the shallow integration of lowered border trade barriers, and coping with the limited interdependence of energy and, to a lesser degree, macroeconomic spillovers. Compliance was highest with commitments on international trade (0.734) where government action to reduce border barriers was central, and in energy (0.660) where physical and economic interdependencies and security threats in the post-1973 and post-1979 periods were most intense and visible. Far more modest was compliance with commitments involving macroeconomic management: real GNP growth (0.397), inflation multicountry (0.266), aid and schedules (0.265), fiscal adjustments (0.259), demand composition (0.233), interest rate (0.221), and inflation rate (0.221). In contrast, foreign exchange rate compliance (–0.700) was sharply negative indicating that governments in the year following the summit acted to produce or achieve an exchange value for their currency almost entirely the opposite of that collectively prescribed at the summit. The era of globalization, conceived narrowly as governments unwilling and unable to collectively act against global financial markets to affect the value of their currencies, thus appears to have arrived long before the 'new consensus' of the 1990s took hold.

The more limited evidence available from the 1990s does suggest that in the area of environment and development, and the issues of the global commons and redistribution embedded in them, the record of compliance by G7 members has increased (Kokotsis and Kirton 1997). Moreover, compliance with the 19 key commitments of the 1996 Lyon Summit, across the full array of economic, global and political issues, show a clear rise in overall compliance from the levels of 1975–89 in economics and energy (G7 Research Group 1997). Important to its success in inducing compliance is the intensifying transgovernmental network among G7 officials, grounded in centres within national bureaucracies focused on G7 cooperation and implementation (Kokotsis and Kirton 1997).

This expanding policy breadth and authoritative reach in the 1990s has come as the G7 has generated ambitious, timely and well-tailored agreements on priority issues, and across the broad array of issue areas that constitute its continuing and expanded agenda. The 1996 Lyon communiqué encodes a large number and broad array of concrete 'commitments', which are central to the G7's role as a decisional forum.[18] For example, in the 'global commons' domain of biodiversity and climate change, the G7 summits from 1988 to 1995 generated 15 and 34 commitments respectively, with the annual number rising sharply from zero in 1988 to a peak of 13 in 1992, then a slow fall to a level of five each year from 1993 to 1995. By comparison, in the older and redistributional if much narrower domain of developing country debt, the summits from 1988 to 1995 generated 13 commitments, with activity peaking in 1990–92 (Kokotsis and Kirton 1997).

The success of the G7 in catalysing collective action in the 1990s is even more apparent if one moves beyond its decisional role to include its directional and deliberative functions. A conception of the G7 as a modern global concert, performing the core functions of stability maintenance through ongoing communication, consensus formation and crisis response, suggests that the institution has been highly successful in shaping the post-cold war, rapidly globalizing system of the 1990s. The systemic changes of the 1990s were greater than those which challenged the industrial world and broader international community in the early 1970s and early 1980s. Yet in sharp contrast to the stagflation and 'crisis of governability' of the early 1970s, and the deep recession, immobilized trade liberalization, rise of Eurocommunism and debt crisis of the early 1980s, the G7 has presided over, shaped and sustained an OECD and global economy with much strength.[19] It has substantially accomplished its central objectives of inflation reduction, fiscal consolidation and trade expansion,[20] while maintaining historically above-average levels of growth and employment (see Tables 1.6 and 1.7).[21] It has done so largely by avoiding coordinated interventions aimed at macroeconomic fine tuning, in favour of defending and enlarging the policy framework within which transnational market forces can operate and within which modern microeconomic and social policy adjustments can be shared.

In particular, during the 1990s the G7 can be credited with five major achievements: extending the democratic and market revolution; reinforcing the process of liberalization and globalization; successfully responding to policy and market financial crises; catalysing international economic institutional reform, and engendering microeconomic and social policy reform.

In the broadest terms the G7 has extended the global democratic and market revolution through adroit and adequate provision of financial assistance and the encouragement of political participation with Russia,

Table 1.6   Real GDP of G7 countries, 1970–98 (percentage changes from previous period)

	US	Japan	Germany	France	Italy	UK	Canada	EU
Average								
1970–79	3.5	4.6	2.9	3.5	3.6	2.4	4.9	3.2
1980	0.3	2.8	1.0	1.6	3.5	(2.2)	1.5	1.4
1981	2.5	3.2	0.1	1.2	0.5	(1.3)	3.7	0.1
1982	2.1	3.1	(0.9)	2.5	0.5	1.7	(3.2)	0.9
1983	4.0	2.3	1.8	0.7	1.2	3.7	3.2	1.7
1984	6.8	3.9	2.8	1.3	2.6	2.3	6.3	2.3
1985	3.7	4.4	2.0	1.9	2.8	3.8	4.8	2.6
1986	3.0	2.9	2.3	2.5	2.8	4.3	3.3	2.8
1987	2.9	4.2	1.5	2.3	3.1	4.8	4.2	2.9
1988	3.8	6.2	3.7	4.5	3.9	5.0	5.0	4.2
1989	3.4	4.8	3.6	4.3	2.9	2.2	2.4	3.5
1990	1.3	5.1	5.7	2.5	2.2	0.4	(0.2)	3.0
1991	1.0	4.0	5.0	0.8	1.1	(2.0)	(1.8)	1.5
1992	2.7	1.1	2.2	1.2	0.6	(0.5)	0.8	0.9
1993	2.3	0.1	(1.1)	(1.3)	(1.2)	2.1	2.2	(0.5)
1994	3.5	0.5	2.9	2.8	2.1	3.8	4.1	2.9
1995	2.0	0.9	1.9	2.2	3.0	2.4	2.3	2.5
1996*	2.4	3.6	1.1	1.3	0.8	2.4	1.5	1.6
1997*	2.2	1.6	2.2	2.5	1.2	3.3	3.3	2.4
1998*	2.0	3.7	2.6	2.6	2.1	3.0	3.3	2.7

Note: * Estimates and projections.

Source: OECD, *Economic Outlook*.

the management of relations with other post-communist societies such as Ukraine, and deterring threats from still closed polities such as Iraq, North Korea and China. While all this has preoccupied the G7 during the 1990s, allowing less time to focus on macroeconomic and exchange rate management, the democratic-market revolution has provided a stronger foundation for globalization in finance, trade and investment. Indeed, the task of reconstructing a consensus to replace that created by the original cold war and partly reactivated by the new cold war of the 1980s, and to do so in an era when new security threats offer few galvanizing clear and present dangers, has been a formidable accomplishment. It is all the more remarkable, given the major differences in national interest among G7 members *vis-à-vis* Russia, Japan

Table 1.7   Unemployment rates, civilian labour force basis, approximating US concepts, G7 countries, seasonally adjusted, 1975–97

	US	Japan	Germany	France	Italy	UK	Canada
1975	8.5	1.9	3.4	4.2	3.4	4.6	6.9
1976	7.7	2.0	3.4	4.6	3.9	5.9	7.2
1977	7.1	2.0	3.4	5.2	4.1	6.4	8.1
1978	6.1	2.3	3.3	5.4	4.1	6.3	8.4
1979	5.8	2.1	2.9	6.1	4.4	5.4	7.5
1980	7.1	2.0	2.8	6.5	4.4	7.0	7.5
1981	7.6	2.2	4.0	7.6	4.9	10.5	7.6
1982	9.7	2.4	5.6	8.3	5.4	11.3	11.0
1983	9.6	2.7	6.9*	8.6	5.9	11.8	11.9
1984	7.5	2.8	7.1	10.0	5.9	11.8	11.3
1985	7.2	2.6	7.2	10.5	6.0	11.2	10.5
1986	7.0	2.8	6.6	10.6	7.5*	11.2	9.6
1987	6.2	2.9	6.3	10.8	7.9	10.3	8.9
1988	5.5	2.5	6.3	10.3	7.9	8.6	7.8
1989	5.3	2.3	5.7	9.6	7.8	7.3	7.5
1990	5.6*	2.1	5.0	9.1	7.0	7.0	8.1
1991	6.8	2.1	4.3†	9.6	6.9*	8.9	10.4
1992	7.5	2.2	4.6†	10.4*	7.3†	10.1	11.3
1993	6.9	2.5	5.7†	11.8	10.2*†	10.5	11.2
1994	6.1*	2.9	6.5†	12.3	11.3†	9.6†	10.4
1995	5.6	3.2	6.5†	11.7	12.0†	8.8†	9.5
1996	5.4	3.4	7.2†	12.5†	12.1†	8.3†	9.7
1997	5.3	NA	NA	NA	12.3	7.5	9.6

Notes: * Break in Series. US (1990, 1994), France (1992), Germany (1983), Italy (1986, 1991, 1993). These breaks are reflective of changes in methods of calculations.
† Preliminary.

Source: Bureaus of Labor Statistics, US Department of Labor, May 1997.

(part of whose territory continues to be occupied by Russia) and a Germany eager to accommodate Russia for fear of the direct negative impacts a large and unstable neighbour can bring.

3. INSTITUTIONAL DEVELOPMENT FOR MONETARY AND FINANCIAL COOPERATION

In the realm of monetary and financial cooperation, the G7 in the 1990s has made three major contributions. It has maintained the 'globaliz-ation' consensus in favour of barrier-free transborder monetary flows and freely floating exchange rates, despite the concerns of some about the volatility, misalignments and social instability the regime has caused. Second, its members acted with adequate effectiveness in the 1994 Mexican peso crisis and 1997 Thai baht devaluation to limit contagious panic. And third, it translated the fiftieth anniversary sentiment in favour of international financial institution reform into an action agenda sufficient to meet the new challenges of the present era.

Two challenges lie ahead. The G7 has yet fully to address the future regionalization of finance in the form of the EMU and the emergence of regional forums in APEC (where finance ministers have met annually since March 1994) and through the Asia-Pacific A6 or within NAFTA (where finance ministers met in April 1994, prior to the peso crisis, and continue doing so annually, usually on the margins of IMF meetings).[22] Moreover, especially in the wake of the summer 1997 Asian currency crisis, it faces the task of defining a new global regime for international capital flows, complete with rules for the management of domestic banking and financial systems.

The G7 has played a more restricted role in exchange rate and monetary-financial management in the 1990s, relative to its active con-certed intervention in the Plaza and Louvre accords of the 1980s. This reflects less a consensus among G7 members that they are impotent in the face of globalized financial markets demanding autonomous central bankers, than a shared view that the degree of ad hoc coordinated intervention they have undertaken is appropriate for the degree of volatility they have faced, to exchange rate realignments that have largely reflected underlying economic conditions, and for a process and pace of financial globalization that has been desired and economically and politically sustainable among members.[23] Relative to earlier periods, and with the exception of European regional instability in 1992, there has been little volatility among G7 currencies. The major moments of concern have been caused by President Clinton's public comments about the US dollar on the eve of the 1994 Naples Summit, and the decline of the Canadian dollar amidst the national unity referendum of 1995 (Bergsten and Henning 1996: 50).

Only recently have changes in exchange rates among the big three currencies (the US, Japan and Germany) approached the magnitude of the shifts experienced with the soaring superdollar in the 1980s. Such realignments remain consistent with a US economy in the sixth year of a vibrant non-inflationary expansion, and a Japan and Germany experiencing much slower growth. Although French President Jacques Chirac, as host of the G7 in 1996, displayed some sympathy for a 'Tobin tax'-like instrument to impede international financial flows, and received some initial support from Canadian Prime Minister Jean Chretien, there was little support for such a move on the part of the big three. Chirac's determination proved no stronger nor effective than that his French predecessors traditionally displayed for greater fixity in exchange rates. Nor were Chirac's anxieties about globalization prominently reflected in the Lyon communiqué.[24] There has thus been little real or perceived need and enthusiasm to move towards fixed exchange rates, arrangements for targets and indicators, or Plaza–Louvre-like accords (Bretton Woods Commission 1994; Williamson and Miller 1987; Bergsten and Henning 1996).

The one real threat to the financial system – the Mexican peso crisis of 20 December 1994 and the subsequent collapse of Barings Bank – showed the effectiveness of a US-led ad hoc response, reinforced by a NAFTA, APEC and G7-bred sense of solidarity. This contained the immediate crisis, rapidly restored Mexico to strong economic growth, and catalysed a preventative, and thus far successful, G7-led process of international institutional reform.[25]

The programme of international financial institutional reform defined at the G7 Finance Ministers' meeting in February 1995 dealt with the capacity of the system to respond to shocks, resource allocation and adequacy, policy direction and conditionality, and organizational management and governance. Due largely to G7 dominance of the international financial system and the IMF, this reform programme was substantially implemented within two years. A new process of surveillance, early warning and frank dialogue succeeded in the timely deterrence of bad policies by several smaller countries. The creation, through a flexible formula, of the New Arrangements to Borrow (NAB) effectively doubled the financial resources that could speedily be deployed in a crisis, and brought the emerging financial powers, largely in Asia, into the regime.[26] Moreover, the revolt at the 1994 IMF meeting in Madrid, in which developing country members of the IMF rejected a G7 consensus to increase the allocation of SDRs, soon eroded. Led by the G7, the IMF agreed at its September 1997 Hong Kong meeting to double its allocation of SDRs (thereby adding US$29 million to the globe's capital base) and to increase its members' quotas by 45 per cent.[27] IMF procedures have been adjusted to ensure enhanced respect for the practice of sustainable development. Issues of inter-institutional communication and cooperation, as well as overlap and duplication, have begun to be addressed.

At present, the largest challenge to the international financial system, and the institutions that manage it, flows from the deepening regionaliz-ation of monetary integration, prominently in Europe, but in nascent form in the Asia-Pacific and NAFTA regions. The advent of the EMU, and attempts by three (and perhaps all) of the European big four to meet their Maastricht targets, reduces their flexibility to engage in outward-looking, systemically-oriented G7 efforts at policy coordination in the coming years.

Institutionally, the prospect of EMU as an accomplished reality, with a European Central Bank, suggests the G7 may be replaced by a G3, with Canada and perhaps Britain excluded. It will at least face the added demand for macroeconomic coordination in a world where responsibility for monetary policy resides uncertainly within three or four of the G7's eight members (with the EU), and that for fiscal policy continues to reside within seven (de Silguy 1997).[28] In the shorter term, the transition will cause monetary instability which will require strength-ened G7 cooperation for its management (Henning 1996). Across the Pacific, the G7 confronts the APEC Finance Ministers' forum, and most recently an A6, with the potential to serve as a mechanism for managing the US–Japanese exchange rate and monetary relationship. Within North America, the ministerial-level North American Financial Group provides a forum to deal with the financial relationship of the United States with its two largest trading partners. Together these developments may lead to a process of competitive regionalization that could both threaten the stability of the global financial system, and underscore the potential role of the G7 as a transregional connector.

4. INSTITUTIONAL DEVELOPMENT FOR TRADE AND INVESTMENT COOPERATION

In the area of trade and investment cooperation, the market environ-ment faced by the world's international institutions is relatively benign. Steady gains in world trade have brought benefits to most major powers, and politically consequential disruptions to relatively few.[29] The primary threat, flowing from the end of the cold war, is a decline in the consensus of embedded liberalism, as a new emphasis on competitiveness, strategic trade policy and reciprocity and fairness, has arisen in the United States and other leading trading powers (Higgott 1996). Related to it is the regionalization trend, including commitments to accept or develop full-fledged free trade areas in North America, the full western hemisphere, and the Asia-Pacific region, with the United States and Canada at the common hub.

In the face of such severe challenges the G7 and its trade ministers' Quadrilateral have served as an effective transregional forum for catalysing movement towards multilateral trade liberalization, managing major bilateral trade tensions between the major powers, and ensuring continuing liberalization on a sectoral basis. The major challenges are to develop regimes to link trade with the environmental, labour, government procurement and other policy arenas exposed in deep integration, to stimulate and shape a multilateral regime for the investment that is now so integrally linked with trade, and to guide the future institutional development and membership of the WTO.[30]

In its preparatory process and through the on-site presence of trade ministers, the 1993 Tokyo G7 Summit produced the market access agreement that provided the decisive political impetus to conclude the Uruguay Round of the General Agreement on Tariffs and Trade (GATT) and the General Agreement on Trade in Services (GATS). More broadly, the G7 leaders were vital in maintaining momentum during the early 1990's recession, calling for a strong dispute settlement mechanism, and creating a WTO (Bayne 1995: 495). At Halifax in 1995 and Lyon in 1996 respectively, the G7 provided the solidarity required to contain the bilateral tensions, bred by US assertiveness and extraterritoriality, over US–Japanese automotive trade, and the Helms–Burton Act. Subsequently, its Quadrilateral, assisted by regional institutions such as APEC, has helped overcome America's unilateral defection to secure sectoral liberalization in information technology, telecommunications, and possibly financial services.

The first of the future challenges faced by the international trading system and the G7 as its central manager is to define regimes for the 'new' deeper integration issues of trade and environment, trade and labour, and bribery and corruption (as a component of transparency in government procurement). Progress is likely to come more rapidly in the area of environment. This is despite the prevailing tendency to treat the subject as a question of divisive north–south redistribution, and the limited progress the G7 has made to date in setting directions and defining principles for the nascent regime. Unlike labour standards, the environment is at its core an issue of the global commons. Transborder ecological spillovers are more pervasive, visible and harmful than those of labour migration. There are robust regional regimes, most notably in Europe and North America, to serve as a model and stimulus

(Rugman, Kirton and Soloway 1997). And there is no single multilateral organization, akin to the International Labour Organization, to which the task can be delegated.

The task of developing a Multilateral Agreement on Investment (MAI), long beset by north–south divisions similar to those in the trade–environment debate, received a major impetus from the 1995 Halifax G7 Summit. Here leaders decided that a high-quality agreement would be developed for three years in the consensus forum of the OECD, and then taken for final negotiation into the much broader and diverse arena of the WTO. The production of such an agreement has the overwhelming support of the global business community, who face a plethora of restrictions and patchwork of differing rules in the various countries in which they operate and the Bilateral Investment Treaties through which they deal. It also benefits from the regional stimulus of NAFTA and its important investment provisions (Rugman and Gestrin 1996). Yet the slow progress thus far in generating an MAI, despite the support of the business community, the United States, and the NAFTA model, underscores the continuing power of national governments, and the need for high-level G7 impetus to secure such deep integration.

The intensifying interrelationships between trade, investment, capital flows, and the operation of national financial institutions has underscored the role of the G7, primarily through its finance ministers, in determining which international institutions shall have primacy in managing the broad multilateral investment regime the world has hitherto lacked, and thus the speed and shape of the emerging regime. The work of the OECD, with its emphasis on broad principles, complemented and competed with the WTO's process of securing a liberalization of financial services by the end of 1997 (with detailed disciplines on particular products), and the IMF's attempt to amend its Articles of Agreement to secure responsibility for all capital flows as they crossed national boundaries. That issue was closely related to strengthened prudential surveillance and reforms of private sector financial institutions. For as the 1997 Thai crisis demonstrated, poor banking practices could exacerbate or even cause capital flight and exchange rate devaluations. The central role of the G7 in arbitrating among competing international organizations was evident at Hong Kong in September 1997 where G7 finance ministers agreed to the IMF amendment.

The final trade challenge is developing the WTO as an institution, following its first ministerial meeting in Singapore in December 1996 (Hoekman and Kostecki 1995; Ostry 1997). One issue is whether the future lies in a continuation of sectoral arrangements, incremental improvements, or another major round of negotiations. Here the failure of the US at Naples in 1994 to receive G7 endorsement of its 'Open Markets 2000' initiative is more reflective of the absence of careful US preparation than the new impotence of the G7 to play its traditional role. However the current debate between regionalism and multilateralism within each of the G7's major trade liberalizing leaders – the United States, United Kingdom and Canada – and the lack of leadership in the trade field shown by the United States at the Denver Summit promises slow progress in this area. Movement will await, at a minimum, President Clinton's attainment and use of fast track authority.

The G7 has proven more efficacious in developing the WTO as the fourth pillar of the international economic system, by including its head along with those of the IMF, IBRD and the United Nations in the lunch with G7 leaders at Lyon in 1996. It has also taken up the question of WTO membership, notably, when and on what terms the WTO will admit Russia, a democratic power and partial G7/G8 member, and China, and bear the burden of absorbing both. At Denver in 1997 the G7 called for Russia's early admission, pledged support, and relaxed the earlier condition, established publicly and unilaterally by the US, that Russia would have to enter on 'commercially acceptable' terms.

5. CONCLUSION

Despite its many successes in the 1990s the G7 as an institutionalized system of overall global governance faces several challenges, all of which were manifest in the preparation and execution of the 1997 'Denver Summit of the Eight', held 20–22 June 1997.

The first is the need for an institution, led by a new country, at times with a new leader, serving as host each year, to sustain the momentum on those thematic emphases such as international institutional reform and multilateral trade liberalization that require a multiyear programme rather than a one-year push to accomplish. President Chirac at Lyon in 1996 did relatively little to carry through on the Halifax emphasis on institutional and particularly UN reform, leaving the G7 members most dedicated to this cause to act alone within the IMF and other international institutions. It is also noteworthy that in choosing enhanced Russian participation, global environmental protection and African development as the dominant themes at Denver, President Clinton set aside the issue of international institutional reform that he did so much to initiate at Naples in 1994. Although African development did constitute a continuation of the development emphasis at Lyon 1996, such a variable focus on major issues reduces the impact and credibility of the G7 commands.

A second challenge is to regularize and integrate more tightly into the summit preparatory and follow-up process the work of the many ministerial forums which have emerged, particularly those dealing with the microeconomic agenda. In part as a result of the low US unemployment rate in 1997, and its lack of popularly-elected ministers or those with independent power bases within coalition governments or party factions, the US in its year as host chose not to mount an unemployment ministerial, notwithstanding the fact that it had pioneered the forum at Detroit in 1994. Such choices compound the problem of variable focus, and deprive the G7 of a valuable mechanism for comparing best practices (such as those of the Netherlands), and for implementation and compliance review.

A third challenge is to overcome the abandonment at Denver of any effort to have the leaders engage in serious examination of topics from the classic economic agenda of the G7: exchange rate management, macroeconomic management, microeconomic policy, trade and investment, and north–south relations (outside the narrow African initiative that President Clinton mounted). With only a single hour and a half session 'at seven' devoted to core economic subjects, Denver was largely devoid of economic content.[31] This is a serious problem at a time when issues of exchange rate intervention, European unemployment, the advent of the EMU, the progress of MAI and the relationship of an investment regime with associated environment and labour issues warrant leader-level attention. It is especially problematic when new leaders lacking finance ministry experience, as from the United Kingdom in 1997, need to be socialized into the collective economic framework. It also inhibits anticipatory review and precautionary action, for example, to cope with the Asian currency crisis that erupted in the months following Denver.

A factor in this abandonment of a core economic agenda constitutes the fourth challenge – to find a durable means to cope with Russia's constant pressure for greater inclusion, while maintaining an ability to manage emerging macroeconomic and structural issues in a forward-looking way. The United States' central purpose at Denver was to make Russia appear as a full member of a newly-named 'Summit of the Eight'. This left little time for any economic discussions among the seven, and led to an emphasis on an issue – global environment conventions – where the Russians are functionally relevant. It stands in sharp contrast to the French formula for assuaging Russian pride and supporting President Yeltsin's re-election prospects with a separate, issue-specific summit in Moscow on an issue of central relevance to Russia. It also suggests, paradoxically in a post-cold war globalizing era, a return to the primacy of high politics, deference to the pride of a much lower status country, and a predominant concern with offering the Russians a concession for the enlargement of NATO. Looking ahead, only if the G7 is maintained as an effective economic institution will Russia have an incentive to become and be socialized into a power with a modern market economy. Full participation in an ineffective institution carries no prestige of use to the Russians at home or abroad.

The immediate cause of the prospective low performance of Denver on the emerging structural issues bred by deepening integration in the global economy was a poorly engaged, domestically-distracted US President missing an opportunity to display leadership at the outset of his second and still fresh electoral mandate. Yet the deeper cause lies in the dynamics of relative capability. Vibrant US growth and a soaring US dollar in 1996 and into the first quarter of 1997 caused a strong concentration rather than equalization of capabilities among the G7. This produced a powerful disincentive for the US to listen, learn and adjust, and a reduced ability for the other G7 members to make President Clinton, now equipped with the prerogatives of host, to respond to their concerns. All this was translated into action, and its effects compounded by President Clinton's call at Denver for G7 members to celebrate and adopt the American model of economic success. Yet within the summit institution, with its norms of effective equality, it led not to a deference to American leadership and collective decision, but to resistance to American arrogance and stalemate.

Looking ahead, the summit process is likely to quickly recapture its prevailing status in the 1990s as an effective international institution. Denver did not produce a decision to transform the G7 into a full G8, thus retaining its capacity to deal with economic issues at seven until the time when the Russians are able to contribute, on the basis of economic strength and market experience, to the dialogue. The responsibilities of host will pass to countries, beginning with Britain, deeply committed to the summit process. The advent of strong economic growth in several G7 countries, including Britain, will lead to the equalization of capability among G7 members that leads to high performance.[32] The long-awaited return of real growth in Russia could reinforce this trend, by making it over time a genuine economic power worthy of membership in the concert. Finally, the sequence of hosting, through Britain in 1998, Germany in 1999, and Japan in the year 2000, will bring to central attention the structural issues of deeper integration that are of pressing domestic concern in G7 members other than the United States.

NOTES

1. I am grateful to Professors Gavin Boyd, John Dunning, Yale Ferguson and Carol Evans and to Laurette Glasgow for their comments and to Gina Stephens, Cecilia Brain, Litza Smirnakis, and members of the University of Toronto G7 Research Group for their research assistance.
2. Bergsten and Henning's analysis does note such successes as the falling inflation, stable US dollar exchange rates, full employment in the US, the conclusion of the Uruguay Round and creation of the WTO, regional trade liberalization initiatives and the global spread of outward, market-oriented economic strategies. But it highlights the very modest growth in the industrialized countries, unemployment far above traditional levels in Europe and for the G7 as a group, stagnant average income levels in the US for over two decades, and a rapid rise in unemployment in Japan (Bergsten and Henning 1996: 49–50). In their analyses, the causes of the G7's broad failure are traditional differences among the members, especially the US and Germany, on key issues, America's declining economic and security power, inconsistent policies and inept performance, and above all, an inaccurate 'new consensus' among members that ambitious coordination is impossible given massive global flows of private capital, pervasive large fiscal deficits, the increased importance of independent central banks and poor memories of past achievements in G7 coordination.
3. The exception argues that in the 1990s ' . . . the momentum towards a rule-based system already begun in trade, investment and the environment is being maintained . . . new progress is being made in international financial relations . . . There is fresh impetus to reform the UN's operations . . . much of the innovatory pressure has come from the leaders of the G7 countries, at their Summits in Naples in 1994 and especially at Halifax in 1995. There they launched a systematic policy of working through international institutions, in a way never attempted before' (Bayne 1995: 493–4). Bayne argues the G7 judged that 'strong and effective international institutions would help them to resolve the tensions of globalization, between domestic and international pressures' and 'counter protectionist and inward-looking tendencies' but required the G7 to lead by example by 'drawing up multilateral rules, observing them strictly and co-operating in their enforcement' (Bayne 1995: 500–501).
4. Cooperation can be conceived of as a scale, ranging from consultation, through co-ordination, then harmonization and finally confederation, with each step progressively reducing national independence and weakening political accountability (Lawrence et al. 1996: 45). Cooperation, as used by Bergsten and Henning, refers to 'all collaborative activities among governments', whereas coordination is 'the process by which national policies are adjusted to reduce the adverse consequences (or reinforce the positive consequences) that the policies of one or more states have on the welfare of other states' (Bergsten and Henning 1996: 13; Putnam and Henning 1989: 15). The classic work on the G7, followed here, defines cooperation as 'episodes in which the policies of one or more states are modified to reduce the costs (or increase the benefits) that those policies entail for the welfare of other states, so that national policies differ from those that would have been expected from purely unilateral or autarkic policymaking', and offers wider scale mutual enlightenment, mutual reinforcement, mutual adjustment, and mutual concession (Putnam and Bayne 1987: 2, 261–5).
5. It has been further suggested, following the logic of Mancur Olson, that the slower

growth in the second half of the post-1945 half century is a result of the accretion of international institutions which the international community is quick to create and eager to continue, but almost never ready to abolish (Portes 1994). By this logic the G7 compares favourably as a lightly institutionalized body devoid of an organization, that providing impetus in eliminating or downsizing the multilateral institutional inheritance.

6. On the critical importance of small size and shared values in creating and rendering effective the major multilateral institutions of the immediate post-world war two period see Eichengreen and Kenen, 1994.

7. It was the 1997 Denver Summit of the Eight, under American leadership, that mounted a major programme to bring to Sub-Saharan Africa the growth that other regions of the developing world had experienced.

8. It was only at the trade ministers' meeting in May 1997 that APEC agreed to identify sectors that it could proceed to liberalize among itself and then within the broader WTO.

9. For example, on such performance (as opposed to power) indicators as the UN Human Development Index (measuring life expectancy and literacy as well as production), Japan and Canada regularly outrank the US.

10. In a change from an earlier position recommending more weight for China, India, Mexico and Brazil, Bayne (1995: 497) now argues that the G7 should retain its current membership, as 'the present G7 members need more than ever the close links provided by the summit process to defuse disputes among themselves and to counter the strains of globalization. The present G7 membership provides the best opportunity for exerting reciprocal pressure between the highly developed countries of Europe, North America and Japan, which would be lost if the composition were changed.'

11. The list includes the dinner the G7 had with 15 developing country leaders invited by French President Mitterrand on the eve of the 1989 Paris Summit, the dinner the Japanese Prime Minister and President Clinton had with the Indonesian President (then chair of the Non-Aligned Movement) on the eve of the 1993 Tokyo Summit, and the broad and intense series of consultations Canada held in the lead-up and follow-up to the 1996 Halifax Summit.

12. Ideological cleavage and consensus, as measured by the party in power in the G7 governments, has little effect in predicting the ability of the G7 to reach ambitious agreements. This is probably due to the presence of number two, Japan, with its Liberal Democratic Party hegemony, as the great stabilizer that prevents a divide into two powerful poles with few consequential countries in the middle (Kirton 1989).

13. 'The fundamental reason for heads of government to meet has always been that they can reconcile the domestic and external pressures of national policy, in a way that other ministers cannot. As the overlap between domestic and external policies has increased within globalization, so the requirement to reconcile conflicting pressures has grown . . .' (Bayne 1995: 494).

14. This argument thus sustains that of Eichengreen and Kenen (1994) who note the importance of flexibility in propelling the success of the 1945 institutions during their first 25 years, and the greater success enjoyed by the lightly organized GATT in contrast to the heavily organized IMF and IBRD.

15. This forum has now become an annual institution as environment ministers met again in Florence in 1994, Hamilton in 1996, Cabourg in 1996 and most recently in Miami, Florida on 5–6 May 1997. This last meeting focused on climate change, the forthcoming United Nations Special Session reviewing the Rio commitments, international efforts on environmental enforcement and compliance, and environmental hazards and children's health. As this forum involves only environment and not development ministers, it is an institution directed at the 'global commons' rather than 'sustainable development' embracing issues of north–south redistribution. As

with the 1945 galaxy, the G7 has been slow to evolve a component institution for development at the ministerial level.

16. There are pressures to broaden the microeconomic, ministerial-level focus, as Japan pressed in 1997 to host a ministerial-level G7 meeting of the 'Caring Society', focused on social policy (pensions and health care).

17. The terrorism ministerial, an extension of the G7's longstanding concern with this issue, can be seen as the leading edge of the G7's attempt to respond to the globalization of migration, while the information society meetings embrace both border and domestic barriers. The 1997 interruption is best seen as a temporary result of US hosting, rather than an end of the impulse towards institutionalization in these domains.

18. A 'commitment' is defined as 'a discrete, specific, publicly expressed collectively agreed statement of intent; a "promise" or "undertaking" by Summit members that they will take future action to move toward, meet, or adjust to an identified target' (Kokotsis and Kirton 1997).

19. There is certainly no 'crisis of governability' in the 1990s. The apparent 'wholesale rejection of incumbents throughout the G-7' (Bergsten and Henning 1996: 51) is a 'post-cold war success' rather than a 'G7 failure' effect. It is no greater than the transition centred on 1980 which largely brought the 'new cold war' (including Mitterrand) or 'neo-conservative' generation into power. The Bush–Clinton transition of 1992 is equal to that of Carter–Reagan, the LDP has returned to power in Japan after a brief interlude, and Kohl has continued in Germany.

20. Projections for 1997 place inflation (as a percentage of consumer price index increases) within the G7 as follows: US 2.9; Japan 1.3; Germany 1.8; France 1.6; Italy 2.4; Britain 2.6; and Canada 1.7. Fiscal balances (as a percentage of nominal GDP) are: US –1.5; Japan –2.9; Germany –3.3; France –3.3; Italy –3.3; Britain –3.1; Canada –0.3 (sources: International Monetary Fund, 23 April 1997, OECD, December 1996). By May 1997, the US budget deficit for 1997 was widely forecast to be less than 1 per cent of GDP, paving the way for the bipartisan balanced budget agreement reached that month. In Canada, the government was well ahead of its deficit reduction targets and widely expected to be in surplus by 1998. While Germany and Japan, afflicted by slow growth, faced cyclical budget deficit difficulties, the fiscal foundations for the 'new consensus' among the G7 had disappeared.

21. Projections for 1997 place real GNP growth (percentage increase) for 1997 for G7 members as follows: US 3.0; Japan 2.2; Germany 2.3; France 2.4; Italy 1.0; Britain 3.3; and Canada 3.5 (International Monetary Fund, 23 April 1997). Real GNP growth in the G7 as a whole, weighted by members' GNP levels at then current exchange rates, was +0.982 in the 'peak' low growth year of 1980, and almost double at +1.78 in the 1990s peak low growth year of 1991 (see Table 1.6). Unemployment in the USA peaked at 9.7 per cent in 1982 compared to 7.5 per cent in 1992 (and a level of 5.4 per cent in January 1997); in Canada at 11.9 per cent in 1983 compared to 11.2 per cent in 1992 (and 9.7 per cent in January 1997); in Britain at 11.8 per cent in 1983 compared to 10.5 per cent in 1993 (and 7.7 per cent in January 1997). In Germany a peak of 7.2 per cent in 1985 compares with 6.5 per cent in 1994 and 1995, rising beyond 7.2 per cent only by the fourth quarter of 1996 (to reach 7.8 per cent by January 1997). In Japan peaks of 2.8 per cent in 1984 and 2.9 per cent in 1987 compare with 2.9 per cent in 1994 (and a level of 3.3 per cent in January 1997). Only in France and Italy is there a rise, with a French peak of 10.8 per cent in 1987 compared with one of 12.9 per cent in January 1997, and Italy's earlier peak of 7.2 per cent in 1985 compared with a recent peak of 12.5 per cent in 1996Q2 (and 12.3 per cent in January 1997) (source: Bureau of Labor Statistics, US Department of Labor, May 1997).

22. The A6 is a group of six Asia-Pacific countries assembled under US leadership in 1997 to address financial and economic issues within the Asia-Pacific region.

23. This non-interventionist fostering of globalization has brought low interest rates across the G7. In December 1996 short-term rates (in per cent) stood at: US 5.3;

Japan 0.6; Germany 3.1; France 3.3; Italy 7.6; Britain 6.1; and Canada 3.0; while long-term rates stood at US 6.5; Japan 3.1; Germany 6.1; France 6.1; Italy 7.7; Britain 7.4; and Canada 6.8 (source: OECD, December 1996). In both cases, correcting for inflation and growth rates (and allowing for the politics of the OECD process), the interest rate differentials provide a strong incentive for the rapid appreciation of the US dollar against most G7 currencies, as experienced over the past year. For example, the OECD's 1997 projected real short-term interest rate for the US was 2.4 per cent and for Japan –0.7

24. The economic communiqué was entitled 'Making a success of globalization for the benefit of all'.

25. In taking up international financial institution reform as the centrepiece of the 1995 Halifax Summit the G7 displayed a preventative as well as reactive capacity. The issue was identified at the Naples 1994 Summit, and promoted by Halifax host Jean Chretien, well before the peso devaluation added impetus to the process (Kirton 1995a).

26. The IMF has the General Arrangements to Borrow (GAB), a credit facility of about $27 billion, and prospectively the New Arrangements to Borrow (NAB) created in 1994. While the GAB–NAB is not enough to handle another Mexico and a Russia at the same time, the G7, through the IMF, is handling Russia through regular relaxations of IMF conditions for the provision of financial assistance. There is thus no need for a major new allocation of SDRs. Indeed, the need had disappeared well before the apparent repudiation of the G7's proposal at the Madrid meetings of the IMF.

27. The 45 per cent quota increase, agreed to by the IMF's Executive Committee in Hong Kong, represented a compromise among IMF Managing Director Michel Camdessus, who sought a 100 per cent increase, most G7 members, who were willing to accept 60 per cent, and Germany and Japan, who wanted much less for fear of sparking global inflation. The result shows the influence of other G7 members even at times of relative weakness, in driving G7 outcomes.

28. The more likely institutional evolution, based on the precedent of the trade ministers' Quadrilateral, is the creation of a G4 or G5, with Canada and Britain included.

29. In 1997, projected current account balances (as a percentage of GDP) among G7 countries were as follows (with 1995 figures in brackets): US –2.3 (–2.0); Japan 1.8 (2.2); Germany –0.5 (–0.9); France 1.6 (1.1); Italy 3.7 (2.5); Britain –0.9 (–0.5); and Canada –0.0 (–1.4) (source: IMF, 23 April, 1997). In contrast, the 1980 peaks were as follows: US –3.4 per cent in 1987; Japan 4.4 per cent in 1986; Germany 4.8 per cent in 1989; France –2.0 per cent in 1982; Italy –2.4 per cent in 1981 (and 1992); and Britain –4.4 per cent) in 1989 (Bergsten and Henning 1996: 60–62). The current range is thus much narrower, and more closely clustered around balance within the G7, than in earlier periods.

30. For example in the world's largest trading relationship, that between the United States and Canada, an estimated 40 per cent of trade takes place between different affiliates of the same multinational corporation while an additional 30 per cent takes place between corporations linked by joint ventures, technology licencing arrangements, or strategic alliances (Weintraub 1997).

31. Without the last-minute intervention of the US Treasury in the US preparatory process, even this session 'at seven' would not have been held.

32. The September 1997 IMF World Economic Outlook raised its projected 1997 growth rate for the US and lowered that for Japan, but forecast for 1998 that Canada would lead (with 3.7 per cent), with the US at 2.6 per cent, Japan at 2.1 per cent, Britain at 2.6 per cent, the European Union as a whole at 2.9 per cent, and Russia at 4.1 per cent (up from 1.8 per cent in 1997).

REFERENCES

Bayne, Nicholas (1995), 'The G7 summit and the reform of global institutions', *Government and Opposition*, **30** (Autumn): 492–509.

Bergsten, Fred and Randall Henning (1996), *Global Economic Leadership and the Group of Seven*, Washington, DC: Institute for International Economics.

Bretton Woods Commission (1994), 'Bretton Woods: looking to the future', *Commission Report, Staff Review, Background Papers*, Washington, DC; Bretton Woods Commission, July.

Commission on Global Governance (1995), *Our Global Neighbourhood: The Report of the Commission on Global Governance*, New York: Oxford University Press.

De Silguy, Yves-Thibault (1997), membre de la Commission, responsable des affaires économiques, monétaires et financières, 'The impact of the creation of the euro on financial markets and the international monetary system', Institute of International Finance, Washington, Tuesday, 29 April.

Eichengreen and Kenen (1994), 'Managing the world economy under the Bretton Woods system: an overview', in Peter Kenen (ed.), *Managing the World Economy*, Washington, DC: Institute for International Economics, pp. 3–57.

Esty, Daniel and Damien Geradin (1997), 'Market access, competitiveness and harmonization: environmental protection in regional trade agreements', *The Harvard Environmental Law Review*, **21** (2): 265–336.

Feldstein, Martin (1988), 'Distinguished lecture on economics in government: thinking about international economic coordination', *Journal of Economic Perspectives*, **2** (Spring): 3–13.

Frankel, Jeffrey (1988), *Obstacles to International Macroeconomic Policy Co-ordination*, Princeton Studies in International Finance No. 64, Princeton: Department of Economics, Princeton University.

G7 Research Group (1997), *The 1997 G7 Compliance Assessment*, University of Toronto, G7 Research Group.

Gummett, Philip (ed.), *Globalization and Public Policy*, Cheltenham, UK: Edward Elgar.

Henning, Randall (1996), 'Europe's Monetary Union and the United States', *Foreign Policy*, **102** (Spring): 83–100.

Higgott, Richard (1996), 'Beyond embedded liberalism: governing the international trade regime in an era of economic nationalism', in Philip Grummett (ed.), *Globalization and Public Policy*, Cheltenham, UK: Edward Elgar, pp. 18–45.

Hodges, Michael (1994), 'More efficiency, less dignity: British perspectives on the future role and working of the G-7', *The International Spectator*, **29** (April–June): 161–77.

Hoekman, Bernard and Michel Kostecki (1995), *The Political Economy of the World Trading System: From GATT to WTO*, Oxford: Oxford University Press.

Ikenberry, John (1993), 'Salvaging the G-7', *Foreign Affairs*, **72** (Spring): 132–9.

Ikenberry, John (1996), 'The myth of post cold war chaos', *Foreign Affairs*, **75** (May–June): 79–91.

Ionescu, Ghita (1995), 'Reading notes, summer 1995: from international to global reform', *Government and Opposition*, **30** (Summer): 394–7.

Jayawardena, Lal (1989), 'World economic summits: the role of representative groups in the governance of the world economy', *Development: Journal of the Society for International Development*, **4**: 17–20.

Kenen, Peter (1994), *Managing the World Economy*, Washington, DC: Institute for International Economics.

Kenen, Peter (ed.) (1995), *Understanding Interdependence*, Princeton: Princeton University Press.

Keohane, Robert (1984), *After Hegemony: Cooperation and Discord in the World Political Economy*, Princeton, NJ: Princeton University Press.

Keohane, Robert (1994), 'Comment', in Peter Kenen (ed.), pp. 58–63.

Kindleberger, Charles (1973), *The World in Depression, 1929–39*, Berkeley: University of California Press.

Kirton, John (1989), 'The seven power summit as an international concert', Paper presented at the International Studies Association Annual Meeting, London, England, April.

Kirton, John (1993), 'The seven power summit and the new security agenda', in David Dewitt, David Haglund and John Kirton (eds), *Building a New Global Order: Emerging Trends in International Security*, Toronto: Oxford University Press, pp. 335–57.

Kirton, John (1994), 'Exercising concerted leadership: Canada's approach to summit reform', *The International Spectator*, **29** (April–June): 161–76.

Kirton, John (1995a), 'The G-7, the Halifax Summit, and international financial system reform', *North American Outlook*, **5** (June): 43–66.

Kirton, John (1995b), 'The diplomacy of concert: Canada, the G7 and the Halifax Summit', *Canadian Foreign Policy*, **3** (Spring): 63–80.

Kirton, John (1997a), 'Canada and APEC: contributions and challenges,' *Asia Pacific Papers*, **3** (May): 1–27.

Kirton, John (1997b), 'Le Rôle du G7 sur le Couple Intégration Régionale Sécurité Globale', *Etudes Internationales*, **28** (June): 255–70.

Kirton, John and Rafael Fernandez de Castro (1997), *NAFTA's Institutions: The Environmental Potential and Performance of the NAFTA Free Trade Commission and Related Bodies*, Montreal: Commission for Environmental Cooperation.

Koekman, Bernard and Michel Kostecki (1995), *The Political Economy of the World Trading System*, Oxford: Oxford University Press.

Kokotsis, Ella and John Kirton (1997), 'National compliance with environmental regimes: the case of the G7, 1988–1995', Paper prepared for the Annual Convention of the International Studies Association, Toronto, 18–22 March.

Krasner, Stephen (ed.) (1983), *International Regimes*, Ithaca, NY: Cornell University Press.

Labbohm, Hans (1995), *G7 Economic Summits: A View from the Lowlands*, The Hague: Netherlands Institute of International Relations Clingendal.

Lawrence, Robert Z., Albert Bressand and Takatoshi Ito (1996), *A Vision for the World Economy*, Washington, DC: Brookings Institution.

Lewis, Flora (1991–92), 'The G-7½ Directorate', *Foreign Policy*, **85** (Winter): 25–40.

Llewellyn, John and Stephen Potter (eds) (1991), *Economic Policies for the 1990s*, Oxford: Blackwell.

Odom, William (1995), 'How to create a true world order', *Orbis*, **39** (Spring): 155–72.

Ostry, Sylvia (1990), *Governments and Corporations in a Shrinking World: Trade and Innovation Policies in the United States, Europe and Japan*, New York: Council of Foreign Relations.

Ostry, Sylvia (1997), *The Post-Cold War Trading System: Who's On First?*, Chicago: University of Chicago Press.

Pauly, Louis W. (1997), *Who Elected the Bankers? Surveillance and Control in the World Economy*, Ithaca: Cornell University Press.

Portes, Richard (1994), 'Comment', in Peter Kenen (ed.), pp. 64–8.

Putnam, Robert and Nicholas Bayne (1987), *Hanging Together: The Seven Power Summits*, Cambridge, MA: Harvard University Press.

Putnam, Robert D. and C. Randall Henning (1989), 'The Bonn Summit of 1978: a case study in co-ordination', in Richard N. Cooper, Barry Eichengreen, Gerald Holtham, Robert D. Putnam and C. Randall Henning, *Can Nations Agree: Issues in International Economic Co-operation*, Washington: Brookings Institution.

Ruggie, John (ed.) (1993), *Multilateralism Matters: The Theory and Praxis of an International Form*, New York: Columbia University Press.

Rugman, Alan and Michael Gestrin (1996), 'A conceptual framework for a multilateral agreement on investment: learning from the NAFTA', in Pierre Sauve and Daniel Schwanen (eds), *Investment Rules for the Global Economy*, Toronto: C.D. Howe Institute, pp. 147–75.

Rugman, Alan, John Kirton and Julie Soloway (1997), 'NAFTA, environmental regulations and Canadian competitiveness', *Journal of World Trade*, **31** (2): 129–44.

Shafer, Byron (1996), *Postwar Politics in the G-7: Orders and Eras in Comparative Perspective*, Madison, Wisconsin: University of Wisconsin Press.

Smyser, W.R. (1993), 'Goodbye, G-7', *The Washington Quarterly*, **16** (Winter): 15–28.

Snidal, Duncan (1985), 'The limits of hegemonic stability theory', *International Organization*, **39** (Autumn): 579–614.

ul Haq, Mahbub (1994), 'The Bretton Woods institutions and global governance', in Peter Kenen (ed.)

USTR (1997), *Study on the Operation and Effect of the North American Free Trade Agreement*, Washington, DC: United States Trade Representative, 1 July.

Von Furstenberg, George and Joseph Daniels (1992), *Economic Summit Declarations, 1975–1989: Examining the Written Record of International Cooperation*, Princeton: Princeton University Press.

Weintraub, Sidney (1997), *NAFTA at Three: A Progress Report*, Washington, DC: The Centre for Strategic and International Studies.

Whyman, William E. (1995), 'We can't go on meeting like this: revitalizing the G-7 process', *The Washington Quarterly*, **18** (Summer): 139–65.

Williamson, John and Marcus Miller (1987), 'Targets and Indicators: A Blueprint for the International Coordination of Economic Policy', *Policy Analyses in International Economics 22*, Washington, DC: Institute for International Economics.

2. Corporations and structural change in the world economy*

Peter J. Buckley

INTRODUCTION

The major agents of change in the world economy are corporations. Firms do not act in a vacuum and the context – set by government, consumers, suppliers, the level of extant technology and the culture of the countries in which the firms operate – plays a key part in determining the outcome of the changes they initiate. Further, firms are reactive as well as proactive. They react to the context and to other firms. This chapter examines current controversies in comparative economic structure, including the nature of competitiveness, the nature of the 'Asian miracle', the public/private sector divide, the role of trade blocs and the notion of the competition of cultures. These issues are presented as 'new stylized facts' which need to be explained by successful models of multinational firms as we approach the millennium (Buckley and Casson 1976, 1985). Finally, extant models of multinationals are discussed and extended by questioning traditional notions of ownership, exchange, competition and information.

The foregoing discussion enables us to examine the stylized facts listed below as key issues in the changing global economic structure and to subject them to a process which leads from (1) overall trends to (2) specific market changes and (3) an analysis of the competences which firms need to meet the challenges of these changes. This will lead to (4) changes in the optimal boundaries of firms and finally to (5) changes in the internal organization of firms.

* I would like to thank Gavin Boyd and Mark Casson for comments on an earlier draft.

COMPARATIVE ECONOMIC STRUCTURE

What has changed in the world economy since the 1980s? What are the new stylized facts which need to be explained by models of multinational enterprise? A number of key stylized facts are presented here in order to confront the challenges to the theory of the multinational enterprise as we approach the millennium.

The key updated stylized facts may be broken into empirical and conceptual issues: four empirical issues and four conceptual issues demand attention.

Empirical issues:
1. The rise (and relative recent decline) of Southeast Asian economies.
2. The lack of development in the poorest countries.
3. The change in the balance between private and public sector, with the former in the ascendant.
4. The dominance of trade blocs in the world economy: the integration of markets internationally and the trend towards 'globalization'.

Conceptual issues:
1. The conceptualization of competitiveness – is this a phenomenon which can be described meaningfully at the aggregate (national) level?
2. The integration of culture into (economic) models.
3. Welfare.
4. Ownership as a signalling process.

Empirical Issues

1. The rise of Southeast Asian economies
International business theory has a tradition of responding to (incorporating) 'stylized facts'. The most profound incorporation is the response to the rise of Japan, whose distinct culture and non-Judeo-Christian tradition meant that simplistic theories of the dominance of 'the West' had to be rejected. This development led to the refutation of models of the world economy which posited 'the West' as a singular exemplar of development and the rest of the world as 'other'. A critical outgrowth of this recognition was much soul-searching that led to an outpouring of concern over 'competitiveness' – a relative term, since there was now something to be relative to! In addition, it led to the search for differences between 'successful' western economies – bank-

based versus market-based financial systems, unitary versus federal states are examples.

The rise of Southeast Asia (not, as usual, a precise spatial term – a conceptual term covering Hong Kong, Taiwan, Korea and Singapore (the four little tigers or dragons) and now including a second wave: Malaysia, Thailand, Indonesia to be followed by Vietnam and the huge somnolent dragon, China) has caused further intellectual frissons.

The latest revisionist view, that of Krugman (1996) is essentially that this was an accident waiting to happen. His view is that this involved a transfer of labour from the traditional (agricultural) sector to the modern (industrial) sector but that, crucially, total factor productivity in the modern sector has not improved.

For international business scholars, the rise of these new competitors raises interesting new issues concerning the international transfer of technology and changing competitive strategies. Many firms in East and Southeast Asia have achieved the transfer of technology from advanced countries without the necessity of accepting foreign direct investment (FDI). Indeed, they have found ways of circumventing the need to pay market prices for proprietary technology. One method has been to initiate best practice by hiring consultants from 'the West' to send their best human capital abroad for training. Thus, a transfer of technology has been achieved without inward investment. Methods such as sending key personnel to be trained in western universities circumvents proprietary control of technology. Emerging country competitors have found institutions which underprice technology and have created mechanisms to transfer this technology relatively costlessly, to their own emergent multinational firms. Advanced country, established multinationals are now faced with a problem of non-appropriability of technology and management skills. This is a far broader issue than the classic 'foreign direct investment versus licensing' issue and it places the knowledge transfer and appropriability issues right back at the heart of international business theorizing.

A second new competitive challenge lies in the new competitor's use of labour and the spin which this gives to 'flexibility of labour' as a key competitive weapon. Typically, in the West, flexibility of labour implies deregulation of the labour market, removing minimum wage standards, reducing unionization and other barriers to labour mobility. This concept is challenged by the Asian company's use of flexible labour *within* the firm, rather than between firms. This intra-firm flexibility – moving workers around jobs within a firm rather than between firms – allows the building of loyalty to the firm and greater internalization of labour efficiencies.

2.   The lack of development in the poorest countries

The least developed countries in the world (LTDCs) are not catching up with the newly industrializing economies (NIEs) and, indeed, are slipping both relative to the rest of the world and in many cases, absolutely. The LTDCs do not attract FDI in any quantity. FDI is very skewed firstly towards advanced economies and then towards a small minority of less-developed countries, with a particular current bias to China.

The motives for FDI reveal why this is so. FDI is targeted on: (1) markets (preferably large and rapidly growing); (2) key inputs, notably scarce natural resources; and (3) plentiful cheap labour. Although motive (3) would seem to favour LTDCs it does not do so because these typically lack the key complementary inputs – a good (transport) infrastructure, political stability, good educational standards and a culture of hard work and compliance with multinational firms' standards. Countries which are resource poor, small in GDP terms and landlocked are particularly disfavoured.

3.   The change in the balance between public and private sectors

Transfer of assets from the public to the private sector has become a widespread panacea for governments seeking to increase efficiency and growth. However, this policy of privatization has only been tractable where well-established property rights exist. Frydman and Rapacynski suggest that the meaning of privatization in East Europe 'has turned out to be complex and ambiguous. Instead of the clarification of property of a capitalist society, the privatization process has, so far, led to a maze of complicated economic and legal relations that may even impede a speedy transition to a system in which the rights of capital are clearly delineated and protected' (1993:13). This is quoted by Williamson (1996:324) who points out that getting property rights correct is too narrow a conception of institutional economics.

The privatization of whole swathes of previously publicly-owned assets has set in train the creation of a set of emerging multinationals in telecommunications, railways, utilities (water, electricity distribution, power generation, refuse collection, and so on). Some will argue that new principles are required to explain these 'new (new) multinationals', but the analysis below shows that this is unnecessary.

4.   The dominance of trade blocs in the world economy

The success of the European Union (EU) in achieving greater European integration, the deepening and extension of NAFTA and the rise of free trade areas such as Mercosur, point towards an accelerating trend in world trade – the growth of trade blocs. These trade blocs are also investment and technology blocs, encouraging closer ties between member economies.

The concept of globalization has become devalued by the ascendancy of use over meaning. Perhaps we should return to markets to give meaning. Broadly, if we envisage three levels of markets – financial markets, markets in goods and services and labour markets – we can envisage each of these moving at a differential speed towards global integration.

Financial markets are already very closely integrated internationally, so much so that no individual 'national market' can have independent existence. Goods and services markets are integrated at the regional level and this coordination is largely policy driven through institutions such as the European Union, NAFTA, ASEAN, and so on. Labour markets, however, are functionally separate at the national level and here integration is largely resisted by national governments (the UK's opt-out of the EU Social Chapter to 1997, examples from NAFTA).

The beneficiaries of this differential speed of integration are multinational firms. They can raise capital at the lowest possible cost, reap economies of scale in regional goods and services markets and segment labour markets by choosing least-cost inputs for different spatially separate activities (Buckley 1997).

It is somewhat ironic that issues of economic geography have not been to the fore in international business theorizing. Perhaps this is because of the difficulty of modelling in this area (Krugman 1995) or an unfortunate byproduct of the academic division of labour. However, spatial issues should not be underrated in constructing more satisfactory and comprehensive approaches to international business theory.

The key to progress is to elide from geography to the spatial division of labour. Geographical barriers (mountains, deserts, large land masses with no sea coast) represent difficulties of transportation (which vary with historical time because of technological innovations in transportation) which inhibit trade and the emergence of specialization and cooperation in effecting a division of labour. The political division of economic space into nations results in countries having an internal division of labour which differs from that prevailing externally. Primarily, this difference is mediated through trade and so the existence of an entrepôt becomes a crucial factor in stimulating exchange and development (Buckley and Casson 1991).

In the modern world economy, this entrepôt function is provided by the MNE. In this sense the MNE compresses space by its organization – the mountain comes to Mahomet. The internal and external divisions of labour meet at the boundary of the multinational firm. The spatial boundaries of the state are crucial in international trade, but in a world economy dominated by MNEs, this boundary becomes much less important. The borderless world (Ohmae) results from exchange across the different divisions of labour becoming spatially internal to every national member of the global economy. Mediation of different divisions of labour is no longer trade through an entrepôt but through the mediation of the different resulting price signals by the managers of multinational firms. This gives rise to issues such as the 'Who is us?' issue posed by Robert Reich (1990). Is 'us' British firms wherever they are located or all firms in Britain whoever the ultimate owners are? On this issue hangs much of modern economic policy.

Perhaps the permeable boundaries of multinational firms have relegated the importance of geography, as have technological developments in telephony which make the management of spatially diverse entities, such as the multinational firm, so much more efficient. If so this puts much more emphasis on the coordination problem. The importance of the multinational firm arises from the fact that it is a system for integrating and coordinating intermediate product flows arising from activities concentrated at different locations. It is in this sense that the multinational firm represents a real challenge to the nation state, which attempts to coordinate activities within a given spatial area defined by politically and historically determined national boundaries (now completely permeable to intermediate product flows of information by telegraphic communications).

Conceptual Issues

1. The conceptualization of competitiveness
Competitiveness (or 'international competitiveness') is an elusive concept which has generated controversy amongst commentators on international business. Obviously, competitiveness is difficult to measure for numerous practical reasons which make quantification problematic, including the measurement of quality, taking account of changing exchange rates, purchasing power parity deviations and differences in ends as well as means. There are two important issues in clarifying these problems: one is the essential comparative component of competitiveness, the other is the multifaceted and dynamic nature of the concept (Buckley, Pass and Prescott 1988).

There are essentially three methods of assessing competitiveness – by reference to the past (the historical comparator) to another area of economic space (spatial comparisons) and by reference to a counterfactual position (what would have happened if some crucial event had not occurred or some crucial decision not been taken). Competitiveness has to be measured against some other state of the world – over time, across space or against a well-defined 'straw man'. The critics of the way that competitiveness is presented in more 'popular' versions (Thurow 1992) such as Krugman (1996) object largely to the concept being applied to countries (or aggregations larger than the single firm) – 'firms compete, not countries'. Krugman's attack is well grounded. It points to the essentially benevolent outcome of free trade based on comparative advantage and the welfare-enhancing nature of specialization and trade – going back in the tradition of Ricardo.

This is, however, to take a narrow view of the situation. The international business literature, here as elsewhere, scores in terms of its wider remit. Countries do, in fact, compete in that they provide public goods on which firms located so as to take advantage of this provision can draw. This might be location specific (subsidies to R&D in their territory, for example) or might provide a base for launching an attack on the world market (education and training for managers). The difficulty for governments is to create public goods for 'our' firms, but to prevent leakage of these benefits to 'their' firms. The creation of such 'selective' public goods not available to outsiders is a major dilemma – as is the decision as to which firms are 'our' firms (Reich 1990). The creation of the oxymoron 'selective public goods' emphasizes this problem and is the essence of the analytic difficulties on which Thurow and others have imperfectly seized.

Perhaps this issue is best dealt with by distinguishing between transferable and non-transferable assets. If firms located in a given territory are highly competitive in ways which do not depend on cheap labour, then they are drawing on intangible assets. Competition based on assets which are not transferable from the 'home' territory will predispose the firm to move towards integrating forward into distribution or backwards into long-term contracts for raw materials and key inputs to maintain the home base. Examples of the latter include Japanese backward integration into raw materials and colonization in Africa. Thus these non-transferable resources in the home country lead to an export base in the home country which needs complementary resources. This leads to an export platform type of development with integration both backward and forward, maintaining control of a vertically integrated global structure. Contrast this situation with firms reliant on transferable

Table 2.1   Comparative measures of competitiveness

	Firm	Nation
Historical comparisons	1. ✓	2. ✓
Spatial comparisons	3. Inter-regional and international comparisons	4. Problems of international comparability. 'Firms compete, not nations'.
Counterfactual comparisons	5. Conceptually possible, but difficult.	6. Possible, but very difficult at the aggregate level.

resources. Such firms can substitute FDI for exporting from the home base by the transfer of technology or expertise to a cheaper labour country, leaving the home base with a vertically disintegrated economy, subject to the vagaries of shifting, footloose FDI and dependent upon depressing wages to attract new inward FDI and keep existing firms from exiting. Thus competitiveness of nations is an issue – and one that existing International Business (IB) theory can illuminate.

These points are well taken. However, as Table 2.1 shows, there is an aggregation problem when we move to Cell 4, where it is difficult to compare nations spatially. It is possible to track the competitiveness of a nation over time (Cell 2), leading to notions of a 'loss of competitiveness' but there are myriad problems in comparing, say, Japan with Germany at a given point of time. Similarly, the counterfactual comparison is difficult within a firm (what would have happened if you had not invested in a new plant?), but the order of magnitude ascends dramatically when we examine counterfactuals for a whole nation (what would have happened if you had not increased the education budget?).

The second difficulty concerns the wide-ranging nature of competitiveness – it is clearly more than simply performance, it must contain the idea of sustainability. After all, the easiest way to gain world market share is to give your product away! Thus some measure of future potential (investment) must be incorporated. Given that there are trade-offs between performance (consumption) and potential (investment), the concept must include some element of choice of ends (objectives) and not just means. Because there has to be a balancing of ends and means, management becomes important.

Competitiveness thus requires a blend of hard data and more judgemental inputs, which makes modelling difficult.

2. The integration of culture into models

If the above section is correct, it provides a crucial insight into the current preoccupation with culture in international business. This is because a shared culture, through its role in reducing transaction costs, can determine the relative efficiency of alternative types of organization – firm and nation are two such examples. The injunction 'render unto Caesar what is Caesar's', may be opposed by 'render unto Toyota what is Toyota's'. In the case of cultural affiliation, the balance may have shifted, and be shifting to the firm rather than the political entity.

There can be no gainsaying the fact that culture is not amenable to simple modelling. Its holistic nature demands attention as do the awkward attempts to 'draw lines' from a box with 'culture' written on it to a box with 'economy' or 'firm' written on it! Buckley and Casson (1991) attempted to examine 'scientific outlook and systems thinking' and 'competitive individualism versus voluntary association' as key determinants of development and to link them to geographical aspects of a trading system. The key links here are the development of a sustainable specialization through a division of labour and falling transaction costs through repeated interactions and shared cultural values (see also Fukuyama 1996).

3. Welfare

Economic models permit judgements about efficiency to be made. The efficiency calculus is generally based on maximizing consumer welfare using market-determined prices to value individual satisfaction. This measure of efficiency has become a moral imperative for economists who have stood accused of regarding individualist hedonism as the only criteria for judging human society (Buckley and Chapman 1996). However, the core assumption of economics – that people optimize – leaves open what enters into their objective function. Since people cannot meaningfully optimize unless they can rank alternatives in order of preference, it is assumed that optimization is with respect to a well-behaved objective function. It may be simply consumption goods, alternatively it may not be selfish materialistic wants. The utility function can represent altruistic feelings and emotional needs (Buckley and Casson 1993).

Another feature of the welfare function is that it is usually specified where everything in it is controlled by the individual concerned. There is no interdependence, such that one person cares about something which another person decides: there are no vicarious components. Selfishness is thus a convenient assumption for economic modellers, because it is feared that the additional complications of altruism would undermine the theory's predictive power. However, the inclusion of preference interdependence is often a straightforward means of modelling issues such as morale and motivation (Buckley and Casson 1993). This has strong links to informational issues in welfare (Casson 1997; Buckley and Carter 1996).

4.   Ownership as a signalling process

In models of multinational enterprises, ownership has been conceived largely as a management governance mechanism. Where transactions cost configurations so dictate, hierarchy (ownership) will be preferred to market transacting. The transfer of ownership to foreign countries creates multinationals.

Ownership may be conceived of in an entirely different, but complementary fashion. The ownership of an enterprise can be seen as a signalling mechanism, drawing on characteristics associated with the parent firm, and often therefore on characteristics associated with the country of origin of the parent firm. Thus when the Rover car company of the UK is taken over by BMW of Germany, Rover takes on the characteristics of style, efficiency and engineering quality of its new parent by osmosis. Similarly, the establishment of a greenfield plant by Toyota conveys to the new (potential) workers, investors and consumers the kudos of quality and reliability of product and the view that it will be managed in a Japanese style (concerned, democratic, using modern techniques of personnel management). To some extent these are myths. Ownership signals, like any other asset, though, require investment. It is incumbent upon MNEs to instil precisely those qualities which ownership signals presage.

In this respect, ownership is akin to branding, patenting and image making. It confers a premium upon paper issued by a firm which possesses it – thus a higher price will be paid for the same income stream issuing from Rover when it is owned by BMW. This is a microeconomic version of Aliber's multiple currency theory of FDI (Aliber 1970, 1971). In this crude version, it relies on investor myopia, for of course rational investors would see that the firm retains the same income stream. Some degree of consistent improvement of performance and more importantly the expectation of this continuing into the future must underpin this belief for it to be a sustainable hypothesis.

We can take this further by relating the reputation for maintaining and increasing value to the issue of who takes over whom. A reputation of this kind creates 'blue chip' status for a company which can be leveraged to ensure that the financial markets back firms with such a reputation against those without one. We can build this into a theory of acquisition and account for the stylized fact of the growing importance of mergers and acquisitions as a means of foreign market entry and development by examining the nuances of 'the way assets are managed' as a reputation capable of being leveraged. Such a reputation reflects the broad-based perception of a firm's management. This is subtly different from the value of goodwill, physical assets, brands and patents, because we are now putting value on the managerial system for extracting values from given assets. The quality of the system of internal coordination and entrepreneurship is more difficult to value than the assets enumerated above.

MODELS OF MULTINATIONAL ENTERPRISES

The Modelling Process

As signalled above, this chapter illustrates the process by which we can move from the analysis of general trends to specific propositions (see also Buckley 1988).

Several major trends were identified in the section on comparative economic structure above. These trends (the rise of East Asia, lack of development in the poorest economies, privatization and trade blocs) have induced specific market changes. These changes include: new competitors in mass production and high technology sectors from countries such as Korea and Malaysia; the failure of import-substituting investments, for example in Africa; new competitors and competitive structures in newly privatized industries; and, combined with the driving down of transport costs (through containerization, and so on) the result is the possibility of new competitive strategies such as just-in-time production internationally.

The specific market changes require new competences from companies facing these challenges. In general, the competences required are of the more general entrepreneurial type than the previous generation of technological skills required for efficient mass market production. In final product markets, more competition is experienced. In intermediate product markets the transport cost revolution makes dispersed activities more feasible, and in labour markets the adoption of policies of deregulation means that more aggressive management policies can introduce increasing flexibility to labour management. In

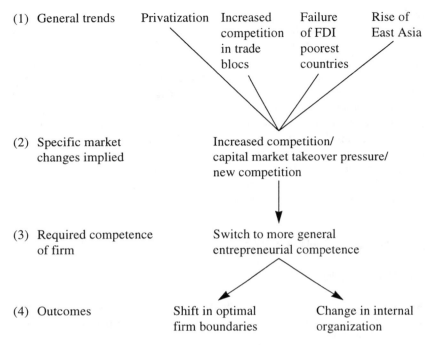

Figure 2.1   Modelling trends in the international economy

capital markets, the mushrooming of stock markets means that the increasing threat of hostile acquisition puts more pressure on company managements to perform above the norm.

These specific market changes affect the boundaries of the firm and impact upon the internal organization of the firm.

Figure 2.1 shows that the *principles* of the analysis are timeless, but that the context differs and so does the empirical outcome of the given trends. The process can be traced through a variety of potential scenarios, given well-established stylized facts. New theories are not required, but the intelligent application of well-established models and frameworks are necessary.

The Choice of Contractual Arrangements

The forces outlined in Figure 2.1 can be expected to have a major impact on the current and future institutional arrangements in the international economy. This chapter suggests that international business theory leads to several predictions of changes in the global economy.

Asset ownership by firms

		Conventional assets	Appropriable skills
Country of location	Labour costs	1. Vertical disintegration volatile home economy	2. Mixed outward FDI and inward labour cost seeking FDI
Competitive base	Public assets	3. Inward investment – home firms as takeover targets	4. International vertically integrated structure with powerful home base

Figure 2.2   *Interactions between country of location and the ownership of assets by firms*

Asset ownership

		Conventional assets	Appropriable skills
Country of location	Labour costs	Less developed countries of Africa, Asia and Latin America in low-tech industries	UK industry 'old European industries'
Competitive base	Public assets	British car industry	Japanese export platform and *keiretsu* companies

Figure 2.3   *Examples of interaction between country of location and the ownership of assets by firms*

These will include: a greater share of international business activity being focused on mergers and acquisitions; increasing volatility of foreign direct investment based on cheap labour seeking; differential success of firms and firms of given nationality, creating value from a reputation for managing assets, leveraging of generalized skills to create powerful globally integrated groups and competition of national territories to create non-transferable asset bases.

This will lead to the configuration of the world economy as pictured in Figures 2.2 and 2.3. Quadrant 1 represents the situation where the country of location is competing on labour costs (or labour flexibility in the external market sense), interacting with firms which have asset skills (physical assets, patents, brands). This leads to a vertically disinte-grated structure with a volatile 'home' economy where the firms' transferable skills can combine with cheap labour at home or elsewhere. Quadrant 2, similarly, has a country of location competing on low-cost

	Rise of new economies		Privatization		Trade blocs
	Inward	Outward	Inward	Outward	
Non-contractual modes					
Imitation	✓				
Educational transfers	✓				
Piracy/counterfeiting	✓				
Contractual modes					
'Licensing'			✓	✓	
Control modes – FDI					
Joint ventures	✓	✓	✓	✓	✓
Greenfield ventures		✓			
Acquisition			✓	✓	✓

*Figure 2.4   The changing configuration of modes of international
business activity*

labour but this time interacting with firms which have appropriable
generalized management skills. This leads to a mix of outward FDI
seeking locationally fixed public assets together with a fluctuating flow
of cost-seeking inward investment. Quadrant 3, which combines
locationally fixed public goods with firms with asset skills, will represent
prime targets for inward takeovers of indigenous firms. Quadrant 4
represents the powerful home base of a vertically integrated structure,
both forward and backward.

Figure 2.4 examines the implications of the changes identified by
plotting their effect on the change of contractual arrangements made
by multinational firms. East Asian and other 'new' multinationals favour
non-contractual means of acquiring assets and knowledge and also have
a penchant for joint ventures with foreign-owned multinationals. In
their outward involvements, they favour greenfield ventures, often on a
wholly owned basis, but also using joint ventures. They are insufficiently
integrated, so far, into the world capital market and are culturally
unfamiliar with takeovers, so that the acquisition mode favoured by
western multinationals does not appeal to them. The newly privatized
companies have had recourse to inward licensing and joint ventures in
order to acquire skills and technology previously unavailable to them
(or of which they previously had little need, such as generalized marketing skills). They have also come under the acquisition spotlight, as
foreign predators see them as ripe targets because of their undervalued

assets and unreleased potential. In their outward activities, they have favoured licensing and joint ventures, to access capabilities which they do not possess but some of them have sought complementary packaged assets by acquisition.

Finally, the development of trade blocs has facilitated and been facilitated by joint ventures and acquisitions between multinational firms.

Thus, we can observe a different emerging configuration of modes of doing international business (compare Buckley 1981). Non-contractual modes are increasing in importance as (covert) means of technology transfer but in areas where higher levels of competitiveness and market development exist, joint ventures and acquisitions are in the ascendant because these are key means of acquiring capabilities.

Implications for the Organizational Structure of Multinational Firms

The pressures analysed in this chapter will have a profound impact on the organizational structure of multinational firms. They are presented with two key imperatives – to create appropriable assets, especially those based on generalized management skills (and, by analogy, to prevent leakage of returns from assets where appropriability is difficult) and to derive rent by internalizing locationally specific public goods. These imperatives require radical restructuring and will alter the scope of such firms.

Leakages in appropriability can be stemmed in two ways: by moving into assets which do not leak and by stopping leakages in conventional assets (Buckley 1983). As Figure 2.4 showed, non-appropriability is a key issue in 'non-contractual transfers'. Largely, because of institutional difficulties, multinationals have hitherto found it difficult to control these transfers – they are mainly occurring under the auspices of governments, universities, other non-commercial entities and through grey and black markets. Our analysis leads us to expect that multinational firms will increasingly seek to control these areas. This will involve political action to internalize some governmental activities (or at least quasi-internalize them by representation in government and on the governing bodies of non-commercial organizations) to seek to extend patent rights, licensing arrangements, copyright, branding design and technological protection and to clamp down on piracy and counterfeiting.

Our analysis further suggests that acquisition in particular and joint ventures will become more important as FDI modes. Acquisition results from companies capitalizing their general entrepreneurial skills – backing their valuation of what these skills can achieve with post-takeover assets against the markets valuation of this value. This will lead to a new breed of financier, whose key skills will be to value generalized entrepreneurial and management skills residing in a firm's system of control. Company valuation will become even more of an art and even more well rewarded for those at the successful apex of activity. One key part of these skills will be cultural sensitivity, for foreign acquisitions require this quality in abundance in order to release the value promised to the financiers in the post-acquisition integration phase.

CONCLUSION

This chapter has examined the process of modelling multinational enterprises. It has sought to show that the significant stylized facts of the near millennium global economy can be explained satisfactorily by a combination of timeless principles together with a careful and judicious selection of special assumptions suited to the local and temporal situation that is to be explained.

The five-stage process outlined in Figure 2.1 enables analysts to make progress whilst working in a common paradigm. Specific models with different specialist assumptions can be developed and these can compete to explain and predict changes in the global economy as they are confronted with empirical evidence. So, working from general trends to the specific market changes implied by these changes, to the required competences of the firm and the implied impact on the firm's optimal boundaries and changes in internal organization, a clear modelling procedure can be followed. Given the rapid rate of change in the world economy, it is likely that adaptations of models will be needed frequently. We should beware of jettisoning key principles whilst this is occurring.

REFERENCES

Aliber, Robert Z. (1970), 'A theory of direct foreign investment', in C.P. Kindle-berger (ed.), *The International Corporation*, Cambridge, MA.: MIT Press.

Aliber, Robert Z. (1971), 'The multinational enterprise in a multiple currency world', in J.H. Dunning (ed.), *The Multinational Enterprise*, London: George Allen & Unwin.

Buckley, Peter J. (1981), 'New forms of international industrial cooperation', *Aussenwirtschaft*, **38** (2): 195–222. Reprinted in Buckley and Casson (eds), (1985) *The Economic Theory of the Multinational Enterprise*.

Buckley, Peter J. (1983), 'New theories of international business: some unre-

solved issues', in M. Casson (ed.), *The Growth of International Business*, London: George Allen & Unwin.
Buckley, Peter J. (1988), 'The limits of explanation: testing the internalization theory of the multinational enterprise', *Journal of International Business Studies*, **19** (2): 1–16.
Buckley, Peter J. (1997), 'Trends in international business research: the next 25 years,' in I. Islam and W. Shepherd, *Current Issues in International Business*, Cheltenham: Edward Elgar.
Buckley, Peter J. and Mark C. Casson (1976), *The Future of the Multinational Enterprise*, London: Macmillan.
Buckley, Peter J. and Mark C. Casson (eds) (1985), *The Economic Theory of the Multinational Enterprise*, London: Macmillan.
Buckley, Peter J. and Mark C. Casson (1991), 'Multinational enterprises in less developed countries: cultural and economic interaction', in P.J. Buckley and J. Clegg, *Multinational Enterprises in Less Developed Countries*, London: Macmillan.
Buckley, Peter J. and Mark C. Casson (1993), 'Economics as an imperialist social science', *Human Relations*, **46** (9): 1035–52.
Buckley, Peter J. and Malcolm Chapman (1996), 'Economics and Social Anthropology – Reconciling Differences', *Human Relations*, **49** (9): 1123–50.
Buckley, Peter J. and Martin J. Carter (1996), 'The economics of business process design: motivation, information and coordination within the firm', *International Journal of the Economics of Business*, **3** (1): 5–25.
Buckley, Peter J., C.L. Pass and Kate Prescott (1988), 'Measures of international competitiveness: a critical survey', *Journal of Marketing Management*, **4** (2): 175–200.
Casson, Mark (1997), *Information and Organization: A New Perspective on the Theory of the Firm*, Oxford: Clarendon Press.
Frydman, Roman and Andryej Rapacynski (1993), 'Privatisation in Eastern Europe', *Finance and Development*, June: 10–13.
Fukuyama, Francis (1996), *Trust*, Harmondsworth: Penguin.
Krugman, Paul (1995), *Development, Geography and Economic Theory*, Cambridge, MA.: MIT Press.
Krugman, Paul (1996), 'The myth of Asia's miracle', in *Pop Internationalism*, Cambridge, MA.: MIT Press.
Reich, Robert B. (1990), 'Who is us?', *Harvard Business Review*, **68** (1): 53–65.
Thurow, Lester C. (1992), *Head to Head: the coming economic battle among Japan, Europe and America*, New York: Morrow.
Williamson, Oliver E. (1996), *The Mechanism of Governance*, Oxford: Oxford University Press.

3. Contestability and concentration in world markets

Gavin Boyd

INTRODUCTION

In international business studies and international political economy literature questions about the contestability of markets, and about the relative strengths of firms exploiting, increasing, or reducing that contestability, are considered from several perspectives. There is interest in overall trends, resulting from interactions between national policies and corporate strategies, which raise or lower degrees of competition in all the markets which are being internationalized through trade and transnational production. The overall trends are responsible for changes in the spread of gains from deepening integration in the global economy, and thus activate corporate and policy-level responses which form mixed patterns of competition and cooperation. Specialized policy studies focus on the trade, structural, competition, foreign direct investment and financial policies of governments, identifying especially problems of cooperation, viewed as justifications for nonintervention in the working of market forces or as challenges to build strong transnational links between policy communities. Work on the operations of international firms mainly assesses their performance in diverse contexts of contestability and concentration, with sensitivity to the opportunities and problems of continuing globalization.

Through much of the literature, especially in the international political economy area, the opening of markets through reductions of barriers to trade and investment is presented as a systemic advance, facilitating increased corporate competition across national borders, and thus raising levels of efficiency in specializations which ensure higher gains from commerce. There are expectations of balancing effects as firms contend for enhanced market strengths, but optimism is qualified because of general awareness of major contrasts in the competitiveness of firms and in the structural competitiveness of national political economies.[1]

Comprehensive orientation in the study of market contestability has to be based on recognition that competitive processes in markets linked across borders tend to result in the displacement or absorption of less efficient and less officially favoured firms, and that concentration accordingly increases while contestability diminishes.[2] Questions about cooperation between governments in the implementation of their competition policies thus demand consideration, but there is general consensus that political will to cope with this difficult task is lacking. There are varying degrees of understanding that governments are reluctant to impose restraints on the foreign operations of their firms, and to accept obligations to collaborate with other governments for the implementation of coordinated competition policies. Jurisdictional problems, moreover, are recognized, in view of the ways in which transnational enterprises can extend their global operations through foreign affiliates and alliance partners.[3]

Patterns of contestability can be distinguished at sectoral, country, regional and global levels, with references to cross-border linkages and to differing configurations of partnering or adversarial relations between intercorporate systems and governments. Sectorally, low levels of contestability are evident in high technology industries,[4] notably aircraft, as entries can be made only with very high-volume investments for research-intensive production and for competition against the informal connections of major firms with leading airlines. Country contrasts, aggregating sectors, evidence the consequences of relative economic openness and of cooperative or noncooperative interactions between the corporate and policy levels. The country contrasts, notably those between the USA, Japan, and Germany, are factors in regional and global contexts, and evolving trends in those contexts are reflected in the dynamics of policy processes and of intercorporate activity which shape further structural change, with falls and rises in contestability.

Patterns of concentration, related to the differences in contestability, exhibit contrasts resulting from the market changes and structural changes caused by firms and national policies. Overall, liberalization policies implemented by governments facilitate concentrations of corporate power, while their structural policies, intended to benefit national firms, have mixed effects, generally allowing national and foreign firms to acquire more scope for independent regional and global operations in the contests for markets, resulting in greater concentrations of corporate strength. In this vast process the implementation of liberalization and structural policies is affected by the pressures of large states against each other and against smaller states, notably in the North America Free Trade Area, the European Union, and East Asia.

Large asymmetries in bargaining strength enable the USA to press Canada and Mexico for accommodative liberalization which allows extensive scope for virtual exercises of structural power by its firms. Because of a weak structural policy capability the principal regulatory influence is antitrust enforcement, which has a domestic focus and which has evidenced a liberal trend, partly in response to policy-level concerns with enhancing the USA's global competitiveness.[5] Within the European Union a more even spread of bargaining strengths and substantial advances in regional institutional development make for more symmetry in the practical effects of market integration,[6] but externally the Union's bargaining strength tends to secure accommodative liberalization by individual trading partners. This bargaining strength is balanced only by the USA, in a transregional context in which the Union is disadvantaged by lagging competitiveness and by a low structural policy capability. In East Asia, Japan is distinctive as a political economy with strong but guided internal competition, resistance to foreign intrusion, and a substantial structural policy capability.[7] This is exercised in the East Asian environment with emphasis on structural partnering, which involves informal quests for accommodative liberalization by industrializing East Asian states, but restraint is necessary because of competitive US and European involvement in the area.

MARKET OPENNESS

Much current economic advice to governments encourages the adoption of policies that widen the scope for market forces, domestic and international, and that open the way for increasing cross-border linkages between production and distribution processes, for general increases in efficiency through the specializations of the more competitive firms that gain strength as national economies become more open to each other. The rationality of trade and investment liberalization is affirmed with apparent expectations that competition between firms will continue to have efficiency effects after all domestic and external obstacles to commerce are removed.[8] Attention tends to be directed away from problems of market failure, which assume cross-border dimensions as overall economic openness increases. The confidence in market forces entails optimism about the performance of transnational enterprises, whose international production has become increasingly more important than arm's-length trade for the service of markets.

Anticompetitive behaviour by firms and governments, however, is recognized to be a problem, but with some apparent reluctance to acknowledge that this tends to increase as rivalries for world market shares intensify and as transnational enterprises expand their global operations, with growing capacities for securing favourable treatment of their interests by governments. There is also some apparent reluctance to recognize that the bargaining strengths of firms and governments alter with shifts in the spread of gains from international commerce, and that these changing bargaining strengths affect the terms on which markets become more liberalized or less liberalized. Liberalization arrangements, it seems to be insufficiently understood, are outcomes of generally unequal bargaining processes, and their practical significance is continually affected by market entry barriers set by firms that may not be explicitly anticompetitive.[9]

The implementation of liberalization policies tends to be accompanied by increases in regulatory measures that can in effect restrict competition without being unambiguously anticompetitive. The regulatory measures typically include the setting of product standards, forms of environmental protection, stipulations about labour practices, and restraints intended to maintain the national character of vital industries. Antidumping measures have to be listed in this context, and they have special significance as unilateral responses to forms of price competition concerning which economic analysis tends to be ambiguous as a guide for policy, and for its justification. The enforcement authority's biases and the relative bargaining strength of its government mostly determine the outcomes of antidumping cases.[10]

Competing imports tend to activate special interest groups seeking protection of their domestic market shares through the introduction of regulatory measures that act as nontariff barriers. Such measures tend to multiply as the perceived costs of globalization affect sectors and communities; as restraints on competing imports, however, the measures taken increase incentives for transnational enterprises to produce within the countries under forms of regulatory protection. Investment bidding by host countries typically encourages this choice while the special interest groups remain active. Advocacy by these groups can increase because of the continuing effects of competing imports and also because of sectoral disruptions resulting from the rationalization of operations by incoming firms.

The retention of regulatory barriers to imports can be considered politically advantageous by governments valuing the support of special interest groups yet seeking to attract foreign direct investment. Degrees of leverage available for use against trading partners pressing for increased openness to trade largely determine the scope for resistance or accommodation. What tends to result is adversarial concentration by policy communities on strategies for leverage. The possible efficiency and welfare benefits of alternative agreements tend to be relativized, and can be considered impossible to measure. Governments pressing for liberalization commonly use public rhetoric about common interests in free trade, but the political culture of the world trading system is adversarial.[11] Basically, it must be stressed, the imbalances and uncertainties of globalization, in conditions of unevenly negotiated liberalization and of protective regulatory arrangements, tend to motivate more competitive rather than more cooperative foreign economic policies. Relatively disadvantaged states, under pressure from industry associations and communities, seek to enhance their gains from world commerce through protective and promotional measures. Relatively advantaged states seek to preserve their strong positions in world markets through restraints on the penetration of their economies and through more active export development.

The overall trend evolves in a setting dominated by unequal cooperation and rivalry between the European Union and the USA. A complex compromise agreement between them was primarily responsible for the conclusion of the Uruguay Round of Trade Talks and the establishment of the World Trade Organization (WTO), in place of the General Agreement on Tariffs and Trade, at the beginning of 1995. Dependence on the large European and North American markets virtually obliged most other participating countries to accept commitments to liberalization embodied in that settlement: there was no effective coalition of Third World or other industrialized states capable of representing its interests.

The USA is the most active promoter of liberalization in the world trading system, seeking general increases in market openness through promotional endeavours in the WTO, working to negotiate an Atlantic preferential trade area, and attempting to form free trade arrangements in Latin America and the Pacific. The Atlantic venture clearly has high priority, and can be pushed forward in somewhat exclusive trade policy networks outside the WTO, including notably working groups within the Organization for Economic Cooperation and Development (OECD) and the International Monetary Fund (IMF, but most importantly through dialogues between the European Commission and US government agencies. The WTO is of limited utility as a structure offering possibilities for building consensus with policy communities in major trading partners.[12] There is in effect broad scope for unilateral efforts to negotiate free trade arrangements at the regional level, and these efforts can involve reliance on superior bargaining strength to secure accommodation from prospective partners in such preferential arrangements.[13]

Quests for free trade arrangements in regional contexts can be more productive ways of furthering US liberalization objectives than managing trade talks at the global level. In the regional settings the great importance of the US market for prospective partners and the related sensitivities to US capacities for unilateral assertions of trading interests can be very decisive factors. The Uruguay agreement imposes no restrictions on the formation of free trade areas, and does not set any restraints on the use of unilateral measures which the USA and other large states may adopt to secure compliance with their trade policy preferences. The internal dynamics of the US trade policy process, however, may prevent an administration from seizing opportunities to negotiate regional free trade agreements.[14] Congressional unwillingness to grant 'fast track' negotiating authority severely restricted the Clinton administration's trade diplomacy in Latin America during 1997, which was intended to enlarge the North America Free Trade Area.

COMPETING FIRMS AND COMPETING GOVERNMENTS

The operational significance of the basic rationale for general increases in market openness concerns foreign direct investment as well as trade, as it is argued on efficiency grounds that such investment tends to have increasingly significant competitive effects. These can become more important than those resulting from arm's-length trade, but assessment of the separate consequences is difficult because large proportions of that commerce tend to be replaced by intrafirm trade and intra-alliance trade, much of it in intermediate products. Outside the USA and the European Union this intrafirm trade is associated with dispersals of production specializations across several countries, moreover, and the resulting patterns of subcontractors and suppliers tend to be restricted. Technological transfers and other contributions to the efficiencies of host country firms can thus be small, while the market strengths of those firms can be severely weakened by the marketing strategies of the transnational enterprises, which technically may not involve resorts to anticompetitive practices.

The treatment of competition policy issues in some of the literature on trade liberalization conveys quite limited understanding of the dimensions of the problems of assessing efficiencies in markets which are being unevenly linked through commerce facilitated by asymmetrically negotiated arrangements for increased economic openness. In a small or medium-sized country under pressure to liberalize, the economic openness which has to be accepted can cause an efficient established national pattern of concerted entrepreneurial activities to become vulnerable. This problem has been evident in Taiwan's experience. The danger that has to be stressed is that transnational enterprises implementing regional strategies for several small or medium-sized countries can severely weaken host country firms that may have superior long-term innovative potentials. The regional strategies of the transnationals may well have a short-term focus, and may not be open to integrative partnering with host country enterprises.[15]

The references to competition policy issues that urge governmental efforts to develop common approaches to these problems also commonly underestimate the losses of economic sovereignty experienced by national administrations as international firms extend their operations and interact with numerous host governments. There is often little acknowledgement, moreover, that the competition policies of the large states out of which the major multinationals have been operating are of course focused domestically, and are generally not concerned with any anticompetitive practices by those firms in foreign markets.[16] The host governments, of course, can attempt to assert authority on competition issues within their markets, but the literature generally avoids reference to the constraining effects of bargaining leverage available to the large states which are the home countries of numerous major multinationals.[17]

Governments are encouraged to cooperate, for general adoption of increasing liberalization measures, in the common interest. Competition between governments, however, tends to be given more and more stimulus by intensifying corporate contests for world market shares. The growth and employment effects of increases in national gains from involvement in the world economy become more and more vital for the domestic political fortunes of national administrations. At the same time these gains tend to become more uncertain, because of switches in the strategies of large global enterprises and changing trends in the economies of countries linked by the operations of those enterprises.[18] Hence there are rivalries to raise levels of structural competitiveness, support and protect key sectors, and enlist the cooperation of international firms. Where there are low structural policy capabilities, it must be stressed, regulatory measures and resorts to strong bargaining leverage tend to be all the more important elements in a policy mix.

With the changes in patterns of relative bargaining strengths that are resulting from the consolidation of the USA's role as the central power of NAFTA, and the enlargement of the EU, the scope for competition between governments is being altered. The possible efficiency effects of such policy-level competition moreover can be seen to assume differing likely configurations. There are incentives for states outside the two major blocs to form new regional associations for collective bargaining with those blocs and for collectively more self-reliant economic growth. The alternative is to risk becoming individually more exposed to leverage on trade and investment issues by either or both blocs as they compete in the world economy.

The scope for policy-level competition is changing as the USA and the European Union assert their interests in holding the initiative on issues of further global liberalization. Ongoing Atlantic discussions of these issues indicate to the rest of the world that the launching of any negotiations under WTO auspices on those issues, and the adoption of related agendas, are intended to be primarily outcomes of US–EU decisions, and that steering roles based on those decisions would be assumed, despite possible conflicts of interest.[19] Japan is the only industrialized state outside the Atlantic relationship, and, notwithstanding exceptional prominence in the world economy, is politically not able to assert a competing role as the leader of a coalition of non-Western states with common interests in the world trading system. The Japanese scope for global economic diplomacy is limited by distinctive cultural factors and by heavy dependence on access to the US market.[20] Japanese interests in global liberalization negotiations sponsored by the USA and the EU would have to be given expression in ways that would take advantage of differences between EU and US preferences on the details of proposed market opening arrangements. On questions of access to the Japanese market the EU and the USA are rivals as well as cooperators.

For several decades Japan has been under pressure from the form of Atlantic collaboration that has been promoting liberalization in the global economy. This pressure has in effect increased because of the disruptions of Japan's interests in industrializing East Asia since the 1997–98 currency crises. Those economic reverses have weakened regional partners and have made Japan more dependent on the US market. The response that would seem imperative is to strive for even greater structural competitiveness, using a policy capability that has been a source of superiority over the main Western rivals. The likely effects would be further increases in the competitiveness of Japanese firms, evidenced in deeper penetration of medium and higher technology sectors in Europe and the USA. The corporate-level competition could in turn benefit Japan's involvement in government rivalry, in part because of European interest in attracting Japanese direct investment. Such investment can help to overcome the EU's technological lag behind the USA and balance the strong American corporate presence in Europe.[21]

Altogether, in the dominant pattern of policy-level competition, some diverging trends seem likely. Competition between governments tends to force macromanagement improvements but can occasion protective measures as well as increases in subsidies. The significance of market opening arrangements can thus be reduced. The scale of such arrangements entered into by the USA and the EU, however, may give considerable impetus to competitive trends between firms. Mergers, acquisitions and displacements of weaker enterprises may accelerate, with uncertain efficiency effects, and meanwhile may cause the formation of new representations of interests, with resultant changes in all the policy-level competition. Yet international enterprises which have acquired very powerful positions and which can operate with oligopolistic allies can of course be affected by bureaucratic inertia: the efficiency effects of competition can thus be reduced. Governmental competition, meanwhile, may prevent cooperative policy-level activity that could engage with the problem of international oligopoly power. This may happen because, after policy-level cooperation that initiates major advances in trade and investment liberalization, for example in the Atlantic context, goodwill encouraged by the anticipated benefits may dissipate because of asymmetries in the actual outcomes.

MARKET CHANGES AND STRUCTURAL CHANGES

Degrees of regional and global trade and investment liberalization, facilitating expansions of international operations by firms, have had significant effects on the markets of major industrialized states as these have become increasingly linked through transnational production and arm's-length commerce. In 1990 Germany, France and Britain had import penetration ratios in their markets for manufactures of about 30 per cent, and their ratios of penetration through local production by foreign firms varied between 15 and 25 per cent. All these figures reflected interdependencies which had been rising within the European Union as well as linkages which had been growing with the USA and Japan. The USA's corresponding degrees of penetration in its market for manufactures were considerably lower – about 15 per cent through imports and about 15 per cent through local production by foreign firms.[22]

Through the 1990s and especially since the completion of the Single Market project there have been large but difficult to measure increases in the contestability of the markets which are being integrated in the European Union. Numerous national barriers to intrazonal and external commerce have been removed, principally through extensive technical harmonization and standardization, and the elimination of intrasectoral restraints that had been implemented by diverse formal and informal methods. A substantially open regional business environment has developed.[23] Mergers and acquisitions have been increasing, and those involving partners outside the Union have been more numerous than those between firms in member countries. The Union's competition policy is relatively liberal, guided in part by concerns to facilitate the emergence of large internationally competitive European enterprises. Lagging global competitiveness remains a difficult problem for the Union, especially because the development of a substantial structural policy has not been possible at the Union's present stage of institutional evolution.

The combined effects of regionalized competition and increased concentration have been evident in a trend toward price convergence across the Union and a substantial fall in price–cost margins. Associated with these changes has been a general increase in the size of firms, and more active external penetration of the Union market, interacting with the increased rivalry between Union enterprises. The competitive effects of the external penetration have been substantial, and in some sectors the linkages with the rest of the world have developed faster than intra-EU integration processes, due to the persistence of rivalries between national business communities.[24] This appears to have been the case in the automobile and air transport industries.

In the much more highly integrated US market advanced degrees of contestability, resulting mainly from antitrust enforcement and the influence of a very individualistic business culture, have generally increased. Imports as shares of consumption in numerous manufacturing industries have risen substantially: in 1995 the ratio for transportation equipment was 24.3 per cent, and for electronics it was 32.5 per cent; in 1985 the ratios had been 18.4 per cent and 17 per cent, respectively. For industrial machinery and equipment the corresponding ratios had reflected somewhat larger increases – from 13.9 per cent in 1985 to 27.8 per cent in 1995. Higher ratios were recorded in low technology sectors which had become internationally less competitive. Meanwhile the use of imported inputs by US manufacturing industries rose across several sectors: for transportation equipment these inputs amounted to 15.7 per cent of production in 1995, a rise of about 50 per cent since 1985; a similar rise was recorded in electronics, where the imported input ratio reached 11.6 per cent in 1995.[25]

The proportion of US manufacturing output that is exported has on the whole followed the trend in import penetration, rising from an average of 7.9 per cent in 1985 to 13.4 per cent in 1995. The export shares of production in the industrial machinery, electronics, and instruments sectors were 25.8 per cent, 24.2 per cent and 21.3 per cent in 1995, reflecting increases roughly in line with the average for all manufacturing sectors since 1985, except in the case of electronics, where the export share doubled during that period.[26] The conjunction of increases in import penetration and export orientation within higher technology sectors has accorded with general rises in intraindustry trade between the USA and the EU, and these have evidenced complementary specializations in conditions of very open competition. The import penetration in the USA appears to have been possible largely because contests in the home market between US firms have precluded collaborative responses, to a considerable extent. In this process complementary specializations induced by strong contestability have become a significant trend. To some degree, then, tendencies towards concentration in the markets linked across the Atlantic may have been moderated.

Assessment of the overall figures for US manufacturing sectors, however, has to take into account Japanese contributions to the levels of import penetration, especially because the USA is the main destination of Japanese exports, and these are concentrated in the US industries which have experienced major increases in such intrusion. The Japanese involvement has clearly been a major factor in the contestability of the US market, while contestability within the Japanese market has remained almost entirely a domestic affair.[27] Japan's intraindustry trade has been at low levels, thus in effect allowing the intraindustry Atlantic trade to assume greater significance as an outcome of competitive processes facilitated by relatively balanced liberalization.

Competitive pressures associated with liberalization have had very complex effects in East Asia, contributing to price convergence only in moderate degrees. There have been strong intermediate goods price linkages between Japan and industrializing East Asian states, because of extensive Japanese manufacturing in those states. Much of this, however, has been oriented towards service of the US market, and has resulted in relatively modest increases in exports from the host countries to Japan. Japanese firms have sought to maintain and increase market shares in the USA by holding down export prices while keeping prices high in their home market. These home prices have been going down, but slowly, and this has reflected the longstanding strength of networks of national firms in that market. Across most of Japan's manufacturing sectors the level of import penetration in 1995 was about 6 per cent, accounted for mainly by raw materials imports.[28]

RIVAL SYSTEMS

Liberalization, as a general shift towards market-based policies, has resulted in more active contests between national systems of corporate governance, business cultures, and intercorporate systems. Impetus has been given to the development of collaborative practices for the development and use of complementary specializations that have been facilitated by cultural ties, common experiences in dealing with home country administrations, and shared access to flows of commercial intelligence. The cooperation within national patterns has been a source of reciprocal pressures for adaptive changes in those patterns, in the interests of improved competition. Meanwhile market strengths gained or lost have been associated with shifts in contestability and in degrees of concentration.

The state of the major patterns of corporate culture and organization sets them in uneven rivalry. The very large American pattern is challenged first by the Japanese pattern and second by the German pattern, while between the Japanese and German patterns there is lower-level competition. The American pattern extends deeply into Europe, where the German pattern retains its distinctive identity within the integrating regional economy. In other members of the European Union corporate cultures and organizations are not yet beginning to merge across borders and link up with the German pattern. A new regional configuration could be conducive to greater efficiencies throughout the Union, and to further development of its institutions, but local attachments and loyalties severely hinder such systemic evolution.

The American pattern has been profoundly influenced by regulatory arrangements which severely restrict cooperation between firms, maintain separation between manufacturing and financial enterprises, prevent cross-holdings and concentrations of ownership, and exert pressure for managerial performance through active markets for corporate control. Shareholder demands for substantial returns on investment tend to force emphasis on short-term profitability, in effect encouraging investors to resort to trading methods which push up stocks.[29] The speculative contestability threatens to become unsustainable, through losses of investor confidence.

The social organization of trust tends to be at low levels in the American pattern, and it tends to motivate strong quests for concentrated market power, sought through mergers and acquisitions. There are no significant spontaneous restraints on these in the national business culture, and accordingly the level of concentration in several sectors, notably automobiles, tends to be higher than in Japan, where spontaneous restraints in the intercorporate system ensure pervasive respect for the independence of weaker firms whose counterparts in the USA would be insecure. US quests for concentrated market power extend very much into international operations, where mergers and acquisitions, notably in Europe, can of course assist consolidations of positions in the home economy.

The European pattern exhibits lagging adaptation, with continuing opportunities for US corporate involvement, attracted by the size of the Union market. The institution of a common Union system of corporate governance, which would facilitate the formation and operation of regional firms, is prevented by the influence of strong national attachments and loyalties in the policy communities of European countries. Considerable concentrations of ownership in the major firms which retain their national character tend to be sources of political pressure to maintain continuity, despite functional considerations for change which would provide a rationale for introducing a market-based system to serve the entire region.[30] The central feature of the European configuration is the German system, in which solidarity is preserved with relatively high levels of concentrated ownership, strong cross-holdings, very active financing and monitoring roles by banks, and pervasive ties with peak economic associations.[31]

The German system in effect benefits from the smaller size and weaker efficiencies of the intercorporate patterns in other Union states. Their diversity limits potential for cross-border collaboration, while the larger dimensions and home economy ties of German firms are advantageous for regional operations. In contests for Union market shares, however, the challenge from the American corporate presence is formidable, especially because of the competitive strength of that presence in other Union members whose intercorporate systems are more open to penetration.

The Japanese pattern of corporate activity, distinguished by dynamism generated through intensive emphasis on solidarity and through applications of internalization logic at the industry group and intercorporate levels, introduces large asymmetries into the global configurations of contestability. In the home economy the substantial exclusion of foreign corporate involvement is a well-established imperative, while virtually unlimited access to other industrialized economies is recognized as a condition for outward-oriented growth. The main external contestability effects are in the USA, where national concentrations of market strength have been given somewhat less scope for expansion, and have been challenged to achieve greater efficiencies. The Japanese competitive pressure has evoked vigorous US corporate quests for higher achievement, thus contributing to overall growth. Meanwhile the US system of corporate governance, as a consequence, has been under pressure to change, especially through relaxations of legal restrictions on interfirm collaboration.[32]

The growth potentials of the major national patterns of corporate activity have evidenced sharpening contrasts while general liberalization has been continuing in most industrialized states. Slackening growth in these states has raised questions about the efficiencies of enhanced competition, as these have promised service of markets by the most productive international firms, operating in rivalries which push them towards higher levels of performance. Efficiencies resulting from more active corporate rivalries have had general growth effects but, with concentrations of international market strengths, restructuring strategies have enabled large enterprises to maintain and extend their positions with leaner organizations, and with shifts of operations to lower-cost Third World locations. High social insurance costs have discouraged the maintenance of large staffs at centres in industrialized states. Meanwhile prospective increases in those costs, due to continuing shifts of production operations to lower-cost areas, have obligated higher redistributive and protective allocations by governments, with resultant tax increases which transnational enterprises have been endeavouring to avoid, through further relocations of production operations. Finally, the ageing and shrinking of populations in industrialized states has weakened demand, imposing conservative limits on the planning of firms.[33]

The basic developmental issues indicated by trends in the contestability of advanced country markets thus demand consideration of structural policy options in which partnering with third world countries will clearly be required. The agenda for dialogues on further trade and investment liberalization, while brought into policy-level discussions enlarged by structural policy perspectives, will also have to be extended through openness to interactions with transnational enterprises. The increasingly significant structural consequences of their largely independent operations will have to be examined not just on the basis of competition policy concerns but with reference to fundamental problems of performance in the markets which they are linking. While assessments of competition policy problems remain judgemental, resting on ambiguities of economic analysis, problems of internationalized market failure with more profound implications for growth are likely to become more prominent in policy debates. This is likely to happen mainly because of the economic and political effects of externalities associated with globalization.[34]

TRADE, INVESTMENT AND COMPETITION POLICIES

Expanded perspectives are becoming necessary in discussions of trade, investment, and competition policies because of the multiplication of complex structural interdependencies in the deepening integration that has been facilitated by general liberalization. The interdependencies complicate the efficiency considerations that have justified the adoption of liberalized trade and investment policies. These efficiency considerations have to be related to concerns with competition policies because international oligopoly power can be used to serve very effectively the markets which it links. The efficiency considerations also have to be related to antidumping practices that can restrict the scope of trade liberalization commitments. Such antidumping practices, supported by very active lobbying groups, can be clearly anticompetitive, and thus can merit scrutiny in interactions over competition policy issues.

Trade liberalization in the more developed areas of the world trading system is driven principally by the efforts of the USA to open markets in Europe and East Asia. Influential groups in US policy communities see home country firms in those markets profiting from diverse forms of governmental support and from collusive practices tolerated under lax competition policies. American trade policy activism is thus felt to be justified in the national interest, and also in the global interest.[35] Imperatives for this activism are not seen to be diminished by the establishment of the WTO. This structure does not generate broad aggregations of interests that could be given expression in more comprehensive liberalization. General increases in market openness have to be achieved through bargaining in the Atlantic relationship, while most states in the global trading system implement cautious reactive policies and make few efforts to build collective bargaining strengths.

The American concern with perceived trade-distorting European and East Asian practices is sustained in part by impressions that US antidumping cases do provide evidence of the significance of such practices, but also, it appears, by awareness that the volume of these cases, and the high proportion of findings (above 90 per cent) against foreign firms, tend to discourage trade, in effect making liberalized markets less contestable.[36] Commerce is similarly discouraged in the European side by large numbers of antidumping cases, which also lead mostly to findings against outside firms. In the USA and Europe the penalties imposed tend to be high, and the negative effects on trade flows have been substantial, notably in the sectors in which high proportions of complaints have originated – chemicals, primary and fabricated metals, nonelectrical machinery, and electrical and electronic equipment.[37]

Antidumping measures are permitted under the WTO, which imposes no accountability regarding their use, and does not restrict the rights of member governments to take unilateral actions in defence of their commercial interests.[38] Because of this freedom, it must be stressed, the strong bargaining strengths of the USA and the European Union, based on the sizes of their internal markets, are sources of attitudes attuned more to exchanges of concessions in Atlantic commerce than to problems of building support for liberalization in the global trading system. Progress in Atlantic interactions, however, is difficult because of preferences on each side for continued independence in the use of antidumping measures: there is no willingness to set up a common authority that would review the anticompetitive effects of antidumping measures and assume authority for obligating the treatment of antidumping cases in line with Atlantic concepts of fairness and welfare.[39]

In the USA, and to some extent in the European Union, high penalties imposed on foreign firms held to be selling below cost, together with the pronounced bias against such firms reflected in the findings of most antidumping cases, encourage intensive lobbying activity, and proliferations of complaints.[40] Adversarial attitudes which tend to develop in trade policy communities thus tend to be stronger than might otherwise be expected. Economic rationales for increased liberalization are thus in danger of being relativized as attentions focus on strategies for extracting concessions from trading partners through aggressive demands backed by implicit threats of allowing greater scope for antidumping complaints. Meanwhile the discouraging effects of antidumping decisions on commerce tend to be extended because the imposition of penalties on foreign suppliers introduces distortions into markets for closely related products.[41]

The increasing numbers of antidumping cases and their diversity, together with operations by lobbying groups, increase the complexity of competition policy issues, tending to make these politically more intractable. Discussions of these issues in OECD over the past two decades have failed to yield consensus on how they should be approached in Atlantic relations, and have evidently made the USA and the European Union reluctant to consider entrusting such issues to the WTO. Meanwhile the strains and uncertainties in trade relations are evidently increasing the incentives for firms on each side of the Atlantic to serve their major markets through production in those markets. In this way an indirect effect of the trade difficulties is to strengthen the roles of transnational enterprises, to the disadvantage of firms whose limited resources oblige them to serve external markets mainly through exports.

Transnational enterprises, because of the scale of their direct investments in host countries and the advantages derived from investment bidding by those countries, are motivated to observe caution in price competition against host country firms, and in the use of imported inputs which for purposes of intrafirm trade are covered by transfer prices that can disguise artificial valuations. Public attention that is taken up by antidumping cases can of course be diverted from price discrimination strategies implemented by firms producing in host markets. The larger the scale of such production the stronger is likely to be the political influence which can be exerted to moderate complaints about the effects of price discrimination. Meanwhile, however, as the international production and marketing operations of transnational enterprises expand, with superior efficiencies relative to the activities of domestic firms, the sensitivities of those firms to perceived cases of dumping by corporations penetrating the local markets through exports are likely to increase. More impetus may thus be given to the expansion of operations by transnational enterprises, because of the trade frictions.

Altogether, the complex structural issues which are being posed for governments are assuming larger dimensions while international competition policy issues remain unresolved and foreign direct investment policies encourage transnational production more than arm's-length exports for the service of markets.[42] Governments competing in the implementation of trade policies tend to lose structural policy capabilities as transnational enterprises make more and more independent strategic choices while inducing more active investment bidding rivalries. In the internationally linked sectors high technology industries are becoming more prominent as concentration trends increase,[43] and in the Atlantic context US international firms are tending to be more and more advantaged, because of the continuing effects of technological lags in Europe and the slow emergence of regional firms through intra-Union mergers and acquisitions.

For the US administration, endeavours to achieve further liberaliz-ation in Atlantic commerce can offer prospects for increased exports that will reduce trade imbalances and the development of production in Europe rather than at home. These are major considerations because of concerns about the costs of globalization that have entered into national economic policy debates. If a preferential system of Atlantic trade can be formed, moreover, the USA will be more advantaged in its rivalry with Japan. Optimism about what can be achieved in that rivalry has been encouraged by the weakening of the Japanese regional production system in East Asia since 1997.

Uncertainties about further liberalization of Atlantic commerce, however, are likely to discourage US international firms from basing their strategies on such a prospect. Their established emphasis on investing in production within Europe is likely to remain strong, and may well increase if Atlantic frictions over monetary and financial issues become acute after the formation of the European Monetary Union. The risks of such frictions may be expected to be serious because of the difficulties of cooperation between policy communities on each side.[44]

TRADE IN SERVICES

A General Agreement on Trade in Services (GATS), negotiated as part of the Uruguay Round, sets general principles for the liberalization of trade in services and provides for sectoral negotiations in which, in effect, industrialized states are expected to bargain with each other and with third world governments for reciprocal concessions. No significant restraints are imposed on the freedom of governments to implement services trade policies independently. Little liberalization of services trade has resulted. The USA has been the principal advocate of liberal-ized services trade, seeking progress through sectoral bargaining with emphasis on securing favourable degrees of reciprocity. In global services trade US firms have superior competitiveness, because of strengths in their internal market and deep involvement in the Euro-pean Union, as well as because of extensive operations in Latin America and East Asia. The main focus of US quests for liberalization has been the European Union. The large presence of US manufacturing firms in the Union has encouraged much related development by US service enterprises. Service firms based in Union member states had difficulties in expanding outside their national territories until the Single Market

Programme became effective in 1992, and still have to contend with the cumulative effects of the previous fragmentation in the Union market.

National regulatory arrangements for services trade are generally restrictive, and can be changed virtually at will by governments without technical violations of GATS, which includes many exceptions that have allowed national administrations to concentrate on negotiating bilateral and regional deals for sectoral reciprocity.[45] Financial, communication, and air transportation services have been the sectors of most significance for the USA and the European Union. The US interest in financial services has been especially active because the establishment of the European Monetary Union may well lead to attempts to form a regional system for the regulation of banking and securities firms.

The Single Market Programme has intensified competition between financial institutions within the European Union, increasing a concentration trend in which mergers and acquisitions involving firms in member countries have been accompanied by mergers and acquisitions involving US and other outside enterprises. A very high proportion of the activities by US financial institutions has been in Britain, and from there the expansion of operations into the rest of the Union has been facilitated by the Second Banking Directive, implemented by member countries during the mid-1990s, which enables financial institutions licenced in any EU state to operate throughout the Union. For the European Union there are complex reciprocity issues because of a highly pluralistic pattern of financial regulation in the USA, in which authority is fragmented between several agencies, including the Federal Reserve, the Federal Deposit Insurance Corporation, and the Securities and Exchange Commission.[46]

US financial institutions have a recent history of acute fragility, due to the weaknesses of numerous banks and the failures of many Savings and Loan Associations, which have been very costly for the US administration. Strong speculative compulsions have been evident in the sector, notably with the growth of securities firms whose operations are difficult to regulate. There is a danger that speculative activities will become unsustainable, leading to a crisis.[47] In such an event releases of funds by the Federal Reserve, which helped to overcome a crisis in 1987, might well be an inadequate remedy as the sector is now at a much higher level of internationalization, offering greater opportunities for capital flight.

A strong trend towards concentration is under way in the US financial sector, due to relaxations of restrictions on banking across state borders, and gradual reductions of legal barriers separating the operations of banks and securities firms.[48] Increasing concentration in the sector will lead to deeper and more potent international involvement, especially in Europe where the emergence of regional enterprises through mergers and acquisitions is likely to continue at a slow pace, because of the divisive effects of national loyalties and the persistence of slack growth in the European economies. A weakening of the financial sector in Japan, meanwhile, following the crises in industrializing East Asia, will enable US financial institutions to compete more effectively in the Asia-Pacific region.[49]

Changes in relative bargaining strengths associated with the stronger roles of US financial institutions in Europe and East Asia can be expected to enable the USA to press for increased liberalization, on more favourable terms, in the European Union. On the European side cautious responses are likely, not only because the competitive advantages of US institutions are becoming greater but also because the fragmentation of authority in the US system of financial regulation hinders negotiating strategies that could make full use of the nation's potential for leverage.

The growth of trade in financial services, especially across the Atlantic, has been greatly facilitated by advances in communications technology and a liberalization of communication services. The technological advances have tended to make national regulatory restrictions ineffective, despite endeavours by governments to preserve the national character of their communications industries. Communication services, liberalized within the European Union and in the USA, have multiplied Atlantic business connections on a large scale, in effect giving prominence to regulatory issues over which US and European interests can conflict. A European regulatory system may evolve with an emphasis on facilitating the development of Union communication services. On the US side there is concern to maximize opportunities for the expansion of American communication firms in Europe, especially through links with the financial sectors.[50] Use of these opportunities, in a context of Atlantic cooperation and competition, assists operations by US communications firms in the rest of the world, aiding especially rivalries with Japanese communications firms.

High volume cross-investment in financial services is a source of restraints on resorts to leverage in Atlantic relations, and ensures continuity in current levels of contestability, as well as relatively favourable prospects for collaborative adjustment to strains that may follow the establishment of the European Monetary Union.[51] The interdependence in financial services also contributes to the acceptance of rationales for further liberalization in Atlantic communications services. In air transport services, however, there are major asymmetries which give rise to conflicts of interest. The European Airbus consortium, with large subsidies from member countries, has challenged the global market strength of the leading US aircraft manufacturer, Boeing, causing US administrations to exert pressures for the elimination of official support for Airbus. Meanwhile US airlines enjoy rights to provide services between Union countries, while European airlines do not have corresponding rights to provide services within the USA. For more balanced interdependence the European Union could demand reduction of the intrazonal rights of US carriers in Europe, while pressing the USA to allow European carriers to serve routes within the United States.

Political will to form a regional air transport system with rights for mainly Union carriers does not appear to be developing in the European Union, and for the USA there are no major incentives to seek further access to Union routes. National airlines in the Union value their individual rights to serve Atlantic routes, and could see their access to US cities endangered by efforts to reduce US air services between Union member states.[52] For US airlines retention of the rights enjoyed in Europe becomes more important as the Union admits new members and as it increases its commercial links with East Asia. US air transport interests in East Asia have been asserted rather effectively in negotiations with Japan, in which bargaining strengths have been altered because of the financial stresses in industrializing East Asia.

REGIONAL AND GLOBAL CONTESTABILITY

Trends in market contestability which were associated with an apparently stress-free globalization process have been altered by the financial distress in East Asia. Globalization was raising interdependencies between major industrialized states in ways which preserved a rough balance between the USA and the European Union, while both were challenged by high growth in a Japan-centred East Asian economic system. With the weakening of that system, political and economic links between it and the European Union have become more distant and less active, while the USA has in effect acquired greater bargaining strength in relations with Japan. At the same time recoveries from slack growth in Europe have become more dependent on increased commerce with the USA. With these changes, and with continued growth in the US economy, the resources of US international firms for support of their global operations have assumed greater significance, making possible more active quests for world market shares.[53]

In perspectives on market functions which influence policy communities in industrialized states, the East Asian reverses have been seen to strengthen the logic of aligning economic policies with competitive processes, for maximum efficiencies and for the imposition of market discipline on those processes. The scope for effective structural policies is considered to have been reduced, in view of the East Asian evidence that problems of governance tend to cause deficiencies in technocratic functions, with tolerance of excessive risk-taking by favoured firms. Prospects for consensus on the need for a common structural policy in the European Union have become unfavourable, although the Union's technological lags and weak growth remain formidable problems. The impressive structural policy consensus in Japan, however, has been preserved with some modifications to increase contestability for greater efficiencies, and to restrict diversions of resources into speculative operations. In the USA longstanding emphasis on market-friendly policies has been strengthened in ways that have discouraged interest in structural policy initiatives. Trade policy activism has accordingly assumed more significance as a key to export performance that can promise higher growth. Meanwhile the dangers posed by high levels of speculation, however, have tended to force greater recognition of regulatory imperatives that can impose caution on market-friendly policies.

The USA has, in effect, acquired more scope for international policy initiatives because of diminished European expectations of growth-enhancing commerce with East Asia, Japan's increased dependence on the US market, and the enhanced importance of that market for distressed East Asian industrializing states. The dynamics of US economic policy making, however, continue to operate with strong pluralism that can induce stagnation, while issues concerning the costs and benefits of globalization are demanding coherent responses. Compulsions to increase trade policy activism can thus motivate the administration, especially because of the strength of protectionist pressures in the legislature.

In the European Union the dynamics of policy making allow considerable scope for the representation of protectionist demands, and these may well become stronger as slow growth disappoints expectations of higher performance in the single market. The European Commission's extensive consultations with interest groups across the Union, for the aggregation of representative demands as a basis for policy initiatives, has resulted in openness to concerns about outside penetration of the integrated market.[54] Protectionist pressures have been responsible for a 1991 understanding with Japan which restrains its motor vehicle exports to the Union until the end of 1999. Demands by clothing and footwear groups have also ensured continued protection of these sectors.

The widening of opportunities for US international policy initiatives, which may be of less consequence than would otherwise be possible because of problems of governance, has reflected structural and bargaining changes that have expanded opportunities for American transnational enterprises. Japanese competitors have lost degrees of status because of strains in their home economy, and caution has been imposed on their planning because of the disruptions of East Asian economies that were becoming closely linked with Japan. A general effect appears to have been weakened Japanese corporate involvement in Europe, together with reduced Japanese interest in Latin America. Adjustments and recoveries in industrializing East Asia must be expected to have high priorities for the major Japanese firms that have been deeply involved in that area.

The European focus of American transnational enterprises suggests that the most significant uses of new opportunities by these firms will be intended to consolidate positions in the Union market, especially in advance of changes likely to follow the establishment of the European Monetary Union. This will tend to facilitate growth by Union firms, and the development of more numerous intrazonal mergers and acquisitions. It will probably also give some impetus to the expansion of links between interest groups in member countries, and to an intensification of their consultative interactions with the European Commission.

US international firms are thus likely to lead a stronger Atlantic and, to a degree, global concentration trend. The persistence of slack growth in Europe will probably contribute further to this trend, that is because of increasingly significant technological lags and lags in competitiveness, the negative effects of heavy debt burdens and high unemployment, and the degrees to which regional entrepreneurial endeavours are hindered by divisive national loyalties in member countries of the European Union. It must be stressed, however, that high levels of speculation in the US economy have considerable destabilizing potential. Authoritative warnings of this can indicate needs for monetary restraint and more efficient regulation of the financial sector, but remedial action can be made difficult by problems of governance, which can have more serious negative effects during critical election years.

NOTES

1. See Robert Z. Lawrence, 'Trade liberalization issues in industrial countries', in Chorng-Huey Wong and Naheed Kirmani (eds), *Trade Policy Issues* (Washington DC: International Monetary Fund, 1997) pp. 69–86 and *Trade and Development Report, 1997* (Geneva: United Nations Conference on Trade and Development, 1997).
2. Reduction of trade barriers by governments gives impetus to this trend. On the trend in the EU see Stephen Davies and Bruce Lyons et al., *Industrial Organization in the European Union* (Oxford: Oxford University Press, 1996) chapters 2 and 4.
3. See Bernard Hoekman, 'Competition policy and the global trading system', *The World Economy*, **20** (4), July 1997, 383–406, and Alexis Jacquemin, 'Towards an Internationalisation of Competition Policy', *The World Economy*, **18** (6), November 1995, 781–90.
4. On the problem of technology collusion see William J. Baumol, 'Horizontal collusion and innovation', *Economic Journal*, **102** (410), January 1992, 129–137. See also Giovanni Dosi, Keith Pavitt and Luc Soete, *The Economics of Technical Change and International Trade* (New York: New York University Press, 1990) chapter 8, and Nathan Rosenberg, Ralph Landau and David C. Mowery (eds), *Technology and the Wealth of Nations* (Stanford: Stanford University Press, 1992) chapters 7 and 15.
5. See Lawrence J. White, 'Competition policy in the United States: An overview', *Oxford Review of Economic Policy*, **9** (2), Summer 1993, 133–50; B. Dan Wood and James E. Anderson, 'The politics of US antitrust regulation', *American Journal of Political Science*, **37** (1), February 1993, 1–39; and Marc Allen Eisner, 'Bureaucratic professionalization and the limits of the political control thesis: the case of the Federal Trade Commission', *Governance*, **6** (2), April 1993, 127–53.
6. See *Industrial Organization in the European Union* (op. cit., note 2), part II.
7. See Masahiko Aoki and Ronald Dore (eds), *The Japanese Firm* (Oxford: Oxford University Press, 1994) and Jonathan Morris (ed.), *Japan and the Global Economy* (London: Routledge, 1991).
8. See *Towards a New Global Age: Challenges and Opportunities* (Paris: OECD, 1997).
9. Large states tend to extract concessions from small states, seeking advantages through hub and spoke trade liberalization arrangements. See Ronald J. Wonnacott, 'Trade and investment in a hub and spoke system versus a free trade area', *The World Economy*, **19** (3), May 1996, 237–52. Comments by Lawrence (op. cit., note 1) on the roles of international firms in deepening integration, have implications regarding entry barriers.
10. See Brian Hindley and Patrick A. Messerlin, *Antidumping Industrial Policy* (Washington, DC: American Enterprise Institute, 1996), Alan M. Rugman and Michael V. Gestrin, 'US trade laws as barriers to globalisation', *The World Economy*, **14** (3), September 1991, 335–52, and Donald A. Hay, 'Anti-competitive practices, market access and competition policy in a global economy', *Market Access after the Uruguay Round* (Paris: OECD, 1996) pp. 81–100.
11. On the dynamics of protectionist policies see Sanoussi Bilal, 'Political economy considerations on the supply of trade protection in regional integration arrangements', *Journal of Common Market Studies*, **36** (1), March 1998, 1–32, and John B. Goodman, Debora Spar and David B. Yoffie, 'Foreign direct investment and the demand for protection in the United States', *International Organization*, **50** (4), Autumn 1996, 565–91.
12. See Allen V. Deardorff, 'An economist's view of the World Trade Organization', *Joint US–Korea Academic Studies, 7, 1997: The Emerging WTO System and Perspectives from East Asia*, 11–36.
13. On the scope to negotiate preferential trade arrangements see brief comments in Deardorff.

14. On protectionist dynamics in the US system see Goodman, Spar and Yoffie (op. cit., note 11), and Douglas Nelson, 'Domestic political preconditions of US trade policy: liberal structure and protectionist dynamics', *Journal of Public Policy*, **9** (1), Jan.–Mar. 1989, 83–105.
15. Problems for Taiwan and other East Asian industrializing states in their rivalries with Japan are discussed in Michael Hobday, *Innovation in East Asia: the Challenge to Japan* (Aldershot: Edward Elgar, 1995).
16. See references to domestic factors in antitrust policy in Wood and Anderson (op. cit., note 5), and comments on the orientation of competition policies in Jacquemin (op. cit., note 3).
17. Jacquemin refers to this problem.
18. See references to imbalances in *Trade and Development Report, 1997* (op. cit., note 1) and to the costs of globalization in Dani Rodrik, *Has Globalization gone too Far?* (Washington, DC: Institute for International Economics, 1997). See also Ethan B. Kapstein, 'Workers and the world economy', *Foreign Affairs*, **75** (3), May/June 1996, 16–37.
19. See Bruce Stokes (ed.), *Open for Business: Creating a TransAtlantic Marketplace* (New York: Council on Foreign Relations, 1996).
20. Japan's foreign economic relations are managed under considerable foreign pressure. See Yumiko Mikanagi, *Japan's Trade Policy* (London: Routledge, 1996).
21. On Japanese direct investment in Europe see John H. Dunning, *Alliance Capitalism and Global Business* (London: Routledge, 1997) chapter 13.
22. See Jose Campa and Linda S. Goldberg, 'The evolving external orientation of manufacturing: a profile of four countries', *Federal Reserve Bank of New York Economic Policy Review*, **3** (2), July 1997, 53–82.
23. See *The Single Market Review*: Subseries V: *Impact on Competition and Scale Effects*, Vol 3: *Competition Issues*, and Subseries IV: *Impact on Trade and Investment*, Vol. 4: *External Access to European Markets* (European Commission, 1997).
24. Ibid., and see *Industrial Organization in the European Union* (op. cit., note 2), Part II.
25. See Campa and Goldberg (op. cit., note 22).
26. Ibid.
27. Ibid.
28. Ibid.
29. See W. Carl Kester, 'American and Japanese Corporate Governance: Convergence to Best Practice?', in Suzanne Berger and Ronald Dore (eds), *National Diversity and Global Capitalism* (Ithaca: Cornell University Press, 1996) chapter 4.
30. See Erik Berglof, 'Reforming corporate governance: redirecting the European agenda', *Economic Policy*, **24**, April 1997, 91–124, and Benn Steil et al., *The European Equity Markets* (London: Royal Institute of International Affairs, 1996) chapter 5.
31. See Steil (op. cit., note 30).
32. See Kester (op. cit., note 29).
33. The demographic change has contributed to slower growth, which is discussed in Lawrence (op. cit., note 1). On the costs of protecting vulnerable sectors see Rodrik (op. cit., note 18).
34. See comments by Rodrik (op. cit., note 18), on the costs borne by workers and on the capacities of international firms to reduce their tax burdens by relocating their operations.
35. See Laura D'Andrea Tyson, *Who's Bashing Whom? Trade Conflict in High Technology Industries* (Washington: Institute for International Economics, 1992).
36. See Hindley and Messerlin (op. cit., note 10).
37. Ibid. See references to these sectors in Campa and Goldberg (op. cit., note 22).
38. See Deardorff (op. cit., note 12).
39. See Hindley and Messerlin (op. cit., note 10).
40. Ibid., and see Alan M. Rugman and Andrew D.M. Anderson, 'NAFTA and the

dispute settlement mechanisms: a transaction costs approach', *The World Economy*, **20** (7), November 1997, 935–50.

41. On the difficulties of restraining antidumping actions see Michael J. Finger, 'Subsidies and countervailing measures and antidumping agreements', *The New World Trading System: Readings* (Paris: OECD, 1994) pp. 105–12.

42. On investment bidding see Thomas L. Brewer and Stephen Young, 'Investment incentives and the international agenda', *The World Economy*, **20** (2), March 1997, 175–98. The structural issues for governments are related to the costs of globalization, discussed by Rodrik (op. cit., note 18).

43. See *Conflict and Cooperation in National Competition for High Technology Industry* (Washington, DC: National Academy Press, 1996, for the Hamburg Institute for Economic Research, the Kiel Institute for World Economics, and the National Research Council).

44. See C. Fred Bergsten, 'The dollar and the Euro', *Foreign Affairs*, **76** (4), July/August 1997, 83–95.

45. See Deardorff (op. cit., note 12), and Laura Altinger and Alice Enders, 'The scope and depth of GATS commitments', *The World Economy*, **19** (3), May 1996, 307–32.

46. See William D. Coleman, *Financial Services, Globalization and Domestic Policy Change* (London: MacMillan, 1996) chapter 7.

47. On the dangers of a financial crisis see Frederic S. Mishkin, 'Preventing financial crises: an international perspective', *Manchester School Papers in Money, Macroeconomics and Finance, Supplement*, **LXII**, 1993, 1–40, and references to the USA in Frederic S. Mishkin, 'Understanding financial crises: a developing country perspective', *Annual World Bank Conference on Development Economics, 1996* (Washington, DC: World Bank, 1997) pp. 29–62.

48. See Coleman (op. cit., note 46).

49. See comments on the Japanese financial sector in *World Economic Outlook, Interim Assessment, December 1997* (Washington, DC: International Monetary Fund).

50. See *External Access to European Markets* (op. cit., note 23), 85–6.

51. See figures for cross-investment in financial sectors in Sylvia E. Bargas, 'Direct investment positions for 1996', *Survey of Current Business*, **77** (7), July 1997, 34–55.

52. The European Commission is advocating collective negotiations with the USA, involving all EU airlines, and has begun legal proceedings against EU carriers that have bilateral arrangements with the USA – *The Economist*, 14 March, 1998, 5.

53. On US growth see *World Economic Outlook* (op. cit., note 49), 25.

54. See Bilal (op. cit., note 11).

4. Structural competitiveness and interdependencies: regional patterns*

John de la Mothe and Gilles Paquet

' . . . national productivity levels depend on a quality which [Abramovitz] labels "social capability" but freely admits that no one knows what this means.' E.L. Jones (1995)

1. INTRODUCTION

There has been considerable debate in recent years about the notion of competitiveness. Some have discarded it altogether as being rather 'a poetic way of saying productivity' at best, and at worst as being 'a matter of time-honoured fallacies about international trade being dressed up in new and pretentious rhetoric' (Krugman 1996a: 24). Others have provided an array of definitions that consider competitiveness to be gauged by unit costs or market shares. A broader and (perhaps) more useful definition might be the one that Krugman has proposed somewhat ironically: 'a combination of favorable trade balance *and something else*' (Krugman 1996b: 6, emphasis added). While Krugman uses this expression in a somewhat derogatory sense, it focuses helpfully on the capacity of a country to meet the test of foreign competition whilst ensuring a presence in certain key economic sectors, or a growing standard of living, or 'something else' that is regarded as being desirable from a social welfare or other efficiency point of view.

In this chapter, we are interested in 'structural competitiveness'. Chesnais has defined it as 'the strength and efficiency of a national economy's productive structure . . . the global efficiency of the national economy, proficient and flexible structure of its industries, the rate and pattern of capital investment, its technical infrastructure and other factors determining the "externalities", i.e. the economic, social and institutional

* The assistance of Chris Wilson in preparing this chapter and Chapter 5 has been most important, and the comments of Jeffrey Roy have been most appreciated.

frameworks and phenomena which can substantially stimulate or hamper both the productive and competitive thrust of domestic firms' (Chesnais 1986: 86–7).

The key word here is *externalities*. The notion of structural competitiveness acknowledges that the capacity of firms to compete effectively does not depend only on factors that are internal to the firm, but also on more *systemic* and *environmental* features of the firm/sector, frameworks and phenomena that are external to the firms that have a significant impact on their performance. The challenge here is to characterize how this great diversity of systemic and environmental forces impact on and modify the productive and competitive thrust of domestic firms.

In the next section, we identify the various channels through which the capabilities of firms might be enhanced or hampered, the interdependencies among the stakeholders of each firm and among firms might be enriched or empoverished, and effective knowledge production and value creation might be catalysed or paralysed. We then examine some examples of the different ways in which this nexus of processes operates in Europe, North America and East Asia in order to be able to elicit the relevant contrasts between zones and to conjecture the likely drift in the nature of their structural competitiveness over the next decade. In conclusion, we identify the most important pressure points and blockages that are likely to tilt the level playing field among these three economic zones.

2. STRUCTURAL COMPETITIVENESS: CAPABILITIES, INTERDEPENDENCIES AND VALUE CREATION

Structural competitiveness is a systemic attribute of the national economy. It has an asymmetric impact on efficiency at the firm, sector and corporate levels. This asymmetric impact is built on a complex interactive structure (Dosi, Pavitt and Soete 1990). It depends on the structure of the national economy and the way it functions, but it also depends on its governance and its gumption as it emerges from the aggregation of, and the interaction between, the different components, as well as on the extent to which these contextual forces generate levels (high or low) of energization and entrepreneurial drive from the component units.

Consequently, it is not possible to understand the channels through which structural competitiveness forces operate to make firms more or less competitive without (a) getting a fair appreciation of the ways in which firms as knowledge systems operate to create value, and (b) understanding the complex ways in which the stakeholders are connected to their environment.

Meso-Business Systems

The firm is a knowledge system, a complex web of systemic relationships between suppliers, customers, partners, and so on who co-create value through their interactions. In the traditional conception, this value creation process may be stylized as a sequence of three knowledge processes: the *generative* process through which new knowledge is produced by activities aimed at problem-solving; the *productive* process which manifests knowledge in the form of a product or service; the *representative* process which transmits manifest knowledge to the customer. But this stylization does not account very clearly for the extraordinary intensity and complexity of interactions between actors in business systems: relations are less sequential and more reciprocal and synchronous, and underpin an intricate and complex network of collaboration involving customers, suppliers, competitors and many other allies in an integrated value-creating partner system in which much knowledge is tacit (Wikstrom and Normann 1994).

This complex web of relationships translates into various capabilities. One may distinguish those rooted in forms of knowledge that are 'idiosyncratically synergistic, inimitable, and noncontestable' – the intrinsic core capabilities – and those that are easily imitable and contestable – the ancillary capabilities (Langlois and Robertson 1995: 30). Such capabilities are obviously augmentable and this may be done depending on the range of abilities that a firm has in terms of learning and of picking up information from external sources. But, there may also be failure to learn through inertia, through the operations of environmental systemic factors, or through blockages that limit the absorptive capacity.

Transaction costs have been evoked as the central feature in this nexus of interfaces amongst agents, or groups of agents, within the meso-business system (MBS) or between the MBS and its environments. When there is true interdependence, it leads to inseparability, indivisibility and super-additivity. As interdependence deepens and becomes more intense, synergies become more important and idiosyncratically synergistic resources become also increasingly central. As a result, the value creation process becomes more and more impossible to disentangle. This intense interdependence binds together more and more complex organizations encompassing ever broader sets of intrinsic capabilities. In this modern business world, networks (as the locus of interdependent processes) are the new unit of analysis.

Interdependence is also the result of broader systemic forces in the environment that promote and sustain regimes, rules, conventions, forms of cohesion or ensembles of market and non-market relationships generating tighter and more intensely welded networks. These are the families of forces that are generally referred to as the source of structural competitiveness. They are generally identified as sources of external economies or dis-economies for these nexuses of processes defining the meso-business system.

Learning business systems are nested in a broader 'learning economy' as Lundvall (1996) labels it. In this learning economy, the focus is less on allocating existing resources and more on the creation of new value, products and services through innovation and learning. The most important feature of the learning economy is its capacity to increase the rate of learning, especially in sectors facing direct international competition. Structural competitiveness is thus an apt phrase to capture the ensemble of regimes, rules and broader characteristics of the learning economy that ensure in a diffuse but most important way that there is much collective learning in the business system. Structural competitiveness is a shorthand for the prevailing *learning code* that is in place, even though it is not easily captured by structural features. It represents a synthetic way to refer to a variety of features of the economy, society and polity that impact on the learning capabilities of the firm and its capacity to transform. To fully itemize this array of forces is, of course, difficult, and to exactly gauge its impact in quantitative ways is impossible. But one may at least identify broad families of features that are likely to help or hinder this meso-business system learning. The 'New New Deal' that Lundvall is calling for has to do with the coordinated systemic efforts to strengthen the learning capabilities of knowledge-based business systems.

An Organizing Metaphor

This very complex notion of *learning business system* and the very looseness of features like global efficiency, flexibility, infrastructure, 'social capability', patterns of investment (all subsumed under the general heading of structural competitiveness) make them too elusive to be analysable unless one can use a framework that is capable of sorting out, to some degree, the kinds of forces at work.

A variety of approaches are available when one is interested in partitioning both a business system and its environment in such a way as to determine the most important interfaces. Gareth Morgan (1986) has reviewed the set of metaphors in good currency in organizational analysis. The one we propose to use is a hybrid of a few of Morgan's models and is built on a view of the organization as an organism. The rough image sketched in Figure 4.1 presents the main features of a business system and draws freely from Laurent, Paquet and Ragan (1992).

In the approach which we suggest, network organizations might best be defined as the combination of five subsystems of relationships:

1. the *metabolic* subsystem (1) through which the network feeds on its environment and interacts with the external field of forces. The environment is fundamentally informational, but, through this information system, the network taps resources. The richer the informational context the stronger the metabolic relationships *ceteris paribus*;
2. the *technological* subsystem (2) imposed on the network by physical and social technology. These are not absolute constraints, for there are many ways in which one can trade off location and organization against technology (de la Mothe and Paquet 1994). However, there are also untraded interdependencies and synergy effects in the 'filière technologique' (or stream of technological activities) that shape the dynamics of socioeconomies and cannot be ignored except at great costs (Dosi et al. 1988);
3. the *process/functional* subsystem (3) underpins the operations of the network. It weaves physical, informational, and interpersonal resources into a *force de frappe* with commitment that stimulates social learning, probing, enacting, cooperation, alliances, and so on through activating interdependency capabilities and interpersonal resources and trust (Foa 1971);
4. the *structural* subsystem (4) connotes the organizational and institutional features of the business system; these emerge from interaction between the operations of the network and its guidance system but also reflect a significant impact from the other subsystems. This subsystem institutes the core learning capability of the strategic network, its carrying capacity. The more modular, holonic, decentralized, and polycephalous the network, the more likely it is to function well and to stay the course, and also to engage the external environment and to trigger evolution (Weick 1979);
5. the *governing* subsystem (5) embodies the shared values that hold the network together in a dynamic pattern of interaction and

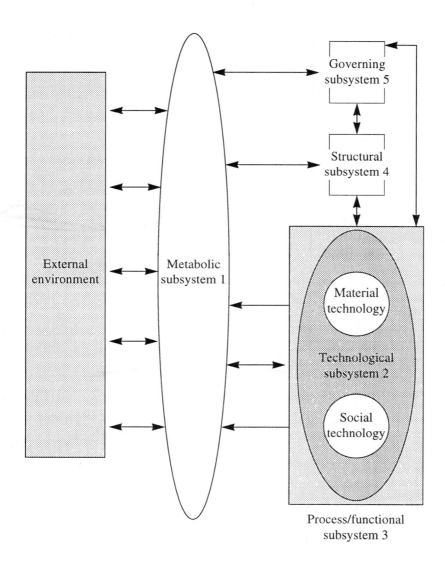

Figure 4.1   A meso-business system

provide it with a guidance system. This is an evolving set of information and control relationships embodying the brain of the
organization (Beer 1976). The governance subsystem may be par-
titioned in two subsets: the executive relationships to maintain the
course of affairs in line with current values and standards; and
the policy-making relationships to modify values and switch standards as organizational learning occurs (Vickers 1965).

These five sets of relationships are strongly interrelated and are co-
evolving. But they have sufficient specificity to serve as a port of entry
for different external effects. At any time, such external effects may
either reinforce existing features of the network or generate some
strains between the different processes and trigger all sorts of adjustments. The ensuing evolution of the business system will, however,
proceed rather slowly most of the time. This is the case because network
organizations (public or private) are 'dynamically conservative social
and intellectual systems built around prevailing technology': it is not
necessarily likely that a major technological innovation, or an important
structural change, or a significant change in the theory of the firm *in
isolation* will trigger a massive reconfiguration unless complementary
processes are also modified (Schon 1971).

One cannot understand how the MBS interacts with its context unless
one fleshes out this context somewhat. This is not easy because the
MBS is embedded in a complex set of Russian dolls-type echo boxes
at the global, national and subnational levels. This loose context is
mapped in a very rough way in Figure 4.2.

The global context is only structured in a minimal way by reminding
the reader that national/regional shells are not necessarily all equal:
there are important asymmetries between dominant and dominated
nations/regions. The MBSs are coalescing in different ways in that
context: some at the local/regional level, others into a national network,
others still transversally across national/regional borders. They also
interact with each other and with governments and sociocultural entities
either within or outside their jurisdiction.

The nature of the intercorporate links, of the industry structure, of
the interface with the civil society, and the intensity of the enervation
that flows from these relationships will influence dramatically the degree
of structural competitiveness. Indeed, it is the super-additivity of the
internal links within the MBS (Figure 4.1) and of the external links
between the MBS and its context (sketched in Figure 4.2) that generates
the *structural competitiveness effect* observed in different zones of the
world.

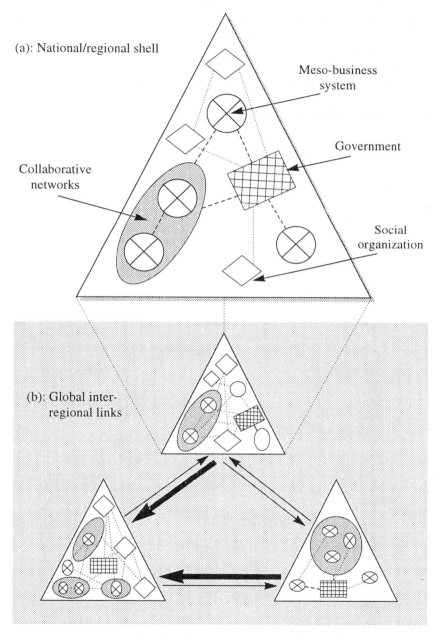

Figure 4.2   External milieu of a meso-business system

While we focus here on the five dimensions of the MBS as *sensors* through which external effects are likely to be appropriated, it should be clear that the very complexity of the environment is the *source* of the externalities which are more or less fully captured depending on the goodness of fit between the the *milieu interne* and the *milieu externe*.

Five-Dimensional Structural Competitiveness

It is extremely difficult to gauge precisely the nature and extent of existing external economies, but the problem is more complex now than it used to be, for external economies are becoming increasingly intangible in developed economies, more 'mobile' (Langlois and Robertson 1995: 99). So our effort to examine the five subsystems of relationships as sensors, as receptor channels for external effects on the business systems, does not presume to be exhaustive.

Our purpose in this subsection is to illustrate the sort of conventions, rules or processes that might deserve some attention under each heading, to illuminate some of these *different ways of doing* across regions that have played an important role in shaping the competitiveness of business meso-systems.

For instance, innovation pertains to all aspects of the network organization but most particularly to subsystem 2. The regime of competition, of provision of infrastructure and social overhead capital, and whatever institutions may prevent inertia and channel behaviour in the direction of a faster pace of innovation and of a greater capacity to generate new ideas and to diffuse them – all this is bound to impact on subsystem 2, and, through it, on the whole business system.

In the same manner, the legal framework and the ruling concept of property have a determining impact on subsystem 4, for it is built on these foundations. The more this system (and the jurisprudential and common-usage practices that have developed around it) promotes a de-absolutization of property rights, facilitating greater collaboration and sharing among stakeholders, the greater the capacity to transform of organizational forms. The business system is a learning system, and to succeed it must develop a great capacity to transform. This means that much importance must be given to the ease with which the governance system can effect transition and adjustment (subsystem 5). Anything that accelerates the process of executive or policy adjustment will improve the governance of the firm. However the link between governance and performance is far from simple: a greater facility to adjust may ease the transformation process of the meso-business system, but it may also lead to it having a lower ability to pre-commit and therefore may hurt the organization (Basu 1995).

Consequently, decisions about types of investment (those that commit more or less to certain directions or to certain types of activities) may have important impacts on the future of the system. This is a problem that is similar to the need for balancing knowledge exploration and knowledge exploitation: too much effort invested in the former may lead to failures in taking full advantage of the existing knowledge (March 1991).

The need for the business system to appropriate material, human, informational and financial resources from the external environment is so central that it makes it dependent on an effective capability to appropriate the needed resources (subsystem 1). A multitude of rules and impediments may paralyse these relationships. Indeed, some of the efforts to promote efficient coordination and networking may impair the process of appropriation of resources.

Finally, the business system also needs to maintain itself in a workable shape. Any failure at this level translates into a malfunctioning and drag. This is what subsystem 3 tries to capture. Any transformation in the rules of the game that facilitates alliances and cooperation or increases the power of mobilization of personal resources by the firm increases significantly its structural competitiveness.

These examples are meant to illustrate how our approach would deal with certain aspects of different socioeconomies and incorporate them in the framework. The central challenge, however, is to identify the main sources of structural competitiveness and to contrast these sources in the different regions. This is difficult since many of the significant features of the socioeconomies that generate some external effect on competitiveness have emerged (mostly) for purposes that have little to do with competitiveness. Moreover, such spillovers are often not fully appropriable. This means that some of the spillovers may end up strengthening the intrinsic core capabilities of national firms, while others will simply be free goods available to all and may only be bolstering ancillary capabilities or at worst be imitated/borrowed even more quickly by competitors. Finally, even though structural competitiveness is an interdependent national attribute, its effects will be mediated by a variety of filters on its way down to the firm: its final impact will depend on the different cultures and structures influenced by the systems of governance, and on the synergies in entrepreneurial cooperation, risk sharing, technological advance and alignment with structural policies.

This entails that structural competitiveness may have differential impacts on the different sectors but also at the different levels (firm, sector, intercorporate, national) on dimensions like gains from trade or investment.

3.   A LOOK AT REGIONAL PATTERNS

The central question is whether one can use this sort of partitioning and this sort of stylization of interfaces to identify important characteristic features of the socioeconomic systems in Europe, North America and East Asia, and to determine whether such differences are sufficient to explain the differential performance of enterprises in learning and value creation.

We have to be satisfied with a set of illustrations of what the externalities might be like and of the different channels through which they may affect the performance of firms and the competitiveness of the socioeconomy as an aggregate of economic agents. We focus on the Triad for comparative purposes, but it should be clear that there are important differences among countries in and around each of these three nodes.

To help in this comparative work, we have used a synoptic table synthesizing a number of important features of the different systems (Table 4.1). This summarizes some of the features of the different subsystems for each node of the Triad. While this table does not represent a comprehensive review of all the sources of structural competitiveness, or stylize rigidly the regime at any one node, it provides a provisional look at some central features of the different regimes. The table should help us to show how interdependencies among subsystems have materialized differently in the diverse regions and how interactions among the subsystems are at the core of structural competitiveness.

Metabolic Relations

Meso-business systems are open systems operating in an environment. This environment has a texture which constrains the flows of materials, energy and information between the business systems and the environment. In that sense, the metabolic relationships depend significantly on many factors that lie beyond the confines of the business systems. There has been some exploration of this interface by analysts interested in sustainable development. They have examined the material and energy uses in products and processes of industrial sectors and economies. But this *industrial metabolism* perspective is unduly restricted in scope (Ayres 1994).

Metabolic relationships do not pertain only to energy and material flows. They encompass a wide variety of exchanges of information and of financial, human and intellectual resources between the business systems and their environment. This symbiotic interface depends much on the type of absorptive capacity and tonus of the business systems – the US business system has an 'aerobic' nature, that is, it thrives in free oxygen, while the Japanese business system has more of an 'anaerobic' nature, that is, it would appear to have flourished in a much more constrained environment, and the European system would appear to nest somewhere in between – but also on the fit between these features and the evolving texture of the environment. As the environment becomes more turbulent and organizations become more and more interdependent, as well as catalysed by the increase in the speed, scope and capacity of the communication system, it may well be that the very advantages of a controlled environment *à la* Japan (fit for anaerobic business systems) can turn out to be disadvantages.

Herbert Simon has explored how different environmental structures impact the features of rational choice (Simon 1956), and Emery and Trist have proposed a stage-development of causal textures for the environment of business systems: placid random, placid clustered, disturbed reactive, and turbulent (Emery and Trist 1965). Placid random environments approximate the classical market environment in which opportunities and noxiants are distributed randomly and independently. Placid clustered environments approximate the world of imperfect competition where noxiants and opportunities are clustered. Disturbed reactive environments approximate the world of oligopolies in which the causal texture of the environment comes much from the interactions of the competing systems. Turbulent environments are dynamized not only by the interactions of competing systems but by new dynamic properties emerging from the field itself: the ground is in motion (Emery and Trist 1973). While simpler and less textured environments call for simple tactics and limited learning, more complex and dynamic environments call for complex strategies and alliances in the face of higher relevant uncertainty. More textured and turbulent environments adopt business systems capable of developing new forms of collaboration and cooperation among organizations with contrasted objectives but whose fate is correlated.

There is no simple metric to gauge the complex set of institutions that mediate relationships between the business systems and the environment, but one may loosely characterize the different regimes in

Table 4.1 Synoptic table illustrating characteristics of different socioeconomic systems

Subsystem	US	Europe	Japan
Metabolic	• Open market • Foreign MNCs significant and accepted • Low savings rates • Low investment and R&D rates • Declining productivity growth	• Selective, but basically open market • Foreign MNCs significant and accepted • Low savings rates • Medium investment and R&D rates • Stagnant productivity growth	• Restrictive access – no access to areas where Japan is exporting • Foreign MNCs not significant and not accepted • High savings rates • High investment and R&D rates • Increasing productivity growth
Physical technology	• Focus on product innovation, and the effective use of IPR to control access to those products. Similarly the US seeks to set standards to control product rents or to control software which runs hardware. In a number of cases the US has walked away from hardware markets when faced with strong competition from Japan or EU • Diffusion by hiring technology, FDI, buying personnel, or buying company	• Some focus on product innovation, particularly with niche applications. Limited control of either standards or processes to the extent that they are assembler of others' goods. • Diffusion by hiring technology, FDI, buying personnel, or buying company	• Focus on production process innovation to control market on price and quality. Strong hardware emphasis, particularly on industrial products. Seeks to have monopolistic control of essential leading-edge components to control downstream markets. • Diffusion by buying product, licensing technology, by government design

Social technology	• Individualism • Consumerism • Declining investment and quality of education • History of voluntary social activism • Anti-interventionist • Social mobility • Knowledge is private good	• Fraternalism • Investment in quality of life • Familialism • Tolerance of intervention • Limited mobility • Knowledge is private/public good	• Collectivism • Invest in future • High investment and quality of education • Strong voluntary and business associations • Expectation of intervention • Social immobility • Knowledge is public good
Process/functional	• Strong antitrust • Inward-looking regionalism • Domestically led development • Low unemployment/low wage • Limited safety net and regressive income distribution	• State-sponsored oligopoly/monopoly • Preoccupied with EU integration • Domestically led development • High unemployment/high wage • Generous safety-net	• Acceptance of oligopoly • 'Open regionalism' in trade • Export-led development • Low unemployment/high wage • Self-reliance
Structural	• Strong IPR and licensing of standards • Regional production networks • Adamant refusal to align FDI with national objectives • Refusal to develop strategic comparative advantage	• • • Unused capacity to align FDI to national objectives •	• Use of patent system for diffusion • Cross-national production networks • Strong capacity to align FDI with national objectives • Strategic developmental state
Governing	• Policy responses deregulation, macroeconomic and post-industrial transition	• Policies toward regional integration and post-industrial transition	• National strategies aimed at enhancing production quality and capacity in next generation industries

the Triad for they have more or less succeeded in managing to shape different metabolic subsystems that ensure some aligment between the environment and the business systems.

One of the main advantages of the North American system has been its almost doctrinal commitment to open markets. But also, advantages stem from the extent to which it has nurtured flexibility and smoothness in access to resources like venture capital, and it has neutralized the barriers to downsizing, restructuring and Schumpeterian creative destruction initiatives. This has translated into a high entrepreneurial capacity and of a much greater ease of access to resources of all sorts by North American business systems than for their competitors in the more regulated or controlled environments of Asia and Europe.

The same may be said about the different forms of regional integration in each zone of the Triad: in North America, regional integration is mainly rule-based, while in East Asia it is much more based on formal hierarchy (parent–subcontract industrial relations) and, in Europe, on supranational institutional cooperation (Davis 1994). These different approaches provide environmental textures which carry a much greater capacity to learn in Asia and America than in Europe.

But it would be simplistic to focus exclusively on sheer access to resources. Resources may be more easily mobilized in certain zones but may also be extremely volatile and quickly lost. The degree of commitment of human resources and the availability of financial resources differ dramatically, depending on the sociocultural system or of the legal system. It is clearly lower in North America than in East Asia where there is a more effective capacity to make the best use of mobilized resources. Corporatist continental Europe would appear to stand halfway between the other two nodes on this score.

The 'contextualist' environment in East Asia, the relatively 'solidaristic' environment in Europe and the relatively 'individualistic' environment in North America nurture very different partnerings among stakeholders within the business system, and shape different forms of alliances and joint ventures with external partners. As these environments become more and more turbulent, they influence more fundamentally the social architecture of the value-creation process, and the different value systems are not only echoed in the legal system but also in the conventions facilitating or making more difficult the operations of the value-creating partner system.

So the metabolic relations permeate the numerous subsystems, impact on their structure and functioning, but also adapt to the strategies that emerge from the various subsystems. The metabolic relationships are major targets of macroorganizational policies by national governments.

But the organizational complexity that results from the dynamic inter-actions described above makes such intervention extremely daunting. Examination of the economic systems within the Triad suggests that no simple mechanical formula is available to design a perfect structural competitiveness fit.

The self-organizing structures are *process structures* and depend on the functioning of the system: a balance between coherence (structure) and innovation (flow) must be achieved. This is no simple feat. An additional difficulty stems from the fact that it has been extremely difficult to extricate macroorganizational policies from the realm of political value judgments. Consequently, the theory and policy of mac-roorganizational intervention has remained an underdeveloped field (Dunning 1997).

Material and Social Technologies

The metabolic relationships determine to a great extent which external economies emerging from the national context will be tapped by the business systems. This is done through adoption of business systems features that better fit the existing metabolic system. But countries differ also greatly in their technological capabilities, in their underlying 'organizing principles' of work, and, as a result, in their learning capa-bilities, that is, in the capacity to improve the learning to learn (Kogut 1994).

There are three forms of 'technology' (material/artefact, social/cul-tural, process/functional) and they are subject to increasing returns – but not necessarily at the same rate. Technical innovations diffuse faster than organizational innovations and they in turn diffuse faster than improvements in the capacity to learn. But we do not always know why. It may have much to do with the 'conditions of appropriability', that is, the required amount of transformation necessary in other subsystems for the innovation to work. But the ability to learn depends on identifi-able features – the nature of competition, the ability to identify opportunities, the deciphering of the sources of improvement in per-formance and quality, and the economic, social and political feasibility of change (Kogut 1994). These factors are partly shapeable by public policy.

We focus in this section on the first two dimensions that deal with the characteristics of technologies: the interactions between material and social technologies constitute an important source of differences between the regimes of the Triad.

The US technological regime is typified by the breakthrough economy fuelled by 'creative destruction' in which new firms act as agents of change. These firms have access to important external resources and are focused on in-house technical efforts aiming at innovation. In Japan, the regime is typified more by the follow-through economy, is more evolutionary, and is more akin to 'creative discovery' based on efforts to ensure incremental progress through cooperative R&D networks because of the limited access to top experts (Baba and Imai 1992). For those reasons, the R&D organizing principles in US business systems emphasize the creation of new knowledge while their Asian competitors emphasize learning and knowledge diffusion (Kogut 1994).

The US-type technological regime is dependent on local employee turnover, on a good fit of the company's capabilities with the external sources of innovation (universities, consortia, and so on), and on much centralized efforts in project management to generate cutting-edge technology. This formula, to some, outlines 'how the West grew rich' (Rosenberg and Birdzell 1994). The Japanese system focuses on the long-term continuity of the firm, exploits long-term employment, the links with suppliers and customers, and requires only small loose groups for coordination (Iansiti and West 1997). Evidence of this abounds, as, for example, when the President of Sumitomo Electric discussed his firm's innovative history in terms of centuries (CSIA 1991). European business systems tend to be closer to the US systems – often for cultural and institutional reasons – but with the additional twist that they are yet more influenced by framework strategies based on strong top-down macromanagement (Baba and Imai 1992), facilitated by the push towards a common market but accelerated by the pressures of globalization and bloc competition.

These systemic differences entail different processes of knowledge diffusion. In the US, knowledge can be acquired through personnel mobility and is easily diffused across borders, while in Japan technology is closely held and does not diffuse easily across borders (Hall 1998). Often, if access is required, reverse-engineering is the only way (Borrus 1993) combined with a closed intellectual protectionism that captures and internally diffuses ideas and technologies. Europe has developed, through the early versions of the EU Framework Programme, some networking across Europe; but it is only recently that it has re-balanced its actions in favour of more diffusion-oriented policies within the EU (Kind 1998).

Most of these dimensions of the technological regimes reveal the 'social embeddedness' of technical change (Dosi 1997). Indeed, under the vague label of *social technology*, a large number of institutions – including international non-governmental organizations like Greenpeace (Strange 1997; Ostry 1998) – have a fundamental importance in the evolution of structural competitiveness. These factors range from managerial competence, corporate flexibility, absorptive capacity, culture and sociability to regimes of ownership of knowledge. And in all those domains, the US would appear to be in a relatively less favourable position, while Japan is advantaged, with the European Union falling somewhere in between, according to the dimension examined. Despite the macroeconomic appearance of convergence between the Triad on a variety of knowledge-intensive indicators (for example, GERD/GDP, number of patents per capita, and so on) the meso-economic shake-out reveals quite different patterns. The 'level playing field' rhetoric often heard in trade negotiations has thus not in fact been borne out in reality (Ostry 1997).

The lack of technical competence is especially important in North America where there are (officially) nearly half a million unfilled high technology jobs and where a certain aversion to acquiring in-depth technical understanding translates into an aversion to organizational learning and adaptability. Indeed, the lack of flexibility of US corporate systems is ascribed in good part to the lack of technical training and to a significant underinvestment in worker skills, upgrading skills and continuous learning/training (Jaikumar 1986; Chaples and Keever 1994). This has translated into a lower broad absorptive capacity in the US *vis-à-vis* new material/artefact technology (and an even lower absorptive capacity in Europe where one observes a greater difficulty in learning high-volume flexible production and in orchestrating cross-national production networks, Borrus and Zysman 1997a).

Important cultural and sociability dimensions differentiate the nodes of the Triad and have impacts on the capacity to evolve toward the rules of new competition like Wintelism and cross-national production networks (Borrus and Zysman 1997b).

First, the individualistic culture of North Americans as opposed to the communitarian fraternalism in Europe and the communitarian collectivism in Japan help to explain the relatively poor performance of the US in a new setting requiring investment in the future and clan-type organizations based on high trust (Fukuyama 1995).

Second, change in material technology is significantly impacted by institutional arrangements. The patent system in Japan is clearly geared to the goal of importing, containing and 'distributing proprietary information as a public good to Japanese industry as a whole, or as a private good to industries whose continued success is viewed as vital to national development strategies' (Girouard 1996: 13; Hall 1998). Girouard shows, as does Hall, how administrative delays in handling foreign patents have a strategic intent and how the career patterns of senior patents officials provide evidence of the patent office being used as an intelligence unit and as a pivotal instrument in an elaborate system for the diffusion of technology. The emphasis in the US has rather been on promoting invention. This is in turn ascribable to some structural features of the business system such as the large dependence on impatient equity capital and the use of patent law and property rights to gain or protect temporary first mover advantage in contestable trade actions. Recent examples can be found in the auto sector and rules of origin issues with Japan, entertainment industry and copyright infringement issues with China, and patenting and biopharmaceutical issues with Brazil.

Third, collective support for relational contracting and networking has much impact (Hollingsworth 1993). In North America, strong anti-trust laws and a long tradition of adversarial relationships between government and business have made relational contracting, partnering and alliances among stakeholders more difficult and this in turn has discouraged the creation of large oligopolistic structures. In parallel, a stronger venture capital market has allowed more new firms to enter the knowledge industry areas and has heightened competition (Ostry and Nelson 1995). The point is made forcefully by Naisbitt (1996) in his comparisons between East Asia and North America.

Process/Functional Subsystem

There is no simple fit between the material and social technologies and the environment that holds the key to the smooth functioning of the business system, even if the broad 'features' of the socioeconomy influence the day-to-day operations of the business system. Both beneficial or deleterious effects on the performance of the system are mediated through a large number of conventions, norms, tacit agreements and moral contracts. This sort of tacit knowledge is recognized as fundamental in the innovation and diffusion of new technologies. Indeed, this explains why 'the process of experimentation proceeds in some settings with enthusiasm, skill and persistence, while in other settings experimentation and creative problem-solving take place only slowly and ineptly' (Murnane and Nelson 1984). The same thing holds for the functioning of the business system as a value-creating partner system (Wikstrom and Normann 1994).

While the emphasis on greater individual freedom and action in North America is likely to be beneficial in providing a fuller measure of flexibility, it makes cooperative and collaborative behaviour more difficult and makes it less easy to mobilize interpersonal resources as effectively as one might within a more cohesive system. This raises the question of trade-offs between economic liberalism, social cohesion and political freedom in the socioeconomy, and the external effects of particular mixes on the business systems (Dahrendorf 1995). While in Asia, social cohesion has been a dominant value and both economic liberalism and political freedom have been more willingly sacrificed (at least to some extent), in America, economic liberalism and political freedom have been promoted while social cohesion has been sacrificed somewhat (Sandel 1996). In Europe, the American values have been attenuated significantly in the name of corporatist cohesion.

A competitive market system may well be an effective way to stimulate change and learning, but hyper-competition may also lead to underinvestment in R&D and a lower economic growth than might be expected when there is only 'workable' competition, that is, where some government intervention limits or tempers the degree of competition. The capacity to improve the ability to learn continuously may require a mindset that encourages imitation and that is more likely in cohesive Japan than in Europe and America.

More or less flexibility, like more or less competition, affects the functioning of the business system by shaping different incentive reward systems that may accelerate or decelerate the process of ideas generation. But there is much inertia and path dependence in the drift of the socioeconomy, and often the process of social learning is derailed or trapped in suboptimal arrangements for reasons that have much to do with features of the value system: systematic risk-avoidance, localized learning, complexity of the process of change and difficulty in identifying the source of enhanced performance (Kogut 1994).

The strong antitrust sentiment in North America (as can be seen in events involving, for example, Microsoft and Netscape), when contrasted with the ease with which state sponsorship is accepted in Europe, and how oligopoly is regarded as a superior market structure in Japan, may explain why certain practices have developed more readily in one node of the Triad.

One central feature of the process/functioning subsystem is its performance. The fuzziness of the notion of competitiveness entails that the notion of operational effectiveness is not always clear. For instance, the new dimensions of 'systemic' competitiveness embodied in the European approach (Coriat 1997) have led to a high wage/high unemployment regime, and to much less interest in efficiency-driven measures like downsizing. The operational priorities have had much impact on the way things are done. Much less convergence than might have been expected has occurred because of the differences in the unstated assumptions about the very notion of operational effectiveness from one node of the Triad to the other.

The limited safety-net in the US and the self-reliance philosophy in Japan have stood in sharp contrast with the generous welfare philosophy in Europe. The principle-oriented trade negotiations by the US and the result-oriented negotiated access approach by the Japanese have contrasted with European strategies fueled much more by quality of life, equity and standards of living concerns as seen in the EU and OECD debates (European Commission 1996). These illustrate different approaches with regard to cross-national production networks: cautiously introduced by Japan, they have been copied by the US in ways that have often been very costly to local communities that had become 'disposable', while Europeans have remained reluctant to adopt them not only because of strategic myopia as Dosi suggests (1997), but also as a matter of choice based on the priority of social cohesion. The same important impact may be ascribed to loosely stated income redistribution commitments that have limited considerably the diffusion of material and social technologies in good currency elsewhere in Europe. Indeed, the process/functioning subsystem has adapted quite differently to globalization in the Triad and has significantly influenced national responsiveness to globalization.

Structural Subsystem

The day-to-day life of the business system (given the environment and the technologies) is a bubble of numerous interactions that tends to put pressure on existing formal structures and triggers an evolution in these rules. The relative importance of research universities, industrial associations, and of a focused legal framework are only a few of the features that define the architecture of the business system, and they are bound to evolve as a result of the functioning of the system.

The structural subsystem codifies and institutionalizes social learning in organizations and institutions. This is the subsystem which stands most clearly as the basis for comparison among the different zones of the Triad, because the stylized and instituted features of the different systems are both better known and better explained than the differences in the other subsystems.

The structural subsystem is a result of pressures to constrain the functioning of the business systems in ways that are in keeping with their broad objectives, but they are also dramatically constrained by the environment and the sociocultural system.

The US does not have a coherent structural system: its structural subsystem is a patchwork of fixes and levels rather than the result of a comprehensive plan (Noll 1991). On the contrary, in Japan, the structural subsystem is in place much more by design, strategy and tradition (Shimada 1991), while in Europe the structural subsystem is the result of reactive collegial coordination within a broad and still emerging EU Framework Programme.

An X-ray of the structures of the different business systems reveals fundamental cleavages between the zones of the Triad. These often echo fundamental differences in historical patterns and value systems. But they also reflect different sorts of industrial strategies: generic, uncoordinated and untargeted at the federal level in North America, programmatic and loosely targeted in Europe, and flexible, eclectic, but pragmatically targetted in Asia, as in the case of the Human Frontiers Initiatives.

Different theories of technical change and of entrepreneurship underpin the diverse practices and structures of the Triad. While North American entrepreneurs are perceived as heroic agents of 'creative destruction' and their work is stylized as frontier seeking and departing from accepted routines, Japanese entrepreneurs are focused on 'creative discovery' on the basis of cooperative, continuous and marginal progress in techniques (Baba and Imai 1992), while the European style would appear to be an intermediate case: grounded in stiffly reactive strategies of 'creative maintenance' (Pavitt 1984).

Another important structural feature is the nature of the relationships between government, business and society in each region. While in Japan government and business have forged very strong ties in the background of strong contextualist and tacit social cohesion, in Germany the strong alliances are between business and labor, and in North America business has held hegemonic power (Hart 1992). These different structures obviously entail much different behavior by governments as strategic oligopolists in the three zones (Dunning 1993). A third important structural feature pertains to antitrust legislation and rules. While in North America, and to a lesser degree in the United Kingdom, it is believed that great market power and cartels are dangerous features, in East Asia and in Europe excessive competition is regarded as dangerous, and inter-firm cooperation is encouraged.

Moreover, the difference between the structural and behavioral instruments is even greater than the differences in objectives. North America stands alone in 'its emphasis on private avenues of enforcement, triple damage suits, and a greater predisposition to extraterritorial application' (Ostry and Nelson 1995: 97). Over time, Europe (with the exception of the UK) has drifted significantly toward the Japanese position. The Framework Programme has provided the basis for a loose and limited supportive role of the state when necessary.

Governing Subsystem

Governance is the process through which a socioeconomy or any other complex organization is steered. Business systems have seen their governance evolve over time. But the governance subsystems have not evolved in parallel or at the same speed in the different zones. In Japan, the closed contextualist setting and the internal cooperative ethos have generated a network/transversal type governance subsystem with a strong learning capability. In North America, the individualistic ethos and the spirit of competition have led to a process of governance that remains rather decentralized even though 'temporary' monopolies are current and stable oligopolies often viable. The European systems are again occupying the middle ground with much greater centralization than in America but not as much social cohesion as in East Asia.

Whatever the degree of fit between the governance subsystem and the new realities, there is an agreement about (1) the new importance of coordination, (2) the need to effect this coordination in a 'localized' way to a much fuller extent than has been the case before, and (3) the need for government–business–society collaboration in such a governance system. But there has been much less convergence, at the ideological level at the very least, amongst the three zones on the philosophy of governance. Market principles dominate in the US and the UK, fairness looms large in Europe, and a result-based consensual framework drives Asia. All this has translated into a quasi-refusal to develop national comparative advantage strategies in the US, a limited and strategic state support for business in Europe, and a comprehensive and systemic predatory strategic developmental strategy in Asia (Dunning 1993).

In North America and in Europe, the 'centralized mindset' still prevails and has prevented the development of the new decentralized systems to the extent that it should have (Resnick 1994). For the same reason, there has been a great slowness in shifting the governing to the meso-level. Indeed, the bloc-creation process has often led to a recentralization of the governance of multinational firms, notably in North America (Litvack 1990).

To the extent that strong elements of communitarianism exist in Asia and Europe, some have argued that with increasing interconnectedness in the world economy, the world trading system will become more communitarian (Lodge and Vogel 1987). To the extent that cross-national production networks have blossomed, this is a trend that has made managed competition an increasingly important supplement to free trade, and has triggered the development of new forms of cooperation between government, business and society.

Subsystems' Interdependencies

We have thus far identified differences among the nodes of the Triad at the level of subsystems. But this hardly does justice to the regional patterns. For there is an inner dynamic in each region that cannot be reduced to a simple addition of these subsystemic dimensions.

Some may be tempted to decompose the overall performance in one country or in one node of the Triad into different components ascribable to the different subsystems as is done in shift-share analysis. In such calculations, one tries to decompose the changes in market shares into structural (market effect, commodity effect, specific effect) and residual effects (Guerrieri and Milana 1995). For instance, an analysis of the exports in high-tech products reveals that in Asia two-thirds of the increased market share are ascribable to structural effects (developing a greater market penetration in fast-growing commodity and market segments) and one-third to a residual 'competitiveness' advantage. For the US, two-thirds of the market share loss would appear to be ascribable to competitiveness disadvantages, while for European countries, the same would appear to be the case.

This sort of analysis identifying 'competitiveness' residually may give a rough sense of its relative importance but it throws no light on the 'real' sources of competitiveness. It simply constitutes a quantifiable metric of our ignorance so to speak, that is, of the changes in the relative competitiveness position of a country or region that we know nothing about.

Structural competitiveness emerges from a confluence of forces in the same manner as Bernouilli cells spontaneously emerge when oil is heated; the number and shapes of these cells depend on the energy flowthrough – at temperature X, four hexagonal cells are created, at temperature $X + i$, eight octagonal cells are created (Prigogine and Stengers 1988). In such a context, not only does one face two different structures for dissipating heat through oil, but it makes no sense to try to manage the first (less efficient) structure so that it can be as efficient as the second, for the structure acquires its form in response to the energy flowthrough. The central question is not which structure is comparatively better, but what is the energy flowthrough that is generating this type of structure.

If, indeed, as we suggest, the economy is made of process structures, the challenge is finding the balance between coherence (structure) and innovation (flow). But since we know so little about innovation and creativity, we are without meaningful levers to control it, and therefore without much possibility of controlling or modifying the multitude of structures which depend on it. Consequently, one cannot hope to ascertain the degree of structural competitiveness through a simple capitalization of interstitial coordination gains *à la* Ozawa (Chapter 7, this volume) or through the multiplication of relational contracts *à la* Kay (1995) although these are important components. In a learning economy, the source of structural competitiveness must be sought in the process of cognition and tracked down using 'pattern rationality' in the investigation of collective learning. This is working like a plumber, tracing back 'a leak to its source ... through a chain of possible causes ... at different locations in the system ... on the basis of a background knowledge of the system which is commonplace and largely tacit' (Schon 1995: 83).

Only with the help of such a diffuse pattern causality can one expect to develop insight into the process of cognition and learning, and gain some insights into the best way to structure knowledge production to foster structural competitiveness (Paquet 1998). One can imagine 'ways' to gauge, however roughly, some of the Schumpeterian efficiency gains or some of the innovativeness ascribable to trust and 'social capital' *à la* Coleman–Putnam, but it would be futile to expect that much precision can be gained in ascribing a portion of the socioeconomic performance to such 'causal' factors in a dynamic full of non-linearities where emergent properties are the new rule.

Our sense is that such work is bound to converge toward certain grey zones of economic theory like X-efficiency and entrepreneurship – zones where process is dominant and where cognition is omnipresent. But, this probing may not generate immediate policy dividends. It is more likely that for quite a while one may have to be satisfied with playing out likely scenarios, examining their plausible consequences for certain broad patterns of relationships among the subsystems, and probing the sort of dynamization one may expect from the emerging new process-structure contours.

As learning, knowledge and innovation become the new drivers of the economy, structure, functions and technologies will become more malleable, and even if discontinuities may not be predictable precisely, it will become normal to anticipate an erosion of national norms, standards and conventions, and the emergence of subnational entities better able to count on a better fit between technologies, structures and cultures (de la Mothe and Paquet 1998). This drift into 'glocalization' (that is, a process of localization evolving in parallel with the globalization movement) will in turn tend to weaken yet more the national contexts and to elicit different forms of looser and more distributed governance and to recast dramatically the sources of structural competitiveness.

4.   CONTRASTS AND TRENDS

Even though the world scene has become turbulent for all, and the challenges to the three zones have a certain similarity, the openness of the North American zone and the immense flexibility and adaptability of its rule-based fabric have probably not bestowed as many external benefits on its business systems as the structures of corporatist partnering in Europe or the tacit contextualist integration observed in East Asia. In the latter two cases, some important government–business– society cooperation has provided the European and East Asian firms with definite comparative advantages.

At the technology level, some sociocultural elements have been quite influential. The North American individualistic, competitive and adversarial tomus has led to a strong drive to explore, and the innovation process has thereby been fueled immensely. Competition has been the engine of progress and the material and social technological drives that have ensued have been impressive, but largely as a result of sheer combativity. The East Asian thrust has been quite different. The emphasis there on the imitation and diffusion of technology, and the strong support given to partnerships and alliances, have led to a much greater capacity for governments to provide national firms with competitive advantages. Europe has displayed a much greater capacity for solidaristic arrangements than North America, but without either reaching the consensus in East Asia or the urge to innovate in America.

Much benefit has obviously flowed from technological competition in North America. However, in the other two zones the national and zone partnership agreements may have generated often less rapid technological change but a more socially profitable one (redistributing the benefits to a greater extent toward the nationals). The degree of coordination by governments has often enabled European and East Asian business systems to exploit the better innovations generated in North America.

The central emphasis on competition in North America has led to the prevalence of Schumpeterian 'creative destruction' built on maximum freedom for economic opportunities, in a decentralized structure.

The East Asian business systems, building on social capital and trust, have been betting on a process of creative maintenance and discovery that has proved much less disruptive. Moreover, the capacity to mobilize without coercion in a multiple number of interacting ways has been the basis of a much more robust system of coordination and cooperation. One has therefore the very strong sense that structural competitiveness has been a much more important source of externalities in East Asia than in North America.

The European case is again halfway between the other two. Much partnering at the supranational and at the national levels has generated forms of institutional cooperation which have benefited many European enterprises, but not to the full extent that had become possible in East Asia. Even here, fast-moving software firms in Milan prefer to avoid the additional bureaucracy of the EU (Rome plus Brussels) and thus choose to forgo the pecuniary levers that are available through BRITE, EUREKA, ESPRIT, or other programs in order to compete quickly and partner with university laboratories or firms of their choice in Stanford, Montreal, or Newark.

Many of these differences have been ascribed to contrasts in the governance of the business systems. While there exists much variety, numerous levels and many speeds within each zone, the governance system has been generally more hierarchical and bureaucratic in Europe, more decentralized and market driven in North America, and more clannish and transversal in East Asia. This has provided the East Asian enterprises with greater flexibility to take advantage of the externalities generated by cooperative ventures. In North America the external benefits have often been dissipated as rents are when there is excess competition. The European governance system has on the other hand been often too cumbersome and inflexible to take full advantage of the external benefits generated by the actions of the European Union or of the national governments.

The complex alchemy of subprocesses might cause some convergence in the different zones, but, while the broader environment tends to be more and more similar, the metabolic relationships are firmly different, the structure/functioning relationships are converging in a more superficial than fundamental way, and between the governance mechanisms there remain fundamental differences that are unlikely to be easily erased. So it is more likely that there will be a coalescence of the three zones into loosely integrated but truly separate facilities with a much different if compatible institutional order.

5. CONCLUSION

This very simple sketch remains much of an hypothesis that needs to be validated by additional work. However, it has the benefit of identifying the nature of the blockages in the five dimensions of the business systems that may hold the key to useful interventions by governments interested in generating external benefits for their national enterprises and in helping them to appropriate these externalities.

Up to now, structural competitiveness has been regarded as a source of organic externalities very much as it is suggested that social capital is a source of economic and social progress in certain socioeconomies as a result of centuries of maceration (Putnam 1993). However, there is no reason to be satisfied with whatever this historical process cranks out. One may therefore craft strategies that are designed to increase the external benefits accruing to domestic firms and take action to help them appropriate them.

BIBLIOGRAPHY

Ayres, R.U. (1994), 'Industrial metabolism: theory and policy', in B.R. Allenby and D.J. Richards (eds), *The Greening of Industrial Ecosystems*, Washington: National Academy Press, pp. 23–37.

Baba, Y. and K. Imai, (1992), 'Systemic innovation and cross-border networks', in F. Scherer and M. Perlman (eds), *Entrepreneurship, Technological Innovation and Economic Growth*, Ann Arbor: The University of Michigan Press, pp. 141–51.

Basu, K. (1995), 'Flexibility in economic theory', in T. Killick (ed.), *The Flexible Economy*, London: Routledge, pp. 64–78.

Beer, S. (1976), *The Brain of the Firm*, London: Wiley.

Borrus, M. (1993), 'The regional architecture of global electronics: trajectories, linkages and access to technology', Berkeley Roundtable on the International Economy, mimeo 31p.

Borrus, M. and J. Zysman, (1997a), 'You don't have to be a giant: how the changing terms of competition in global markets are creating new possibilities for Danish companies', BRIE Working Paper 96A, 21p.

Borrus, M. and J. Zysman, (1997b), 'Wintelism and the changing terms of global competition: prototype of the future?', BRIE Working Paper 96B, 22p.

Centre for Science and International Affairs (CSIA) (1991), *Sumitomo Electric Innovates*', Cambridge, MA: John F. Kennedy School of Government.

Chaples, S.S. and D.B. Keever, (1994), 'Cultural contradictions impeding

American high-tech competitiveness in global markets', in S. Aahra and A.J. Ali (eds), *The Impact of Innovation and Technology in the Global Market Place*, New York: The Haworth Press, pp. 15–36.

Chesnais, F. (1986), 'Science, technology and competitiveness', *STI Review*, **1**, Autumn: 85–129.

Coriat, B. (1997), 'The new dimensions of competitiveness: towards a European approach', *IPTS Report*, No. 15: 7–14.

Dahrendorf, R. (1995), 'A precarious balance: economic opportunity, civil society, and political liberty', *The Responsive Community*, **5** (3): 13–39.

Davis, C. (1994), 'Competitiveness, sustainability, and the North American system of innovation', Background Paper for the Trinational Summer Institute, Whistler, B.C.

de la Mothe, J. and G. Paquet, (1994), 'The technology–trade nexus: liberalization, warring blocs or negotiated access?', *Technology in Society*, **16** (1): 97–118.

de la Mothe, J. and G. Paquet, (1998), *Local and Regional Systems of Innovations*, Boston: Kluwer Academic Publishers.

Dosi, G. (1997), 'The new socio-economics of organization, competitiveness and employment', *IPTS Report*, No. 15: 15–20.

Dosi, G. et al. (1988), *Technical Change and Economic Theory*, London: Pinter.

Dosi, G., K. Pavitt, and L. Soete, (1990), *The Economics of Innovation and International Trade*, Brighton: Wheatsheaf.

Dunning, J.H. (1993), *Multinational Enterprises and the Global Economy*, Reading, MA: Addison-Wesley.

Dunning, J.H. (1997), 'Governments and the macro-organization of economic activity', *Review of International Political Economy*, **4** (1): 42–86.

Emery, F.E. and E.L. Trist, (1965), 'The causal texture of organizational environments', *Human Relations*, **18**: 21–32.

Emery, F.E. and E.L. Trist, (1973), *Towards a Social Ecology*, London: Plenum Press.

European Commission (1996), *Building the European Information Society for Us All*, Brussels.

Foa, U.G. (1971), 'Interpersonal and economic resources', *Science*, **171** (3969): 345–51.

Fukuyama, F. (1995), *Trust*, New York: Free Press.

Guerrieri, P. and C. Milana, (1995), 'Changes and trends in the world trade in high-technology products', *Cambridge Journal of Economics*, **19**: 225–42.

Girouard, R.J. (1996), '*U.S. Trade Policy and the Japanese Patent System*', BRIE Working Paper 89, 55p.

Hall, I.P. (1998), *Cartels of the Mind: Japan's Intellectual Closed Shop*, New York: Norton.

Hart, J.A. (1992), *Rival Capitalists*, Ithaca: Cornell University Press.

Hollingsworth, R. (1993), 'Variation among nations in the logic of manufacturing sectors and international competitiveness', in D. Foray and C. Freeman (eds), *Technology and the Wealth of Nations*, London: Pinter, pp. 301–21.

Iansiti, M. and J. West, (1997), 'Technology integration: turning great research into great products', *Harvard Business Review*, **5** (3): 69–79.

Jaikumar, R. (1986), 'Post-industrial manufacturing', *Harvard Business Review*, **64** (6): 69–76.

Jones, E.L. (1995), 'Economic adaptability in the long term', in T. Killick (ed.), *The Flexible Economy*, London: Routledge, pp. 79–110.

Kay, J.A. (1995), *Why Forms Succeed*, New York: Oxford University Press.

Kind, P. (1998), 'International cooperation in the EU Framework Programs', presentation to the American Association for the Advancement of Science, Philadelphia, February 18.

Kogut, B. (1994), 'The permeability of borders and the speed of learning among countries', in J.H. Dunning, B. Kogut and M. Blomstrom (eds), *Globalization of Firms and the Competitiveness of Nations*, Lund: Institute of Economic Research, University of Lund, pp. 59–90.

Krugman, P.R. (1996a), 'Making sense of the competitiveness debate', *Oxford Review of Economic Policy*, **12** (3): 17–25.

Krugman, P.R. (1996b), *Pop Internationalism*, Cambridge: MIT Press.

Langlois, R.N. and P.L. Robertson (1995), *Firms, Markets and Economic Change*, London: Routledge.

Laurent, P., G. Paquet and T. Ragan (1992), 'Strategic networks as five-dimensional bricolage', in Salle R., R. Spencer and J.P. Valla (eds), *Business Networks in an International Context: Recent Research Developments*, Proceedings of the 8th IMP Conference, Lyon, pp. 194–206.

Litvack, I.A. (1990), 'U.S. multinationals: repositioning the Canadian subsidiary', *Business in the Contemporary World*, Autumn: 111–19.

Lodge, G. and E. Vogel (1987), *Ideology and National Competitiveness*, Boston: Harvard Business School Press.

Lundvall, B.A. (1996), 'The social dimension of the learning economy', DRUID Working Paper, April, 24p.

March, J.G. (1991), 'Exploration and exploitation in organizational learning', *Organization Science*, **2** (1): 71–87.

Morgan, G. (1986), *Images of Organization*, London: Sage Publications Inc.

Murnane, R.J. and R.R. Nelson (1984), 'Production and innovation when techniques are tacit', *Journal of Economic Behavior and Organization*, **5**: 353–73.

Naisbitt, J. (1996), *Megatrends Asia*, New York: Simon & Schuster.

Noll, R. (1991), 'Structural policies in the United States', in S. Kernell (ed.), *Parallel Politics: Economic Policy-Making in Japan and the United States*, Washington: The Brookings Institution, pp. 230–80.

Ostry, S. (1997), *Who's On First: The World Trading System*, New York: Twentieth Century Fund.

Ostry, S. (1998), 'Globalization and the Nation State', in J. de la Mothe and G. Paquet (eds), *Challenges Un-Met in the New Production of Knowledge: The Third PRIME Lectures*, Ottawa.

Ostry, S. and R.R. Nelson (1995), *Techno-Nationalism and Techno-Globalism: Conflict and Cooperation*, Washington: The Brookings Institution.

Paquet, G. (1998), 'Cognitive evolutionary economics', *Information Economics and Policy*, (in press).

Pavitt, K. (1984), *Technological Innovation and Britain's Economic Decline*, Oxford: Blackwell.

Prigogine, I. and I. Stengers, (1988), *Entre le temps et l'éternité*, Paris: Arthème-Fayard.

Putnam, R.D. (1993), *Making Democracy Work*, Princeton: Princeton University Press.

Resnick, M. (1994), 'Changing the centralized mind', *Technology Review*, **97** (5): 32–40.

Rosenberg, N. and L. Birdzell, Jr (1994), *How the West Grew Rich*, New York: Norton.

Sandel, M. (1996), *America and its Discontents*, New York: Knopf.

Saxenian, A. (1998), 'Regional innovation and the blurred firm', in J. de la Mothe and G. Paquet (eds), *Local and Regional Systems of Innovation*, Boston: Kluwer.

Schon, D.A. (1971), *Beyond the Stable State*, New York: Norton.

Schon, D.A. (1995), 'Causality and causal inference in the study of organizations', in R.F. Goodman and W.R. Fisher (eds), *Rethinking Knowledge*, Albany, NY: State University of New York, pp. 69–101.

Shimada, H. (1991), 'Structural Policies in Japan', in S. Kernell (ed.), *Parallel Politics: Economic Policy-Making in Japan and the United States*, Washington: The Brookings Institution, pp. 281–321.

Simon, H.A. (1956), 'Rational choice and the structure of the environment', *Psychological Review*, **63** (2): 129–38.

Strange, S. (1997), *The Retreat of the State*, Cambridge: Cambridge University Press.

Vickers, G. (1965), *The Art of Judgment*, London: Chapman & Hall.

Weick, K.E. (1979), *The Social of Organizing*, Reading, MA: Addison-Wesley.

Wikstrom, S. and R. Normann (1994), *Knowledge and Value: A New Perspective on Corporate Transformation*, London: Routledge.

5. Governments, macroorganizational policies and structural change: contrasts within the Triad

John de la Mothe and Gilles Paquet

' . . . relationships matter more than perfect plumbing, and trust is cheaper than lawyers'.   Charles Handy (1994)

INTRODUCTION

Globalization has generated a new mobility of economic activity as transnational firms re-align their production patterns. This has led to dysfunctions or frictions within national economies. Governments have responded in two major ways. First, they have engaged in international economic cooperation on an altogether new scale, as John Kirton has shown in Chapter 1. Second, they have implemented new macroorganizational policies, 'affecting the organization of resources and capabilities within their jurisdiction' (Dunning 1993). These new macroorganizational policies have been identified as being 'essentially complementary' to those policies geared to maintaining efficient markets and have been broadly designed to ensure 'the organization of created assets as a key success factor and (to deal with) transaction costs in the value added process' (Dunning 1993: 195).

These macroorganizational policies have not been sufficiently debated by economists or policy makers, nor have they been used with the same strategic thrust or flair by different countries. Indeed, many traditional economists and policy makers continue to deny that such a family of policies can increase positive externalities or their appropriability and argue (rather forcefully) for a dramatic reduction of government action. Ironically, this reduction is advocated while other economists and policy makers suggest that government intervention is becoming increasingly more important. Clearly, there is such a lack of understanding and appreciation of the importance of these relatively new types of policies.

In this chapter, we first explore the range of macroorganizational policies and the different roles that they might play. Second, we present a composite portrait of the ways in which these policies combine to define a new policy possibility framework. Our intent is to identify a few key dimensions along which such policies are likely to transform the wealth-creation process. Third, we sketch different clusters of organizational policies in order to contrast different patterns in the Triad. This leads us to gauge the drift of these policy clusters over the last decades and to suggest the general directions in which parts of the industrialized world are likely to proceed over the next decades.

ORGANIZATIONAL POLICIES: THE MODERN ARSENAL

Analyses of the processes of globalization over the past decade have highlighted the growing awareness on the part of governments of 'the need for them to evolve and sustain well articulated systemic organizational strategies, the specific intention of which is to consciously promote the long-term competitiveness of the firms and resources within their production by a series of interdependent market-supportive policies' (Dunning 1993: 195). Even though many economists and policy makers have argued for a minimalist version of these sorts of policies, a broad consensus has developed in the community of experts on international business that this should entail, at minimum, strategic efforts to correct market failures, and to provide infrastructure with a strong public good component. Moreover, many have called for the creation of those assets which are necessary to ensure the competitiveness of domestic firms, the reduction of the information and transaction costs that distort markets, and the development of regimes, rules and conventions that would enable firms to make optimal use of complementarities and synergies.

Such macroorganizational policies are fundamentally meant to help firms adapt, as smoothly as possible, to new circumstances. Moreover, they are directed to the structure, conduct and performance of the business system, as an adaptive learning system. These policy interventions may aim in general at increasing the flexibility of firms and sectors, but most of the time they are directed to one of the five sets of relationships presented in Chapter 4 to analyse the regional patterns of structural competitiveness. Table 5.1 categorizes the organizational policies, and identifies the main lever and the subsystem

Table 5.1 Taxonomy of organizational policies

	Main lever targeted		
	Structure	Conduct	Performance
Main subsystem targetted			
1. Metabolic			
2. Technological			
3. Process/functional			
4. Structural			
5. Governing			

of relationships in the business system that they are mainly directed to affect.

The structure–conduct–performance framework is a fairly standard classification that has been used in the industrial organization literature since the days of J.S. Bain (1959). It separates the features of the business systems defining the rules of the game, the barriers to entry, the role differentiation, the nature of the coordination and integration of the system (structure) from those pertaining to behavior, strategy and tactics (conduct) and from those dealing directly with the different measures of efficiency in the allocation resources (performance).

The subsystem classification illustrated in Figure 4.1, adapted from Laurent, Paquet and Ragan (1992), corresponds to a partitioning of the business system into five basic subprocesses and their interaction with the environment.

Each of the cells in Table 5.1 corresponds to a range of organizational policies. This does not mean that all those policies are effectively used or even that they *can* be used effectively. For instance, it is not necessarily easy for governments to determine exactly what structural architecture might best energize the technological innovation process in a sector, or any effective way to modify decision rules and firm strategies in such a process. Nor is it easy to ascertain what infrastructural support might accelerate the whole process of learning and innovation in the business system. But most governments see it as their business to orchestrate an ensemble of interventions under the general rubric of technology policy that purports to energize the knowledge production–adaption–diffusion process.

This is no easy feat in an 'age of side-effects' where non-linearities are everywhere, and where the five sets of relationships of the business system network are continuously in interaction and co-evolution. We have tried to map this complex environment in Figure 4.2.

At the global level, business networks are nested in a world system full of asymmetries between dominant and satellite national economies. Each of these national systems comprises various firms or business systems interacting in various ways and coalescing around meso-institutions that facilitate their interactions at subnational, regional, sectoral and transversal levels.

These firms interact not only with other domestic firms or systems but also directly, or through meso-institutions, with enterprises and socioeconomic entities in the same or in other jurisdictions. Indeed, transnational firms design world networks that are constrained very little, if at all, by national shells.

Organizational policies engineered by national, regional or supranational governments will have to take into account this complex set of echo boxes, for the complexity of interactions generates a high degree of unpredictability in impact or effect. Side-effects or unintended consequences play a most important role as global alliances, national policies and local industrial/institutional/cultural features interplay. Of course, not all governments are equally attentive to each of the subsystems, and not all governments agree that there should be policies directed with equal force at structure, conduct and performance. There is little done by government to effect different governance structures or to facilitate more cooperative relations among stakeholders in North America but on both fronts much has been done in Europe and Asia.

Moreover, not all governments take fully into account the complex texture of the world economic system. Some small economies are satisfied to free ride without paying any attention to the unintended consequences of their actions. This is not the case for dominant economies within power blocs. In the case of the US, Japan and Germany, paying attention to the echo boxes is of central importance.

We have stated earlier that these organizational policies are meant to complement broad policies directed mainly to the operations of efficient markets. This is not to imply that all such macroorganizational policies are the source of inefficiencies, but rather that they are meant to ensure better performance (not exclusively in allocative efficiency) by helping the business system to design improved structures, decision-rules and strategies. In certain cases, government intervention may entail some coercion, but most of the time takes the form of incentives and enticing regulations crafted to get the business systems to modify their operations voluntarily.

THE ORGANIZATIONAL POLICY POSSIBILITY FRAMEWORK

The scope of organizational policies has changed dramatically over the last century. In the era of *hierarchical capitalism* that Dunning identifies with the period 1875–1980, governments were confronted with structural distortions generated by suboptimal market structures, extensive use of monopoly power, and the failure of the private sector to provide social overhead capital. This led governments to become *participators* in the socioeconomy to correct distortions, to control undue power and to provide infrastructure (Dunning 1997).

As *alliance capitalism* has increasingly come to define new rules of the game, the scope of organizational policies has changed. There has been less emphasis on corrections to structural failures and a new importance has been attached to the correction of endemic and systemic failures ascribable to heightened levels of uncertainty and to the new importance of externalities. This has called for macroorganizational interventions especially in areas where effective business systems require such assets as an educated labor force, innovative capabilities, organizational competencies and a sophisticated legal and commercial infrastructure – all assets that have a strong public good component (Dunning 1997: 70).

Such macroorganizational policies are bound to be modest and subtle in a global economy where the mobility of most intangible resources (capital, ideas, technologies) is extremely high, and they are likely to focus on creating location-bound assets and on enhancing the capabilities of nation or region-based networks. They depend: (1) on the societal fabric within which market and state are anchored, for a high degree of social cohesion and a high degree of collective coordination based on solidaristic values are likely to make such interventions much easier; (2) on the nature of governance in the socioeconomy and on the role assigned to the state in this governance process; and (3) on the extent to which there are important structural and endemic learning failures and much relevant uncertainty in the economy.

These three dimensions (culture, governance, learning failures) delineate the major dimensions of the organizational policy framework. The more 'contextualist' or communitarian the culture (as in Japan), the more important the state role and the more distributed the governance;

and the more endemic and systemic the learning failures, the more potentially robust the macroorganizational policies (Kumon 1992; Imai 1992; Hollingsworth 1993).

Culture

Extensive surveys like those undertaken by Hampden-Turner and Trompenaars (1993) have revealed that the values systems and the economic, social and political systems vary widely across OECD countries.

Alliance capitalism cannot develop as well in a world of doctrinaire individualism as in a world with strong solidaristic traditions (Gerlach 1992). The nature of the *hexagon contracts* within the business system (between financiers, employees, suppliers, customers, environment, and society) that are permissible or encouraged differ depending on the sociocultural system (Handy 1994). The same may be said about the sort of *partnerships* among firms and between government and business, and about the sorts of *regimes* that might be arrived at among business systems of different countries on matters of common interest (Preston and Windsor 1992).

The basic reason why culture matters so much more in *alliance capitalism* is that it is based on a large number of handshakes, and that such handshakes depend much on trust and on the commitment to cooperation. Fukuyama has probably simplified matters unduly by aggregating all countries into a naive dichotomy – low-trust and high-trust societies – but he has made an important point in distinguishing the societies where voluntary associations beyond the family are weak (Korea, Italy, France) and strong (Germany, Japan) (Fukuyama 1995).

Governance

The governance system is more difficult to probe because of the very complexity of the notion of governance (Mayer 1996). Organizational policies are more likely to be adopted when the state is important in shaping the architecture of the economy, but this does not mean that a more centralized state will be a more effective social architect. In the new economy based on knowledge and learning, the most relevant territorial unit for learning is the region. So a governance process that provides for distributed authority and available levers at the regional level is more likely to be effective. Indeed, the 'learning region' has become the meaningful unit and distributed governance the most fitting pattern of governance (Ohmae 1993; Saxenian 1994; Florida 1995; Acs, de la Mothe and Paquet 1996).

In a world dominated by the economy of ideas and continuous learning, the institutional order designed for material goods is out of kilter. Whereas a centralized mindset dominates the scene in the old economy (Resnick 1994), in the new economy thinking is dominated by a better appreciation of the 'natural systems' instituted according to principles that run very much against the grain of the centralized mindset. Kevin Kelly has summarized 'the ways of nature' in a number of principles that would appear to synthesize the main characteristics of the new institutional order: distributed intelligence, bottom-up control, omnipresence of increasing returns, growth by creating multiple layers of simplicity and chunking, encouraging diversity, eccentricity and instability, seeking persistent disequilibrium, organizing around self-changing rules (Kelly 1994).

In such a world, successful organizations are those that find ways to accommodate and resolve the contradictory needs of promoting competitive pressure and network cooperation at the same time. These countervailing pressures raise the question of the source of the requisite amount of trust, unrequited transfers and the like that are necessary for such islands of cooperation to be built in a sea of competition. Tom Peters has focused on 'communities of practice' – the locus where learning occurs most easily because of the fact that the 'motivation to learn is the motivation to become a member' (Peters 1994: 174).

Anthropologist Virginia Hine has used the clumsy phrase 'segmented polycephalous network' (SPN) and has emphasized the central role of the 'ideological bond' or 'the power of a unifying idea' as adding the sort of glue that is necessary to make the organization live and prosper. To underline this key dimension, Hine has labelled the new form of organization SP(I)N where I stands for ideology (Hine 1977).

While there may be a tendency toward convergence in forms of organization and governance systems as the Triad countries experience profound interpenetration by enterprises from each zone into the others, significant differences between any pair of the Triad remain. But one may detect the emergence of a trend toward decentralization and cooperation in all portions of the world economy as it becomes clear that a new paradigm becomes dominant: the one based on the centrality of the interactions between the component subsystems of the socioeconomy (financial, production, innovation, governance) and of the value-creating partner system (Bradford 1994; Wikstrom and Normann 1994).

Learning Failures

The seriousness of learning failures is of central importance. It is when there are signs of learning failure, of inflexibility, of poor capacity to transform or adjust, that macroorganizational policies are most useful. When the production of knowledge and the process of innovation are stalled, intervention at the organizational level is often the only meaningful way to effect the necessary repairs. Yet such failures are very difficult to diagnose, and often a meaningful diagnosis may appear counterintuitive. For instance, maximal flexibility is not optimal flexibility, for it may lead to low levels of commitment and to a very poor exploitation of the available knowledge.

One may expect learning failures to increase significantly in the alliance capitalism era. Coordination and transaction costs have increased so much that a whole new field of study has emerged in the 1990s: *coordination science* (Malone and Crowston 1994). As the ground comes to be in motion and the environment becomes turbulent, coordination even between groups that have contradictory goals becomes imperative. Coordination has been defined in this context as 'managing dependencies between activities' and identifying the processes that can be used to manage them.

Without some provisional assessment of the differences among the Triad countries in terms of culture, governance and learning failures, it becomes difficult to establish clearly the full range of circumstances and challenges that organizational policies might be asked to face. This can be done at many levels: either in a most general way *à la* Dahrendorf (1995) through the general mix of institutions – economic liberalism, social cohesion, political freedom, or with a great deal of detail through monographic work at the level of each country. The former approach is bound to be relatively unsatisfactory because it is too general, but since the latter is impossible in the confines of a short chapter, we must strive for a compromise between the two through singling out what appear to be the main features of the cultural underground, of the governance process and of the learning/innovation process in the different parts of the Triad.

ORGANIZATIONAL POLICY POSSIBILITY AND STRATEGIES

There has been much work done on the Triad over the last decades. The more serious the analyses, the more differentiated the countries at any one node have appeared, but a number of general propositions would still appear to hold about the countries in each node. For instance, the North American culture remains bravely individualistic while the East Asian culture is more contextually communitarian, and the continental European culture remains relatively more solidaristic than the North American one but without the full social cohesion shown by the East Asians.

The governance systems have some general characteristics. There is a relatively more centralized governance system in East Asia but one that uses less the coercive Taylorian levers than the more subtle levers of social control in the contextualist society. The North American scene is rather paradoxical in that it proclaims a gospel of decentralization and deregulation while exerting much raw power through central agencies. Europe is even more confusing. It has a tradition of centralized power and strong top-down government intervention, and yet is distilling a new federalism in which power and authority are devolved slowly to regions. As for the world of learning failures, they appear to be most evident in Europe, while the great flexibility of markets in North America and the great social cohesion in East Asia would appear to have played important roles as facilitators and catalysts of social learning.

This diagnosis is meant to be a provisional characterization to help sort out the rationale for the different patterns of organizational strategies in each node of the Triad. To put the matter most vividly, we have tried to represent the constraints imposed by culture and governance and the opportunities generated for organizational strategies by important learning failures in Table 5.2.

Table 5.2   Constraints and opportunities for organizational policies

Region	Culture	Governance	Learning failures
North America	−1	+1	0
Europe	+1	+2	+2
East Asia	+2	0?	0

Note: +ve indicates relative ease in developing organizational policies and −ve indicates relative difficulty.

There has been a broad acceptance in every node of the Triad that the competitiveness of firms depends on the actions of the firms themselves, on the work of their associations and on the supportive action of the state. Countries with different cultures, governance structures and learning failures are obviously bound to make differential use of organizational policies. Our provisional diagnosis would appear to indicate that Europe is the most likely candidate to use extensively organizational policies while the other two areas are probably less likely to use them because they have alternative mechanisms of adjustment that are working not too badly. Yet this relative reluctance to engage in organizational policies is not likely to continue as governance becomes more distributed and learning failures accumulate. Indeed, it is possible already to identify uses of organizational policies that are clear enough to enable one to discriminate among zones and to point to likely directions in which social architects in these different zones might develop (Perlmutter 1965). These clusters are in large part the result not only of objective constraints but also of ideological schemes which allow more or less the possibility of making use of such instrumentalities.

In order to provide a very broad perspective on the constraints on macroorganizational policies (culture, governance, learning failures) and on the instruments most likely to be used to improve structural competitiveness (policies directed to structure, conduct or performance), we have proceeded in three stages. First, we present in Table 5.3 a broad list of elements in which the countries of the different poles of the Triad can be shown to be somewhat contrasted. Second, from this list and the literature available in support of it, we develop a broad-brushed portrait of the character of each node of the Triad. Thirdly, we try to synthesize in a final tableau the comparative contours of the patterns of organizational policies in use in the different portions of the Triad.

A Comparative List

This list is not meant to be exhaustive but rather to remind the reader of the relatively important number of factors that differentiate the *weltanschauungen* of the three broad zones.

A Broad-Brushed Characterization

The North American cluster
The major point about the North American cluster is the lack of 'a coherent, comprehensive structural policy' (Noll 1991: 230). In the face of increasing internationalization of the economy and of increasing structural complexity, there is only 'a decreasing social cohesiveness

and an enervation in the capitalist spirit' (Pryor 1996: 7). This explains the greater difficulty in ensuring the requisite degree of coordination or government–business partnering except in the defense sector and in specific industries.

The general thrust of organizational policies in North America has been to ensure acceptable behavior and performance through competition in product and factor markets. The same logic explains the search for policies directed toward free trade and deregulation. The dynamics of the North American system is based on the simple process of exit and entry of firms driven by competition.

Culturally, there is an underlying distrust of coordination but also often a lack of technical interest in networking unless it proves absolutely essential to superior performance, because knowledge is primarily regarded as a private good. The aggressive pursuit of antitrust policy (witness the March 1998 Congressional Hearings concerning Microsoft) emphasizes particularly the notion of a 'level playing field' and leads to the support of small independent firms. But the US culture generates important impediments to competitiveness to the extent that it leads to an exclusive focus of policies (regulations, R&D, and so on) on structural conditions. As Chaples and Keever (1994) indicate, this has fostered an overemphasis on frontier or breakthrough research and a corresponding neglect of performance considerations. This has contributed to myopic process organization, to 'lone wolf' attitudes and to a lack of participative and networking behaviors.

In a sense, there has been a significant weakness in the governance structures that has had a deleterious effect on systemic competitiveness. While the 'transformation capabilities' generated by competition are impressive, the delinking between the state and societal actors has prevented the emergence of new forms of governance where the government could act as coordinator, moderator, *animateur*. Ideology and distrust have prevented the emergence of practices consistent with better performance because of their basic unacceptability (Lodge and Vogel 1987). Reliance on support for basic research, tax policy to encourage investment and risk-taking, and a stabilizing monetary policy does not suffice and has impaired the ability to learn organizationally. One may obliquely gauge the extent to which the US remains handicapped by this when examining the evolution of other economies which have begun to take advantage of new forms of governance based on greater reliance on alliances and networking (Meyer-Stamer 1997).

This does not mean that the US has remained insensitive to the challenges. There has been recently some critical examination of the regulatory framework and feeble efforts to sketch elements of a

Table 5.3 Triad comparison

	Japan	US	Europe
Resource			
Capital time orientation	Patient capital	Impatient capital	Purposeful capital
Resource access	Restricted	High	Medium
Cultural			
Social cohesion	Homogeneous/coherent	Heterogeneous/incoherent	Heterogeneous/coherent
Trust	High	High (declining)	Low (increasing)
Acceptance of authority	High	Low	Medium
Ideology	Contextualistic	Individualistic	Solidaristic
Fate	Shared	Divided (Mng't–labour, economic–polity)	Divided (Mng't–labour, economic–polity)
Organization			
Economic integration	Formal hierarchy (parent/sub-contractor)	Rule based	Supranational
Business system	Clan	Market	Bureau
Collaborative networking	High	Contractual	State guided
Governance			
Style	Coordinated	Decentralized	Centralized
Political orientation	Partnership democracy	Liberal democracy	Social democracy
Business–Gov't–Labour	Government as facilitator	Adversarial	Partnership

Competitiveness			
Competition policy	Oligopoly tolerated	Pure competition	State monopoly/oligopoly
Competitive strategy	High-tech + high standard of living	High-tech + lower standard of living	Selective technology + high standard of living
Competition emphasis	Creative discovery	Creative destruction	Creative maintenance
Adjustment orientation	State supported transition and movement of old industries offshore	Support of old industries	Enhancement/upgrading of old industries
Technology			
Innovation	Exploitative – emphasis on utilization and ancillary innovation capacities	Explorative – emphasis on innovation and invention capacities	Niche exploitative – emphasis on niche applications
Diffusion	High internal diffusion/low external diffusion	High internal diffusion/ medium external diffusion	Low internal diffusion/high external diffusion
Patents	Public good	Private good	Private good
Absorptive capacity	High	Low	Medium
Technology focus	High-tech	High-tech/low-tech	Medium-tech
Industrial Policy			
National strategy	By design	Random	Constrained
Regional development	Technopolis	Meso-level driven	Regional innovation systems
Trade access	Asymmetric	Open	Selective openness

macroorganizational policy. US legal and regulatory barriers to industrial R&D and domestic production are being examined closely. The
US Framework Program (1996) for stimulating industrial investment is
aimed at improving the flexibility of the US financial services sector.
This is being mirrored by extensive investment measures or incentives
at the State level. But the central focus of science, technology and
industrial quasi-strategies is the active pursuit of trade and foreign
investment liberalization (National Export Strategy 1993; Interagency
Trade Promotion Coordinating Committee 1995; Big Emerging Market
Program 1996 which is run by the Department of Commerce). Science
policy is being tipped increasingly towards technology application and
diffusion (*Science in the National Interest* 1995), particularly via such
mega-project mechanisms as the Information Highway Initiative, the
International Space Station *Alpha*, and the Human Genome Project
(HUGO). The Manufacturing Extension Partnership (MEP) is aimed
at increasing technology diffusion in SMEs; while the Cooperative
R&D Agreements (CRADAs) promote inter-sectoral technology linkages (Cheney and Hill 1998; Hill 1998). Indeed, this orientation is being
accelerated, towards 'dual-use technology' programs aimed especially
at the old military–industrial complex such as the Los Alomos Weapons
Lab. (Alic *et al.* 1991).

But these initiatives run against a prevalent anti-interventionist sentiment. So, efforts to change conduct directly via some government
intervention at the process level (for example, through manipulation of
the incentive–reward system, to increase R&D or some investment in
process skill learning through tax incentives) remain very tame (Dickson
and Czinkota 1996). Indeed, if one had to sketch the North American
pattern within the taxonomy of organizational policies, it would take
the form of a triangle with its base covering the whole range of structural
policies along the five target fields but growing laterally into the conduct
level when it comes to the process/functional subsystem.

The myopic and short-term time horizon of meso-business systems
explains some important learning failures: a lack of manpower training,
of foreign direct investment as a strategic variable, and the development of income inequality levels that can only discourage networking,
alliances and collective decision making for innovation that might generate long-term gains. The reliance on creative destruction and the
relative neglect of new knowledge that requires joint ventures and other
forms of alliance, have left the US in a position where it is witnessing
an erosion of its hegemonic position (Luttwak 1993; Nye and Owens
1996; Teece 1990).

The European cluster

The European Union is built on a search for macroorganizations likely to yield scale economies and social cohesion through carefully selected cooperative programmes (Soete 1997). Given the multitude of national governments with their 'slightly' different policy stances, this calls for 'managed multilateralism'.

To be sure, the European cluster has 'learning disabilities'. Despite its tolerance for intervention, it is only a 'medium-trust community' in which cooperation is important but still difficult. The EU remains a patchwork of diverging policies coalescing behind the principles of parallelism, subsidiarity and plurality (Salvatore 1991). While this entails 'common structural and regional policies', it must be clear that the EU remains something of a construction site (Dahrendorf 1997; Skidelsky 1995).

The EU Framework Programmes have been one of the most successful initiatives. These programmes are built on the recognition that there are important advantages to risk and burden sharing through cooperation. This represents an important 'experimental advantage' in supranational policy-making when it comes to strategic macroorganizational policies for the medium and long terms, that are broadly based, and have built-in support for learning and social cohesion (Soete 1994).

But the pervasive concern for *fairness* and very generous social support policies have stood in the way of accelerated learning and transformation. Cross-national production networks which developed in Asia and were imitated in the United States have been accepted only to a very limited extent by European meso-business systems. While some have ascribed this to 'learning disabilities' proper, it may be suggested that the reluctance to move in this direction may be due to the social disruptions and dislocations that such networks might entail.

The mix of collegiality and state importance in the governance structure, the importance of alliances between MNEs–governments, and the many-layered policy making within the EU have considerably modulated the transformations of the learning economy. Even when learning failures have been noted, they have not necessarily been noted as failures. Often, they have been labeled the costs of particular policy choices determined by higher social priorities.

Macroorganizational policies in Europe are built on the powers of *associationism*. But according to the country, there is a greater or lesser amount of *dirigisme*: more in France, Spain or Greece (Ortero Hildago 1997), less in Germany (Krull and Meyer-Krahmer 1996), even less in the United Kingdom (Cunningham 1998). For instance, Germany's S&T and industrial policy – in the White Paper *Report on Securing Germany's*

Economic Future – and as part of an overall regulatory reform (announced in 1995) have set out to amend its Cartel Act to conform with current EU competition law. German federal R&D spending has been moved to align with the EU Framework Programme between 1987 and 1993 in such areas as information and communications technologies, industrial and materials technologies, environment, life sciences and technologies, energy, and human mobility. Indeed, as Krull and Meyer-Krahmer put it, 'EU financing has gained considerable significance in Germany' (1996: 25) to such an extent that from the EU Framework I, II and III Programmes, ICT expenditures, for example, have moved from 17 to 40 per cent of expenditures in an effort to harmonize. German alignment with Europe is taking place now in science policy, transportation policy (railways), telephone service policy, SMEs, and labour mobility. Similar effects are being felt in other European states such as, Spain, whose R&D programs received 2500 million ECUs in 1994 (up from 800 MECU in 1987); Portugal, which in 1994 participated in 321 EU S&T programs; Greece, whose R&D expenditures represent about 0.6 per cent of the EU total but which attracted 6 per cent of the IV Framework Programme in 1995; or Italy which attracted in 12,300 million ECUs in 1995.

Different European countries are following somewhat different strategies, even if there is some convergence and an emerging homogeneity as a result of the broad framework that has been adopted. This homogenization process is accelerated somewhat by efforts to construct a broad macroeconomic framework (*monnaie unique*, and so on), and to ensure that new institutional capacity is developed around negotiated community contracts.

The intent is to provide support for networks at the regional/sectoral levels as a basis for improving performance (Amin and Thrift 1995). But the degree of 'social embeddedness' (that is, the way behavior is shaped by factors such as the local labour markets, workforce and financial institutions, and so on) varies significantly from country to country, and it evolves as modes of learning and modes of governance co-evolve (Dosi 1997).

So Europe presents a rich variety of environments: from the 'archetypal' German firm to the British firms *à l'américaine*, to the Italian district. Macroorganizational policies capable of generating systemic competitiveness accordingly remain differentiated. What is most notable about the European strategies is that they have focused largely on the process/functional level across the board but have supported also intervention on every aspect of the process/functional subsystem.

The East Asian cluster

Japan is at the other end of the spectrum (Sigurdson 1995). It has a coherent and systematic macroorganizational strategy of intervention based on *alliance capitalism* (Gerlach 1992). This sort of consultative capitalism is a natural extension of the communitarian culture with its notion of knowledge as a public good, its very self-reliant population, and the long time horizon of its business systems. In this system, institutionalized mechanisms of coordination are omnipresent and based on networks of 'credible commitments'. The ambience of trust and communitarianism makes private, public and social actors work in concert and tends to re-enforce the continuity of relationships.

Macroorganizational policies in East Asia pertain to the technological, the functional/process and the structural subsystems. The focal point is to work on risk-sharing in order to create a mix of competition and cooperation without losers (Tezuka 1997). This approach is a natural extension of clan-type governance and leads to horizontal integration as a mutual insurance system and vertical integration as a way to create competitive teams. Rather than focusing on simple efforts to modify the structure in order to influence obliquely conduct and performance (as in the US), these strategies are efforts to modify conduct and performance directly through negotiation and moral suasion.

These interventions are not ad hoc but rather the fruit of considerable discussions and negotiations among all the stakeholders, with the state playing the role of *animateur*. This strategy is pragmatic, comprehensive, based on very well-articulated goals, and very coherent. Government acts differently at different periods, but its actions are meant to be pro-market and symbiotic with the goals of the business systems, to reduce endemic transaction costs, and to increase the capabilities of the business systems (Dunning 1994). Moreover, its progresses are well documented in numerous policy guidelines from MITI that *accompany* (so to speak) the discussions in the multiple forums and inform and guide them.

The Japanese government has taken a strong role in providing information, organizing projects and in directing both the allocation of resources and the learning trajectories. In so doing, it has used systematically foreign direct investment to serve its national policy, but has not allowed the MNEs to acquire a predominant role. It has built a very strong presence in the private sector to promote training and to facilitate the development of networks, but also to redirect efforts and reframe issues from time to time. For instance, Japanese science policy has rapidly evolved in the very recent past. It now emphasizes strongly the performance of basic research – (S&T Basic Law coupled with the Basic

Structural change and cooperation

Plan for Public Investment fiscal stimulus package valued at 3 per cent of GDP). Such R&D programs include, for example, the interoperable database system, the Manganese Nodule Mining System, the Super/Hypersonic Transport System, and the underground space development technology. Fine ceramics are also targeted, as are bio-electronic devices, functional protein complexes, and medical equipment. Under the Temporary Law Concerning Measures for the Promotion of Creative Business Activities in SMEs, assistance is provided for enhancing management skills and helping firms diversify into new business areas.

Patterns of Organizational Policies

Figure 5.1 synthesizes the different ways in which the three regions have approached the problem of macroorganizational policies. It

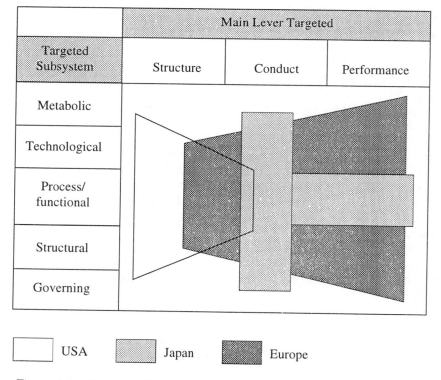

Figure 5.1   Patterns of organizational policies

emphasizes that the US has mainly relied on competition to influence the different subsystems. This is a choice largely determined by culture and by the governance system. It has only been tempted to interfere subtly especially via the tax system in the process/functional subprocess and neither with great vigor nor with great success. At the structural level, much has been done through the defense budget and through specifically defined sectors (for example agriculture) to provide important infrastructure and protection. But in general, the organizational policies have remained somewhat untouched by particularly difficult learning failures. This is because the ideological power of the economic culture has prevented the US government from intervening as much as it might have wished.

On the EU front, a multiplicity of governments are involved and they have intervened massively through rules of all sorts, but they have also done so through direct pressures to modify behaviour and to improve performance. This has not been done, however, in a coherent way, and it is not at all clear that it has been very fruitful. This is in part ascribable to the cacophony of supranational and national agendas, and cultural and governance constraints on state action. While there is an appearance of broad and comprehensive action, it is largely unfocused, open to local/national distortions and is not particularly effective. Yet Europeans are extremely conscious of the learning failures and through the Framework Programme are developing or moving towards coherent macroorganizational intervention.

On the Japanese and East Asian front, there is much variety and much turbulence, but the pattern of intervention is highly focused and based on a very high trust level. It is therefore not necessary to use formal rules and broad structural constraints.

By acting directly on conduct, one is able to have much impact on performance. There is, however, a change in Japanese macroorganizational policy. It is becoming less informal and is slowly adopting some of the rule-based approach in vogue in the US – partly as a way of anchoring the region around Japan as hegemon. This is most certainly clear in the new emphasis on basic research, legal profession associations, and journalistic access which was not introduced as usual through informal channels, but more formally through a rule. Yet, the whole culture-cum-governance background leads to a focus on conduct through informal negotiations (Hall 1998). This is bound to remain the centre of gravity of the organizational policies for the near future.

GAPS, CONTRASTS AND TRENDS

Any likely set of organizational policies would aim at increasing positive externalities flowing toward the business systems from the environment and at increasing the appropriability of these external effects by domestic firms. The interventions in North America, Europe and East Asia are the echo effect of different sociocultural backgrounds but also of the blockages preventing the production of externalities or their appropriation by national firms, and of the type of governance mechanisms in place.

The major pressure for organizational interventions comes from learning failures and these have been much more important in Europe than in the other two zones where coordination through competition (North America) or through consensus (East Asia) has proven to be effective. In North America, this has helped to aggrandize the importance of competition policy and of free trade policy. But, given the weaker pressure on North America as a result of lesser learning failures, these policies have been pursued with a degree of nonchalance. The North American policy framework has not attempted to be more active on this front except through a regulatory framework that attempts to modify conduct and behavior largely at the level of process/function.

Solidaristic values are greater in Europe than in North America. So one may expect that in the world of alliance capitalism, organizational policies may be realized via some direct intervention at the structural level (mainly at the level of process/function) but mainly through detailed regulations on performance at the national level. The pressures created by learning failures have enhanced considerably the taste for organizational policies and the interventionist tradition has made it possible to use many levers that would be resented in the other zones. The Colbertist culture and the hierarchical governance have generated an incredibly complex and intrusive regulatory framework which may appear awesome from the outside but which provides the European firms with external benefits. Industrial policies, innovation policies, regional economic policies and very close partnerships between government and business have permeated the whole field and have provided strategic support to the European business systems.

In Japan and East Asia, much has come to be built on trust and on the multiplex relationships of contextualist and communitarian environments. Again, this has meant more direct action at the level of conduct and performance. However, the focus has been much more on conduct than in Europe through subtle mechanisms like the one mentioned earlier about the ways in which the granting of patents is administered in the interest of domestic firms. It would be extremely difficult to influence conduct in this manner without the extraordinary consensual base on which this network society functions. There are certain features that are handled by intervention at the level of performance directly, but they pertain mostly to the technological and the structural subsystems. Certain types of rules guide the process of licensing and the nature of the *keiretsus* mainly based on performance criteria. But East Asia is particularly apt at appropriating all these externalities for the benefit of domestic firms. On that count, this zone is much more effective than the other two in using macroorganizational policies. It is also better able to immunize itself from intrusion through an array of defensive mechanisms based on religious values (rice) or health considerations.

These trends do not entail that the organizational policies in use are those that would be the most effective. The very limited amount of discussion about macroorganizational policies has kept them more or less occult as a strategic tool. The disadvantage of this lack of wide-ranging and critical discussion is that little is known about the most important blockages leading to learning failures. Consequently, it is not clear that the North Americans have not overused the structural levers and that the East Asians are not vulnerable for counting too much on behavioral pressure.

As convergence proceeds among the countries of the Triad, and as the World Trade Organization extends discussions in the policy fields, it is likely that the margin of maneuverability for organizational policies will narrow considerably and will need to become ever more subtle. In Canada, the national health-care scheme is now celebrated as a source of competitiveness in the automobile sector because of the significant cost savings for the car manufacturers as a result of not having to shoulder directly the health-care costs of their employees.

One may therefore anticipate some reshuffling of the organizational policies in each zone of the Triad and a quest for ever more creative ways to generate externalities and to appropriate them for the benefit of nationals.

CONCLUSION

The growing interdependencies and synergies of the new world of information and flexible production have already generated more or less important externalities that national business systems have attempted to appropriate. But there are important ways in which governments may use organizational policies to craft new competitive advantages. These ways depend much on the features of the socioeconomy and on the challenges posed by learning failures.

We have suggested that one can identify some in the use of these organizational policies in the countries of the Triad. But it may be argued that the strategies in use may not be necessarily those most likely to be of greatest benefit to the countries in question because of the lack of critical discussions of the different foci through which such action might be channeled. Moreover, it is most likely that much borrowing between zones will occur as the WTO puts pressure to harmonize on all.

In the end, the different countries may be forced to fall back on their idiosyncrasies (organically generated or crafted) for strategies to help their domestic firms and may become ever more creative to ensure a steady stream of externalities and to ensure that it is appropriately tapped by national business systems.

BIBLIOGRAPHY

Acs, Z., J. de la Mothe, and G. Paquet (1996), 'Local systems of innovation: toward an enabling strategy', in P. Howitt (ed.), *The Implications of Knowledge-Based Growth for Microeconomic Policies*, Calgary: University of Calgary Press, pp. 339–58.

Alic, J. et al. (1991), *Beyond Spin-Off*, Cambridge, MA: Harvard Business School Press.

Amin, A. and N. Thrift, (1995), 'Institutional issues for the European regions: from markets and plans to socioeconomics and powers of association', *Economy and Society*, **24** (1): 41–66.

Bain, J.S. (1959), *Industrial Organization*, New York: Wiley.

Bradford, C.I. Jr (1994), *The New Paradigm of Systemic Competitiveness*, Paris: OECD.

Chaples, S.S. and D.B. Keever, (1994), 'Cultural contradictions impeding American high-tech competitiveness in global markets', in S. Aahra and A.J. Ali (eds), *The Impact of Innovation and Technology in the Global Market Place*, New York: The Haworth Press, pp. 15–36.

Cheney, D. and C.T. Hill, (eds) (1998), *Science and Technology in the U.S.A.*, London: Cartermill.

Cunningham, P. (ed.) (1998), *Science and Technology in the U.K.*, London: Cartermill.

Dahrendorf, R. (1995), 'A precarious balance: economic opportunity, civil society, and political liberty', *The Responsive Community*, **5** (3): 13–39.

Dahrendorf, R. (1997), *After 1989*, London: Croom Helm.

Dickson, P.R. and M.R. Czinkota, (1996), 'How the United States can be number one again: resurrecting the industrial policy debate', *The Columbia Journal of World Business*, Fall: 76–87.

Dosi, G. (1997), 'The new socio-economics of organization, competitiveness and employment', *IPTS Report*, No. 15: 15–20.

Dunning, J.H. (1993), 'How should national governments respond to globalization?', *The International Executive*, **35** (3): May–June, 187–98.

Dunning, J.H. (1994), 'Governments and multinational enterprises', in L. Eden (ed.), *Multinationals in North America*, Calgary: University of Calgary Press, pp. 277–308.

Dunning, J.H. (1997), 'Governments and the macro-organization of economic activity', *Review of International Political Economy*, **4** (1): 42–86.

Florida, R. (1995), 'Toward the learning region', *Futures*, **27** (5): 527–36.

Fukuyama, F. (1995), *Trust*, New York: Free Press.

Gerlach, M.L. (1992), *Alliance Capitalism*, Berkeley: University of California Press.

Hall, I.P. (1998), *Cartels of the Mind*, New York.

Hampden-Turner, C. and A. Trompenaars (1993), *The Seven Cultures of Capitalism*, New York: Currency/Doubleday.

Handy, C. (1994), *The Age of Paradox*, Boston: Harvard Business School Press.

Hill, C.T. (1998), 'Technology Policies for Industrial Innovation', in J. de la Mothe (ed.), *Science, Technology and Governance*, London: Pinter.

Hine, V.H. (1977), 'The basic paradigm of a future socio-cultural system', *World Issues*, April/May: 19–22.

Hollingsworth, R. (1993), 'Variation among nations in the logic of manufacturing sectors and international competitiveness', in D. Foray and C. Freeman (eds), *Technology and the Wealth of Nations*, London: Pinter, pp. 301–21.

Imai, K. (1992), 'Japan's corporate networks', in S. Kumon and H. Rosovsky (eds), *The Political Economy of Japan*, Vol. 3, *Cultural and Social Dynamics*, Stanford: Stanford University Press, pp. 198–230.

Kelly, K. (1994), *Out of Order*, Reading, MA: Addison-Wesley.

Krull, W. and F. Meyer-Krahmer (eds) (1996), *Science and Technology in Germany*, London: Cartermill.

Kumon, S. (1992), 'Japan as a network society', in S. Kumon and H. Rosovsky (eds), *The Political Economy of Japan*, Vol. 3, *Cultural and Social Dynamics*, Stanford: Stanford University Press, pp. 109–41.

Laurent, P., G. Paquet and T. Ragan (1992), 'Strategic networks as five-dimensional Bricolage', in R. Salle, R. Spencer and J.P. Valla (eds), *Business Networks in an International Context: Recent Research Developments*, Proceedings of the 8th IMP Conference, Lyon, pp. 194–206.

Lodge, G. and E. Vogel (1987), *Ideology and National Competitiveness*, Boston: Harvard Business School Press.

Luttwak, E. (1993), *The Endangered American Dream*, New York: Simon & Schuster.

Malone, T.W. and K. Crowston (1994), 'The interdisciplinary study of coordination', *ACM Computing Surveys*, **26** (1): 87–119.

Mayer, C. (1996), 'Corporate governance, competition and performance', OECD Economics Department Working Paper No. 164.

Meyer-Stamer, J. (1997), 'New patterns of governance for industrial change: perspectives for Brazil', *Journal of Development Studies*, **33** (3): 364–91.

Noll, R. (1991), 'Structural policies in the United States', in S. Kernell (ed.), *Parallel Politics: Policy Making in Japan and the United States*, Washington: The Brookings Institution, pp. 230–80.

Nye, J. and W. Owens, (1996), 'America's information edge', *Foreign Affairs*, **75**, March/April: 20–36.

Ohmae, K. (1993), 'The rise of the region-state', *Foreign Affairs*, Spring: 78–87.

Ortero Hildago, C. (1996), *Science and Technology in Southern Europe*, London: Cartermill.

Perlmutter, H. (1965), *Towards a Theory and Practice of Social Architecture*, London: Tavistock Institute.

Peters, T. (1994), *Crazy Times Call for Crazy Organizations*, New York: Vintage Books.

Preston, L.E. and D. Windsor, (1992), *The Rules of the Game in the Global Economy*, Boston: Kluwer Academic Publishers.

Pryor, F.L. (1996), *Economic Evolution and Structure – The Impact of Complexity on the US Economic System*, Cambridge: Cambridge University Press.

Resnick, M. (1994), 'Changing the centralized mindset', *Technology Review*, **97** (5): 32–40.

Salvatore, D. (1991), *National Economic Policies – Handbook of Comparative Economic Policies Vol. 1*, New York: Greenwood Press.

Saxenian, A. (1994), *Regional Advantage*, Cambridge, MA: Harvard University Press.

Sigurdson, J. (1995), *Science and Technology in Japan*, London: Cartermill.

Skidelsky, R. (1995), *The World After Communism*, London: Papermac.

Soete, L. (1994), 'European comparative innovation systems', mimeo, 6p.

Soete, L. (1997), 'The Impact of Globalization on European Integration,' *The IPTS Report*, No. 15: 21–8.

Teece, D. (1990), 'Capturing value through corporate technology alliances', in J. de la Mothe and L.M Ducharme (eds), *Science, Technology and Free Trade*, London: Pinter.

Tezuka, H. (1997), 'Success as the source of failure? Competition and cooperation in the Japanese economy,' *Sloan Management Review*, Winter: 83–93.

Wikstrom, S. and R. Normann (1994), *Knowedge and Value: A New Perspective on Corporate Transformation*, London: Routledge.

6. Technocratic–corporate partnering: extending alliance capitalism[1]

Rajneesh Narula and John H. Dunning

1. INTRODUCTION

One of the distinctive features of globalization has been the growth of cross-border value added activities by firms, and the subsequent increasing interdependence of economies. However, the growth of globalization has led to a chain reaction, in that there has been an increasing trend for the activities of firms – domestically and internationally – to be undertaken not just through internalization of intermediate product markets ('hierarchical capitalism'), but through 'alliance capitalism' (Gerlach 1992; Dunning 1995a, 1997).

Specifically, alliance capitalism, as used here, refers to the growing use of non-market, quasi-hierarchical modes of corporate activity, whereby firms do not completely (or formally) internalize their value added activities, but utilize a variety of cooperative and collaborative associations with other firms to achieve the same goals, especially to augment their own competitive advantage (Dunning 1995a).

While alliance capitalism is endemic, its application is most pervasive in the case of firms from advanced industrialized countries and, to a lesser extent, among fast-growing newly industrializing countries (Hagedoorn and Narula 1997). Indeed, as has been noted elsewhere (Dunning and Narula 1994, 1995), the emergence of alliance capitalism as a socioeconomic phenomena is a characteristic of the fifth stage of the investment development path.

The economies of the industrialized countries are generally based on value added activity that is capital and knowledge (that is, created asset) intensive. The generation and maintenance of these assets is crucial in determining the competitiveness of firms as well as the competitiveness of countries as locations for economic activity. As national governments are frequently involved in promoting the competitiveness of human and physical resources and capabilities within their jurisdiction, they are, *pari passu*, also involved, directly or indirectly, in their creation or utilization.[2] One of the critical aspects of created assets concerns the generation and subsequent diffusion of intellectual capital,[3] and particularly that arising from investment in research and development (R&D) and human resource development.

Knowledge capital, however, and the problems of fully appropriating its benefits has two aspects. First, it is partly a public good, but in high technology sectors it is also highly tacit and context-specific. Due to its inherent uncertainty, there tends to be suboptimal R&D investment (including training programmes) by firms. Hence, one of the primary roles of governments is reducing the risks and costs and increasing the social benefits of the generation and diffusion of intellectual capital. However, although most national governments agree on the need to intervene to improve and sustain created assets, not all agree on the most optimal method to do so.[4]

Reluctant partnership between governments and companies, often at the behest of the former, is not entirely new: Ministry of International Trade and Industry (MITI) officials have explicitly tried to influence corporate strategies in Japan during most of the post-war era. Our current interest is sparked by its increasing popularity rather than its novelty, as well as the growing cooperative spirit typical of technocratic–corporate partnering today. There has been an increasing tendency towards direct intervention favouring domestic firms, in what has been described as 'techno-nationalism' (Ostry and Nelson 1995). We delve into understanding the logic of techno-nationalism in this age of alliance capitalism.

The purpose of this chapter is thus threefold. First, we wish to enquire, from the firm's perspective, why it has an increasing propensity to undertake R&D alliances, with particular focus on international alliances. Second, we try to understand the role of governments in promoting and engaging in the generation and diffusion of intellectual capital, and in facilitating inter-firm technological alliances. Third, we wish to evaluate the efficacy of techno-nationalism, in light of the welfare and social responsibilities of governments. The remainder of this paper is organized as follows. Section 2 will discuss the growth of alliance capitalism. Section 3 will concentrate on the growth of R&D alliances by firms, and theorize on its nature. Section 4 will address the development of cross-border alliance activity. Section 5 discusses government interests in the R&D activities of firms, while Section 6 examines the interaction between governments and international R&D alliances. Section 7 will evaluate the various means (both direct and indirect) by which governments are involved in strategic alliance activity. Section 8 will present conclusions and discuss some policy implications.

2. ALLIANCE CAPITALISM

Although cooperative and collaborative methods of protecting or advancing the competitiveness of the firms is not new, the propensity of firms to engage in such activities has increased dramatically in recent years. There has been a virtual explosion of *strategic* alliances, with the number of agreements having increased at an average rate of 9.8 per cent annually between 1980 and 1994 (Hagedoorn and Narula 1997). This has prompted suggestions that economic activity through inter-firm alliances is no longer inferior to the use of hierarchies, and is in many cases the *first-best* option (Ciborra 1991). It has been suggested elsewhere (Dunning 1995a, 1997) that this represents a paradigm shift, in which economies are moving away from hierarchical capitalism towards alliance capitalism. Moreover, where firms do engage in hier-archies, it is increasingly through the use of mergers and acquisition (M&A), which, like strategic alliances, are undertaken not so much to reduce transaction costs but to protect and augment competitiveness, and can also be regarded as an *extreme form of collaboration*. Indeed, there is a strong link between M&A and strategic alliances, in that firms often establish a strategic alliance with a prospective M&A target.[5]

There are five interrelated phenomena at work here. First, there has been an increase in such activity across all of the advanced industrialized economies; it is not peculiar to certain countries, such as Japan. Second, there is an increasingly strategic aspect, as alliances are no longer simply undertaken as a means of avoiding transaction and coordination costs, but rather as a first-best 'voice' strategy to reduce market failure due *inter alia*, to barriers to entry,[6] where this is thought preferable to the complete internalization of these markets, or where complete internaliz-ation is not possible. Third, one of the original motives for alliance formation was to acquire market access and/or overcome supply bottle-necks, that is, to achieve vertical integration where such integration was not possible through hierarchies. Firms engaged in very little horizontal alliance formation, unlike today. Fourth, inter-firm alliances are increas-ingly being undertaken, through various modes, as a direct response to pressures brought about by contemporary technological developments and globalization. Fifth, until recently, alliances were primarily under-taken for the purpose of achieving or improving market entry and presence, an increasing number are now being undertaken to protect or enhance the created assets of the participating firms.

The advent of alliance capitalism is in keeping with what the theory might predict, and is associated with stage five of the investment development path[7] (IDP) (Narula 1995; Dunning and Narula 1994, 1996), of advanced industrial countries. As countries enter the fifth stage of the IDP, there is a tendency for their outward and inward direct investment positions to balance, and to fluctuate around this position over time. At this stage, firms from these countries are increasingly involved in intra-industry and intra-firm trade and investment, as they restructure their activities on a global or regional basis. At the same time, the ownership and territorial boundaries of firms become obscured as they increasingly engage in trans-border cooperative agreements. This is as a result of increasing competition across borders between multinational enterprises (MNEs), and the tendency for the competitive advantages of both countries and firms to be dependent on created assets and capabilities which are highly tacit in nature. Indeed, the concept of globalization is very much a reflection of the changes associated with stage five of the IDP.

Globalization as used in this chapter signifies the deepening economic interdependence between these countries and the growing convergence of income levels and consumption patterns between industrialized and several industrializing countries (Dunning and Narula 1997). The three main forms of interdependence are foreign direct investment (FDI), cross-border alliances and networks, and intra-firm and intra-industry trade resulting from the growth of FDI and alliance activity. These have resulted in global supply and demand pressures across borders as firms increasingly compete not just with firms in the home country, but also those in the same sectors in different countries. It is not our intention to review the factors contributing to globalization, which we summarize in Figure 6.1.

3. THE GROWTH OF R&D ALLIANCES: ACQUIRING TECHNOLOGICAL COMPETENCE

The growth of strategic alliance activity mirrors the changes taking place across countries and sectors towards a convergence of technologies, and supply and demand conditions, which is simplistically referred to as globalization. However, despite these macro-level phenomena, it is important to understand firm-specific explanations of the growth of

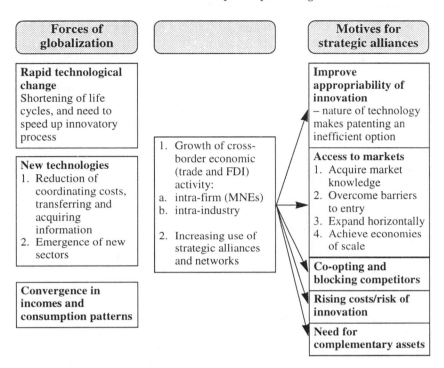

Sources: Hagedoorn (1993), Dunning (1993), Narula (1996), Glaister and Buckley (1996), Dunning and Narula (1997).

Figure 6.1   Relating globalization to the motives for strategic alliances

strategic alliances in general, and strategic technological partnering (STP) in particular. This distinction is important, since STP represents a special case of alliances, given the unique nature of innovating and creating especially through R&D activities.

R&D activities create and develop knowledge creation and development, either in a formalized process, or through incremental learning, which assists the development and/or upgrading of the ownership specific (O) advantages of firms. All other value adding activities represent the utilization of these O advantages. R&D activities are undertaken at the various stages of the value added chain, and are essential for the continued existence of the firm. All O advantages are generated in a similar way, either through formal R&D, or through other informal means. Knowledge is generated through routines, since the firm is boundedly rational and path-dependent. In other words, firms engage in 'localized searches' which are directly related to their current activities. Hence, technology is, to a great extent, both firm- and context-specific (Nelson and Winter 1982). This has always been regarded as one of the main reasons why MNEs prefer to create their O advantages in their home countries but exploit them in foreign countries. Further, even where another firm is able to do so efficiently, the public good nature of technology will mean that the innovating firm will not receive compensation for its R&D output commensurate to its value. This tendency would be greater the higher the tacit and non-codifiable aspect of the technology.

In addition, the benefits of innovations are only partly appropriable through markets given the public good nature of technology.[8] The seller cannot get a buyer for his innovation without revealing it, and thus losing some of its value. On the other hand, the buyer cannot make a rational decision regarding the value of the innovation without full disclosure, thus making a suboptimal offer for it. Thus this implies that the innovator can only generate maximum rents from technology by internalizing its use, based on exclusive awareness.

In summary, since the level of tacitness of knowledge generated through routines is higher, it is logical to expect that newly generated O advantages are more firm- and context-specific than current O advantages of the firm. It may then be reasonably argued that firms, *ceteris paribus*, will have a higher propensity to internalize the market for R&D-related output than for intermediate products generated through production activities at other parts of the value added chain. Likewise, it can be argued that firms will prefer to centralize their R&D activities to a greater extent than production.

The evidence on internalization of R&D activities, however, remains ambivalent – not only are firms engaging in a growing number of STP agreements that explicitly involve joint technology development, but a large percentage of these are in knowledge-intensive sectors (Hagedoorn and Narula 1996). Further, it would also be reasonable to expect that if full internalization is impossible, firms might prefer to use organizational modes that provided the maximum amount of control over the innovatory process. This, however, does not appear to be the case; recent evidence indicates that there is an increasing propensity to utilize non-equity type of agreements, and this trend cuts across sectors and countries (Narula 1997).

Recent evidence on the decision-taking locus by MNEs continues to indicate a preference for centralization of formalized R&D activities (see for instance, Patel 1996; Dunning and Narula 1995). Moreover, there is mounting evidence that the location of these centralized activities need not be confined to home countries. For example, ABB, Ciba Geigy, Philips Electronics and IBM are among the leading MNEs which contribute some type of R&D in their foreign subsidiaries. Although the internationalization of R&D continues to be considerably less than that of production, there has nonetheless been a distinct shift towards internationalization of R&D activities, one reason for which has been the sharp growth of strategic asset-seeking FDI activity (Dunning and Narula 1994, 1995).

In other words, the economic imperative to internalize markets for knowledge-based activities and to locate these activities in the home country is being challenged by changes in the way firms view the global marketplace. What we are trying to emphasize here is that the forces underlying globalization have considerably influenced the way in which firms locate their R&D activities and the organizational modes used. There have been several attempts to develop a taxonomy of reasons why firms are gradually challenging the conventional wisdom about the modality and geography of R&D activities, and these are summarized in Figure 6.1.

4. WHY ALLIANCES OCCUR ACROSS BORDERS[9]

The above paragraphs do not explicitly direct attention to *international* alliance formation. What now of the additional factors to be taken into account in cross-border activity? The transaction costs approach has been extensively studied (for example, Kogut 1988, and Hennart 1993, among others) and suggests that pure hierarchies are sometimes a more costly strategy than alliances, due to the associated higher financial risks and barriers to entry. However, there is another aspect to this from FDI theory. The eclectic paradigm (for example, Dunning 1993) suggests firms engage in foreign-based value added activity if they possess O advantages that they wish to utilize in conjunction with the location advantages of the host region or country. In the case of technology development, however, these advantages are often non-codifiable and, given the firm-specific nature of such assets, it may be that the location advantages *cannot* be completely captured by the foreign investor because they are specific to domestic firms rather than the country they are located in. Therefore, firms are obliged to engage in STP rather than subsidiary (that is, majority-owned) FDI activity.

This particular point has been developed by one of the current authors (Dunning 1995a). In short, firms from one country with O advantages may seek to utilize them in a foreign country either in conjunction with immobile but generally available assets of the host region, *or* with the ownership advantages of firms in that location, when advantages it seeks are firm-specific. Such a firm may be a competitor, supplier or customer to the foreign firm.

However, what we have described here could very well also apply to a network, or other transaction-cost economizing agreement. The difference between a cost-economizing agreement and a strategic alliance is the presence of a 'strategic' element, 'an agreement which affects the long term product-marketing positioning of the firm' (Hagedoorn and Narula 1996), or, in other words, which does not simply minimize the net costs, but also improves the future value of the firm.[10] Focusing our sights once again on the special case of the strategic technology partnering agreement, 'strategic' implies the transfer of some degree of knowledge, on at least a unilateral basis, by at least one of the partners as part of the agreement. In other words, an R&D alliance may be undertaken in a *location with a complete absence of 'traditional' location advantages*, when the objective is primarily to acquire firm-specific O advantages through partnering.

While the presence of this firm may signify a concentration or agglomeration of firms in a given location (an L advantage), this is not necessarily always the case. That is, while L advantages may have determined the nature of the O advantages of the domestic firms, their transfer to a foreign partner within an alliance constitutes the utilization of the domestic partner's O advantages, and not the L advantages from which they may have originally derived. It is pertinent to note that STP does not necessarily imply that it is not simply technology that is being shared or created, but generally also includes a market-related knowledge, be it intra-firm, intra-industry or country-specific. That is, STP may also include the transfer of knowledge which is normally associated with transaction cost-minimizing activities, referred to as O advantages in the FDI literature.

Nonetheless, there is a caveat, as the preceding discussion might suggest, that both partners should not have a particular preference for the location at which their partnership might be consummated. As we have earlier explained, the knowledge base of any given firm is context-specific, since the O advantages, being path-dependent, are a direct result of the comparative and competitive advantage of the home location (Cantwell 1989; Archibugi and Pianta 1992; Narula 1995). As such, where the foreign partner wishes to internalize these O advantages through STP, *it can more efficiently do so in the location where they were generated*. This is equally valid for market-oriented STP and R&D-oriented STP.

So far we have sought to explain why firms prefer to engage in non-market mechanisms to develop technology, because of the nature of technology creation *vis-à-vis* technology exploitation. This is in line with the results of several studies (for example, Pearce and Singh 1992; Patel and Pavitt 1992; Dunning and Narula 1995) that have demonstrated that MNEs prefer to conduct much of their R&D activities in their home countries. Firms, however, are developing multiple home bases for these activities and engaging in foreign-based R&D activities to augment as well as to exploit their competitive advantages (Keummerle 1996). It is therefore logical to expect that where firms find it necessary to engage in alliances to develop technology (R&D) (rather than gaining market knowledge), they will prefer to engage in alliances with 'local' partners given the costs of adapting the context-specific nature of their ownership advantages. Duysters (1996) demonstrates that R&D-related STP tends to be less international than market-oriented STP.

5. THE ROLE OF GOVERNMENTS: A WELFARE PERSPECTIVE

It should, by now, be obvious that national governments have a strong interest in the ability of firms in a given location to conduct competitiveness-enhancing activities, particularly those associated with the creation and deployment of knowledge capital. The reasons can be identified under two main headings, namely, the promotion of wealth-creating assets of its firms (O advantages), and maintaining and improving indigenous resources and capabilities (L advantages). By doing so, a government can help maintain and improve its own locational attractiveness to mobile and footloose investors (of whatever nationality) to conduct high value adding activity. These two concerns are strongly related, since the presence of highly competitive firms at a given location acts as an L advantage, often prompting a virtuous circle. Conversely, strong L advantages, such as the presence of support institutions and firms, infrastructure and skilled manpower (that is, the national systems of innovation) will enhance the O advantages of firms located there.

The reduction of market imperfections in the creation and utilization of knowledge capital has considerable welfare benefits, which stem both from a direct result of these activities, and from externalities generated by them. It is also to be noted that governments may intervene for at least three other reasons, each of which is only indirectly related to advancing competitiveness. The first of these is to protect or advance economic or political sovereignty. The second is for strategic reasons, as in defence-related issues. The third is where investment in R&D is primarily undertaken to promote social goals, such as in the health and environment sectors. In both of these cases, even though R&D may be undertaken by private firms for commercial application elsewhere, the interest of government is to limit diffusion (for example, in the defence sector) of the technology to non-national firms, or to maximize diffusion (such as the health and environment sectors) of innovations, by, for example, acquiring the property rights and providing them at marginal cost to all firms.

Governments have three main concerns in fostering R&D activities.

1. First, there is the question of *level of investment* in R&D. Countries with low expenditures in R&D tend not to be competitive (for example, Archibugi and Pianta 1992). As such, governments have an incentive to encourage R&D activities. Without government intervention, firms may tend to underinvest given their bounded rationality and the path-dependent nature of their activities. Since firms prefer to engage in new ventures closely linked to their current activities, they may invest too little in R&D, *relative* to other kinds of investment (Hall 1986). Further, greater uncertainty may arise from competition: another firm may be doing similar research. Neither the time that the research will be completed, nor the identity of the winner of the race to innovate, is known. The risk from these and other problems is often reflected in the cost of capital to the firm intent on undertaking R&D, and the higher the risk, the more difficult it may be to acquire capital to undertake it. Finance may be unavailable for risky research projects. On the other hand, it is possible that too many, rather than too few, resources may be applied to R&D (Barzel 1968). Where several firms are in a 'race' to solve a technological problem, this may lead to overinvestment in R&D. In other words, there is (1) the danger of firms underinvesting in new technologies with which they are unfamiliar, or are too risky; (2) the risk of overinvestment in a given project due to duplication of investment by several firms.

2. *Problems of appropriability.* Society is faced with the difficulty of sustaining economic growth by providing monopoly power to the inventor so that he may continue to innovate at a socially optimal level, but also by encouraging competition to maximize the diffusion and availability of products at the lowest possible costs. Firms will underinvest in R&D when they are uncertain of appropriating sufficient returns. This occurs for three reasons. First, because the value

of an innovation is not always apparent to the market *ex ante*. Second, even where the value of the innovation is known to the inventor, he cannot convince others without revealing the details of the innovation, which means it loses some its value because of its public good nature. Third, even where the firm overcomes these two hurdles, it cannot charge the market the actual value of the innovation but the opportunity cost, or the value of the next best option available on the market (Barzel 1968). Hence, it will remain uncertain as to whether it can recuperate its costs, unless the government is able to act as a broker in this process. Governments can administer and issue patents, but these are highly imperfect tools to assign property rights, and are also inefficient. It is to be stressed that while government intervention is a possible solution it is not the *only* solution, and indeed, there are several instances and situations where the market is able to rectify its own deficiencies. Firms that are unable to patent utilize secrecy and lead times as methods to protect their property rights (Levin et al. 1987), but are also unlikely to spread the risks and costs of R&D among the potential users of the innovation.

3. *Industry structure and concentration*. The third government concern is the prevention of oligopolistic and/or monopolistic behaviour in asset creation and utilization. It is axiomatic that demand is necessary as a catalyst to innovation, and that competition to survive among firms in a given industry drives the generation and diffusion of technology. However, it remains unclear what the optimal level of competition is. Dasgupta and Stiglitz (1980), among others, have shown that there is a positive relationship between competition in R&D and the level of innovation, but it is as yet unclear what the appropriate level of innovatory activity is. There is evidence that when there are a larger number of firms engaged in R&D in a given industry, the average level of R&D investment per firm falls, but the total investment in the industry rises. On the other hand, there is also evidence confirming the Schumpeterian idea that innovative activity may be encouraged by industry structures in which firms are few and concentration is substantial. This is a complex issue that remains unresolved, and is very much a question of country-specific policy. Certainly, it would appear that, given the cost and risk of R&D in the age of globalization, a few large firms are more likely to be successful than a large number of small ones. How the implementation of R&D alliances affects the optimum industry structure is unclear, but in general, governments have preferred to

limit strategic alliances of firms in a given industry to pre-competitive research (for example, SEMATECH, ESPRIT).

6. GOVERNMENTS AND INTERNATIONAL R&D ALLIANCES

The discussion so far has illustrated the importance attached by national governments to the creation and diffusion of knowledge capital, which is regarded as the bedrock upon which the prosperity (that is, the competitiveness) of the advanced industrial countries is built. However, the influence of governments on the competitiveness of their economies has been somewhat diluted with the advent of globalization and, in its wake, alliance capitalism. Globalization has meant, *inter alia*, (1) an increasing interdependence and convergence in consumption patterns and technologies across countries; (2) the increasing internationalization of production through networks of MNE affiliates; (3) an increasing overlapping and merging of industrial sectors, and (4) increasing capital and knowledge intensity as well as a concurrent shortening of technology life cycles (Figure 6.1). There is increasing difficulty in identifying and determining where R&D investment is made, and who reaps its benefits. Ostry and Nelson (1995) suggest that because of the difficulties of monitoring and enforcing international compliance to property rights as well as the declining efficacy of patents, government support of R&D is the best way to induce industrial innovation, rather than relying on the market to provide an adequate return.

This line of reasoning has a considerable following, not least among economists who advocate 'strategic trade theory', as well as most neo-Schumpeterian economists. Essentially the argument is that technology defines competitiveness, and with the cost of R&D activity rising, an oligopolistic market structure would be optimal. A small number of firms would reap higher profits, which would support higher wages. However, since every government would like its firms (or one of them) in each high-tech, capital-intensive sector to be among the surviving firms, this has led to a sort of 'techno-nationalism' where every country supports its national champions through various means to maintain technological competitiveness.

However, this techno-nationalism has resulted in a sort of prisoner's dilemma, as globalization makes it much more difficult to identify what constitutes a national champion, as has proved to be the case with ICI or Rover. Indeed, Ostry and Nelson (1995) argue that policies that have sought to create national champions have actually furthered the process of transnationalization, since barriers to imports have encouraged foreign MNEs to establish local value adding activities, and undertake alliances in order to receive national treatment.

Governments do not have to regard STP as a first-best option, or even a second-best one: it is debatable whether R&D investment through alliances is quite at the same level as that achieved through internalized R&D activity by national firms. Certainly, it would seem obvious that government financial support to a collaboration between a national champion with a firm of another nationality may represent a subsidy to the foreign firm. Likewise, a firm may see R&D subsidies by the government as a substitute for its own R&D efforts rather than as an additional source of investment, leading to a net reduction in R&D expenditures on a national level. However, the question is not whether R&D investment through STP is a better solution than R&D investment by domestic firms, but whether it represents a better solution than that offered by the free market, and there is good reason to suspect that the market will be unable to achieve a welfare optimum.[11] Moreover, it is important to realize that it is not simply a question of maintaining the *level* of R&D investment, but also the *efficiency* of this investment.

Our discussion up to this point underlines the unresolved question of the prudence of government intervention in R&D activity. With R&D activity highly uncertain in nature, especially when such R&D activity is close to or at the technology frontier, and where the R&D is basic and conceptual in nature, the efficacy of government intervention is unclear. This is for two reasons. First, governments need to target industries and sectors which offer promise in the medium and long term, and are not 'sunset' industries. Besides, there may be several different, competing technologies, but only limited funds. In such cases, choices have to be made, and firms do not have incentives to reveal their true opinions, especially where the most 'deserving' firm is a rival one. As Farrell (1987) has emphasized, a central authority is bound to have less complete information than the firms in question. When firms are engaged in R&D some distance away from the technological frontier, the direction in which investment is to be made is obvious since firms at the frontier (that is, the technology leaders) have already done so.[12] The astounding success of MITI in picking winners in the 1950s and 1960s, and their less successful interventions in the 1980s and 1990s, illustrates this point well. However, non-intervention is not the answer either, since firms that are risk averse will avoid investments in highly risky, economically less viable, 'blue sky' projects.

Second, where a 'worthy' project is defined, there are clear difficulties in identifying whether the government subsidies are being utilized for the purpose for which they were provided, or simply as a mechanism for cross-subsidization of other R&D projects. This arises from the tacit nature of basic R&D in high technology industries, since the output may not be patentable or have an identifiable, tangible form.

It is not our aim in this chapter to evaluate the wisdom of government involvement in promoting R&D activity, or to criticize techno-nationalism.[13] Our position is based on the assumption that these are the implicit goals of governments in advanced countries (for a review, see Ostry and Nelson 1995). However, the evidence reviewed so far indicates that firms must necessarily engage in asset-exploitation on a global (or at least regional) basis if they are to remain competitive, and albeit to a lesser degree (but to a growing extent), develop and acquire new assets globally. The evidence reviewed would also indicate that, in general, firms are more willing to engage in collaborative R&D activities in overseas locations than in wholly-owned R&D activities, and this has much to do with techno-globalism (Archibugi and Michie 1994).

Having said this, however, there is no consensus on the optimal way to boost the competitive advantage of firms through strategic alliances. On the one hand, countries such as the US have hitherto attempted to deal with the root causes of market failure by attempting to make markets more efficient, but only directly intervening on a reactive, case-by-case basis (for instance, in sectors in which defence applications may exist). On the other hand, countries such as France and Japan have taken a more active, or direct, role.[14]

7. OPPORTUNITIES FOR GOVERNMENTS: DIRECT VS. INDIRECT INTERVENTION

We have so far illustrated that insofar as governments are concerned, their primary interests lie in strengthening the competitiveness of their national firms. The evidence would suggest that the role of governments, at least in investment path stage five countries, is most effective as a facilitator of competitive advantage, in terms of providing the comp-lementary assets needed by firms rather than through direct intervention. These assets are best described as the national systems of innovation (NSI), and are defined as the network of institutions in the public and private sector in a given country that support the generation and diffusion of innovations (Freeman 1987). In the parlance of the eclectic paradigm, the NSI represent the location-bound resources and capabilities that sustain, complement and enhance the O advantages of firms. In other words, indirect intervention takes the form of improving the O advantages of firms by affecting the L advantages of the country. By direct intervention we mean the actions of governments that directly influence the O advantages of firms. It must be noted that few countries desist completely from direct intervention. Direct intervention includes attempts by governments to enhance the O advantages of firms by fiat, through restrictions on domestic operations of foreign MNEs (for example, the US airline industry), through exclusive contracts to develop products for the use of governments (for example, the French TGV, eurofighter project, space shuttle, and so on), and through exclusive (or subsidized) access to public sector research facilities. We will briefly discuss the options available to governments in connection to encouraging R&D alliances under these two headings.

Direct Intervention

First, governments can engage as direct participants in R&D alliances as a partner. This is especially common in basic research projects, as public research institutes and universities have the human and capital resources to undertake fundamental R&D, or what is referred to as pre-competitive research by the EU. This is one of the means used by the EU to improve the competitiveness of European firms – indeed, 12 billion ECUs, almost 60 per cent of funding within the second and third framework programmes which covered the periods 1987 and 1994 was directed towards universities and public institutes (Geuna 1996). An additional advantage of direct participation is that it is better able to monitor the utilization of the resources and act as an honest broker, and prevent the misallocation of funds by commercial (and profit-oriented) partners. NTT, the Japanese telecommunications giant, has played a similar role in enforcing the partnership agreements undertaken by firms in telecommunications and computers, by sponsoring research complementary to that of MITI, and allowing the consolidation of national champions in each of these industries (Levy and Samuels 1991)

Second, governments can guarantee a market for the output of the alliance. This can be undertaken in at least three ways: first, by providing project-specific contracts to consortia of firms, as is the case with most EU aerospace projects, and US defence-related projects. This substantially reduces the risk associated with R&D, and improves the appropriability of the innovation; second, by directly affecting the returns to the innovator by creating a market for the product. For example, in the 1970s, the Japanese government established the Japan Robot Company which bought all the output of the robot manufacturers, and then leased the robots to its customers; third, by establishing a particular technology standard which may be proprietary to a particular firm, and requiring general adherence to it, has the added advantage that it prevents duplication of investment in other, inferior, alternatives. This is achieved through establishing cross-licensing agreements. The most successful of these, the aircraft patent agreement among US firms which remained in force between 1917 and 1968, was established at the behest of the US government during the First World War in order to standardize the use of the 'best-practice' technology in airframes across the various manufacturers (Bitlingmayer 1988). A difficulty in so doing is that first, governments may not necessarily select *ex ante* the most superior technology, and second, they may sometimes be required to suspend (or modify) antitrust regulations. In fact, the aircraft patent agreement was eventually terminated by the US supreme court, when it was deemed as contrary to antitrust regulations.

Third, governments can provide market access in exchange for technology to a domestic firm. They can do this, for example, by insisting that a foreign-based MNE should comply with certain minimum local content provisions, or that it take a domestic partner in exchange for its access to the domestic market. The case of both European and US Voluntary Export Restrictions with Japanese firms led to an increase in FDI (and alliance formation) during the 1980s. A similar approach was taken by Korea during the 1960s (Amsden 1989), where technology transfer was made a condition for market access.

Fourth, governments can make participation in alliances a pre-condition for future government contracts. Both the direction of research and the availability of subsidies can be used as leverage to encourage firms to undertake collaborative research. This is the case with the Japanese computer industry, in which major Japanese firms were asked to collaborate on joint R&D, with the understanding that it affected future subsidies from MITI. Levy and Samuels (1991) note that when Matsushita left the computer industry in 1964, it was unable to enter MITI-sponsored computer alliances for two decades.

Indirect Intervention

The literature is replete with policy prescriptions to improve the L advantages and the quality of location-bound resources, and there is no reason to revise this literature here. The enhancement and improvement of L advantages has received considerable attention in various guises: see Porter (1990), Dunning and Narula (1996), Lundvall (1992) and Nelson (1993) among others, and is relatively uncontroversial: there is, therefore, no need to develop an exhaustive typology of options here. We shall, however, highlight two important issues.

First, although governments are unable to prevent alliances from being unstable, or indeed, from reducing the inherent risk of R&D activity – whether collaborative or otherwise – there is a role for them in providing information to help identify synergies, complementarities and opportunities, since there are market imperfections in the *market for partners*. Governments can help diffuse the results of basic research output produced either by government research institutes or private establishments to interested parties by creating a sort of 'marketplace' where potential partners can meet and exchange information. This is undertaken on a regular basis through trade fairs, but also directly through governmental institutions (Niosi 1995). Even where governments do not own the technologies, they can play an important role in matchmaking firms.

Second, there is an important and growing role for governments in encouraging and monitoring cross-border R&D alliances, and reducing the uncertainty attached to this. First, this can be done by the development of binding multilateral intellectual property rights protection through agencies such as the World Trade Organization (WTO), thereby improving appropriability of innovation, both domestically and internationally. There is a very real danger of cross-border duplication of activity, especially in terms of multiple (and not necessarily compatible) standards which can be potentially suboptimal in terms of expenditure on a global basis. Recent initiatives by the G7 members to jointly subsidize space research is such an example. The failure to develop a common standard on HDTV has largely affected its successful commercial launch. However, intergovernmental initiatives are, in general, the exception rather than the rule.

Areas in which Government Intervention is Futile

Despite the best efforts of governments, there nonetheless remain considerable risks associated with success or failure of an alliance (see Inkpen and Beamish 1996). Das and Teng (1996) suggest that such risks are of two types, namely, *relational* and *performance* risk. Relational risk occurs as a result of one or more of the partners in an alliance being unwilling to work towards the mutual interest of the partnership, thereby breaching the agreement. Such behaviour may be rational or irrational, and include asymmetrical learning, or a lack or trust. There is limited scope for government intervention in such instances, since we would have to assume perfect information *ex ante* of the failure of a partner to provide inputs in the prescribed manner. Given the nature of R&D alliances, such an assumption is clearly unrealistic, and in the case of basic R&D, the asymmetrical learning may not be evident in the short term. Nor, it must be said, does relationship risk arise only from the failure of partners to maintain the agreement, but also where they interpret the agreement literally. Lastly, relational risk may be unintentional, since partners may have different objectives.

Performance risk, on the other hand, occurs when all partners have cooperated fully, but the partnership has not achieved its objective, and represents the opposite problem. The role of government here is also limited, except where such alliances had received government subsidies, since the question is whether in fact the failure of the partnering was due to inefficient and/or inappropriate use of the funds, or that the research trajectory was 'too far' from commercialization for any tangible output to be generated. Such questions have been raised about the ESPRIT programme of the European Commission (Mytelka 1991).

8.   CONCLUSIONS

Globalization has led to profound changes in which business activities are conducted, not least because of the growing use of networks and alliances by firms from the advanced industrial countries. This process, dubbed 'alliance capitalism', represents a new phase in the evolution of the market economies, and is associated with the fifth stage of the IDP.

There has also been a concurrent growth in the use of alliances to acquire and develop knowledge capital. The growth of strategic technology partnering is somewhat strange, in that firms have hitherto preferred to internalize their R&D activities. Further, they have tended to geographically concentrate these activities in their home countries. We have attempted to provide an explanation for these new phenomena within existing paradigms of FDI activity and neo-Schumpeterian theory. Furthermore, we have tried to explain the welfare and social rationale for government involvement in promoting and partaking in R&D activities in general and alliances in particular, paying special attention to the evolution of *international* strategic technology partnering.

It would seem that governments are increasingly engaged in promoting the competitiveness of their domestic firms, in what can be loosely described as 'techno-nationalism' (Ostry and Nelson 1995), with the intention of developing 'national champions'. Most of the major industrial economies practise some sort of government intervention to boost the O advantages of their firms. While some governments do so through indirect means that improve the quality of location-bound resources and capabilities to attract mobile O advantages of domestic- and foreign-owned firms, others attempt more direct intervention by directly participating in O advantage-generating activities.

Much of this intervention was initially a response to globalization, with the desire of protecting weak domestic firms from international competition. Ironically, this has led to a greater use of alliance and network-forming activity; hence, this techno-nationalism is doomed to failure, as the question of 'who is us' and 'who is them' makes such policies increasingly redundant. National champions are equally willing to act as free agents, and are in some instances receiving national treatment (and support) from several governments, both national and regional. The example of IBM being involved in several research con- sortia funded by the EU and the US governments best illustrates this point.

As for the underlying motive of improving levels of R&D activity, this too would seem to be in doubt. It should be noted that R&D alliances are even more footloose than traditional majority-owned pro- duction or R&D activities, nor, it must be stressed, do R&D alliances provide significant levels of spillovers to the host economies where they might be located. Funds invested in joint research by governments are notoriously hard to evaluate in terms of their application, both in a geographic and a technical (that is, project-specific) sense. Furthermore, firms are more interested in establishing themselves near centres of agglomeration, regardless of where these might be located. This indi- cates a very real danger of entering into an incentives tournament, with so many countries willing to subsidize R&D (Niosi 1995), and with so little obvious spillovers therefrom.

The advice to governments is to view strategic technology partnering as complementary to domestic R&D, rather than as a substitute. Fur- thermore, a distinction needs to be made regarding the various aspects of R&D: basic research, applied research and development. There is relatively little controversy about basic research and the need for governments to subsidize it, although the ability of governments to pick who to subsidize is another matter. However, strategic technology partnering is also relatively uncontroversial in basic research.

The debate primarily revolves around applied research and develop- ment. In a roundabout sense, Krugman (1994) is right, albeit for the wrong reasons – countries don't compete, companies do. It is not the role of governments to try and enhance the O advantages of its firms to the exclusion of foreign-owned establishments, nor can they expect to do so in this age of alliance capitalism. Instead, the onus should be on improving the location advantages of countries and the O advantage – augmenting resources such as education and training, infrastructure, institutions, intellectual property rights protection, and other non-specific R&D support. Nonetheless, in another sense, Krugman was wrong: competitiveness does matter, since markets are imperfect and resources are mobile, thereby making government intervention necessary. Its urgency is further enhanced by the fact that the current extent of involvement by governments represents a sort of prisoner's dilemma, since no country is likely to back down from the current competitiveness-enhancing 'war'. We would be safe to conclude that in this age of strategic trade policies and targeted industrial development, nations that rely only on market forces to determine outcomes are not just not playing on a level playing field, but are playing on a different playing field altogether.

We believe that the evidence on globalization and alliance capitalism points towards a role for governments in improving the efficiency of R&D activities on an international basis. It is understandable that countries duplicate R&D investments for strategic and political reasons, especially in basic research, but the failure to create international standards in many instances leads to considerable misallocation of resources, particularly in applied research and development. Further, different countries are often unknowingly engaged in subsidizing the same projects by transnational firms. There is clearly a growing need to address these and other issues at a multilateral level, as is currently attempted within the framework of the WTO for intellectual property rights.

NOTES

1. This chapter has benefited from comments by Terutomo Ozawa, Gene Slowinski and Gavin Boyd.
2. For instance, by being involved in the generation and diffusion of knowledge, both in the sense of technology and acquiring access to foreign markets.
3. Intellectual capital is a generic term which includes knowledge, information and experience embodied in both human and physical resources.
4. It should be noted that a distinction needs to be made regarding the difference between three elements of R&D: basic research, applied research and development. There is relatively little controversy regarding the role of government in basic R&D. Fundamentally, our discussion centres around the extent and nature of government involvement in applied research and development activities.
5. Although Hagedoorn and Sadowski (1996) indicate that only about 2.6 per cent of strategic alliances lead to M&A, this number is quite significant given that they

are primarily focusing on alliances whose primary purpose is strategic technology partnering.

6. For a discussion of exit and voice strategies of firms to markets, see Dunning (1995a).
7. The IDP suggests that the international direct investment position of a country (that is, the outward less the inward direct investment) goes through various stages according to its economic development (measured both by its GNP per capita and changes in the structure of its economic activity). For further details see Narula (1995) and Dunning and Narula (eds) (1996).
8. It should be noted that, throughout the remainder of this chapter, our arguments apply to the more formalized process of R&D rather than the informal processes of R&D.
9. See Osborn and Hagedoorn (1997) for a review of the literature.
10. The important considerations between the transaction cost school (which emphasizes cost) and the organizational capability school (which emphasizes value) is succinctly summarized in Madhok (1997).
11. The argument against intervention suggests that governments may not be able to do better than markets, and that since innovation occurs in response to market demand, it cannot be seriously suboptimal. This line of reasoning is succinctly summarized in Hall (1986), pp. 9–14.
12. It is necessary to emphasize the difference between firms that are a distance from the technology frontier, and those that are simply experiencing X-inefficiency. The latter group are simply using an inferior technology, while the former are operating at an earlier stage of the product life cycle.
13. See Krugman (1994) for such a critique. For a counter-argument, see Dunning (1995b)
14. For details, see contributions to Nelson (ed.) (1993).

REFERENCES

Amsden, A. (1989), *Asia's Next Giant*, New York: Oxford University Press.

Archibugi, D. and J. Michie (1994), 'The globalisation of technology: a new taxonomy', *Cambridge Journal of Economics*, **19**: 121–40.

Archibugi, D. and M. Pianta (1992), *The Technological Specialisation of Advanced Countries*, Dordrecht: Kluwer Academic Publishers.

Barzel, Yarom (1968), 'Optimal timing of innovations', *The Review of Economics and Statistics*, **50**: 348–55.

Bitlingmayer, George (1988), 'Property rights, progress, and the aircraft patent agreement', *Journal of Law and Economics*, **31**: 227–48.

Cantwell, John (1989), *Technological Innovation and Multinational Corporations*, Oxford: Basil Blackwell.

Ciborra, Claudio (1991), 'Alliances as learning experiments: Cupertino, competition and change in high-tech industries', in L. Mytelka (ed.), *Strategic Partnerships and the World Economy*, London: Pinter, pp. 51–77.

Das, T. and B.-S. Teng (1996), 'Risk types and inter-firm alliance structures', *Journal of Management Studies*, **33**: 827–43.

Dasgupta, P. and J.E. Stiglitz (1980), 'Uncertainty, industrial structure and the speed of R&D', *Bell Journal of Economics*, **11**: 1–28.

Dunning, John H. (1993), *Multinational Enterprises and the Global Economy*, Wokingham: Addison-Wesley.

Dunning, John H. (1995a), 'Reappraising the eclectic paradigm in the age of alliance capitalism', *Journal of International Business Studies*, **26**: 461–91.

Dunning, John H. (1995b), 'Think again, Professor Krugman: competitiveness does matter', *The International Executive*, **37**: 315–24.

Dunning, John H. (1997), *Alliance Capitalism in Global Business*, London: Routledge.

Dunning, J.H. and R. Narula (1994), 'Transpacific direct investment and the investment development path: the record assessed', *Essays in International Business*, March: 1–69.

Dunning, J.H. and R. Narula (1995), 'The R&D activities of foreign firms in the US', *International Studies in Management and Organisation*, **25**: 39–73.

Dunning, J.H. and R. Narula (1996), 'The investment development path revisited: some emerging issues', in J. Dunning and R. Narula (eds), *Foreign Direct Investment and Governments: Catalysts for Economic Restructuring*, London: Routledge, pp. 1–41.

Dunning, J.H. and R. Narula (1998), 'Developing countries versus multinationals in a globalising world: the dangers of falling behind', in P. Buckley and P. Ghauri (eds), *Multinational Enterprises and Emerging Markets*, London: Dryden Press.

Dunning, J.H. and C. Wymbs (1997), 'The sourcing of technological advantages by multinational enterprises', mimeo, Rutgers University: Newark.

Duysters, Geert (1996), *The Dynamics of Technical Innovation: The Evolution and Development of Information Technology*, Cheltenham: Edward Elgar.

Farrell, Joseph (1987), 'Information and the Coase Theorem', *Economic Perspectives*, **1**: 113–29.

Freeman, Christopher (1987), *Technology Policy and Economic Performance*, London: Frances Pinter.

Gerlach, Michael (1992), *Alliance Capitalism*, Oxford: Oxford University Press.

Geuna, Aldo (1996), 'The participation of higher education institutions in European Union framework programmes', *Science and Public Policy*, **23**: 287–96.

Glaister, K. and P. Buckley (1996), 'Strategic motives for international alliance formation', *Journal of Management Studies*, **33**: 301–32.

Hagedoorn, John (1993), 'Understanding the rationale of strategic technology partnering: inter-organizational modes of Cupertino and sectoral differences', *Strategic Management Journal*, **14**: 371–85.

Hagedoorn, J. and B. Sadowski (1996), 'Exploring the potential transition from strategic technology partnering to mergers and acquisitions', MERIT working paper series 96–010.

Hagedoorn, J. and R. Narula (1996), 'Choosing modes of governance for strategic technology partnering: international and sectoral differences', *Journal of International Business Studies*, **27**: 265–84.

Hagedoorn, J. and R. Narula (1997), 'Globalisation, organisational modes and the growth of international strategic technology alliances', MERIT working paper series.

Hall, Peter, H. (1986), 'The theory and practice of innovatory policy: an overview', in Peter Hall (ed.), *Technology, Innovation and Economic Policy*, New York: St Martin's Press, pp. 1–34.

Hennart, J.-F. (1993), 'Explaining the swollen middle; why most transactions are a mix of market and hierarchy', *Organization Science*, **4**: 529–47.

Inkpen, A. and P. Beamish (1997), 'Knowledge, bargaining power, and the instability of international joint ventures', *Academy of Management Review*, **22**: 177–202.

Keummerle, W. (1996), 'The drivers of foreign direct investment into research and development: an empirical investigation', Boston: Working Paper No. 96–002.

Kogut, Bruce (1988), 'Joint ventures: theoretical and empirical perspectives', *Strategic Management Journal*, **9**: 319–32.

Krugman, Paul (1994), 'Competitiveness: a dangerous obsession', *Foreign Affairs*, **73**, 28–44.

Levin, R., A. Klevorick, R. Nelson, and S. Winter (1987), 'Appropriating the returns from industrial research and development', *Brookings Papers on Economics Activity*, No. 3: 783–820.

Levy, J. and R. Samuels, (1991), 'Institutions and innovation; research and collaboration as technology strategy in Japan', in L. Mytelka (ed.), *Strategic Partnerships and the World Economy*, London: Pinter, pp. 120–48.

Lundvall, B. (ed.) (1992), *National Systems of Innovation: Towards a Theory of Innovation and Interactive Learning*, London: Pinter Publishers.

Madhok, Anoop (1997), 'Cost, value and foreign market entry mode: the transaction and the firm', *Strategic Management Journal*, **18**: 39–61.

Mytelka, L. (1991), 'States, strategic alliances and international oligopolies', in L. Mytelka (ed.), *Strategic Partnerships and the World Economy*, London: Pinter, pp. 182–210.

Narula, Rajneesh (1995), *Multinational Investment and Economic Structure*, London: Routledge.

Narula, Rajneesh (1996), 'Forms of international Cupertino between corporations', in C. Jepma and A. Rhoen (eds), *International Trade: A Business Perspective*, Longman: Harlow, pp. 98–122.

Narula, Rajneesh (1997), *International Strategic Technology Partnering by EU Firms: Globalisation or Regionalisation*, mimeo, Universiteit Maastricht.

Nelson, R.R. (ed.) (1993), *National Innovation Systems*, New York: Oxford University Press.

Nelson, R. and S. Winter (1982), *An Evolutionary Theory of Economic Change*, Cambridge: Belknap Press.

Niosi, Jorge (1995), *Flexible Innovation: Technological Alliances in Canadian Industry*, Montreal: McGill-Queens University Press.

Osborn, R. and J. Hagedoorn (1997), 'The institutionalisation and evolutionary dynamics of inter-organizational alliances and networks', *Academy of Management Journal*, **40**: 261–78.

Ostry, S. and R. Nelson, (1995), *Techno-Nationalism and Techno-Globalism: Conflict and Cooperation*, Washington: The Brookings Institution.

Patel, Pari (1996), 'Are large firms internationalising the generation of technology? Some new evidence', *IEEE Transactions on Engineering Management*, **43**: 41–7.

Patel, P. and K. Pavitt, (1992), 'The innovative performance of the world's largest firms: some new evidence', *Economic Innovation and New Technologies*, **2**: 91–102.

Pearce, R and S. Singh (1992), *Globalising Research and Development*, London: Macmillan.

Porter, M.E. (1990), *The Competitive Advantage of Nations*, New York: The Free Press.

7. Organizational efficiency and structural change: a meso-level analysis

Terutomo Ozawa*

MULTI-LEVELS OF ORGANIZATIONAL EFFICIENCY

When we talk about economic activity as a collective endeavor in this globalizing economy, there are basically the five levels of organizational efficiency we should be concerned with: the micro–micro (intra-firm), the meso (inter-firm), and the macroeconomy (intra-economy), the regional (cross-border, intra-regional), and the world economy (global) strata. These levels of efficiency may be named X efficiency, Y efficiency, and Z efficiency, Beta efficiency, and Alpha efficiency, respectively.

A hierarchy of efficiencies thus exists, but how consciously – hence, how effectively – each stratum of economic activity is organized depends on the degree of coherence or integration of the stratal group involved as an aggregate, and above all, on the degree of sharing an understanding of, and commitment to, common goals. In capitalism, the firm or the corporate person is the most coherent and purpose-focused economic entity because of the singularity of its *raison d'être*, that is, the pursuit of profits by minimizing costs and maximizing sales. The firm constitutes the core of the hierarchy as a unit of activity. All other strata are the ecosystems within which the firm pursues its own goal of making profits by attaining maximum possible X efficiency.

The level of X efficiency is also externally constrained by complex sets of factors in the meso, macro, regional, and global strata, whose organizational efficiencies are in turn determined/affected by the behaviours of the firms. As will be seen below, X efficiency itself, along with Y efficiency, is now increasingly pursued *cross borders*, as the firm

* The author is grateful to John Dunning and Gavin Boyd for their helpful comments and suggestions which are incorporated in this chapter.

is transformed into the multinational enterprise, often at the cost of Z efficiency but to the benefits of Beta and Alpha efficiencies.

As economic activity expands beyond the firm level and outward in wider organizational strata, the coherence and density of economic objectives/goals weaken and the *raison d'être* of the stratum diversifies. Economic efficiency is usually compromised in pursuit of non-economic goals, hence it can never be maximized and attained in a first-best fashion.

Since my assignment for this chapter is to examine the issues of inter-corporate or inter-institutional governance such as industrial groups and inter-firm coordinations, I should focus only on the meso stratum. It is useful, nevertheless, to locate my area of exploration in the total scheme of things. Besides, the multi-levels of organization interact with each other in various ways, sometimes complementarily and sometimes at cross-purposes. Considerations of the meso stratum are unavoidably intertwined with other stratum. Therefore, a few paragraphs are in order to describe an overall picture.

NEOCLASSICAL NIRVANA AND STRATAL GOVERNANCE

Mainstream economics posits that the market mechanism, when free from imperfections/distortions, is capable of achieving maximum efficiency in a Pareto-optimal way at each level of economic activity and organization – that is, there exist *neoclassical firms in a neoclassical industry in a neoclassical economy – all perfectly governed by the market.* Under these ideal conditions, the regional economy (Beta efficiency) and the global economy (Alpha efficiency) are similarly at Pareto optimality by the extension of the same logic; each national economy is completely market-governed and acts as a price-taker in the global economy. All the multi-levels of coordinations are thus automatically and optimally achieved via the market mechanism without any conscious planning and control, that is, without any non-market governance structure.

The above 'first-best world' or 'dream world' is an intellectual edifice in which neoclassical nirvana is attained, completely liberated from market imperfections. Within the firm, for example, this perspective argues that it makes no difference if capital hires labor or labor hires capital. The firm can minimize costs and maximize profits at the fullest possible efficiency. No wonder, then, that the firm has long been considered 'the black box'. At the meso level, no ranking of strategic importance exists with respect to different industries; an industry is an industry is an industry – the 'micro-chip' industry is no different from the 'potato-chip' industry, because the same market rationality governs all industries equally and they are the neutral elements in a vector of industries. At the macro level, industrial policy and strategic trade are anathema to the market economy; they only distort market rationality (Brander 1986). In this perspective, each national economy itself becomes a 'perfect competitor', hence the world economy is organized on a perfectly competitive basis. There is no rationale for regionalism.

In the logic of perfect competition, therefore, there is no need for conscious, planned or strategic decision making to organize economic exchanges; every exchange is *impersonally* and *impeccably* carried out without any trace of mutually interactive (externality-generating) behaviors of individual economic actors. In fact, the marketplace envisioned by neoclassicists in its purest form can be interpreted as a no-man universe, just as the perfect competition model is equivalent to a no-firm universe. For that matter, it is also a no-country universe. That is to say, there is no room for considering how 'social capital' (Coleman 1988) is formed and accumulated in a variety of economic organizations and through their interactive relations.

What is missing in neoclassicism is well described by Fukuyama:

> We can think of neoclassical economics as being, say, eighty percent correct: it has uncovered important truths about the nature of money and markets because its fundamental model of rational, self-interested human behavior is correct about eighty percent of the time. But there is a missing twenty percent of human behavior about which neoclassical economics can give only a poor account. As Adam Smith well understood, economic life is deeply *embedded in social life*, and it cannot be understood apart from the customs, morals, and habits of the society in which it occurs. In short, it cannot be divorced from *culture*. (Fukuyama 1995: 13, emphasis added)

Indeed, culture has lately begun to be increasingly treated by economists as an important variable – a variable of differentiation – that affects economic performance, and a variety of indicators of different cultural traits have been devised to measure econometrically their effects on economic efficiency (Gray 1996). The importance of culture as a market-supportive institution grows as economic activities become ever more knowledge-intensive and based on flows of information as an input, as well as a lubricant, for exchanges. Culture is defined as 'the array of formal and informal rules that guides the members of a society in their selection of appropriate behavior and provides the framework for the construction of ideology', and is regarded as 'a learned and shared information pool':

> It is the context in which all economic and political behavior must make sense. While not determinative of behavior, it does establish the range of choice for action. Another way of putting it is that members of a society behave *in accordance with shared understandings acquired by virtue of shared experience.* Culture, then, can be viewed as *a learned and shared information pool.* (Smith 1992: 13, italics added)

A similar, but more conventional economics-(non-culture)based, observation was made by Ron Coase (1992) in his Nobel Memorial lecture by citing Lionel Robbins (1932):

> from the point of view of the [neoclassical] economist 'organization' is a matter of internal industrial arrangement – if not internal to the firm, at any rate internal to 'the' industry. At the same time it tends to leave out completely the *governing factor* of all productive organization . . . (Coase 1992: 714, italics added)

Coase then interpreted and expanded on it as follows:

> What this comes down to is that, in Robbins's view, an economist *does not interest himself in the internal arrangements within organizations but only in what happens on the market*, the purchase of factors of production, and the sale of the goods that these factors produce. What happens *in between* the purchase of the factors of production and the sale of the goods that are produced by these factors is largely ignored . . .
>
> This neglect of other aspects of the system has been made easier by another feature of modern economic theory – the growing abstraction of the analysis, which does not seem to call for a detailed knowledge of the actual economic system or, at any rate, has managed to proceed without it. (Ibid.: 714, italics added)

In addition to the firm being 'the black box' of economics, indeed, the meso-level and macro-level strata are still left largely unexplored as 'the black hole' of the economic universe, as it were, a sphere of institutional arrangements that still stands as 'nothingness' (inexplicable and irrelevant) to neoclassical economists who tenaciously hold on to the myth of total market efficacy. They all start out with the supposition that 'in the beginning there were markets' (Williamson 1975).

INTRA-FIRM ORGANIZATION (X EFFICIENCY)

Since the day of Robbins's observation, a number of institutionally oriented economists have made significant contributions to our understanding of the logic of the firm and of the intra-firm organization. Thanks to their efforts, the firm may no longer be a black box. Ron Coase's seminal work (1937) theorized an economic organization (the firm) as a substitute for coordinating economic activities via the market. Coase pioneered the development of transaction-cost economics, but his analysis remained at the firm level and did not delve into the efficacy issue of intra-firm (micro–micro) organization. The issue was later taken up by others.

The concept of X efficiency (Leibenstein 1966) captured the level of efforts, that is, mental and physical exertions, expended by managers and workers within the firm. Leibenstein argued that X inefficiency leaves much greater room for improvement than allocative inefficiency, namely a greater degree of deviation from the ideal of the perfect market. If Coase is credited for bringing the firm back into economic analysis as an institutional substitute for the market, Leibenstein should be credited for having the economic profession refocus on individuals as efficiency-determining agents.

> Much of the productive economic life of individuals is carried out through or within organizations, yet the theory of organization is not part of standard economic analysis. The focus of [our] study is the relations of the components of economic organizations to internal efficiency. We will look at organizations from several viewpoints; that of *individuals* making decisions as agents for the organization; that of *individuals* facing, in their work, decisions that entail their own personal interests; and that of the various elements of organizational structures that constrain and influence the decisions made by *individuals*. (Leibenstein 1987: 1, italics added)

In Leibenstein's view, however, X inefficiency basically occurs when the firm is sheltered from the rigor of market competition.

Alchian and Demsetz (1972) looked upon the firm as 'a highly specialized surrogate market' which can satisfy the need of the team methods of production in the modern market economy, but which is confronted with the problems of shirking (less or poor efforts) and monitoring, as well as with their costs.

Yet all these analyses – from Coase to Leibenstein to Alchian and Demsetz – are still couched in 'the myth of the market economy' (Lazonick 1991), since they regard organizational inefficiencies as *deviations* from the dreamed-of norm of market idealism, deviations that cause market infirmities. Nevertheless, Coase was the very first who recognized the 'inefficiencies' of the market transactions governed by the price mechanism as compared to the intra-organizations or hierarchical transactions governed by internal directives or fiats.

Other than, or in addition to, the relative efficiencies of markets vs. hierarchies, there is an issue of the relative efficiencies of differently crafted hierarchies between countries, that is, the heterogeneous hierarchies organized and governed under divergent sociocultural principles. Aoki (1988), for example, explored the way the Japanese (J-) firm is differently organized and governed from the American (A-) firm, and concluded:

> The A-firm emphasizes efficiency attained through fine specialization and sharp job demarcation, whereas the J-firm emphasizes the capability of the worker's group to cope with local emergencies autonomously, which is developed through learning by doing and sharing knowledge on the shop-floor. In the former, the operating task is *separated* from the task of identifying and finding necessary expedients to overcome and prevent emergencies, whereas in the latter the two tend to be *integrated*. (Aoki 1988: 16, original emphasis)

The J-firm is organized in such a way to make the most of the information-processing capabilities of worker groups on the shop-floor, contributing to the dynamic efficiency of firms and surpassing that of the A-firm-type hierarchy built on the principle of specialization, so far as the problem solving related to production processes is concerned.

Many aspects of intra-firm organization have been explored, but the study of firms has until recently evolved with some neglect of entrepreneurship and innovative activity (knowledge creation). In examining the relations between organizational forms and entrepreneurship, Imai (1992) makes a distinction between 'network organization' and 'hierarchial organization'. This distinction can supplement Aoki's J-firm vs. A-firm paradigm, defining the network organization as 'a *place* for interaction between related actors, [where] each obtains positive externalities of created information' (Imai 1992: 221, emphasis added). On the role of entrepreneurs, he further observes:

> When an entrepreneur tries to advance things in a new way, he needs on-the-spot information to suggest the structural information from which he can grasp the new context in its entirety. This is the necessary qualification of an entrepreneur. However, even if an entrepreneur has grasped information that will enable him to discern future developments, he cannot begin work with that information alone. He knows only the direction of change for his immediate vicinity and does not yet have enough details to complete the whole job. For that purpose, he needs more information, which enables

him gradually to identify the total structure of the new context. Entrepreneurs create a *loop* to obtain such information to match the situation at
the moment. In abstract terms, they can be called *information networks*
(Imai 1992: 221, italics added)

Imai goes on to argue (1) that Japan's entrepreneurial activities were
first carried out in the organizational form of the *zaibatsu*
(conglomerates controlled by family-owned companies) in the prewar
period, then in business groups in the postwar period, and most recently
in the network industrial organization,[1] and (2) that 'in each phase,
entrepreneurs have been new men (in a Schumpeterian sense) who
were freed from the constraints of the old paradigm and thus opened
up a new context in Japanese industrial society' (Imai 1992: 229).

Focusing on the network organization, Nonaka and Takeuchi (1995)
similarly state:

What is unique about the way Japanese companies bring about continuous
innovation is the linkage between the outside and the inside. Knowledge
that is accumulated from the outside is shared widely within the organization,
stored as part of the company's knowledge base, and utilized by those
engaged in developing new technologies and products. A conversion of some
sort takes place; it is this conversion process – from outside to inside and
that is the key to understanding why Japanese companies have become
successful. (Ibid.: 6)

This outside–inside interactive flow of knowledge will be revisited below
when we examine the meso-level (inter-firm) transactions and production. In fact, the outside–inside nexus encounters many problems of
entrepreneurial coordination in knowledge creation, investment choices,
and production strategies, which have to be overcome at the meso (Y),
the national (Z) – and especially at the regional (Beta) and the global
(Alpha) levels in a highly globalized mode of business operations.

In the recent past, as seen above, examinations of intra-firm organizational efficiency have increasingly been focused on the dynamics of
innovation, drawing empirically on Japanese experiences, as well as
conceptually on organizational theory. This topic is currently a hot
subject on the frontier of management studies and has already generated a considerable amount of literature. Therefore, this brief survey
may do disservice by omitting many other important studies on this
topic. But this section is merely intended to point out that X efficiency
represents just one – but undoubtedly the most critical – of the multi-
levels of organization, since private enterprises are the drivers of global
capitalism. Before we turn to meso-level organizational approaches, we
take another brief look at the macro mode of governance.

MACROORGANIZATIONAL COORDINATION (Z EFFICIENCY)

The ideology of the market is strongly ingrained in the mindset of mainstream economists. 'The image of a free market has acquired normative significance in the political and cultural value system of the West, quite independent of the extent to which actual markets are really free' (Lowe 1977: 33). The market is a powerful instrument, no doubt. Yet, 'Like fire, the market is a good servant, but a bad master' (Eatwell 1982: 44). The market is basically neither goal-determining nor goal-pursuing; it is goal-neutral at best and sometimes even goal-hindering. In essence, the market is merely a resource-allocative institution, not a goal-setting institution (Ozawa 1997: 382).

It was only after the Great Depression of the 1930s that the market's inability to maintain full employment (that is, the occurrence of 'involuntary' unemployment) was finally recognized by policy makers and that fiscal and monetary policies became accepted in market economies. John Maynard Keynes's *General Theory of Employment* (1936) provided a conceptual foundation justifying the role of government in macroeconomic stabilization. Until then, economists had regarded the market as a fully effective and automatic mechanism capable of achieving full employment while governments adhered to Say's law of markets and the quantity theory of money (tied to the international gold standard). Interestingly enough, however, the efficacy of macroeconomic stabilization policies has recently been questioned by rational expectations theory. Moreover, fiscal discretion has been allowed little scope by huge accumulations of national debt.

Distinct from the concept of macro-stabilization policy, John Dunning (1992b) introduced a new concept of macroorganizational policy for the primary purpose of eliminating market failures. A macro-stabilization policy alone is not sufficient for the success of an economy, especially a developing economy; there is an additional role the government can and should play in assisting both resource creation and allocation. This need is great, particularly when the market itself is not yet developed, as is the case with the developing and transition economies or when the market alone cannot accomplish certain tasks.

Expanding on Dunning's framework, Peter Gray (1995: 61) went a step further by including 'the provision of efficiency-enhancing infrastructure and explicitly [recognizing] the existence of competition among governments to create an efficient economy in order to attract created assets', since there is 'the obvious interaction between general macro-organizational strategy and industry-specific (industrial) policies affecting the attractiveness of the economy to Schumpeterian firms'. Here, Gray did depart from Dunning's original conceptualization which was grounded on the efficacy of the market, that is, macroorganizational measures to correct for market imperfections; Gray took the concept of macroorganization into the realm of *interactive hierarchies* (competing governments), whose policy measures can enhance the individual economy's efficiency – apart from the global economy's efficiency – above and beyond what can be achieved through the market alone. Dunning essentially looked upon the government as a market-abiding, market-enhancing, and market-compatible institution, whereas Gray regarded it as a goal-setting, market-subordinating institution, that is, a master over the market servant. It should be mentioned, however, that Dunning himself did emphasize the role of the individual government as an oligopolist in 'selling' national policies in rivalry with each other, although he did not elaborate on it as much as Gray did: 'Governments have a critical role to play both in setting the framework within which market forces and/or hierarchies can operate and in counteracting practices, either by the participants of the market or by other Governments, of rigging the workings of the market to their own benefit' (Dunning 1992a: 164).

The national focus of macroorganization policy, however, is increasingly shifting to the cross-border, multinational macroorganization at both regional and global levels. This is because any successful national firms cannot remain long as uninational and homebound; they must become *multinational* firms in this age of globalization. Consequently, entrepreneurial functions, especially asset-creating and information-filtering functions have increasingly become cross-border/transnational.

Hence, governments concerned with local growth, employment, price stability, and gains from deepening integration have to recognize needs for policy coordination and cooperation among themselves. A beggar-thy-neighbour stance, such as 'rigging the workings of the market to their own benefit', if taken by all governments, would trap themselves in the lowest-payoff cell of the prisoner's dilemma situation. Cooperation based on trust and goodwill can bring them out of the entrapment to the highest (mutually beneficial) possible payoff cell. Put differently, governments have the dual characters of Dr Jekyll and Mr Hyde. They are undoubtedly oligopolistic competitors who create and reinforce market failures. Simultaneously, however, they are oligopolistic cooperators or joint benefit maximizers eager to solve market failures at regional and global levels. Governments can also create short-term market distortions to bring about dynamic long-term structural upgrading.

Governments may thus form economic blocs to maximize regional gains. The doctrine of free trade and free capital movement is one that only a dominant capitalist country can espouse after a long period of initial protectionism (Eatwell 1982). Such a doctrine is a highly income-elastic 'luxury' good. Although the United States depicts itself as the twentieth-century champion of free trade, its very success of catching up and forging ahead of its rival economies was due to 'the entrepreneurial role of the American state' (Kozul-Wright 1995). NAFTA – and NAFTA-plus – is the manifestation of the continued involvement of the American state in crafting a governance structure for trade and investment in its traditional sphere of influence. The hope is that America's own, as well as the whole Americas', economic welfare is to be raised through economic integration. EU can be considered a similar move to enhance Z efficiency as part of greater Beta efficiency.

MESO-LEVEL 'INTERSTITIAL COORDINATION' (Y EFFICIENCY)

Networks of Alliances

One modality of meso-level organization was conceptualized by G.B. Richardson (1972) as the third method of economic coordination in addition to markets and firms:

> I was once in the habit of telling pupils that firms might be envisaged as islands of planned co-ordination in a sea of market relations. This now seems to me a highly misleading account of *the way in which industry is in fact organized* . . . there are two aspects of it that should trouble us. In the first place it raises a question, properly central to any theory of economic organisation, which it does not answer; and, secondly, it ignores the existence of a whole *species* of industrial activity which, on the face of it, is relevant to the manner in which coordination is achieved . . .
>
> Let me now turn to the species of industrial activity that our simple story, based as it is on a dichotomy between firm and market, leaves out of account. What I have in mind is the *dense network of co-operation and affiliation* by which firms are inter-related. (Richardson 1972: 883–4, italics added)

Indeed, this 'dense network of co-operation and affiliation' has recently become all the more ubiquitous in both domestic and cross-border business activities. We now hear much about *strategic business alliances* in R&D, product development, marketing, and production.

But why is this way of organizing business connections so important?

This third modality of coordination is certainly on the rise in the modern economy, especially with the emergence, and the present dominance, of what may be called 'components-intensive, assembly-based industries' or 'differentiated Smithian industries', such as automobiles, electronics goods, and other high-tech manufactures (Ozawa 1992). These industries are vertically deep and multi-layered in value-added operations of material transformation, and *a variety of organizational techniques and structures can be devised with different consequences of efficiency*.

Thorstein Veblen stressed the importance of 'interstitial coordination' in this civilization of 'the machine process' in his 1927 book, *The Theory of Business Enterprises*:

> each industrial unit, represented by a given industrial 'plant', stands in close relations of interdependence with other industrial processes going forward elsewhere, near or far away, from which it receives supplies – materials, apparatus, and the like – and to which it turns over its output of products and waste, or on which it depends for auxiliary work, such as transportation. The resulting concatenation of industries has been noticed by most modern writers. It is commonly discussed under the head of the division of labor. Evidently the prevalent standardization of industrial means, methods, and products greatly increases the reach of this concatenation of industries, at the same time that it enforces a close conformity in point of time, volume, and character of the product, whether the product is goods or services. (Veblen 1927: 15–16, emphasis added)

Anyone who is familiar with the Toyota production system (Ohno 1978) or *lean production* (Womack, Jones and Roos 1990) knows that this is exactly what the 'just-in-time' method is all about: to achieve a 'close conformity in point of time, volume, and character of the product' between final assemblers and parts suppliers. All the major-parts suppliers are the close affiliates (semi-independents) of the final assemblers so that they can cooperate in fine-tuning the timing of parts production and delivery at the least possible costs. They are all located in the vicinity of final assembly operation sites, and information-connected via on-line computers. They form a dense network of cooperation and affiliation, both spatially and functionally. Indeed, they constitute a 'virtual factory'.

In contrast, conventional mass production or Fordism is another system in which this 'close conformity in point of time, volume, and character of the product' is achieved by means of a large inventory as a buffer for 'just-in-case' contingencies, an inventory of parts mostly produced in-house (that is, internalized production) and also in part purchased from independent outside suppliers (that is, externalized production). The conventional mass production system is thus basically a combination of hierarchy and the market, with less reliance on networking. Under such a system, automobile manufacturers are, to paraphrase D.H. Robertson's famous statement, 'huge islands of hierarchical coordination in this ocean of unconscious co-operation'. Thus, there are two major alternative approaches to components/parts-intensive, assembly-based production. How the inter-process, vertical division of labor is organized determines the relative strength of a system.[2] Organization technology is a decisive competitive determinant, now that product and production technology has become nearly identical and only surface-differentiated between the automobile industries of advanced countries.

Returning to the above quotation, Veblen is clearly referring to relational efficiency or 'interstitial efficiency', or Y efficiency – in addition to the internal productive efficiency of each economic unit attainable through standardization, specialization, and a higher degree of inter-unit coordination. Veblen continued:

> By virtue of this concatenation of processes the modern industrial system at large bears the character of a comprehensive, balanced mechanical progress. In order to [attain] an efficient working of this industrial process at large, the various constituent sub-processes must work in due coordination throughout the whole. Any degree of maladjustment in the *interstitial coordinations* of this industrial process at large in some degree hinders its working. Similarly, any given detail process or any industrial plant will do its work to full advantage only when due adjustment is had between its work and the work done by the rest. *The higher the degree of development reached by a given industrial community, the more comprehensive and urgent becomes this requirement of interstitial adjustment.* (Veblen 1927: 16, italics added)

The costs of interstitial adjustment are basically transaction costs. Hence, it may not be amiss to claim that Veblen was a forerunner of transaction-cost economics.

Transaction-cost economics, initiated by Coase (1937) and expanded by Williamson (1975), was also approached by Victor Goldberg (1980) in terms of what he calls a *relational exchange* framework. He observed,

> Much economic activity takes place within long-term, complex, perhaps multiparty contractual (or contract-like) relationships; behavior is, in varying degrees, sheltered from market forces. (Ibid.: 87)

The reasons why much economic activity is 'sheltered from market forces' (that is, internalized in hierarchies) can be explained, according to Goldberg, by three facts about the real world:

First, people are not omniscient; their information is imperfect and improvable only at a cost. Second, not all people are saints all of the time; as the relationship unfolds there will be opportunities for one party to take advantage of the other's vulnerability, to engage in strategic behavior, or to follow his own interests at the expense of the other party. The actors will, on occasion, behave opportunistically. Third, the parties cannot necessarily rely on outsiders to enforce the agreement cheaply and accurately. (Ibid.: 87)

Hence, 'the parties will find it efficacious to protect one party's reliance on the continuation of the relationship', so long as 'the spectre of opportunistic behavior hangs over the relationship' (ibid.: 89). Furthermore, 'if the parties cannot draw upon *a reservoir of trust* or rely on the discipline of future dealings, they will require some mechanisms for balancing the reliance and flexibility interests' (ibid.: 89, emphasis added), thus calling for some sort of governance mechanism and raising the costs of transactions. Here it is worth restressing the role of trust as an intangible resource that can substitute for a formal governance mechanism. Trust is transaction-cost-reducing. It facilitates *continuous, long-term* transactions without cumbersome governance rules and structures and in which benefits and costs are usually shared only over time, if not at each time of exchange/transaction.

Modern industry is becoming ever more dependent on interstitial efficiency in managing continuous inter-unit relationships, and 'a reservoir of trust' has emerged as a critical determinant of such efficiency. This type of efficiency is no doubt connected with the trust-based formation of 'social capital', inseparable from societies and cultures, as stressed by Fukuyama (1995). Interstitial coordination is thus more prevalently and more effectively carried out via informal dense networks of cooperation and affiliation in a high-contextualist culture (Japan and other East Asian nations) than in a high-contractual culture (Anglo-Saxon nations like the US and UK). (On this point of cultural difference, see also the chapter by de la Mothe and Paquet in this volume.) The latter relies more on internalization, that is, hierarchies, as a way of resolving the problems of market transaction costs associated with interstitial coordination.

Shareholders–Management Nexus

More recently, the issues of both micro–micro and meso-level organizational efficiencies have been simultaneously explored, because of their close interconnectedness, in terms of 'principal–agency' problems between financial shareholders and management. The problems are whether hired managers are making their utmost efforts to maximize the returns on capital put up by lenders, and how effectively their activities and performances are monitored. Examinations of these problems originated with the separation of management from ownership that results in the agency problems of corporate control and external finance, as explored by Berle and Means (1932). These also marked the first transition in the evolution of capitalism from 'entrepreneurial capitalism' to 'hierarchical capitalism' and 'alliance capitalism' (Dunning 1994) – or 'proprietary capitalism' to 'management capitalism' and 'collective capitalism' (Lazonick 1991). Given this transition, we are now in the new phase of managing corporate governance under two broad opposing approaches: hierarchical vs. alliance (in terms of Dunning's typological differentiation). And this distinction serves as a useful frame of reference for inter-firm relations in vertically specialized production, to which we will come back later. In the context of corporate finance, however, another distinction, *bank-based* capitalism vs. *securities-market-based* capitalism, may be more appropriate and useful.

In this connection, Stephen Prowse (1995) studied on a comparative basis the corporate control mechanisms among large firms in the US, UK, Japan, and Germany and concluded:

> evidence to date appears to suggest that corporate governance systems based on the concentrated holding of financial claims by active investors, such as exist in Japan and Germany, may be more efficient means of resolving corporate agency problems than systems which rely on liquid securities markets and the threat of hostile takeover. (Ibid.: 1)

Japanese and German corporations have been more dependent upon banks for capital through long-term loans, that is, debt capital and indirect finance, than upon the securities (stock and bond) markets, that is, equity capital and direct finance. Bank loans enable the firms to take long-term perspectives for strategic business operations and to accumulate internal funds more quickly from the surpluses (residuals), which they can use for further investments in R&D, marketing, and customer services. Since interest rates are fixed, the firms are able to share any residuals with employees – instead of just pleasing only shareholders and boosting share prices via higher dividends. In contrast, equity finance often makes the firms myopically occupied only with the 'bottom line' on a quarterly basis, thereby rendering them excessively short-term oriented.

This type of bank-centered finance in Japan is called the 'main bank system'. The main bank is the one which holds the largest outstanding stock loans extended to a particular firm and is simultaneously a large shareholder of the firm – that is, it plays a dual role of lender and share-holder (Aoki and Patrick 1995). At present, banks' shareholding is restricted to a maximum of 5 per cent of a particular firm's share (10 per cent prior to 1987). But there is no such limit to bank loans. In this respect, debt capital (lending) has played a decisive role in financing corporate Japan, while equity interest holding serves as a symbolic role of affiliation.

On the other hand, Germany's universal banking allows a much broader role for shareholders of nonbank corporations, since there is no restriction on shareholding. 'Deutsche Bank, for example, owns 28.1 per cent of Daimler-Benz's equity. German banks as a group own nearly 9 per cent of all domestically listed shares of German companies, and own more than 25 per cent of at least thirty-three major industrial corporations' (Kester 1992: 32). Furthermore, German banks also act as depositories for stock owned by other classes of shareholders, with the value of bank-held stocks amounting to approximately 40 per cent of the total market value of outstanding domestic shares, at the end of 1988 (Kester 1992: 32). Thus, the German banking industry as a whole owns and stewards nearly a half of listed German corporate shares.

In contrast, Japanese equity interests are relatively more cross-owned among nonbank corporations within the *keiretsu*. For instance, the reciprocal shareholding of the Mitsui group is 18 per cent, that of the Mitsubishi group is 25 per cent, and the Sumitomo group 24 per cent. In this respect, Sweden seems to have a similar pattern: cross-holding of shares issued by publicly listed Swedish corporations is about 25 per cent (Kester 1992: 32).

It is interesting to note the ranking of economies (Table 7.1) with respect to the extent to which firms in different countries take a long-term view in businesses, as judged by the Institute for Management Development (cited in Hampden-Turner and Trompenaars 1993). The Anglo-Saxon economies are regarded as less long-term oriented, whereas Japan, Sweden, and West Germany are considered strongly long-term focused.

As pointed out by Fukao (1995: 83–4), this difference in the time horizon of business activity may have to do with the concentration and arrangement of corporate ownership and governance:

> The strong voting power of shareholders and good communication between them and management seem to have forged very stable ownership of most Japanese and German companies. The ownership pattern of U.S. and British companies is less concentrated and less stable. As a result, the stock markets play the role of the market for corporate control in the United States and the United Kingdom but do not in Japan and Germany. Generally,

Table 7.1   Ranking of countries by long-term business orientation

Japan	1
Sweden	2
Germany	3
New Zealand	4
Finland	5
Switzerland	6
Singapore	7
Norway	8
Netherlands	10
United States	19
Italy	20
Ireland	21
United Kingdom	22

Source: The Institute for Management Development as cited in Hampden-Turner and Trompenaars (1993).

management in Japanese and German companies is more stable and can offer *more credible commitments* to employees and suppliers than can management in U.S. and British companies. Finally, in Japan, Germany, and France paid-in capital is traditionally regarded more as security for creditors and other stakeholders of the company than as the property of shareholders.

These differences in the structure of corporate governance have a number of implications for the performance of companies. The strong voting power of shares appears to lower the cost of equity in Japan and Germany. Weaker voting power raises the cost in the United States and the United Kingdom. Strong restrictions on cash distributions to shareholders in Japan and Germany seem to lower the cost of debt and allow companies to maintain greater leverage. It seems easier for management in Japanese and German companies to maintain long-term implicit contracts with employees than it is for companies in the United States and the United Kingdom. Although the systems in Japan and Germany seem to allow firms in those countries to invest in more employee training, the pattern also makes deploying workers from declining sectors to growing ones more difficult. (Original emphasis)

Meso-Macro Nexus

The preceding differences among the countries can be viewed in terms of two polar models: one is the Anglo-Saxon legal system built on common laws that emphasizes the role of securities markets and hostile takeovers as governing mechanisms, and the other the Franco-German legal system that provides considerable stability. Both systems mold institutions in such a way to manage an economic system as efficiently as possible. Each provides a set of institutional underpinnings for achieving macro-level efficiency or Y efficiency in terms of policy, system, and structure.

The Anglo-Saxon system seems more transaction-cost intensive. More conflicted and confrontational power relationships between a company's board/management and its shareholders prevail because they are autonomous and independent of each other. In the Franco-German system the two parties usually have many overlapping or interlocking positions to enhance coordination. The Anglo-Saxon paradigm entails more litigation and more lawyers in market-making and market-conflict-resolving efforts.

Japanese and Swedish approaches to corporate governance are also close to the Franco-German paradigm. In fact, Japan consciously adopted German commercial codes at the beginning of its modernization efforts: Japanese thinking has been strongly influenced by the German traditions, as Chalmers Johnson (1982) pointed out:

> What do I mean by the developmental state? This is not really a hard question, but it always seems to raise difficulties in the Anglo-American countries, where the existence of the developmental stage in any form other than the communist state has largely been forgotten or ignored as a result of the years of disputation with Marxist-Leninists. Japan's political economy can be located precisely in the line of descent from the German Historical School – sometimes labeled 'economic nationalism', Handelspolitick, or neo-mercantilism. (Ibid.: 17)

While the Anglo-Saxon paradigm places markets above governments whose role allows only minimum regulatory functions, the Franco-German paradigm assigns a key role to bureaucracy. In Peter Evans's words (1995):

> The internal organization of developmental states comes much closer to approximating a Weberian bureaucracy. Highly selective meritocratic recruitment and long-term career rewards create commitment and a sense of corporate coherence. Corporate coherence gives these apparatuses a certain kind of 'autonomy'. They are not, however, insulated from society as Weber suggested they should be. To the contrary, they are embedded in a concrete set of social ties that binds the state to society and provides institutionalized channels for the continual negotiation and renegotiation of goals and policies. Either side of the combination by itself would not work. A state that was only autonomous would lack both sources of intelligence and the ability to rely on decentralized private implementation. Dense connecting networks without a robust internal structure would leave the state incapable of resolving 'collective action' problems, of transcending the individual interests

of its private counterparts. Only when embeddedness and autonomy are joined together can a state be called developmental. (Ibid.: 12)

Referring to the experience of Japan's Ministry of International Trade and Industry (MITI) as an effective orchestrator of catch-up growth, Evans argued that MITI's autonomy and its exceptionally competent cohesiveness through the *gakubatsu* (old-boys' school ties) among classmates, especially the alumni of Tokyo University Law School, were strongly – and still are to some extent – embedded in 'the maze of intermediate organizations and informal policy networks, where much of the time-consuming work of consensus formation takes place' (Okimoto 1989: 155, as cited in Evans 1995: 50) or what the World Bank (1993: 181) calls the 'administrative web' (cited in Evans 1995: 49). This maze or web consisted mainly of: (1) a variety of 'deliberation councils' organized on an ad hoc basis by bureaucrats, business people, and academics (mostly at the initiative of MITI) for policy deliberation; (2) close and constant contact between sectoral bureaus, within MITI, and corporate executives; and (3) the *amakudari* ('descent from heaven') bureaucrats given post-retirement sinecures at corporations as high-paid executives, a practice that provides informal communications channels for policy implementation. Thus, 'embedded autonomy' occurred through a combination of internal bureaucratic cohesiveness and external networks, as shown in Figure 7.1.

It should be mentioned that in government–industrial collaboration in early postwar Japan there was a very active technocratic role in interactive learning with business (policy-targeted as a national instrument of value creation). In Germany, such technocratic involvement in corporate achievement was less significant.

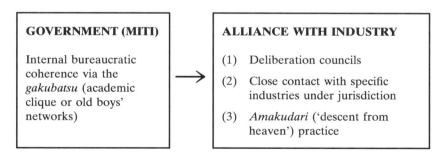

Figure 7.1 Japan's developmental state for catching up

External Architecture and Networks (Meso-level Governance)

Kay (1995: 63) introduces a concept of 'architecture', which means the network of relational contracts with a firm's stakeholders, that is, its employees, suppliers, and customers. The architecture has three subsystems: (1) 'internal architecture', within which firms establish relational contracts with and among their employees; (2) 'external architecture', within which firms maintain relational contracts with their suppliers or customers; and (3) 'networks', through which firms set up intercorporate relationships.

As discussed earlier, Japanese firms are more external architecture–network (EAN) intensive. For that matter, German, Swedish, and Italian corporations are similarly EAN oriented in pursuit of communal or solidaristic interests (see de la Mothe and Paquet's chapter in this volume). This is in sharp contrast to the Anglo-American model of an enterprise which exists in the interests of owners/shareholders; the Anglo-American firms are hindered, legally and institutionally, from organizing and benefiting from EAN. Further, the workers in Anglo-American firms are highly individualistic – and certainly not as collective value-oriented as in the Japanese firms.

In this respect, the Anglo-Saxon approach may be characterized as 'reductionist capitalism', whereas the German and Japanese approaches may be called 'holist capitalism'. This way of distinguishing the two is perhaps most appropriate, since they basically do differ in sociocultural traditions and orientations. Smithian classical economics argued that the pursuit of selfish interests automatically would lead to social harmony, that is, in modern parlance, 'what is good for General Motors is good for the country'. In contrast, the German Historical School essentially denied that the individual good is identical with the national good or 'what is good for the country is good for General Motors'. Of course, these are rather the extreme poles. In his celebrated inaugural speech, John F. Kennedy said: 'Ask not what your country can do for you, but ask what you can do for your country'. Democratization of Germany and Japan has modified the relationship between state and people to a situation where 'what is good for Siemens or Mitsubishi may not be good for the country'.

Be that as it may, in order to be good for the industrial community, if not for the country, individuals and companies (management) need to cooperate with each other in a teamwork fashion to some extent. In reductionist capitalism, such a collaborative approach risks being regarded as 'collusion'. Therefore, firms end up internalizing any operation which requires close coordination and control. On the other hand, holist capitalism promotes a loose form of teamwork and long-term relations. Industrial groups are a manifestation of this collaborative approach.

The following two episodes illustrate how a car maker, Chrysler Corp. in reductionist capitalism, and another, Toyota Motor Corp. in holist capitalism, had contrasting experiences with respect to the different ways their production is organized and governed. Since these episodes occurred concurrently and were reported simultaneously in the same issue of *The Wall Street Journal* (8 May 1997), the contrasts are all the more heightened:

– Chrysler Corp. had a 28-day-old engine-plant strike longest in 30 years. The cause of the strike was Chrysler's move to outsource drive-shaft work at its Mound Road plant in Detroit to Dana Corp. The drive-shaft work currently employs about 280 workers. But this strike cost Chrysler more than $430 million through the lost production of more than 95 000 vehicles.

– Chrysler and national United Auto Workers (UAW) officials wrapped up a bargaining session, reaching a tentative contract agreement:

Chrysler's Promises to the UAW	What Chrysler Didn't Yield
**$100 million in new investments at Detroit Mound Road engine plant, including a new engine-block line that will employ former drive-shaft workers.	**Its right to assign drive-shaft work to Dana for now as part of a strategy of focusing on core engine components.
**The return to Mound Road over the next five years of drive-shaft work that is now being assigned to supplier Dana Corp.	**Its right to defer negotiations over its current plans to obtain commodity-like parts such as oil pumps, water pumps, flywheels and exhaust manifolds for the new engine plant from outside suppliers rather than from Mound Road.
**Two chances for senior Mound Road workers to transfer to a new engine plant nearby that will build Chrysler's next-generation V-6 and V-8 engines starting this fall. Previously, Chrysler had offered only one chance to transfer, based on seniority.	**Cash payments totaling $300 000 demanded by the UAW local as compensation for workers whose hours will be reduced as a result of the assignment of parts work to outside suppliers.

– What made things even more complicated and worse was that UAW local 51 shop chairman and other unionists refused to sign the tentative pact and stormed out of the negotiation by blasting it as a 'cave-in' by national UAW leaders. Thus there was no unity inside the UAW itself.

What is involved are (1) the outsourcing of some parts that used to be done in-house to outside suppliers and the reassignment of a relatively small number of workers (about 250) who are directly affected by such an outsourcing decision, and (2) the internal disunity, at least seeming, of the UAW because of the high degree of autonomy given to locals.

In contrast, another news item was about Toyota's fast rebound after a fire at one of its suppliers.

- The fire (on February 1, 1997) at Aisin Seiki Co.'s Factory No. 1 incinerated the main source of a crucial brake valve (worth $5) that Toyota buys on a just-in-time delivery basis. Without it, Toyota had to shut down its 20 auto plants at home, which build 14 000 cars a day. Weeks were expected to be needed for Toyota's recovery.
- Yet, in an 'Amish barn-raising' fashion, Toyota's suppliers, as well as some which had never produced brake valves before, came to the rescue. The upshot was that Toyota started up again not weeks later but only five days. Consequently, Toyota lost production of 72 000 vehicles – instead of its multiples as reported earlier. Furthermore, Toyota was soon able to recoup the lost output, because Toyota-group firms and workers were willing to do overtime and extra shifts.
- Although it is merely a $5 brake valve called 'p-valve', an abbreviation of a brake-fluid-proportioning valve, it needed 200 p-valve variations. Besides, the valves have many complex tapered orifices that require highly customized jigs and drills.
- By the fifth day after the fire, the 36 suppliers, aided by more than 150 other sub-contractors, and nearly 50 separate lines producing small batches of the brake valve, came to the rescue without thinking about money/costs or business contracts. In one case, a sewing-machine maker that had never made car parts spent about 500 man-hours refitting a milling machine to make just 40 valves a day.
- Suppliers never asked Toyota or Aisin what they would be paid for rushing out the valves. They operated on a trust basis. Indeed, as the first valves arrived at Toyota factories, Aisin told the suppliers it would pay for everything, from drills and overtime pay to lost revenue and depreciation. And Toyota promised the suppliers a bonus totaling about $100 million as a token of its appreciation.

If the same type of accident had happened in the United States, disrupting the supply of a key part, the first thing managers might have done was most likely to call in, and consult with, corporate lawyers about suing the supplier involved for contractual breach. In reductionist capitalism, interstitial coordinations are governed by legal contracts, while in holistic capitalism, they are governed fundamentally by trust and reciprocity.

Meso-level Governance for Knowledge Creation

Nonaka and Takeuchi (1995) argue that Western firms tend to view the organization as a machine for information processing but not as a machine for knowledge creation, and that the Western concept of knowledge is biased toward 'explicit' knowledge, 'expressed in words and numbers, and easily communicated and shared in the form of hard data, scientific formulae, codified procedures, or universal principles' (ibid.: 8). In contrast, Japanese firms are more concerned with 'tacit' knowledge which is 'highly personal and hard to formalize, making it difficult to communicate or to share with others', largely because tacit knowledge is 'deeply rooted in an individual's action and experience' (ibid.: 8).

Most importantly, furthermore, Nonaka and Takeuchi (1995) contend that Japanese companies 'believe that new and proprietary knowledge cannot be created without an intensive outside–inside interaction' (ibid.: 11). To be more specific, they explain: 'Creating knowledge is not simply a matter of processing objective information about customers, suppliers, competitors, channel subscribers, the regional community, or the government. Crew members also have to mobilize the tacit knowledge held by these *outside stakeholders through social interactions*' (ibid.: 234, italics added).

What Nonaka and Takeuchi stress is a holistic or systems approach to knowledge creation via a wide sphere of relational contacts within which all stakeholders' tacit knowledge can be tapped and transformed into explicit knowledge at the group level's efforts. This mode of knowledge creation is inherent in holistic capitalism. This can be achieved only via meso-level interactions inside a broadly defined group of stakeholders.

The above inside–outside system has emerged in Japan since the early 1980s. This development matches Imai's explanation (1992) of Japan's evolved pattern of corporate structure. As briefly touched on earlier, Imai posits the sequence of the *zaibatsu* → business groups → network organizations as the dominant form of meso-structure:

First, in relationships between companies, emphasis has moved from such formal systems as mutual shareholding between companies and the assignment of directors to informal relationships in which the exchange of information is of primary importance. Of course, mutual shareholding to prevent hostile takeovers is still important for core companies, but in general, human linkages based on mutual trust are becoming crucial for information exchange. Second, the handling of information has undergone a drastic change. In the zaibatsu, an organization received information on the affairs of the outside world, and, to use the jargon of the economist, information was *exogenous*. In business groups, however, it is *endogenous* in nature, in that internal transmission and processing of information is important, but, as has been typical in the conventional information activities of trading firms, arbitraging based on information has been the main activity and there has not been a high degree of information creation. (ibid.: 219–20, original emphasis)

We might add that business groups were very active in importing technologies and processing them via adaptive R&D, especially in the early postwar period. No wonder, then, that 'there has not been a high degree of information creation'. Most recently, Imai sees the growth of network organizations as places for interactive innovation:

In network industrial organizations, information is created through interaction, and the creation of information becomes the driving force of business activity ... 'Creation of information' ... refers to the means of creating a new context in the process of normal decision making ... Context is the medium through which new information is generated, and it is the network that creates such context. The market *fails* in such activities. The network industrial organization provides a 'place' for interaction between related actors, and each obtains positive externalities of created information. (Ibid.: 220–21, original emphasis)

This vista of a network of *organizational* relationships matches that of a network of *technological* relationships, in which 'technological progress in one sector of the economy has become increasingly dependent on technological change in other sectors', as emphasized by Kodama (1995: 190). Kodama also distinguished between 'breakthrough' and 'fusion or hybrid' technologies. The latter are cross-industry innovations, and are best represented by mechatronics and optoelectronics, two major fields of fusion technology, in which Japanese industry has strong clear-cut competitiveness (ibid.: 195–207). Put differently, fusion technology is a *meso-rooted technology*, which Kodama identified as the 'sources of Japan's technological edge'.

It should be noted that cross-industry networking in Japan occurs in the context of vigorous competition between network organizations. There is strong intra-network cooperation entailed by vigorous inter-network rivalry. This particular structural combination of cooperation and competition generates dynamic self-renovative forces in Japanese industry, since intra-network (intra-group) cooperation fuels inter-network (inter-group) rivalry, which in turn motivates and consolidates intra-network cooperation. This dynamic dual system of feedback necessitates identification of a new paradigm of what may be called 'rivalrous cooperation'.

In addition, Imai's notion of a place for interaction and an acquisition of positive externalities is similar to that of 'institutions to capture externalities' (Weder and Grubel 1993). Weder and Grubel (1993) identified three major types of such institutions: (1) associations, (2) company structures, especially in the form of multinational corporations, and (3) industry clusters. As empirical examples, they chose Switzerland and Japan, and found some important similarities in the ways knowledge spillovers are internalized in the three forms of institution. As to 'company structures', Weder and Grubel argue that 'efficient multinationals leave very few, non-exploited commercially valuable uses of R&D' (ibid.: 498) and observe:

> Both countries are homes to some of the most successful enterprises in the world, most of which are multinationals whose success is based on the production of high-quality goods that incorporate innovative technologies at the highest level. The success of these industries depends heavily on R&D and... on the existence of the kind of institutions capable of assuring that the externalities from R&D are internalized by firms undertaking the investment. (ibid.: 499)

Weder and Grubel thus view the multinational operations of R&D-active firms as a means of internalizing their own technological spillovers.

On the other hand, Cantwell (1989) regards a process of multi-nationalization as an enhancement of companies' capabilities to create new technologies, that is, to innovate on a global scale: 'carrying out research and production in a variety of international centers of innovative activity increases the capacity for and the complexity of technological accumulation with MNCs [multinational corporations]' (ibid.: 94). The emergence of firms qua multinationals thus inevitably cuts across the different strata of governance and coordination.

Given the rapid multinationalization of firms, the conventional concept of X efficiency itself, as defined in mainstream economics which treats the firm as a uninational firm, is becoming obsolete. As noted earlier in our discussion of X efficiency, entrepreneurial functions were left largely unexplored. This was partly a reflection of the neoclassical tradition that treats technological changes or innovations as *exogenous* variables (as often said as 'manna from Heaven'). Our preceding discussions show that entrepreneurial functions for innovation are *endogenously* created out of interactions between actors at the meso level and through interactions between the inside and outside of the firm – now increasingly across national borders. In this new form of organizing entrepreneurial functions, X and Y efficiencies are interlinked and merged; the micro–meso connections are all the more strengthened in industrial grouping and networking, as is the case with Japan's *keiretsu* groups. Japan's technological competitiveness in particular derives both from meso-level (inter-stakeholders) interactions in exchanges of tacit knowledge and from the micro–micro level of transformation of tacit knowledge into explicit knowledge through team-based R&D activities.

Moreover, multinational firms are operating beyond the stratum of Z efficiency and through the strata of Beta and Alpha efficiencies. They strive to maximize not a nationally confined X efficiency, that is, 'uninational X efficiency', but a multinationally optimizable X efficiency, that is, 'transnational X efficiency'. Multinationals are inter-stratal straddlers. The transnationalization of X efficiency is illustrated in Figure 7.2.

HARMONIZATION ISSUES IN OPTIMIZATION OF Z EFFICIENCY BETWEEN COUNTRIES

Given the fast tempo of globalization, how are the countries going to deal with their divergent structures/institutions of corporate governance and their different macro-organizational approaches, which are often culturally ingrained. Can we really push for the ideal of a 'level playing field'? As seen above, socio-cultural factors play crucial roles in the ways economic activities are organized in different countries. Is it possible to harmonize the different structures of the intra-country strata of X, Y, and Z efficiencies among countries?

Take the case of Japanese organization. Aoki (1988: 298–9) identified small groups and close interpersonal ties and communications among the group members as the 'robust core' of the Japanese organization:

> In the small group, tasks, information, and outcomes are shared by the members (although not necessarily in completely egalitarian ways), and each group interacts with other groups both inside and outside the organization

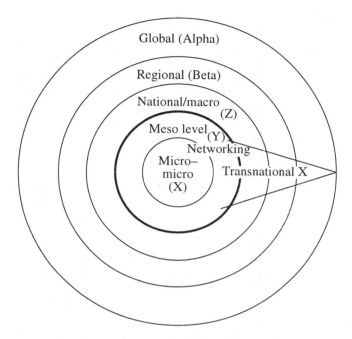

*Figure 7.2   The five levels of organizational efficiency and
transnationalization of the firm*

in a manner designed to preserve its own integrity as much as possible.
(Ibid.: 298–9)

Aoki ascribes to many centuries of agrarian experience such Japanese
traditional customs as mutual help, collective coordination, risk and
output sharing, flexible and continual adaptation to environmental
changes, high work ethic, and acceptance of communal-life obligations.
Although small-groupism thus did play a role in the formation of the
J-firm and their management and production techniques, Aoki argues
that the J-type organization along with some of its unique management
and production methods could be adopted elsewhere in different cultural environments. He thus concluded on an optimistic note:

> Western and Japanese firms can thus learn much from each other that will
> help make their industrial organizations more efficient and more humani-
> tarian in spite of the cultural barrier. The hope is that the symbiotic
> development of human capacity and technology may help to fuse cultural
> differences into a new hybrid in the future.

Aoki's optimism has already proved correct, since we now know that the American automobile makers have adopted many key techniques of lean production and the just-in-time delivery system. Multinationals are quick learners from each other. For example, the New United Motor Manufacturing Incorporated (NUMMI), a joint venture between GM and Toyota set up in Fremont, California, USA, is credited for facilitating the spread of lean production techniques in the US automobile industry. As a result, there has been considerable convergence, so far as micro–micro organizational efficiency on the factory floor in the automobile industry is concerned.

But how about the still-persistent discrepancies in meso-level organizational modalities, which are institutionally prescribed by laws, regulations and business customs? Here, two views are worth noting: Johnson (cited in Edwards and Patrick 1992) observes:

> Regulatory harmonization is obviously desirable. It is, however, a long way off. Regulators are operating pursuant to laws which are adopted by the political bodies of their country; they tend to set the priorities and values that are to be maintained. Although in general terms those values are probably common across many different regulatory structures, the business of how to implement them and what to emphasize, what priorities to give, can differ from one nation or one state or one province to the next. So when it comes to harmonization, each regulator somehow has to justify each compromise from the existing local standards which he or she is prepared to agree to. That is one reason for the reticence to adopt in any substantial measure a different system being proposed by someone else. But I don't think it is private interests of regulators nearly so much as it is *the different philosophies and policies that are driving different regulatory programs*. (Ibid.; 9, italics added)

Gyohten (cited in Edwards and Patrick 1992) similarly pointed out:

> I think under the given reality, it certainly is premature to aim at very extensive and quick harmonization of the regulatory regimes among different markets. There are three elements which are relevant to this issue. One is, to what extent in reality are different markets really globalized. Second, to what extent is each market receptive to this globalization and prepared to be harmonized. Third, *because competition between different national markets is also being intensified, to what extent each national market can afford not to be harmonized without risking some loss of influence in the global market environment*. (Ibid.: 9, italics added)

The battle still continues on the issue of the organization and governance of economic activities within a national jurisdiction. Organizational Y and Z efficiencies are based on nation-specific factors, hence they are more 'national public goods', that is, highly localized organizational assets, than 'borderless quasi-public goods', such as technology and commercial information of the explicit type that has no national boundary. The more globalized the competitive economic forces become, the more mandated national governments become to create and manage national public goods. They themselves thus become 'institutions to create and capture externalities'.

FINAL WORDS

We have classified the levels of organizational efficiency in the global economy into five types: X, Y, Z, Beta, and Alpha. This classification has provided an overall frame of reference within which the issues of the meso-level structural organization related to Y efficiency are examined. The need for meso-level coordination and governance arises from the structural characteristics of modern manufacturing which call for what Veblen (1927) identified as 'interstitial coordinations'. These coordinations can be accomplished by three basic modalities of governance: markets, hierarchies, and networks.

In the recent past, the need for interstitial coordination has grown enormously for three main reasons: (1) the rise of components-intensive, assembly-based manufacturing (that is, a deeper vertical division of labour), which characterizes short-cycle goods/models, notably automobiles and electronics; (2) the use of lean (or flexible) production techniques such as the 'just-in-time' system for parts delivery; and (3) corporate restructuring and re-engineering, resulting in the expanded outsourcing of intermediate goods and services, both at home and across national borders. These trends reflect a shift of global capitalism from hierarchical to alliance; firms are becoming more network organizations. With their globalizing operations, moreover, the firms' meso-level operations necessarily straddle national borders in pursuit of a new type of *X efficiency qua multinational* – distinctly different from the conventional type of X efficiency involving only the uninational firm. Although the five levels of governance are differentiated for analytical purposes, the growth of multinational firms raises complex issues for structural governance and optimization, especially at the national level for Z efficiency. Information and knowledge being 'borderless quasi-public goods', the multinational firms are carrying out their entrepreneurial functions for innovation across the multi-strata of governance. This development is all the more facilitated by the current trend toward trade and investment liberalization. National governments are thus required to act as *institutions to create and capture externalities* if they are to maximize and retain Z efficiency.

NOTES

1. As a catching-up economy, the top-down governance of the *zaibatsu* was instrumental in 'innovative trading' (knowledge imports and absorption), but as the need for 'innovative production' (knowledge creation) increased with the closing of the technology gap between Japan and the West a looser/more flexible form of organization as represented by business groups – and most recently, by network industrial organization – became more suitable as operational structures. The distinction of 'innovative production' from 'innovative trading' I owe to the editors of this volume.
2. The American automobile industry, as well as other Western automobile industries, has adopted many techniques of lean production, notably the just-in-time delivery system, thereby introducing networks of affiliations with suppliers. Nevertheless, they are still less network-oriented than their Japanese counterpart.

REFERENCES

Alchian, Armen and Harold Demsetz (1972), 'Production, information costs, and economic organization', *American Economic Review*, **62**: 777–95.
Aoki, Masahiko (1988), *Information, Incentives, and Bargaining in the Japanese Economy*, Cambridge: Cambridge University Press.
Aoki, Masahiko and Hugh Patrick (1995), *The Japanese Main Bank System: Its Relevance for Developing and Transforming Economies*, New York and Oxford: Oxford University Press.
Berle, Adolf and Gardiner Means (1932), *The Modern Corporation and Private Property*, New York: Commerce Clearing House.
Brander, James A. (1986), 'Rationales for strategic trade and industrial policy', in Paul Krugman (ed.), *Strategic Trade Policy and the New International Economics*, Cambridge, MA: MIT Press, pp. 23–46.
Cantwell, John (1989), *Technological Innovation and Multinational Corporations*, Oxford: Basil Blackwell.
Coase, Ronald (1937), 'The nature of the firm', *Economica*, **4**: 386–405.
Coase, Ronald (1992), 'The institutional structure of production', *American Economic Review*, **82** (4): 713–19.
Coleman, James S. (1988), 'Social capital in the creation of human capital', *American Journal of Sociology*, **94** (Supplement): S95–S120.
Dunning, John H. (1992a), 'Review article: the competitive advantage of countries and the activities of transnational corporations', *Transnational Corporations*, **1** (February): 135–68.
Dunning, John H. (1992b), 'The global economy, domestic governance, strategies and transnational corporations: interactions and policy implications', *Transnational Corporations*, **1** (December): 7–45.
Dunning, John H. (1994), *Globalization, Economic Restructuring and Government*, The Prebisch Lecture for 1994, Geneva: UNCTAD.
Eatwell, John (1982), *Whatever Happened to Britain?*, London: BBC.

Edwards, Franklin R. and Hugh T. Patrick (1992), *Regulating International Financial Markets: Issues and Policies*, Boston and Dordrecht: Kluwer Academic Publishers.

Evans, Peter (1995), *Embedded Autonomy: States and Industrial Transformation*, Princeton: Princeton University Press.

Fukao, Mitsuhiro (1995), *Financial Integration, Corporate Governance, and the Performance of Multinational Companies*, Washington, DC: Brookings Institution.

Fukuyama, Francis (1995), *Trust: The Social Virtues and the Creation of Prosperity*, New York: Free Press.

Goldberg, Victor (1980), 'Relational Exchange: Economics and Complex Contracts', *American Behavioral Scientist*, **23**, reprinted in Louis Putterman (ed.), *The Economic Nature of the Firm: A Reader*, Cambridge: Cambridge University Press, 1986, pp. 86–91.

Gray, H. Peter (1995), 'The modern structure of international economic policies', *Transnational Corporations*, **4** (3) (December): 49–65.

Gray, H. Peter (1996), 'Culture and economic performance: policy as an intervening variable', *Journal of Comparative Economics*, **23**: 278–91.

Hampden-Turner, Charles and Alfons Trompenaars (1993), *The Seven Cultures of Capitalism*, New York: Doubleday.

Imai, Ken-ichi (1992), 'Japan's Corporate Networks', in Shumpei Kumon and Henry Rosovsky (eds), *The Political Economy of Japan*, Volume 3: *Cultural and Social Dynamics*, Stanford: Stanford University Press, pp. 198–230.

Johnson, Chalmers (1982), *MITI and the Japanese Miracle: The Growth of Industrial Policy, 1925–1975*, Stanford: Stanford University Press.

Kay, John A. (1995), *Why Firms Succeed*, New York and Oxford: Oxford University Press.

Kester, Carl W. (1992), 'Industrial Groups as Systems of Contractual Governance', *Oxford Review of Economic Policy*, **8** (3) (Autumn): 24–44.

Keynes, John M. (1936), *The General Theory of Employment, Interest, and Money*, London: Macmillan.

Kodama, Fumio (1995), *Emerging Patterns of Innovation: Sources of Japan's Technological Edge*, Boston: Harvard University Press.

Kozul-Wright, Richard (1995), 'The myth of Anglo-Saxon capitalism: reconstructing the history of the American state', in Ha-Joon Chang and Robert Rowthorn (eds), *The Role of the State in Economic Change*, Oxford: Clarendon Press, pp. 81–113.

Lazonick, William (1991), *Business Organization and the Myth of the Market Economy*, Cambridge, UK and New York: Cambridge University Press.

Leibenstein, Harvey (1966), 'Allocative efficiency vs. X-efficiency', *American Economic Review*, **56**: 392–415.

Leibenstein, Harvey (1987), *Inside the Firm: The Inefficiencies of Hierarchy*, Cambridge, MA: Harvard University Press.

Lowe, A. (1977), *On Economic Knowledge. Toward a Science of Political Economics*, White Plains, NY: M.E. Sharpe.

Nonaka, Ikujiro and Horitaka Takeuchi (1995), *The Knowledge-Creating Company*, New York and Oxford: Oxford University Press.

Ohno, Tai'ichi (1978), *Toyota Seisan Hoshiki: Datsu-kibo no Keiei o Mezashite* [Toyota Production Formula: Toward Non-scale-based Management], Tokyo: Daiyamond.

Okimoto, Daniel I. (1989), *Between MITI and the Market: Japanese Industrial Policy for High Technology*, Stanford: Stanford University Press.

Ozawa, Terutomo (1992), 'Foreign direct investment and economic development', *Transnational Corporations*, **1** (1) (February): 27–54.

Ozawa, Terutomo (1997), 'Japan', in John Dunning (ed.), *Governments, Globalization, and International Business*, Oxford: Oxford University Press, pp. 377–406.

Prowse, Stephen (1995), 'Corporate governance in an international perspective: a survey of corporate control mechanisms among large firms in the U.S., U.K., Japan and Germany', *Financial Markets, Institutions and Instruments*, **4** (1): 1–63.

Richardson, G.B. (1972), 'The organization of industry', *Economic Journal*, **82** (September): 883–96.

Robbins, Lionel (1932), *The Nature and Significance of Economic Science*, London: Macmillan.

Smith, Robert J. (1992), 'The cultural context of the Japanese political economy', in Shumpei Kumon and Henry Rosovsky (eds), *The Political Economy of Japan*, Volume 3: *Cultural and Social Dynamics*, Stanford: Stanford University Press, pp. 13–31.

Veblen, Thorstein (1927), *The Theory of Business Enterprise*, New York: Charles Scribner's Sons.

Weder, Rolf and Herbert G. Grubel (1993), 'The new growth theory and Coasean economics: institutions to capture externalities', *Weltwirtschaftliches Archiv*, **129** (3): 488–513.

Williamson, Oliver E. (1975), *Markets and Hierarchies: Analysis and Antitrust Implications*, New York: Free Press.

Williamson, Oliver E. (1985), *The Economic Institutions of Capitalism: Firms, Markets, Relational Contracting*, New York: Free Press.

Womack, James P., Daniel T. Jones and Daniel Roos (1990), *The Machine that Changed the World*, New York: Macmillan.

World Bank(1993), *The East Asian Miracle*, New York: Oxford University Press.

8. Trade policy and competition law: issues for developing countries

J. Michael Finger and Adriana Castro

INTRODUCTION

The first generation of economic reforms that the World Bank and other international institutions supported in developing countries dealt with the basic framework for a market economy: macroeconomic soundness, price stability, reduction of fiscal deficits, improved balance of payments and opening to external competition via the liberalization of trade restrictions, particularly the removal of quantitative restrictions and the lowering of tariffs.

As countries have moved toward completion of such first-generation reforms, the World Bank has added a second focus: to assist governments to create an *enabling environment* for private-sector-led growth.[1] This enabling environment is a seamless web of government policies and infrastructure within which economic activity takes place, that is, people produce, consume and transact. One of the key lessons of the *East Asian Miracle* (World Bank 1993) is the importance of a government-created business-friendly environment. The business environment includes an effective legal code that provides for intellectual and physical property rights, for contracts and for dispute resolution. The broader environment includes education, health, the honesty of the policeman on the corner, and access by all members of the society to all the elements that make up the seamless web.

Competition *policy* has many constituent parts: privatization, deregulation, trade liberalization – all the dimensions of policy and economic environment that influence the degree and quality of rivalry that will exist among enterprises that operate in the domestic market. All of these are important tools for shaping the enabling environment. Competition *law* is but one of these elements.

In this chapter, our focus will be on the interaction of trade policy (more properly, trade liberalization) with competition law and the institutions that enforce competition law. We will review developing country experience with the enforcement of competition law, arguing as we go that (i) trade liberalization is an essential element in effective competition policy in developing countries, and (ii) competition law brings with it serious risks of misuse.

There are, however, competition problems of an international scope that trade liberalization will not resolve. We review the nature of such problems and the institutional approaches to them that several authors have suggested. We then go on to ask several unfashionable questions about the current interest in the internationalization of competition policy. Is there evidence that competition problems of an international scope are a major impediment to the continuing economic progress of the developing countries? Is the adoption of competition policy by developing countries a clear benefit, that is, are there real possibilities that such policies may have effects other than the benefits that economists normally associate with them? Would the internationalization of competition policy rules strengthen the position of developing countries to deal with the problems that they face? Our conclusion is that international cooperation has particular potential to be useful in two areas: (1) the review of mergers by enterprises that operate in several different countries, and (2) elimination of government-sanctioned export cartels. For developing and transition economies, trade liberalization, privatization and the establishment of an institution–legal structure that defines property and facilitates transactions are more important parts of creating an enabling environment for continuing growth than is an international arrangement to deal with cross-border competition issues.

TRADE LIBERALIZATION AS A MAJOR ELEMENT OF COMPETITION POLICY

From 1981, when the World Bank's policy-based lending began, through 1994, the World Bank made 238 policy-based loans that supported liberalization of trade policy or foreign exchange policy. These loans, made to 75 different countries, specified over 2000 trade or foreign exchange policy reforms as conditions for borrowing, and about 80 per cent of these reforms have been substantially implemented. Through these loans, the World Bank has supported developing country trade reforms that have affected imports of over $500 billion, in 1993 values. At the Uruguay Round, by comparison, developing countries agreed to tariff reductions that will affect 32 per cent or $393 billion of their total merchandise imports (likewise in 1993 values).[2]

In many of these economies the domestic market is not large enough to absorb the output of several enterprises that have achieved efficient scale of production. It is obvious that if these economies remain isolated from international competition, competition policy alone will bring minimal improvements of economic efficiency. For nearly all countries, trade liberalization is a necessary part of competition policy.[3]

Beware of Backsliding

The first round of trade liberalization – the removal of quantitative restrictions and the lowering of tariffs – has not always brought about increased openness to international competition. Governments, under pressure from domestic enterprises, sometimes fudge the removal of trade barriers. They manipulate product and process standards, or business regulations, so that they discriminate against imports. They might also resort to antidumping (see Figure 8.1), or any of a long list of devices, some explicitly GATT-legal, some questionably GATT-legal, all quite effective for keeping out imports. It is obvious but experience indicates that it is worth repeating; genuine opening to trade – not circumvented opening – will be a necessary part of establishing competition.

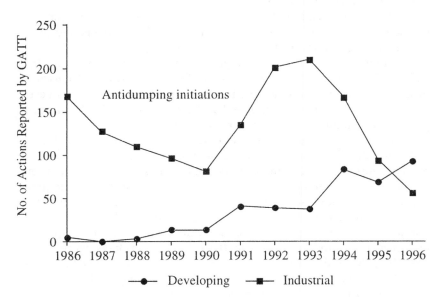

Figure 8.1   Antidumping initiations, 1986–96

TRADE LIBERALIZATION DOES NOT SOLVE ALL COMPETITION PROBLEMS

There are, however, cases in which the removal of governmental restrictions on imports – genuine liberalization – will not eliminate market power enjoyed by local producers. Since 1990, some 35 developing and transition economy countries have either enacted or significantly revised existing competition laws as parts of extensive changes of competition policy – changes in which trade liberalization and privatization carried perhaps more weight.

Non-traded goods, or goods that are difficult to trade internationally because of high transportation costs or perishability, are obvious examples of markets that cannot be made competitive by trade liberalization alone. Furthermore, in markets where products are highly differentiated foreign competition is not very effective in stimulating price competition (Globerman 1990) due to factors such as strong preference for the national brand or exclusive supplier deals. As an example, Globerman cites the markets for office typewriters and farm tractors in the US, where trade liberalization did not encourage price competition. In those cases, foreign competition was faced by highly differentiated markets and well-established distribution channels of American suppliers. On the other hand, in the markets for sheet glass and portable typewriters, foreign competition did serve to increase price competition. Consumers cared less about the nationality of the products and distribution channels were not tightly controlled.

For imports to be able to compete with domestic substitutes, they still need support services such as marketing, distribution networks, product repair and maintenance. In some instances, control over access to international business services has been the basis for local enterprises to maintain a non-competitive arrangement.

Where local producers have integrated forward into distribution, including the distribution of imports, they can use this position to prevent imports from gaining a foothold.[4] Guasch and Rajapatirana (1994) cite the example of Nabisco's attempt to enter the Colombian market. Since domestic producers dominated the food distribution network, Nabisco ended up forming a joint venture with local producers. The joint venture, in turn, lessened the potential effects on competition that imports would have provided. Nabisco's products were priced according to the domestic counterpart, so lower prices never materialized. Increased import penetration, this instance illustrates, does not necessarily bring with it an increase of competition.

Cases have been identified in which all producers in a region were under common ownership – the oligopoly extended past national borders to include nearby sources of potential competitive pressure. A furniture manufacturer in South Africa, who found that he was paying twice the world price for wood from the highly concentrated South African wood industry looked into the possibility of buying wood from neighboring countries. He found that the same enterprises controlled timber and wood production in those countries.[5]

In instances such as those listed in the previous paragraphs, openness to international investment and openness of the market for services to international competition are important complements to trade liberalization and competition policy.

CAUTIONS ABOUT THE USE OF COMPETITION LAW AND INSTITUTIONS

Where there is collusive action by local producers, trade liberalization, to be effective, must be accompanied by appropriate policies to deal with that collusive action. One should caution, however, that application of competition policy correctly identifies the source of the problem. If the legal system is weak (inadequate property rights, contract law and dispute settlement) collective action by local enterprises (horizontal or vertical) may be a necessary part of doing business locally. Trade reform and competition policy, to be effective, must be complemented by legal reform. Along with a clear and enforceable set of national antitrust rules, the institutional arrangement through which national antitrust laws are enforced is a key element in effectively combating anticompetitive practices. Competition agencies can be effective instruments for identifying missing institutions, private actions that are anticompetitive and governmental policies that support or enable anticompetitive actions.

Unfortunately, there have been instances in which competition agencies have seen their first duty as policing the 'fairness' of domestic competition and have strengthened the market power of established enterprises by prohibiting competitive practices that in most countries are considered beneficial to competition and to the public interest. Fingleton et al. (1996), in a study of competition policy in Central European transition economies, found that few competition law enforcement agencies had focused on hard-core collusive practices such as bid rigging, price fixing and market allocation. Furthermore, attempts by newly-created competition authorities to take on such practices by the countries' major enterprises came face to face with the reality that the enterprises had more political power than the competition authorities. In considerable part out of an instinct to survive, these agencies have ended up dealing with soft issues that are, in effect, contract enforcement issues, and which would be handled in the industrial countries as private disputes resolved in the courts, and not as issues of public policy.

Worse, the enforcement agencies have sometimes found a welcome niche by dealing mainly with 'fairness' issues (for example, preventing one enterprise in an industry from hiring managers away from another) and have ended up by strengthening the positions of the dominant companies. The enforcement agencies infrequently had the authority to impose sanctions sufficiently severe as to force the offending parties to follow the law.

Hoekman and Djankov (1997), in a similar analysis of Bulgaria's experience, found again little attention by the competition authority aimed at hard-core anticompetitive behavior. Many cases of 'unfair competition' have dealt with the enforcement of private contracts and property rights, for example, protecting brand names.[6] When hard-core cartels and abuses of dominance that restrict competition have been the target, the impact of competition law enforcement has been minimal, in part because the penalties that the competition agency can impose are not sufficient to induce enterprises to cease their illegal practices. The current legislation prevents Bulgaria's competition authority (the Commission for Protection of Competition or CPC) from imposing fines on firms it finds in violation without the consent of the court system. Such court intermediation has led to many delays in the imposition of sanctions and has contributed to suboptimal findings of violations (Hoekman and Djankov 1997).

DEALING WITH CROSS-BORDER COMPETITION PROBLEMS

Although trade liberalization and effective competition law can counter various restrictive business practices in domestic markets, countries have expressed concerns about anticompetitive business arrangements that stem from outside their national jurisdiction. Competition laws in several countries exempt export cartels. Apart from legally recognized cartels, there are allegations that some multinational enterprises have the power to fix prices and allocate markets internationally. Also, when multinational enterprises merge, divest and/or restructure their international operations, there may be adverse consequences in other countries which may not be explicitly taken into consideration in the decision-making process.

With increased globalization of markets and of enterprises, arrangements that exist in one country will often have effects in other countries. A recent price-fixing case in the United States, for example, was filed against six Japanese firms, one US firm, two US subsidiaries of Japanese firms, the US subsidiary of a Swedish firm, five Japanese nationals and one US national. This example shows that anticompetitive behavior can have a far-reaching multinational dimension.

For convenience, competition issues that have an international dimension can be sorted into three categories (Klein 1996: 2).

1. Transnational mergers, leading to pre-merger review of the same union by several different countries' authorities.
2. International cartel cases, where competitors in one or several countries get together privately to fix prices or allocate territories on a worldwide basis. (Power applied through control of exports.)
3. Market access cases in which anticompetitive horizontal or vertical restraints prevent foreign competitors from being able to compete on a level playing field. (Power applied through control of imports.)

The first category includes mergers among dominant firms which are likely to affect competition in several markets and could affect trade as well. One of the problems that often arises when more than one country has jurisdiction over the matter is the possibility of divergence of judgment on the 'legality' of the merger.

The second category covers complaints about the export behavior of a cartel. On the one hand, the complaint might be that export prices are too high – local consumers or a consumer interest-oriented enforcement agency might protest about costs of artificially high prices charged by cartel members, some of whom might be local producers. There are also complaints that cartel prices are too low – local producers not included in the cartel might complain that they were being set upon, driven out of business by a foreign cartel.[7]

Complaints such as those the US has frequently voiced against Japan are good examples of the third category. Japanese enterprises, these complaints allege, may make and maintain arrangements that prevent foreign access to the Japanese market. In the case of automobiles and parts, a frequent complaint is that Japanese auto manufacturers prevent Japanese dealers from handling US-manufactured vehicles (Washington 1995).

Problems of policing all three categories of practices arise because the anticompetitive action often takes place in one country, while its effects are felt in another. A government has no authority to impose sanctions in another country, nor even to collect the information needed to pursue a case. While there are bilateral agreements among countries to cooperate with each other to develop the evidence needed to pursue an antitrust investigation,[8] such cooperation is far from complete.

There are several reasons behind this lack of completeness. First, antitrust standards differ between countries. In addition, and perhaps more important, cross-border disputes usually bring out mercantilist concerns to protect local producers, for example, to promote the export potential of national champions. An antitrust case within a country pits certain domestic producers against other domestic producers. In such a case, the politics of the government opposing one group of producers can be neutralized by the politics of favoring others, allowing efficiency and consumer benefits to be the dominant concerns. But when Country A wants the government of Country B to use its power to extract from a 'B' business the information necessary to reach a legal decision that would restrain the 'B' business, that is, provide an advantage to 'A' producers over those from 'B', the issue often becomes one of our guys versus their guys – as trade protection cases tend to be. The rhetoric of the unwillingness to cooperate will often dwell on differences of antitrust standards and procedures, even though the motive that propels the unwillingness is the mercantilism that propels trade restrictions.

ANTIDUMPING IS NOT COMPETITION POLICY

One of the more influential delusions of trade policy is the idea that antidumping actions deal with situations in which competition policy – except for the administrative problems of cross-border enforcement – would apply. This simply is not true. Neither in concept, history nor application is antidumping about competition policy. Antidumping is ordinary protection with a great public relations program – nothing more.

History

Jacob Viner, the first scholar to pull together previous writings on the subject, showed that throughout history, accusations of foreign dumping had often been part of the rhetoric of pleading for protection – by whatever means protection was traditionally provided. When the Liberal Party government in Canada in 1904 came up with the world's first antidumping law, it was in a political bind. Cursing the tariff was an important part of the party's politics of getting votes from farmers, while keeping it high was an important way of obtaining contributions from manufacturers. Canadian steelmakers, an important source of financial support, were pressing for higher tariffs on steel rails, but it would have been difficult for the Canadian government to confine any tariff increase to steel rails. Once the tariff was opened for revision, all the producers to which the government owed a political debt would come forward; the tariff increase would spread to other iron and steel products, to textiles, to farm equipment, and on and on.

The Canadian government's response was a new wrinkle to what was, for Canada, an old trick. As the eminent Canadian economic historian O.J. McDiarmid (1946: 8–9) has documented, 'Canada's principal contribution to the technique of trade restrictions has been in giving the executive and administrative branches of government a wide measure of control over the effective rate of duties through artificial valuation of goods for duty purposes'. The Canadian government not only continued to artificially value goods for customs purposes, it added a new tax, equal to the difference between this artificial value and the true, or invoiced, value of imports.

The impact of the new 'special duty of customs' (as it was first called) on steel imports won the enthusiastic support of Canadian industry, and the new measure soon came to be known as the 'antidumping tax'.

While in Canada policing the evils of monopoly power was never more than the rhetoric of the matter, in the United States early antidumping regulations were, in substance, extensions of antitrust law. These laws, incorporating the standards of proof and evidence of US competition law, proved, however, to be an ineffective vehicle for interests seeking import protection, and these interests continued to urge a Canada-style antidumping law.

Though a Supreme Court decision blocked the application of the 1890 Sherman antitrust law to a contract that had been made in a foreign country, the Congress corrected that technicality in 1894. During World War I, protectionists piggybacked on anti-German sentiment to plead for higher tariffs. Viner quotes a propagandist who argued that 'the German government was accumulating vast stocks of goods in order to dump them on the markets of the world . . . and regain in the field of economic warfare what she was losing on the military battlefield' (Viner 1923: 65).

President Woodrow Wilson, like the 1904 Canadian government, would not risk opening the tariff for revision. Instead, he proposed legislation aimed specifically at foreign dumping – the antidumping act of 1916. The 1916 law is part of criminal law, and procedures under it are subject to strict rules of meaning and proof. These rules prevented the expansive application that Canada's administrative mode had made possible there. Pressure thus continued for a 'Canadian-style' anti-dumping law. In 1921, Congress enacted such an antidumping law – the same one President Wilson had vetoed the year before – and President Harding signed it into law. It differed from the previous (1916) US antidumping law (that remained in effect) in two ways:

- it provided remedy through the bureaucracy rather than through the courts, that is, an *administrative*, rather than a *legal* remedy, and
- it aimed to protect *competitors* injured by import competition rather than to protect *competition* itself.[9]

As long as tariffs were high, there was minimal demand for anti-dumping actions. A GATT canvass in 1958 found a total of 37 antidumping decrees in force around the world, 22 of them in South Africa (GATT 1958: 14).

Application

As tariffs were reduced, interests seeking protection began to probe for other means. Under this pressure, the 1921 law proved to be a signal departure from the 1916 law. Trust-busting remained the rallying cry, but the object of regulation shifted from trusts to imports, the instru-ment from law to bureaucracy. The 1916 act asked a *legal* question: 'Is this really a problem caused by dumping?'. As use of the 1921 act has evolved, it asks a *political* question: 'How can antidumping be applied here?'. Or, as legal analysts sometimes put it: 'If you accuse someone of an antitrust violation, you have to prove it. If you use antidumping, you do not'.

The crack about antidumping cases not requiring proof refers to their acceptance in national antidumping regulations and in the GATT/WTO regulations of determinations based on 'best available information'. An investigation that cannot dig up information on the behavior of the sellers accused of dumping can proceed on the basis of information supplied by the accuser. There is, functionally speaking, no minimum standard of proof or evidence in an antidumping case.

Antidumping is not an application of competition policy standards. An OECD (1996) study has found that of a total of 664 antidumping measures imposed by the United States, Canada, Australia and the European Union (1980–91), less than 10 per cent (63 cases) involved any possible violation of antitrust standards. Antidumping harnesses the righteousness of trust-busting to propel the bureaucratics of customs administration in the service of restricting imports. It is ordinary protection with a grand public relations program.

Because antidumping as presently practiced is no more than ordinary protection, it would be useful to restrict antidumping action to those instances in which the standards of competition policy would justify governmental intervention. Of course, as antidumping and competition policy do not overlap, that would amount to eliminating antidumping actions. The improvement of economic welfare would simply be the gains from eliminating protection, the gains from trade. Given, however, the political popularity that antidumping currently enjoys, and the strength of the interests that enjoy trade protection disguised by the rhetoric of antidumping, it is not likely that any proposal to *replace* antidumping by competition policy would be approved. At present, the policy objective should be to prevent the rhetoric of competition policy from justifying additional expansion of the scope of antidumping actions. A less drastic possibility than eliminating antidumping altogether might be to expand the coverage of public interest considerations to allow an antidumping authority to base a negative decision on the effects of the proposed restriction on competition in the domestic market.

PROPOSALS RELATED TO INTERNATIONAL ENFORCEMENT

On one side of the spectrum of recommendations to deal with international competition disputes are those who argue that antitrust issues should be handled by enhancing cooperation between national competition authorities, independent from multilateral agreements such as the WTO. More ambitious approaches call for the creation of an independent institution for the enforcement of multilaterally agreed competition policy rules (for example, Scherer 1994). This institution would be in charge of the enforcement of agreed rules and could also use national competition offices to support its investigations. In between, some authors have proposed agreement on a greater harmonization of competition policies (agreement on minimum standards, for example), as well as the participation of the GATT/WTO in this matter. Existing GATT/WTO mechanisms could be used to address antitrust issues through the non-violation complaints in the Dispute Settlement Mechanism (Hoekman and Mavroidis 1994), and also the scope of GATT's disciplines could be further extended to encompass antitrust.

Bilateral Cooperation

The position of some governments, particularly of the United States, is often that contemporary international competition policy issues can be managed through application of national laws, aided by cooperation among national governments.[10] According to this approach, each country is encouraged to unilaterally adopt and enforce sound antitrust laws. Whenever competition-related actions inside of one country are likely to have an impact on trade and competition in countries outside its jurisdiction, national agencies should cooperate to investigate the matter, and this cooperation would be ensured and regulated by bilateral agreements. The EU–US Antitrust Cooperation Agreement of 1991 and the US–Canada Agreement are examples of such agreements.[11] More generally, the United States International Antitrust Enforcement Act of 1994 authorizes the Federal Trade Commission and the Justice Department to negotiate and conclude bilateral agreements with other governments through which confidential information could be shared. It also allows for agreements that would compel the antitrust agencies of cooperating countries to use their compulsory power to obtain information that the concerned countries need to pursue their investigations. This higher level of cooperation and commitment is likely to put more pressure to curb anticompetitive behavior. Many international cartels which relied on the principle of confidentiality to keep the results of independent investigations by a country's national agency on their activities from being shared, will no longer be able do so.

The Boeing/McDonnell Douglas merger

The merger of Boeing and McDonnell Douglas – recently approved by both the US and the European Union – illustrates several dimensions of a competition policy case involving powerful countries. The merger entailed the acquisition by Boeing of McDonnell Douglas, a direct competitor. Boeing pre-merger already dominated the market for large commercial aircraft, with sales of about 60 per cent of that market. Large barriers to entry and high concentration (the only other significant player being Airbus) characterize the industry.

Though the merger, in the end, was approved by both the US government and the European Union, the proposal generated a great deal of contention between the two governments. Three major concerns were raised by the EU: the alleged dominant position of the new company in the commercial and defense markets; the potential spillover benefits from McDonnell Douglas's defense business to Boeing commercial airplanes; and the exclusivity contracts signed between Boeing and three major US airline companies (American Airlines, Delta and Continental).

Both the general guidelines of competition policy and consequently the criteria that were used to interpret the mergers were different between parties. The US Federal Trade Commission (FTC) determined that the merger would *not* pose a threat to competition in the relevant markets or create the basis for a monopoly. According to the FTC, the commercial aircraft division of McDonnell Douglas had *already* ceased to be a competitor in the international market for commercial aircraft – this because of its past failure to improve the technology and efficiency of its products, and its insufficient investment in new products, infra-structure and research. By 1996, the market share for McDonnell Douglas commercial airplanes had fallen to below 4 per cent of new sales.

The European Union disagreed. They claimed that the proposed merger would give Boeing a dominant position in the aircraft market. The takeover by Boeing would give the company control over 24 per cent of the fleet in service (aircraft built and sold by McDonnell Douglas) and its control over the provision of services and spare parts for that fleet would provide for considerable leverage over new aircraft sales.

Moreover, according to the European Union, Boeing, in its expanded position in the market for military aircraft, would be able to apply technology paid for by defense contracts to its commercial aviation business, giving it an unfair advantage. Likewise, the exclusive supplier contracts that Boeing had signed with a number of airlines effectively closed a significant part of the market from competition.

With regard to the different interpretations of the proposed merger, US FTC Chairman Robert Pitofsky explained that a US Federal Trade Commission investigation emphasizes the effect of the merger on future prices. In the Boeing case, they determined that effect would be minimal.[12] The European Union insisted that its standards require a comprehensive look at all the factors which can influence the market position of a company, including the economic and financial power of the merging companies.

The final approval of the merger by both sides took place only after Boeing agreed to several changes. In response to the EU's concern about the exclusive supplier deals, Boeing promised not to enforce the existing agreements and not to sign any future such contracts (even in approving the initial merge proposal, the US FTC had expressed reservations regarding the exclusive contracts). The civilian airline div-ision of McDonnell Douglas will also remain legally separate from the merged company for the next ten years, thus isolating Boeing from the servicing of the existing McDonnell Douglas fleet. The technological spillover from defense to commercial aircraft will be addressed by making the technology derived from McDonnell Douglas military research available at reasonable royalties to any commercial aircraft company.

This case offers an example where the two parties, the US and EU, were able to reach an agreement without the intervention of an international institution. As provided for by the EU/US agreement on cooperation in competition matters, US and European Union agencies cooperated extensively to share information in conducting their independent investigations, and apparently reached a compromise between the application of US competition policy standards and those of the European Union. Despite differences in the criteria laid down in the European merger regulation and the US, Boeing successfully tried to satisfy both competition authorities.

The process, however, displayed characteristics of a bilateral bargaining situation, in which each government saw its interest in preserving or extending the market position of its national champion. Threats abounded. Had the merger not been approved in the European Union, the European Commission would have had the authority under European Union competition regulations to impose fines of up to 10 per cent on Boeing/McDonnell Douglas sales in the European Union. It could also have fined European companies doing business in Europe with Boeing/McDonnell Douglas, and confiscated aircraft purchased from the merged firm. In the US, President Clinton threatened to report the case to the WTO or to otherwise find grounds to retaliate against European companies operating in the US. Several members of Congress hinted at the possibility of taking direct Congressional action, or of remembering this 'loss' the next time legislation of particular interest to the European Union came forward. At the level of rhetoric, they contended that the United States Federal Trade Commission's approval should have sufficed for the merger to be accepted and condemned the EU's intervention in 'American Business'.

Basic Elements in an International Agreement on Competition Policy

A complete international agreement on competition policy would have to deal with the harmonization of standards. A number of analysts, however, have built their suggestions on the presumption that standards – particularly standards on hard-core antitrust activities – overlap sufficiently that considerable progress could be made with a less encompassing agreement. Following Khemani and Schöne (1997) we turn to a review of the basic elements of an agreement to deal with the three categories of problems listed in the section on cross-border competition, without taking on the harmonization of competition standards. As Khemani and Schöne emphasize, proposals whose key elements involve the use by a party national to one country of the competition policy enforcement mechanism in another country must first assure that each member country will enact and actively enforce competition regulations.

Authorization of mergers of international companies
Mergers of international firms are special cases of spillover effects from different national antitrust policies. Recent examples are the Gillette/Wilkinson and Boeing/McDonnell Douglas cases. Under current practice, such mergers are reviewed by competition authorities in several countries, for example, Gillette's acquisition of Wilkinson had to gain the approval of fourteen distinct merger offices.[13] Cooperation on collection and use of information would obviously be of benefit in such situations (we saw the effectiveness of cooperative behavior in light of the Boeing/McDonnell Douglas case described above). As previously mentioned, it is indeed possible that different authorities will reach different conclusions on the legality of the merger,[14] and at present there is no international mechanism for resolving such differences – even if the authorities are applying, in theory, the same standard. In practical terms, unless a merger is unanimously approved, it must be abandoned.

Anticompetitive behavior by exporters
The second category of problems involves anticompetitive actions that take place in one country while the actors (cartel members) reside in other countries – for example, the case mentioned above, brought in the United States against a combination of six Japanese firms, one US firm, two US subsidiaries of Japanese firms, the US subsidiary of a Swedish firm, five Japanese nationals and one US national. In such cases, the key element is for the enforcing agency or court to have access to information that exists outside of its legal boundaries – international cooperation on the gathering of information.

This is perhaps the most difficult area for reaching international agreement on the application of competition policy. The actions that one government might interpret as anticompetitive behavior might be supported by another as industrial policy. When the standard of industrial policy is to promote and to defend national champions, international problems cannot be eliminated by harmonization of standards. The standard itself implies international conflict – to eliminate international discord requires that nations *change* their standard, not that they harmonize it. Of course, a basic element in a relevant international agreement would require that all national laws authorizing export cartels be abolished.

If a cartel is to be attacked in the country in which its effects are felt, it is obvious that international cooperation on collecting information will be needed. It will be difficult in this area to reach an agreement even to share information. In the past, whether to defend national champions or to defend a different standard of competition policy, governments have often refused to cooperate with an antitrust case in another country and have even made it legally impossible for its national companies to respond. International cartels, mindful of national laws and of governmental attitudes on such matters, arrange their meetings and their archives accordingly.

Anticompetitive behavior that hampers access to a national market
To deal with domestic cartel arrangements that serve to restrict imports, the key elements in an international agreement would be to (i) give legal standing to exporters, and (ii) allow competition policy enforcement via private law suits. The reason for the first element is obvious. The second is necessary, Khemani and Schöne explain, as exporters might be hesitant to file a complaint with administrative enforcement authorities due to the fear that those agencies are not sufficiently independent to objectively represent the interests of a foreign party against nationals. Independent courts, they point out, have a better reputation for applying the law in a non-discriminatory way. As enforcement would be through the enforcement mechanism of the country in which the alleged cartel exists, there would be no need for international cooperation to collect information.

This situation – anticompetitive actions that keep imports out – is one frequently alleged to exist in Japan. The Japanese Antimonopoly Act is very restrictive on the access of private parties to the enforcement mechanism. Their rights are limited to '(1) reporting to the Japanese Fair Trade Commission about anticompetitive practices, with no right to compel the agency to initiate an investigation, and (2) to sue another party for damages caused by anticompetitive behavior once an administrative decision has been rendered determining that the practices are in violation of antitrust law' (Khemani and Schöne 1997: 12).

An international competition authority

Michael Scherer (1994) has developed a plan for an international competition policy authority. While it is not likely that governments will soon approve such a plan, the usefulness of the plan is that it does identify all the elements necessary to handle competition problems that involve several countries.

The Scherer proposal concentrates on the same three areas mentioned above where competition is likely to affect international trade: cartels, mergers and abuses by dominant firms (such as price discrimination, predatory pricing, refusals to deal, distribution restrictions). It emphasizes the appropriate gathering and dissemination of information. The steps Scherer suggests are as follows.

1. Adoption of an international competition policy agreement which would create an International Competition Policy Office (ICPO), within the WTO.
2. One year after the agreement went into effect, all substantial national and international export and import cartels must be registered, and the mechanics of their operations documented, with the ICPO.
3. Following a petition by a member nation(s) that international trade has been restrained or distorted by monopolistic practices, the ICPO will undertake – with the required cooperation of national authorities – a study of the alleged practices. ICPO will publish the results, and its recommendations for correction.
4. Within three years members would agree on a common format for reporting the activities of substantial enterprises that proposed to merge. Afterwards, member governments would have to notify all proposed mergers, along with the agreed format of information about the enterprises. ICPO would distribute the information to all members.
5. Within five years each member country will enact national laws prohibiting export cartels operating from their home territory – with each nation allowed to exempt three industries.
6. Within five years each member country will enact national laws prohibiting import cartels – except those to countervail the effects of export cartels or other trade monopolies.
7. Seven years after ICPO's creation it will begin to accept petitions from member nations of abuse of monopoly power. ICPO – supported by national authorities – investigates, determines if an abuse exists, then recommends corrective action. If national authorities

fail to take that action, the WTO may authorize countermeasures against any country in which the abusive actions take place.

8. Seven years after ICPO's creation it will begin to accept petitions from member nations about proposed mergers. If the ICPO determines that the merger will jeopardize competition in international trade to the detriment of consumers, it will recommend corrective measures. WTO countermeasures are again the last line of enforcement.

9. Should a substantial enterprise continue to control 40 per cent or more of world trade in some four-digit SITC category for a period of longer that 20 years on the basis of validly issued patents or copyrights, any signatory nation may require within its jurisdiction the compulsory licensing of the patents and copyrights, at reasonable royalties.

10. Seven years after ICPO's creation it will begin to accept petitions from member nations concerning monopolistic practices that distort international trade but are expressly covered by the agreement. Investigation, recommendation, and enforcement would follow.

Some authors have argued that the same objectives could be served without the creation of a new organization, for example, by modification or application of GATT/WTO mechanisms. Hoekman and Mavroidis (1994) propose the use of GATT's dispute settlement procedures, more specifically Article XXIII: 1(b) on nullification and impairment, as a means to improve market access. According to that Article, complaints before GATT such as exemptions from or non-enforcement of antitrust rules, which qualify as non-violation complaints, could be used to force governments to take measures against anticompetitive practices by the private sector which interfere with market access previously negotiated in the multilateral agreement. A non-violation complaint could be pursued, for example, if a government allowed domestic firms to impede foreign firms to establish distribution in violation of national antitrust laws.

Trachtman (1993) suggests that exemptions and non-enforcement of competition policy could translate into a 'de facto' subsidy to domestic firms. If that is the case, then foreign non-enforcement would qualify as a violation complaint of nullification or impairment under GATT. In addition, it could be the basis for a countervailing duty action in an importing country.

HOW LARGE IS THE PROBLEM?

Is the impact of anticompetitive actions on international trade a large problem or a small one? Some scattered bits of information are available on which one can base a preliminary judgment. Scherer (1994: 46) reports that at their peak in the 1930s, legally authorized US export cartels (Webb–Pomerene associations) accounted for about 19 per cent of US exports. By 1981, only 39 such associations existed, and handled less than 2 per cent of US exports. The share of German exports from such associations has been estimated at 2 per cent in 1980. The average number (between 1964 and 1873) of registered Japanese export cartels was 202, and roughly half of them were in a single industry, textiles. It is difficult to conceive that in world markets for textiles an association of exporters from any one country, even Japan, would have significant market power.

On the issue of domestic cartels that impede imports, Finger and Fung (1994) have examined the bases for '301' complaints by US enterprises. Failure of a foreign government to enforce reasonable antitrust rules is one of the bases on which a US company can petition (under Article '301' of the US trade act) for the US government to assist it to expand its exports. Of 82 '301' actions taken from 1975–92, in only three was the complaint based on failure to enforce reasonable antitrust standards.

Finally, the growing number of antidumping cases *are not* evidence of competition problems that cross national borders. As noted above, very few of them meet even the most basic criteria of competition policy violations.

EVALUATION

In what areas of competition policy is international cooperation most likely to be attainable and helpful? What sort of international cooperation? International rules of the sort proposed by Scherer that would be enforced by an international agency, or bilateral cooperation to assist with national enforcement (that is, positive comity) – as provided for in bilateral agreements among the US, the EU and Canada?

Until now, bilateral or informal cooperation has been useful in reducing the cost of competition policy enforcement, particularly the ost of evaluating mergers. Even in an instance such as the Boeing/McDonnell Douglas merger, in which the US and the EU applied different principles of competition policy – and in which the politics of defending national champions constrained each government – an agreement was reached. Such cooperation might also make significant progress on other issues, perhaps on the elimination of governmental sanctions for export controls. In the modern international marketplace, there are few products over which the producers of one country can exploit significant market power, hence the mercantilist cost of giving up such cartels is not likely to be great.

International Rules for Competition Policy

An ongoing WTO Working Group on the Relation Between Trade Policy and Competition Policy will look at various options for including international rules on competition policy under the WTO umbrella. Encoding minimum standards as a WTO agreement brings the WTO dispute settlement (enforcement) mechanism into play to assure that the agreed standards are honored. It also, however, brings forward the risks that motivate some to be reluctant to include minimum labor or environmental standards into the WTO: (1) possible imperialism of the industrial countries' view of appropriate standards, and (2) the possibility of protectionist use, that is, that interest groups within countries will accuse other countries of not abiding by international standards as a legal pretext to seek protection from imports from those countries.

Developing countries have in the past justified regulation of foreign direct investment as the only way open to them to deal with the power of multinational enterprises (Jacquemin 1995). Since the Uruguay Agreement on Trade Related Investment Measures (TRIMs) has placed limits on such regulation, some have suggested that the WTO agreements are now unbalanced and should be modified to allow the control of competitive practices by multilateral enterprises. While discussions of such rules-making normally assumes that international rules such as the WTO rules are there to *control* the power of larger countries and larger enterprises, it is also possible to argue that such rules, in reality, apply such power – particularly when their technical complexity prevents the transparency that is an important element in their effectiveness (Finger and Dhar, 1994).

Trade Policy as Competition Policy

Even for industrial countries, the problem of anticompetitive actions significantly interfering with trade does not seem to be a significant one. It is even less likely that developing countries, whose exports tend toward standardized products in which the number of international sellers is quite large, are suffering from having to compete in cartelized export markets. Competition policy, remember, is much broader than competition law and regulation. Openness to international trade, privatization, the availability of institutions and laws necessary to allow markets to function effectively, are important parts of competition policy. For developing countries, the impact of further trade liberalization on the efficiency of resource use in the domestic economy should remain a higher priority issue than the impact of competition policy (or lack thereof) on trade.

NOTES

1. Openness to international trade seems now to be a generally accepted element of development policy. One of the more severe critics of the World Bank's *East Asian Miracle* (1993) report notes that 'the trade strategy debate is no longer alive – the debate is now on the role of the states versus markets [in developing particular industries] in successful export-oriented economies' (Lall 1994: 646).
2. The figure above of $500 billion refers to imports affected by policies that have been substantially implemented.
3. In US history, an important part of the populist argument against the tariff was that it allowed and protected domestic monopolies. Cordell Hull was US President Franklin Roosevelt's first Secretary of State and is considered the father of the US Reciprocal Trade Agreements Act. His first speech as a member of the US Congress attacked the tariff. As Hull (1948) reported the content of his speech, 'I made a vigorous attack on the high tariff and the monopolies and trusts that had grown up behind it. No kind of effort to curb and suppress trust violators [can] succeed unless such effort strides at the main source of their constant creation – the protective tariff – the king of evils, our present tariff, should be given a place near the center of the stage'.
4. The result is higher profits to local producers–distributors (because they now have better access to imports for resale), but no competitive pressure for increased efficiency, and no reduction of prices to consumers.
5. In this instance – one identified in field work for the World Bank – the absence of regular shipping facilities for wood from other sources (for example, South America) pushed up the cost of imported wood to a much higher level than his competitors (manufacturers in North America and Europe) were paying.
6. Hoekman and Djankov also report on another troublesome part of Bulgaria's competition law, a part that prohibits for three years a manager who leaves an enterprise from taking employment with another enterprise in the same line of business. The provision could be a significant barrier to entry – it is an obvious disincentive to the organization of new enterprises.
7. When formalized, such complaints will often take the form of petitions for anti-dumping action to restrict imports. Antidumping however – the following section explains – is in legal structure and in political practice (though not necessarily in political rhetoric) an instrument of trade protection, not of competition policy.
8. For example, the Mutual Legal Assistance Treaties of the United States.
9. Despite the lure of triple damages, only one serious suit has been brought under the 1916 law, and it was unsuccessful.
10. For example, Wood (1995) argues this position.
11. The principle of international comity in enforcing the national laws is an important characteristic of these agreements.
12. The FTC, in contrast, did not approve the proposed Staples/Office Depot merger

which, the FTC concluded, would have significantly hurt competition and consumer welfare. Through a methodology based on comparisons of markets in which both members of the proposed merger operated versus those in which only one operated, the FTC estimated that the merger would increase consumer prices by 13 per cent.
13. Scherer (1994: 2).
14. Khemani and Schöne (1997: 32), give examples of mergers approved in one country but not approved in another. In each, the merger was not consummated.

REFERENCES

Finger, J. Michael and Sumana Dhar (1994), 'Do rules control power? GATT articles and agreements in the Uruguay Round', in Alan V. Deardorff and Robert M. Stern (eds), *Analytical and Negotiating Issues in the Global Trading System*, Ann Arbor: University of Michigan Press, pp. 195–223.

Finger, J. Michael and K.C. Fung (1994), 'Can competition policy control "301"?', World Bank Policy Research Working Paper 1253, February.

Fingleton, John, Eleanor Fox, Damien Neven and Paul Seabright (1996), *Competition Policy and the Transformation of Central Europe*, London: CEPR.

General Agreement on Tariffs and Trade (1958), *Antidumping and Countervailing Duties*, Geneva.

Globerman, Steven (1990), 'Trade liberalization and competitive behavior: a note assessing the evidence and the public policy implications,' *Journal of Policy Analysis and Management*, 9 (1) (Winter): 80–88.

Guasch, J. Luis and Sarath Rajapatirana (1994), 'The interface of trade, investment, and competition policies: issues and challenges for Latin America', World Bank Policy Research Working Paper 1393, December.

Hoekman, Bernard and Simeon Djankov (1997), 'Competition law in Bulgaria after central planning', World Bank Policy Research Working Paper 1789, June.

Hoekman, Bernard and Petros Mavroidis (1994), 'Competition, competition policy and the GATT,' *The World Economy*, 17: 121–50.

Hull, Cordell (1948), *Memoirs*, New York: Macmillan.

Jacquemin, Alexis (1995), 'Towards an internationalization of competition policy', *The World Economy*, 18 (4) (November): 781–9.

Khemani, Shyam and Rainer Schöne (1997), 'International competition conflict resolution: a road map for the WTO,' Private Sector Development Department Occasional Paper, Washington DC: World Bank.

Klein, Joel I. (1996), 'A note of caution with respect to a WTO agenda on competition policy', paper presented at the Royal Institute of International Affairs, Chatham House, London, 18 November.

Lall, Sanjaya (1994), 'The East Asia miracle: does the bell toll for industrial strategy?', *World Development*, 22 (4) (April): 645–54.

Lloyd, Peter and Gary Sampson (1995), 'Competition and trade policy: identifying the issues after the Uruguay Round', *The World Economy*, 18 (September): 681–705.

McDiarmid, O.J. (1946), *Commercial Policy in the Canadian Economy*, Cambridge, MA: Harvard University Press.

OECD, Economics Department (1996), *Trade and Competition, Frictions after the Uruguay Round (Note by the Secretariat)*, Paris: OECD.

Scherer, F.M. (1994), *Competition Policies for an Integrated World Economy*, Washington DC: Brookings Institution.

Trachtman, Joel (1993), 'International regulatory competition, externalization and jurisdiction', *Harvard International Law Journal*, **34** (Winter): 47–104.

Viner, Jacob (1923), *Dumping: A Problem in International Trade*, Chicago: University of Chicago Press.

Washington, Frank (1995), 'Trade settlement could speed supplier globalization', *Ward's Auto World*, Detroit, July, **49**.

Wood, Diane (1995), 'Internationalization of antitrust law: options for the future', *DePaul Law Review*, **44** (Summer), 1289–99.

World Bank (1993), *The East Asian Miracle: Economic Growth and Public Policy*, Policy Research Report, Washington DC: The World Bank.

9. Promoting north–south complementarities

Gavin Boyd and Alice H. Amsden

INTRODUCTION

Because of their resources, efficiencies, and the scale of their operations, transnational enterprises based in industrialized democracies are the principal agents of structural change in the world economy. Their operations are mainly responsible for the deepening integration which is raising levels of structural interdependence between industrialized states, and they are linking third world economies more and more with those states. Firms emerging in third world economies, notably in industrializing East Asian states, compete and cooperate with the northern multinationals. Complementarities are thus evolving, but with imbalances in the gains from trade and transnational production which overall have been tending to widen, especially since the 1997 East Asian financial crises. Associated with the asymmetries in gains have been changes in bargaining strengths, between northern and southern governments, and northern and southern firms. The northern multinationals, especially if influenced, guided, and supported by governments in industrialized states, can contribute substantially to the development of more balanced north–south complementarities, for higher interdependent growth. Problems of governance and of macro and micromanagement in many third world countries, however, will have to be overcome, in part through increased accountability to major industrialized states, committed, hopefully, to partnering in the common interest.

Northern regionalism has been a major factor in the changes of bargaining strengths. The enlargement and deepening of the European Union and the formation of the North American Free Trade Area have increased domination of the world trading system and global investment relations by an Atlantic partnership, which, despite strains, is able to assert extensive shared preferences.[1] Efforts by southern states to form regional economic cooperation systems and to build solidarity for collective bargaining have been mostly unsuccessful.[2] Problems of governance in those states have severely limited productive interactions between their policy communities, and in many cases these communities have been obliged to function under systems of personal rule with low potentials for policy learning.

With the overall shifts in bargaining strengths third world states have become more vulnerable to discriminatory northern trade policies, which have been directed especially against southern exports of textiles and clothing.[3] Vulnerabilities to northern pressures for wider access to southern markets have also increased. Meanwhile the attraction of northern multinationals into export-oriented manufacturing has become more necessary for industrializing states, and investment bidding rivalries between them have in effect added to the bargaining leverage available to those firms. Host country enterprises, some moving into international operations, have had to operate in more and more competitive environments. At the same time global rationalization strategies implemented by the northern multinationals have entailed shifts of industrial capacity from more developed to lower-cost southern countries, with geographic dispersals of production activities that have limited technology transfers. Major structural policy challenges have thus been evident, but engagement with these has been difficult for most southern administrations because of their problems of governance and their generally weak technocratic capabilities.[4]

The basic changes in north–south structural interdependencies have been evolving for several decades, but in a context of increased strains since the 1997 disruptions of the East Asian economies. Several of these economies, especially South Korea, had achieved high outward-oriented growth, aided by incoming direct investment, mainly from Japan, but increasing speculative activity began to destabilize their inadequately regulated financial markets. These markets were being liberalized and internationalized, mainly in response to pressures from the USA, and were disrupted as the speculative activity became unsustainable, due to adverse trends in international currency markets and outflows of foreign capital.[5]

The East Asian problems had some unsettling effects in American and European financial markets, while falls in the currencies of East Asian industrializing countries resulted in export surges that increased deficits in the USA's balance of payments. Meanwhile, through the International Monetary Fund, the United States and other major industrialized countries provided support for adjustment financing to South Korea, Thailand, and other East Asian states in difficulties. The status which these countries had acquired as models of high growth thus declined. Assessments of their achievements before 1997 which placed more emphasis on market forces than on the structural significance of their policies appeared to become more persuasive.[6] Economic advice from the IMF and industrialized states stressed the efficiencies attainable under liberal economic policies as well as the importance of regulating financial markets and facilitating their development.

The status of virtually all third world countries has been weakened by the problems of East Asian industrializing states. There have been related losses of bargaining strengths also, but more to the advantage of northern multinationals than of northern governments, as has been the case in East Asia. For decades before the East Asian financial crises, governments in industrialized states had been losing elements of economic sovereignty as multinationals based mainly in their economies became more active in shaping national economic structures and the interdependencies between them. Meanwhile sectors and communities in those states were experiencing the vulnerabilities and costs of multinational global restructuring strategies. Switches in the locations of transnational production activities and the idling of industrial capacity owned by unsuccessful firms were causing extensive adjustment problems. The resultant burdens assumed by governments were becoming more onerous for immobile labour forces than for international enterprises.[7] Northern administrations were thus motivated to promote more growth by their exporting firms, and therefore to pressure southern governments for increased market access. The northern multinationals, however, while standing to benefit from such access, were able to exploit more competitive investment bidding by northern governments, as well intensified bidding of that kind by third world administrations.

For most southern states the adverse trends in relative bargaining strengths have become more serious because of the East Asian problems. Enterprises in these developing states that have been moving into international operations have tended to encounter greater difficulties in competition against northern multinationals, while the domestic operations of these southern enterprises have been hindered by strains in the home economies. For increased growth in those economies active partnering with their administrations would have substantial benefits, but the pressures of international competition tend to obligate concentration on transnational expansion by the emerging southern enterprises. Like their northern counterparts they have incentives to exploit structural policy rivalries between many governments, and to limit exposure to exactions by their home governments; also they have incentives to lower the costs of coping with the administrative deficiencies of those governments.

Adjustment and developmental imperatives oblige third world administrations to seek increasingly productive cooperation with their own and northern multinationals. Capacities to initiate and manage such cooperation have to be enhanced by overcoming problems of governance. The dynamics of common forms of engagement with northern international firms, however, do not tend to activate resolution of third world problems of governance, except in so far as investment bidding rivalry motivates efforts to improve infrastructures and regulatory mechanisms. Pressures from international lending agencies and industrialized states can induce more significant endeavours to overcome problems of governance, depending especially on the qualities of northern statecraft that may inspire trust, goodwill, and policy learning.

ANALYTICAL PERSPECTIVES

Globalization is a process with many asymmetries – in gains from trade and transnational production, in bargaining relationships at corporate and policy levels, and in capacities at those levels to manage the structural interdependencies which increase as deepening integration continues. These structural interdependencies expand as international firms widen the scope of their transnational production activities. This happens with imbalances between national political economies, in the spread of benefits, and in the evolution of the industrial capacities that are linked, across borders, under the control of competing and cooperating multinational enterprises.

Exploration of the asymmetries in gains from trade and transnational production, and in bargaining and macromanagement capacities, necessitates focus on the functional consequences of differing relationships between firms and governments, and on the development of firms and governments as systems. The benefits of productive cooperation between a country's enterprises and its administration tend to become more substantial as structural interdependencies and the pressures of competition increase in all the markets which are being linked. The cognitive and motivational factors necessary for corporate–government partnering, however, may be lacking. Administrative deficiencies that impose costs on firms and discourage their cooperation increase their incentives to extend their international operations with emphasis on the acquisition of bargaining leverage against numerous host governments and their home administration.

The notable contrasts are between the partnering in the Japanese system of alliance capitalism and the American pattern of individualistic capitalism, in which firms concentrate on the expansion of their foreign activities while relating distantly to their home administration. The Japanese partnering generates efficiencies through extensive entrepreneurial coordination, and ensures bargaining advantages in interactions with foreign governments and firms. In the American pattern intense competition, less restrained by intercorporate ties, results in the emergence of powerful self-reliant international firms, relying very much on their own resources in rivalries with Japanese enterprises clustered mainly in industry groups.[8]

These contrasts dominate the global processes of deepening integration, with complex effects on third world countries, but in a context in which trade and investment policy cooperation develops mainly between the USA and the European Union, because of cultural affinities, the size of the Union, and the large dimensions of Atlantic structural interdependencies. The markets of most third world countries are penetrated mainly by US and Japanese firms, which encounter generally modest challenges from European enterprises. The US–Japan rivalries are intense in industrializing East Asian countries, where Japanese alliance capitalism is active on a larger scale and on a longer-term basis than the American corporate presence. That presence, however, is large and well established in Latin America, where Japanese involvement is on a small scale and European commercial activity is somewhat larger, but below the modest level in East Asia.

For policy learning by third world governments, particularly those in East Asia, Japanese alliance capitalism is a model, demonstrating potentials for rapid outward-oriented industrialization at high technological levels. Superior bargaining strength is associated with this model, because of the size of the Japanese economy and the cohesion in its intercorporate system. The USA, however, ranks higher in terms of bargaining strength on issues of foreign economic relations, because of its greater size and its ties with the European Union. For Latin American countries the USA's bargaining capabilities have assumed much greater significance than the demonstration effects of the Japanese model, which are seen across long social distances. In industrializing East Asia contextual influences are more complex, as the Japanese demonstration effect is immediate and potent, and competitive uses of US and Japanese bargaining leverage are more active.

Japanese, American, and European policy orientations express differing degrees of competitive and cooperative intent in dealing with third world countries, and these differences are to a considerable extent reflected in corporate strategies, especially those of Japanese firms. The mixes of intent at the policy levels reflect varying combinations of inputs in policy communities, and in the Japanese case there is dynamic responsiveness between the technocratic and management levels which is highly functional in terms of shared interests related to the penetration of foreign markets on a long-term basis.[9] The partnering is conducive to stable manufacturing involvement in East Asian and other industrializing states on terms favouring Japanese interests but with consideration of those of host countries. American policy, shaped in strongly pluralistic processes, relates more distantly to third world states, while the very independently managed strategies of US firms are implemented without permanent commitments to engagement in host countries. Such engagement is mainly an individual process, while Japanese firms become involved in host countries in collaboration with other members of industry groups.

Third world interests are affected in complex ways by the degrees to which Japanese, American, and European policies give impetus to, support, and guide the expanding international operations of their firms. These operations tend to result in acquisitions of international oligopoly power, which can be used on an extensive scale for restrictive business practices. Japanese, US, and European Union competition policies each have a domestic focus, and this hinders cooperation for the development of an international competition policy.[10] Third world countries are increasingly vulnerable to restrictive business practices by northern multinationals, and would have to expect that an international competition policy, if it were established, would result primarily from negotiations between the United States and the European Union.

Related to the foreign direct investment policies of the industrialized states are their efforts to encourage increased economic openness in third world countries. Wider market access is advocated to facilitate increased gains from trade and international production. Asymmetries in bargaining strengths, however, determine the terms on which liberalization is negotiated, and these are of concern to southern governments and firms because of the global market strengths of northern multinationals. The leverage that can be applied by the US administration is especially potent, and can be exerted with unilateral activism.

The northern pressures for liberalization challenge southern administrations to implement effective industrial policies, for improved structural competitiveness. The necessary technocratic capabilities, political will, and forms of corporate–government partnering, however, are generally lacking. Problems of governance in third world states thus constitute a special area of inquiry in research on north–south relations. Many of these problems of governance are longstanding, and those which demand close attention are ones which have affected industrializing states in East Asia that had attained high outward-oriented growth.

The costs of problems of governance in all third world states become more serious as their asymmetric linkages with the world economy increase, due mainly to the expanding operations of northern multinationals. The administrative failings have more negative effects on local firms than on the structurally more significant activities of the northern enterprises, and tend to encourage flights of capital.

Perspectives on third world problems of governance have been influenced by contrasts between strong states and weak states, by general recognition that when strong states become more democratic their technocratic capabilities can weaken, and by more specialized understandings that industrialization promoted by strong states, and that achieved in weak states, can open the way for destabilizing rent seeking. The most impressive record of rapid diversified outward-oriented industrialization in the high growth East Asian area has been South Korea's – attained under army-dominated regimes with advanced technocratic capabilities. Use of these capabilities has been subjected to diverse pressures since a transition to representative government. At the same time weaker regulatory functions have allowed rent seeking to increase relative to productive activity.[11]

States that appear strong can be technocratically weak, while drawing political support from the toleration of much rent seeking and corruption, as has been illustrated by Indonesia's experience. In such states administrative dealings with domestic firms tend to have divisive effects, hindering the emergence of independent comprehensive associations for the representation of corporate interests. In a transitional democratic regime which may follow, a clientelist political culture will tend to persist, hindering institutional development and the formation of a broad policy consensus.

The problems of governance, especially in weak states but also in strong ones, tend to prevent engagement with problems of market failure as these assume cross-border dimensions in contexts of globalization. International oligopoly power, as it penetrates opening third world markets, poses larger issues in association with, but also in conflict with, local forms of such power. Externalities include those resulting from relocations of foreign industrial capacity that disrupt sectors and communities in host countries; meanwhile entry barriers posed by market strengths acquired in those countries tend to become higher, to the disadvantage of local firms. In such settings problems of informational market failure can become more serious for those local firms, as incentives for information sharing with such firms become less significant for the foreign multinationals. Finally, the public good of equitable and efficient partnering between local enterprises and the foreign multinationals becomes more difficult to promote: structural policy capabilities remain inadequate, and bargaining inequalities in dealings with the multinationals increase.

The main problems of governance are abuses of power by ruling elites focussed on the maintenance of forms of personal rule through the support of corrupt officials and their clients in business communities. Acute high-level moral failings at the basis of these problems tend to persist, and policy learning is made difficult because of the subservience imposed on administrative staffs and on business associations. Pressures from international lending agencies and industrialized states can force degrees of policy learning, but are often inadequate to induce moral reform. Capacities to inspire such reform are limited because of displacements of moral principles by instrumental values in industrialized states, as outcomes of cultural contradictions in advanced capitalism.[12] These outcomes are reversible, because of potentials for moral progress in those states which have been evident in movements for unity among the Christian churches. Some inspiration for reform can be communicated through high-principled efforts, at the policy and corporate levels, to promote more productive and more balanced complementarities between industrialized and third world states.

COMPLEMENTARITY ISSUES

Questions of equity and efficiency in north–south relations demand urgent consideration by policy makers and corporate managements, especially in major industrialized states, and these questions cannot be deferred pending resolution of problems of governance in third world countries. The questions are posed because of the imbalances, and their cumulative effects, in the global spread of gains from trade and transnational production. These effects include changes in market strengths, structural capabilities, and bargaining capacities which have adverse implications for developing states. The global context is a mix of internationalized market efficiencies and failures without adequate collective management. In this context governments, especially in industrialized states, have to accept extended external accountabilities, because of the direct and indirect cross-border consequences of their policies.

The questions of equity relate firstly to uses of superior global market strengths, structural capabilities, and bargaining capacities by northern multinationals implementing production and marketing strategies. These strategies have very extensive results in third world countries, and demand attention in conjunction with questions about market opening leverage by northern governments against third world administrations. The equity questions regarding corporate and government activities, it must be stressed, have increasingly serious implications for third world states because of increasing northern dominance of the world economy, and because institutions for international economic cooperation mostly reflect that dominance.

The questions of efficiency concern the scope for the use and development of southern productive potentials by third world and northern firms. Overall trends indicate that southern productive potentials, although being exploited, are being underutilized, and that this contributes to the imbalances in gains from asymmetric involvement in the world economy. As northern multinationals compete and cooperate to expand their global market positions there are opportunities for third world enterprises to assume complementary roles, but subject to limitations resulting from the superior resources of the northern firms and the negative structural consequences of third world problems of governance. Administrations with these failings, it must be stressed, severely hinder growth by their own firms, especially through excessive regulation that facilitates the extraction of favours, thus pushing up production costs and transaction costs, while adding to general uncertainties.[13] Administrations with these deficiencies are in several senses inferior partners of northern governments when negotiating on questions of market access. Inequalities of status are associated with the bargaining inequalities, and capacities for knowledge-based dialogue with northern policy communities are weak.

The problems of governance and weak bargaining strengths are reflected in investment bidding to attract northern manufacturing firms. This investment bidding tends to become increasingly competitive, generating compulsions to offer more and more substantial concessions on taxation and trade issues to northern enterprises. Economic strains tend to motivate greater reliance on such concessions, partly because of low estimations of the entrepreneurial capabilities of domestic firms whose growth has been in effect restricted by administrative deficiencies.

The investment bidding, generally unaccompanied by effective structural policy initiatives, allows northern multinationals wide scope to switch sites for third world production operations, so as to maximize the exploitation of shifting location advantages, in line with global rationalization strategies. A common trend is that rising wage costs in more industrialized states cause shifts of assembly-type manufacturing to less-developed, lower-cost countries unless increased concessions are offered in the original host countries. The hopes of those countries for increasingly balanced complementarities with the industrialized states out of which multinationals are operating can thus be disappointed. Recognition of this type of problem and its likely future dimensions can sharpen understandings of imperatives for effective structural policies that emphasize self-reliant growth and the development of selective arrangements for long-term cooperation with incoming foreign firms.

Substantially comprehensive and functional structural policies can enable southern states to build industrial capacities with potentials for increasingly extensive and balanced combinations of competition and cooperation with industrialized states and with the global activities of their international firms. This has been illustrated by South Korea's experience which, despite post-1997 financial strains, has demonstrated how guided and protected industrial growth can advance through complementary links with industrialized states at medium and higher technological levels. A condition for this growth has been delayed economic liberalization, sheltering the domestic market strengths of assisted firms.[14]

Most southern states, because of their problems of governance and their vulnerabilities to northern pressures for economic liberalization, are not able to implement industrial policies for sheltered but increasingly complementary growth. Hence the complementarities which do form continue to be quite imbalanced, and are in danger of becoming disjointed and unstable as northern multinationals implement more extensive and more competitive global rationalization strategies, altering structural interdependencies which they have been mainly responsible for establishing.

The dimensions of this basic southern developmental problem, it must be stressed, have become more serious because of the weakening of southern bargaining capacities and the widening scope for strategic choices by northern multinationals since the 1997 disruptions of East Asian economies. The context is a continuing internationalization of market efficiencies and failures, determined more and more by the operations of the northern multinationals. These alter allocative efficiencies through competitive activities but also through the use of concentrations of economic power acquired by the displacement of weaker firms. Dynamic efficiencies are also altered, notably through synergies generated in alliances between those multinationals. Involvement in these dynamic efficiencies tends to become more difficult for southern firms, because of their generally smaller resources, their technological lags, and the problems of operating in their domestic policy environments.

REGIONAL CONTEXTS

Complementarities are distinguishable according to the degrees to which they are functionally patterned, through cross-border sectoral linkages, and thus according to the ways in which they are being shaped by corporate activities and national policies. Functional patterning tends to be more evident if there is extensive northern intercorporate cooperation in a third world area, but may well develop in such an area through intensive rivalries between northern multinationals.

Industrializing East Asia is the most significant area of functionally patterned north–south complementarities, principally because of the scale of Japanese production and marketing operations, coordinated on a long-term basis through extensive intercorporate bonds. States in this area have been somewhat successful in coping with structural tasks and bargaining inequalities, thereby contributing to degrees of balance in complementarities with Japan, and also to less substantial complementarities with the USA. Despite the 1997 disruptions the functionally patterned complementarities with Japan are assuming more structural significance, although with less balance.

A Japan-centred international manufacturing, marketing and financial system is being formed in industrializing East Asia, through the concerted long-term direct investment and trading strategies of Japanese firms.[15] The bargaining capacities of these firms are very substantial because of their pervasive relational ties with each other, which enhance the significance of their large resources. Host country enterprises are drawn into subordinate partnering roles, mainly through contracting as suppliers, depending on their technological capabilities. This is common in the larger members of the Association of Southeast Asian Nations (ASEAN), where levels of local industrial capacity are low. In South Korea and Taiwan higher levels of industrial development are conducive to more equal partnering between host country and Japanese firms. Structural policies in these two states have responded rather effectively to developmental imperatives while northern pressures for economic liberalization have been resisted. In the operation of collaborative arrangements with Japanese enterprises, however, transfers of advanced technology have been difficult to secure.[16]

The Japanese administration is deeply involved in the expansion of the nation's industrial establishment, through diverse forms of assistance for exports, technology development projects in host countries, and aid for infrastructure programmes. All this activity is informally coordinated with the operations of Japanese firms investing in and trading with industrializing East Asian states, and this partnering expresses long-term commitments to the building of production and trading links. Bargaining relationships with host governments and firms thus tend to be altered in ways which induce acceptance of an increasingly pervasive Japanese corporate presence. The growing influence of this presence, because of the greater dependence of host countries affected by the 1997 financial crises, can reduce its social acceptability, but this does not appear to be a significant problem except in Indonesia. Japanese corporate involvement in that state has led to the development of ties with large Chinese and other local firms enjoying official patronage. Currents of Indonesian nationalism have been directed against the foreign as well as the local Chinese presence, and, although restrained by the army-dominated regime, may be expressed in agitation if its authority weakens.[17]

A more diffuse pattern of complementarities at medium technological levels is developing between industrializing East Asian states through the operations of firms based in Chinese business communities. These are linking ASEAN economies with each other and with a greater China economic area, including Taiwan and Hong Kong. Most of these enterprises are moderately sized family firms, inclined to excessive diversification; some have moved into higher technology manufacturing, mainly in electronics.[18] Cross-border ethnic and cultural ties enable the Chinese firms to maintain market shares while competing against larger, more developed, and more closely linked Japanese firms.

Another diffuse pattern of complementarities, at generally higher technological levels and with extensive global links, is developing because of the involvement of American firms in industrializing East Asia. This activity is on a smaller scale than that of Japanese enterprises, with shorter-term objectives, and with much less official backing; moreover, it tends to be footloose, expressing weaker attachments to host countries, especially because of the stronger focus of major US firms on their European operations. Complementarities develop through competition and cooperation between the Japanese, Chinese, American and host country firms in industrializing East Asia, in a changing configuration. The Japanese enterprises, because of their strong intercorporate ties and their large resources, operate with the most extensive structural effects. They are largely responsible, moreover, for orienting much of the structural change towards service of the US market, which has become more important for them, and for host country as well as for American firms, because of the disruptions of the Southeast Asian economies. These have interrupted, for the immediate future, a structural trend which was linking East Asian industrializing states with Japan on a large scale, at a pace that had been faster than the growth of Japanese trade with the USA.

Latin America ranks next after industrializing East Asia as an area of evolving north–south complementarities. Structural policy endeavours and corporate dynamism have been weaker in this area, northern multinational involvement has been mainly American, and involvement in the world economy has been relatively smaller. Japanese firms have had only a minor presence, and challenges to US firms from a substantial European corporate presence have resulted in less dynamic efficiencies than those produced by the rivalries in industrializing East Asia. The pervasive cross-border operations of Chinese firms in East Asia have not been matched by the activities of affinitive business groups in Latin America. Ventures in regional economic cooperation by states in this area have been more ambitious than those attempted by ASEAN, but have long been affected by macromanagement problems in the participating countries. Nevertheless, there is considerable solidarity which is a source of bargaining advantages in relations with the USA as the principal trading partner of the region. To supplement those bargaining advantages the most important way of balancing dependence on the US market is the development of economic links with the European Union. This has become especially significant for Brazil, and for the future of Mercosur, the principal Latin American regional cooperation system, in which Brazil is the largest member. Efforts by US administrations to negotiate free trade agreements with Latin American states have challenging implications for Mercosur and for the European Union.[19]

The USA's large and virtually dominant direct investment position in Latin America, which has a longer history than that in East Asia, has policy-level effects which maintain a traditional emphasis on asserting US influence in the area.[20] Potentials for collaboration with the European Union in the development of economic cooperation with Latin America thus tend to be excluded. In Atlantic relations US attention focuses on securing wider access to the European market, while seeking common ground on international trade and investment issues for collaborative interaction with Japan and third world states. European Union endeavours to strengthen economic links with Latin America are moderately active, but evidence the Union's technological lags, weak growth, and problems of entrepreneurial cooperation between its business communities.[21]

Latin American complementarities with the USA have been developing at generally lower technological levels than those of industrializing East Asia. There is heavy dependence on exports of textiles, apparel, and leather footware, and, as US tariffs on these are high, substantial increases in external revenue that can help finance investment in higher technology manufacturing are difficult to achieve.[22] Mexico is in an exceptional position as the largest regional exporter of energy to the USA; it has become heavily dependent on the US market for energy and low technology manufactures, while developing only small-scale links with Latin American trading partners.

South Asian and African countries have less prominence in north–south relations because of generally lower levels of development and small roles in world trade. They attract little direct investment, and are severely disadvantaged because of very weak bargaining strengths and, in most cases, because of acute administrative deficiencies. The structural capabilities of northern multinationals have great potential significance for these underdeveloped countries, but direct investment is discouraged by low levels of competence and high degrees of corruption in their governments. Their generally poor location advantages could be improved by large-scale northern aid for infrastructure development, but allocations for this purpose are modest because of Europe's severe unemployment problems and the USA's efforts to reduce its large fiscal deficits. Assistance from the World Bank, reflecting priorities influenced by its major donors, including especially the USA, has offered some relief to many many heavily indebted poor countries, mostly in Africa.

NORTHERN POLICIES

Economic advice and policy proposals from major industrialized states encourage third world governments to increase the openness of their economies, in return for concessions on access to advanced country markets. The rationale which is given most emphasis is that general increases in gains from trade will benefit growth in industrialized and developing countries. This rationale is prominent in publications by the Organization for Economic Cooperation and Development (OECD), and is presented more critically in studies by the United Nations Conference on Trade and Development, which reflect understanding of the significance of major problems of interdependent growth, evident in the costs and vulnerabilities of globalization.[23]

Northern restraints on imports of southern primary products and manufactures are on a scale that hinders export-led growth in developing countries. While tariffs have been lowered, there has been increasing reliance on non-tariff measures and discretionary methods, directed more against manufactures than against primary products, notably in sectors in which developing countries have comparative advantages. There has been extensive use of 'voluntary' export restraints imposed on developing countries and of administered protection to discourage and penalize low-cost imports. Such methods have been used most extensively by the USA.[24]

US economic diplomacy is the main force working for increased market access in third world countries, and it focuses on East Asia as the main area of high growth states with surpluses in bilateral commerce. These surpluses provide occasions for vigorous representations by US exporting firms and, accordingly, for trade policy activism by the US administration. The European Union rather avoids association with this activism, while seeking more spontaneous cooperation from third world governments, and while endeavouring to overcome losses of competitiveness by its firms in East Asia and other developing areas. Japanese policy emphasizes complementarities of interest with East Asian and other third world countries, in terms which invite openness to Japanese exports and investment.

For third world administrations the advice and pressures regarding trade and investment liberalization are significant with reference to bargaining strengths, the protection and support of emerging industries, and issues of competition policy cooperation. All these matters, moreover, have to be considered as they affect problems of operating in the complex adversarial legalism of the World Trade Organization, in which the major industrialized states are advantaged by bargaining strengths and by the expertise of their trade and investment experts.[25]

The inequalities in bargaining strengths, it must be stressed, are large not only because of the overall trade dependence of the southern states but also because of the sizes of the European Union and the North American Free Trade Area. The weaknesses of southern ventures in regional economic cooperation, which are part of this context, are tending to persist, and in industrializing East Asia the inequalities in bargaining strengths since 1997 have become greater, with divisive effects that have made regional cooperation more difficult.

The protection and support of emerging industries becomes increasingly important for southern administrations as northern multinationals secure greater international strengths, especially in higher technology sectors where global oligopoly power is used to sustain large investments in innovations at the frontiers of research.[26] Entries into these sectors are extremely difficult for southern firms unless they receive very substantial subsidies and are aided by very active technology policies. Virtually all forms of assistance that can be provided by southern administrations, subject to their various deficiencies, are more than matched by forms of direct and indirect support received by northern multinationals from their home governments. Pressures for economic openness, in conditions of unequal bargaining, are understandably viewed by southern decision makers as undue restraints on the development of industrial capacity for operations in markets where northern oligopolistic strengths are growing.

International competition policy issues and questions of regulatory policy harmonization are factors in the context of interactions over the opposing interests in economic openness. Between industrialized states problems of cooperation in these two areas have tended to become harder to resolve as deepening integration continues. Competition policy measures and regulatory measures without specifically competitive implications are adopted with various concerns to enhance structural competitiveness, while the international operations of northern multinationals are placed under relatively few restraints by their home governments. The European Union's competition policy is rather liberal, to facilitate the emergence of strong European firms. American competition policy, shaped by more conflicted processes, has a domestic orientation which is in effect tolerant of international oligopolistic gains by US firms. There are degrees of Atlantic competition policy cooperation, and attempts to harmonize regulatory measures, but both kinds of interaction have a very uncertain future.

Third world states have to anticipate that Atlantic rivalries will tend to make European and US policies more liberal, on the basis of subjective preferences regarding the international competitive interests of their firms. This prospect, and the less likely prospect of international competition policy arrangements negotiated between the USA and the European Union, overshadows global trade and investment policy issues confronting third world governments. Associated with this prospect is the danger of increasing use of regulatory measures by northern governments, that have trade effects amounting to forms of 'New Protectionism'. These include health, environmental, and labour policy regulations with restrictive consequences that can take effect in conjunction with antidumping practices.[27] Northern assertiveness in the use of new forms of protectionism has to be reckoned with by southern governments.

CHANGING FUNDAMENTALS

Fundamentals affecting growth prospects and bargaining relationships in industrializing East Asia, Latin America, and less-developed areas, are changing mainly as transnational enterprises based in advanced states extend their trading and international production activities. Fundamentals in East Asia are being changed more rapidly and with higher growth effects than in other southern areas, because of northern competition, at the policy as well as corporate levels, which interacts with organizationally less-developed forms of Chinese capitalism. Opportunities for the promotion of more balanced and more productive north–south complementarities have to be assessed in the emerging new configuration of fundamentals.

Complex interactions between changing fundamentals in north–south relations are dominated by the expanding structural effects of operations by American, Japanese and European transnational enterprises, distinguished principally by size, technological levels, strength of home country affiliations, and the systemic effects of those affiliations. The largest firms are mostly mature and higher technology US enterprises, challenged principally by Japanese higher technology companies. In this rivalry home country intercorporate ties are major advantages for Japanese enterprises, facilitating concerted entrepreneurship and discriminatory management of competition against, and cooperation with, American firms. The competitive weaknesses of most European enterprises limit their value as alliance partners for American firms, but provide opportunities for the large US corporate presence in Europe, where the Japanese presence is smaller.

Global operations by the northern multinationals are expanding under the pressures of intensifying competition which is displacing weaker firms and limiting opportunities for emerging third world enterprises. The expansion is encouraged by the investment bidding of industrialized and developing states, responding to the vulnerabilities and costs of globalization. Investment bidding rivalries have been becoming more active in Europe because of high unemployment and, to a lesser extent, in the USA. Japan, however, has remained apart from this rivalry, because of the high degree of solidarity in its integrated political economy.[28] Third world investment bidding tends to offer northern multinationals – mainly American and Japanese – wider ranges of choices in the implementation of global strategies, and is advantageous for their bargaining with host governments, especially on taxation, trade, and competition issues.

The strong home country ties of Japanese firms cause their strategies to be influenced by policy-level concerns to develop comprehensive long-term cooperation with many developing economies, especially those with rich resources. American firms, however, tend to become more detached from their home economy as they expand their global operations, and relate more distantly to the policy concerns of their home government. These are shaped and articulated in decision processes which, compared with those in Japan, are highly conflicted, with short-term horizons, and with weaker institutionalized professional guidance.[29] European firms tend to have stronger home country ties than their American counterparts, but are not closely identified with European Union policies towards developing countries.

Japanese policy level and corporate engagement in industrializing East Asia has been subjected to severe strains by the 1997 financial crises. Because of the area's importance for the Japanese economy and its opportunities for more constructive and larger-scale Japanese involvement, it is likely to receive very active attention. There is wide scope for Japanese direct investment, because of the depreciation of Southeast Asian currencies and the adverse economic conditions experienced by many Southeast Asian firms. Strong intercorporate ties give Japanese firms superior capacities for collective adaptation to the economic disruptions in industrializing East Asia, and for the concerting of entrepreneurial strategies to strengthen and develop their integrated production system in the area. This collaborative involvement is effecting more potent changes in fundamentals than the smaller and less integrated pattern of US corporate activity, which is more sensitive to the area's unfavourable short-term prospects.

The adaptive capacities of Chinese firms in the area are significant because of pervasive effects on fundamentals at mainly medium technology levels in a pattern that has had weaker links with the world economy but that is less vulnerable to its stresses. The structural interdependencies resulting from the operations of these firms within that zone have considerable stability. These enterprises have very substantial potentials for partnering with the Japanese corporate presence. The development of their cross-border links with each other and of their activities in their home economies, however, continues to be hindered by administrative deficiencies in the larger ASEAN members, especially Indonesia and Thailand.[30]

American firms in industrializing East Asia have incentives to become more footloose, in search of alternative location advantages, because of uncertainties about recoveries of growth in the area and perceptions of unfavourable shifts in host country attitudes after the 1997 crises. The USA has been recognized as the main power behind IMF conditionality terms imposed on East Asian governments, and as the home country of speculators who caused volatility in ASEAN financial markets. The operations of US multinationals in industrializing East Asia are likely to be drawn selectively into global adjustment and restructuring strategies emphasizing the use of more stable location advantages. Increasing interest in the expanding although slow-growing European Union market has been evident in flows changing the US foreign direct investment position.[31]

Prospects for more productive US–Japan interactions, which had been improving gradually through exchanges within the Asia Pacific Economic Cooperation forum, have become unfavourable because of the 1997 crises. Those crises, it must be stressed, have affected vital Japanese interests, indicated requirements for more vigorous commercial involvement in industrializing East Asia, and have made aggressive penetration of the US market more imperative for effective management of that regional involvement and for growth in the home economy. The USA's regional policy is being influenced by increasing protectionist pressures, because of continuing deficits in trade with Japan, and because of surges in low-cost imports from the East Asian industrializing countries.[32]

The Association of Southeast Asian Nations, because of its weaknesses as a regional community and its lack of leadership and institutional development, has tended to become even less united because of the economic strains of its members, especially Indonesia. Individually most of its governments have looked more to Japan than to the USA for cooperation in dealing with those strains, and have thus opened the way for the development of an informal East Asian group in which Japan would be the leading partner. The dynamics of Japanese policy making, however, favour bilateral dealings with each industrializing East Asian state, which are feasible because of the disunity in ASEAN. Such interactions can facilitate further development of the integrated regional production system which Japanese firms have been establishing. Because of the increased dependence of ASEAN members on Japanese direct investment and aid, the preferences of groups of Japanese firms regarding expansion of the regional production system can be expected to receive more consideration from host governments and business communities.[33]

Fundamentals in Latin America are changing with fewer of the complexities affecting structural interdependencies in East Asia, and this is happening more under the influence of American policies and corporate strategies. US commerce with the area is at about the same level as that with industrializing Asia, but is rather balanced and is growing much faster than that with the rest of the world. The volume is much larger than Japan's, and is about double that of the European Union with Latin America. The USA's foreign direct investment position is larger than that in industrializing East Asia: in 1993 on a historical cost basis it was $101 936 million for Latin America and the western hemisphere, while that in industrializing East Asia was $38 643 million. The gross product of US nonbank majority-owned foreign affiliates as a percentage of GDP in Brazil, Mexico and Venezuela ranged between 2.6 and 2.9 per cent in 1995. These figures were similar to those for Indonesia, but below the level of Malaysia and higher than the level for Thailand.[34] The comparisons are significant because in each of those ASEAN countries there is a large Japanese corporate presence, while in the Latin American states that presence is small.

US exports to Latin America comprise principally medium and higher technology products, and are growing much faster than imports from that region, which are mostly primary products and low technology manufactures. Latin American developmental imperatives are to increase exports of medium and higher technology products. This tends to be difficult, because of the weaknesses of many Latin American firms, relatively low levels of technological competence in the region, and the consolidation of market strengths by US manufacturers through exports to and production in the area. American efforts to promote regional trade liberalization, using bargaining power based on regional market strengths and on the size of the American economy, pose problems for Latin American states seeking to protect their emerging industries.

For structural change that would facilitate progress towards balanced intraindustry trade with the USA, a major Latin American option is to increase trade and investment links with the European Union. Discussions of a free trade agreement between the European Union and Mercosur were under way in 1997, and these were especially significant because commerce within Mercosur has been growing rapidly, with increases averaging 27 per cent a year between 1990 and 1995.[35] The discussions, if leading to more active European involvement in the area, could be increasingly advantageous for growth in Mercosur, while contributing to Mercosur's expansion. Members of this major regional association and other Latin American countries would then be able to interact more effectively with the USA on issues of trade and investment liberalization, while benefiting from competition between European and American firms in the development of the area's growth potentials.

Fundamentals in the low-growth areas of South Asia and Africa, where initiatives for regional economic cooperation have been weak, are undergoing little change. Most of these underdeveloped states are small-scale exporters of primary products; they attract very little foreign direct investment, and their modest external links are mainly with the European Union. It is very difficult for most of these states to finance industrialization by increasing their export revenues, and their lack of collective bargaining strengths makes them vulnerable to northern pressures for trade liberalization. Preferential trade arrangements with the European Union have been of minor value for some of these states, mostly former French colonies. European commercial involvement in these states does little to change their marginal roles in the world economy, and is virtually unchallenged by American or Japanese intrusion.

Prospects for growth in most of the South Asian and African states, and for their adjustment to fluctuations in international primary product markets, depend very much on the development of strong systems of regional economic cooperation. The need for these is urgent, especially in Africa, where the separation of numerous small national markets from each other severely restricts growth. More active and more constructive European involvement could aid regional economic ventures in Africa and South Asia, and assist resolution of problems of governance in those areas. Such involvement, and the deeper involvement in Latin America for which there are manifest incentives, could be aided by, and could complement, a structural policy for the European Union. This is clearly needed to overcome the area's acute unemployment problems, and to establish a sound basis for microeconomic cooperation in support of macromanagement at the Union level.[36]

CONCERTING POLICIES AND ENTREPRENEURSHIP

The complex efficiency, developmental, and equity issues in north–south relations obligate some fundamental reconsideration of entrepreneurial potentials, because of the very extensive involvement of transnational enterprises operating out of the major industrialized democracies. Markets and economic structures are being transformed and linked across borders by these firms, and, while they are tending to become stateless, they have increasing scope to elicit favourable treatment of their interests by the numerous host governments which attract their direct investment. The increasing dimensions of cross-border market efficiencies and failures, evolving because of the competitive and collaborative activities of the transnational enterprises, indicate requirements for micro and macro coordination between governments that can draw entrepreneurial cooperation by international firms. This has to be affirmed with reference to the transborder obligations of governments, in conditions of globalization, which can be seen as a basis for extended accountability, especially when north–south issues are seen in the moral perspectives which are vital elements of Europe's heritage.

Entrepreneurial potentials in globalization depend increasingly on the coordination of corporate planning. In the multiplicity of national contexts in which a transnational enterprise operates there are proliferating sectoral and intersectoral interdependencies, in reciprocal causal relationships with the activities of many other transnational enterprises. The most visible interdependencies are immediate, but there are also impending interdependencies resulting from phases in the planning and implementation of strategies that are firm specific. The price signalling associated with allocative efficiencies in the linked markets provides some guidance for entrepreneurial planning, but this is mainly for the short term, and is not sufficient for significantly comprehensive coordination of future research, production, and marketing decisions. This requires high levels of intercorporate trust, and has to adjust to often unpredictable market changes and to the emergence of new technologies. Entrepreneurial coordination requirements increase as national economies become more highly industrialized and structurally more interdependent, and as the structural effects of international production become more extensive.[37]

Managerial cultures in transnational enterprises, especially those with strong global market positions, become open to alliances, especially in high technology areas, but these tend to be managed instrumentally with restricted information sharing at the planning levels. Uncertainties about the longer-term evolution of sectoral and intersectoral interdependencies thus tend to obligate cautious decision making. Uncertainties about overall economic trends, moreover, which relate to the interacting effects of macro and micro policies in numerous states, also obligate cautious entrepreneurship.

The interrelated types of uncertainties have more adverse consequences for southern firms than for northern enterprises, in a context in which the operations of the latter firms are resulting in global concentrations of market power. Southern firms, with weaker resources and less extensive international connections through networks and alliances, have to operate with greater caution, while coping with the disadvantages of inferior bargaining power in interactions with northern multinational firms and of often weaker status than those enterprises in dealings at home. Southern administrations, although generally motivated to aid their national enterprises, tend to be influenced by dependence on the attraction of northern direct investment.

To overcome the problems of slack growth and of imbalanced gains, and of substantial costs in the deepening integration processes of globalization which are of immediate concern to northern administrations, some major structural initiatives have become necessary. Northern administrations are under pressure to enhance the structural competitiveness of their economies, but individually are becoming less able to enlist cooperation from their own and foreign international firms. Meanwhile all the coordination problems affecting the operations of those firms remain serious and, indeed, may be increasing, with consequences that limit growth potentials while perpetuating many of the imbalances of concern to governments. Hence there are clear imperatives for policy-level initiatives by groups of governments to draw international managements into a broad planning consensus, as a basis for elite transnational community formation that will motivate and facilitate extensive concerted entrepreneurial collaboration.

All this can be affirmed as a response to northern aspirations for higher and more balanced, as well as more stable, growth. It can also be affirmed in a way that opens broad opportunities for southern participation, and that can inspire a strong sense of moral purpose on each side, but especially in the northern policy communities and industry groups. The rationale in terms of efficiencies is that, while gains from trade and transnational production tend to be increased by corporate specializations and economies of scale and scope as markets are linked in deepening integration, extensively concerted entrepreneurship is necessary for the gains to be optimal. They may be hindered by coordination failures, cautious decision making because of perceived uncertainties, and destructive competition. The general cultivation of a spirit of integrative cooperation, and of an atmosphere of trust, will be essential.[38]

The corporate collaboration, of course, could become collusive, and this possibility would have special significance for southern governments and firms, whose roles in the international structural cooperation would be inferior, because of technocratic weaknesses and low levels of corporate development. Guidance functions assumed by northern administrations would thus be of vital importance for interdependent growth of a kind that would become more balanced through complementary southern industrial development. The scale of the intended entrepreneurial cooperation, it can be argued, would exceed the monitoring and guidance capacities of participating governments, and their preferences would undoubtedly not be harmonized. Moreover, consultations between them could be expected to lag behind the collaborative corporate planning processes which those consultations would be intended to assist. Further, changes in the composition and policies of those administrations would pose repeated problems of policy coordination.

To cope with these problems the promotion of north–south complementarities could be planned in regional contexts, with a focus on higher technology sectors, and with a special role for the European Commission, as a technocratic structure functioning on a stable basis, with considerable accumulated expertise. The European Commission is well placed to sponsor direct investment planning conferences for structural policy experts and representatives of northern and southern firms. In terms of European interests the appropriate regional contexts would be Latin America and Africa, and in Latin America especially the Commission's sponsoring role could be very significant as a means of opening up opportunities for diversification of the area's foreign economic relations. Collaboration between the Commission and the US Department of Commerce in sponsoring the proposed conferences could be highly productive, through synergies in the deployment of expertise, if there was a shared political will to engage in integrative partnering with Latin American economies.

In East Asia the political and economic context is less favourable for involvement by the European Commission but is advantageous for Japan's Ministry of International Trade and Industry. A very active sponsoring role in regional direct investment conferences would be possible for that Ministry, but would tend to be managed in intense rivalry with US participants. This could have some advantages for representatives from industrializing East Asia, but would limit the development of overall regional complementarities.

An extremely important supplementary function for Japanese participants could be structural policy advising for governments in industrializing East Asia, to ensure progress in outward-oriented industrialization, with protection of emerging industries and the guidance of domestic savings into the funding of those industries. Such structural policy advising would be vital for strong recoveries from the 1997 disruptions of East Asian financial markets. The basic logic of this advising would go against prescriptions for economic liberalization firmly advocated by the US administration and international lending agencies, but would accord with the preferences of governments in industrializing East Asia that wish to see substantially self-reliant growth.[39]

The structural policy advising need not conflict with the broadly collaborative objectives of the regional direct investment conferences. It could be made clear that longer-term southern complementarity with the north, at higher growth levels, would be aided by the collaborative linking of northern corporate investment strategies with southern structural policies aligned with the developmental interests of southern firms. Clear and persuasive articulation of the Japanese structural logic, it must be stressed, has become necessary for East Asian economic recoveries and for effective management of Japan's structural interdependencies in the area. For industrializing East Asian states there is no viable alternative to adoption of this structural logic, and it can be presented on the basis of comparative studies, notably those by the United Nations Conference on Trade and Development.[40]

American policy-level and corporate involvement in the East Asian direct investment conferencing, although it could begin with an orientation opposed to Japan's, could become adaptable through policy learning and corporate learning, related in part to problems of coordination in the home economy, and to the costs imposed on it by globalization. These costs are significant because the coordination problems hinder adaptation for the tasks of managing the nation's rising structural interdependencies, so as to achieve higher and more balanced growth. Coordination achievements at home, bringing competitive practices into patterns of integrative cooperation, and thus concerting entrepreneurship on a long-term basis, for more friendly alliance capitalism, would aid the development of partnering relationships with industrializing East Asia and with Japan.[41]

The European, Japanese and American partnering, while distinctive in regional patterns, could develop as a new form of international alliance capitalism. The most common meaning of this term refers to the compulsions of firms to collaborate in groups, in order to enhance their efficiencies through reciprocally functional specializations, in the expectation of mutual gains that would not be attainable through less coordinated operations and certainly not through totally competitive strategies. Alliance capitalism has a more specific connotation, referring to the stable relational links between firms in the Japanese intercorporate system, and between that system and the major economic ministries of the home economy. In the East Asian, Latin American, and other regional contexts, alliance capitalism can take on a richer meaning through the international concerting of entrepreneurship and policies which would open up opportunities for increasing participation by southern firms and governments.

European, Japanese and American collaboration in the development of a rationale for international alliance capitalism and for its implementation would open up opportunities for higher interdependent north–south growth. This could help resolve problems of governance in third world countries, through the effects of new forms of external accountability, the emergence of cross-border forms of interest aggregation, increased policy-level communication flows, and the synergies induced through trust and goodwill. Southern capacities to make effective responses would be weak, and would remain weak for considerable periods, but could be expected to improve as the constructive external involvement continued. For the northern countries, coping with slow growth because of their declining and ageing populations and the costs of their own problems of governance, the benefits of more extensively productive southern involvement would tend to become more significant. Much, then, will depend on the extent to which northern goodwill can develop and be concerted at the policy and corporate levels.

PROSPECTS

The distinctive patterns of north–south economic relations must be expected to remain primarily regional, because of continuity in investment and trade flows dominated by northern multinationals and the slow widening of the scope for southern corporate and policy initiatives. Northern international firms will undoubtedly acquire wider scope for entrepreneurial innovations, aided and hindered by the mixed effects of northern policies. Policy learning by northern decision makers, strongly influenced by pressing domestic concerns, related especially to the costs of globalization, the costs of macromanagement, and slack internal demand, may not be adequate for the development of more productive and more balanced complementarities with industrializing states.

Industrializing East Asia will almost certainly continue to be the most active area of competitive northern involvement, with very significant consequences for world growth. Japan's superior capacities for systemic adaptation and development will probably have decisive structural effects throughout the area, under stimulus from the less patterned forms of American and European corporate and government activity. The formative influences of northern systems of corporate governance will have further effects, especially in the configuration of Japanese multinational involvement. Contrasts in northern structural policy capabilities will no doubt also be evident, with Japanese advantages based on the national system of alliance capitalism tending to become more decisive for structural competitiveness. American policy will tend to be the main source of pressure for the adoption of market-based systems of corporate governance, resisted with indirect Japanese support by South Korea, Taiwan, Malaysia and Indonesia.

US–Japanese policy-level and corporate cooperation, with substantial benefits for industrializing East Asia, will probably be very difficult to promote through initiatives from either side or within that area, but could develop with very active European promotion. The high growth potential in East Asia is a powerful incentive for deepening European involvement. This could develop with policy-level initiatives based in part on German concepts of economic order that could have increasing influence in the European Union's external relations, especially with reference to problems of interdependent European growth and the management of the European Monetary Union's role in the global monetary system, which will require much cooperation with Japan. There is a configuration of vast structural interdependencies which demand a vision for structuring international alliance capitalism in line with the common good of northern and southern economies, linking them in deepening dynamic integration.[42]

More positive external formative influences on China's political and economic evolution would be in prospect with the new triadic alliance capitalism that can be hoped for. The Chinese authorities have been confronted with requirements for strong internal economic order, especially in the financial sector, since the 1997 disruptions of East Asian markets. Liberalization under pressure from the USA and international lending agencies is now clearly seen to have hazards that could reduce the regime's scope for an effective structural policy. The implications of these hazards, moreover, have become evident for Chinese decision makers studying the problems of transitional economies in Eastern Europe.

Latin America, continuing to rank next after industrializing East Asia in the north–south dimension of the world economy, will remain a less contested and less dynamic area of triadic involvement. The Japanese focus on East Asia will entail less active interest in Latin America, and European interest in East Asia will tend to increase as its economies recover. If Euro–Japanese–US cooperation develops in industrializing East Asia, however, this could lead to similar collaboration in Latin America, especially if Mercosur becomes a more vigorous regional economic association. The record of regional cooperation in Latin America does not encourage this, but it could develop in response to European initiatives.

South Asia and Africa will clearly be much less contested areas of northern involvement, with accumulated growth problems because of market fragmentation, acute social cleavages, and severe administrative failures. Dependence on exports of primary products and low technology manufactures must be expected to be prolonged in these areas because of the difficulties of overcoming northern discriminatory trade policies and of enhancing location advantages for the attraction of foreign investment into manufacturing at higher technological levels. Enlightened northern entrepreneurship directed towards these areas, it is to be hoped, will have a quality of mercy, evolving out of high-principled concerns that will be active in the less imbalanced partnering that can be envisaged for East Asia and Latin America.

In the longer term the alliance capitalism developing through Japanese, European, and American collaboration could ensure increasing stability in a global pattern of north–south interdependencies, with higher and more equally shared growth. The heavy adjustment functions which the International Monetary Fund has had to assume in Latin America and East Asia during the 1990s could thus become less necessary. This would be all the more probable if the triadic alliance capitalism assisted sound development in the financial sectors of East Asian and Latin American countries for the funding of national industries, rather than for outflows of investment into the vast rent-seeking operations of international financial markets.

The triadic alliance capitalism could assume further significance as a source of discipline in US financial markets. Speculation in US stock markets was at unsustainable levels when the 1997 financial crises occurred in East Asia, and the danger of a fall, to which the East Asian problems could contribute, was evident. A reorientation of US entrepreneurial energies towards more productive operations, which could be associated with triadic initiatives in the north–south context, could reduce the excessive speculation in the American economy. This must be said with emphasis in view of the strains which the USA may experience as the formation of the European Monetary Union drastically alters the role of the US currency in world financial markets.

NOTES

1. A major consequence of the shared preferences has been diminishing US and European interest in reducing restrictions on imports of third world textiles and clothing. See Laura Baughman, Rolf Mirus, Morris E. Morkre and Dean Spinanger, 'Of tyre cords, ties and tents: window dressing in the ATC?', *The World Economy*, **20** (4) July 1997, 407–34.
2. See comments in Danny M. Leipziger, Claudio Frischtak, Homi J. Kharas and John F. Normand, 'Mercosur: integration and industrial policy', *The World Economy*, **20** (5) August 1997, 585–604, and Prem-Chandra Athukorala and Jayant Menon, 'AFTA

242 *Structural change and cooperation*

and the investment–trade Nexus in ASEAN', *The World Economy*, **20** (2) March 1997.

3. See Baughman and others (op. cit., note 1).
4. On the problems in East Asia see Andrew MacIntyre (ed.), *Business and Government in Industrializing Asia* (Ithaca: Cornell University Press, 1994). On problems of political development in Latin America see Scott Mainwaring and Timothy R. Scully (eds), *Building Democratic Institutions: Party Systems in Latin America* (Stanford: Stanford University Press, 1995).
5. For an initial review of the problems see Steven Radelet and Jeffrey Sachs, 'Asia's reemergence', *Foreign Affairs*, **76** (6) November–December 1997, 44–59.
6. See symposium in *World Development*, **22** (4) April 1994.
7. See Dani Rodrik, *Has Globalization Gone Too Far?* (Washington DC: Institute for International Economics, 1997).
8. See comments on the influence of cultures and systems of corporate governance in Louis W. Pauly and Simon Reich, 'National structures and multinational corporate behaviour: enduring differences in the age of globalization', *International Organization*, **51** (1) Winter 1997, 1–30.
9. On the Japanese policy orientation's internal dynamics see Michael Gerlach, *Alliance Capitalism: The Social Organization of Japanese Business* (Berkeley: University of California Press, 1992).
10. See Alexis Jacquemin, 'Towards an internationalization of competition policy', *The World Economy*, **18** (6) November 1995, 781–90.
11. See Mark L. Clifford, *Troubled Tiger: Businessmen, Bureaucrats, and Generals in South Korea* (Armonk: M.E. Sharpe, 1994), and Hyung-Koo Lee, *The Korean Economy* (Albany: State University of New York Press, 1996). See also comments in Radelet and Sachs (op. cit., note 5).
12. See reflections on the effects of market economies in Amitai Etzioni, *The Moral Dimension: Toward a New Economics* (New York: Free Press, 1988).
13. See MacIntyre (op. cit., note 4); Hal Hill, *The Indonesian Economy since 1966* (Cambridge: Cambridge University Press, 1996); and Jorge I. Dominguez and Abraham F. Lowenthal (eds), *Constructing Democratic Governance* (Baltimore: Johns Hopkins University Press, 1996).
14. See Clifford (op. cit., note 11), and Lee (op. cit., note 11).
15. See foreign direct investment figures for ASEAN in Chia Siow Yue, 'Regionalism and subregionalism in ASEAN: the free trade area and growth triangle models', in Takatoshi Ito and Anne O. Krueger (eds), *Regionalism versus Multilateral Trade Arrangements* (Chicago: University of Chicago Press, 1997) chapter 10.
16. See references to this problem in Michael Hobday, *Innovation in East Asia: The Challenge to Japan* (Aldershot: Edward Elgar, 1995).
17. See Hal Hill (op. cit., note 13).
18. See Hobday (op. cit., note 16), and Robert Taylor, *Greater China and Japan: Prospects for an Economic Partnership in East Asia* (London: Routledge, 1996).
19. See Patricia Gray Rich, 'Latin America and present US trade policy', *The World Economy*, **20** (1) January 1997, 87–102.
20. Ibid.
21. See Frederique Sachwald (ed.), *European Integration and Competitiveness: Acquisitions and Alliances in Industry* (Aldershot: Edward Elgar, 1993).
22. See Rich (op. cit., note 19) on achievements in trade expansion.
23. See *Trade and Development Report, 1997* (New York and Geneva: United Nations Conference on Trade and Development, 1997).
24. See references to northern discriminatory practices in *Linkages: OECD and Major Developing Economies* (Paris: OECD, 1995).
25. See brief references to this problem in Richard Blackhurst, 'The WTO and the global economy', *The World Economy*, **20** (5) August 1997, 527–44.
26. See comments on the problems for industrializing East Asian states in Hobday (op. cit., note 16).

27. See *Linkages* (op. cit., note 24), chapter 3.
28. On this solidarity see Gerlach (op. cit., note 9).
29. See discussion of trade policy in Charles K. Rowley, Willem Thorbecke and Richard E. Wagner, *Trade Protection in the United States* (Aldershot: Edward Elgar, 1995).
30. See Hal Hill (op. cit., note 13), and MacIntyre (op. cit., note 4).
31. See Russell B. Scholl, 'The international investment position of the United States in 1996', *Survey of Current Business*, **77** (7) July 1997, 24–33, and Sylvia E. Bargas, 'Direct investment positions for 1996', ibid., 34–55.
32. Sharp currency depreciations made exports from industrializing East Asia highly competitive in late 1997 and early 1998.
33. Japanese official aid has assumed special significance as a supplement to assistance from the IMF for industrializing East Asian states.
34. See Raymond J. Mataloni, 'US multinational companies: operations in 1995', *Survey of Current Business*, **77** (10) October 1997, 44–68.
35. See Rich (op. cit., note 19).
36. On the orientation of EU policies and the difficulties of forming a common structural policy see Giandomenico Majone, 'From the positive to the regulatory state: causes and consequences of changes in the mode of governance', *Journal of Public Policy*, **17** (2) May–August 1997, 139–67.
37. See comments on coordination problems in the USA in Frederic L. Pryor, *Economic Evolution and Structure: The Impact of Complexity on the US Economic System* (New York: Cambridge University Press, 1996).
38. The importance of trust for the generation of entrepreneurial synergies has been well demonstrated in Japan. For observations on leadership requirements see Rabindra N. Kanungo and Manuel Mendonca, *Ethical Dimensions of Leadership* (Thousand Oaks: SAGE, 1996).
39. For discreet comments on the risks of financial liberalization see Stanley Fischer, *Capital Account Liberalization and the Role of the IMF* (Washington DC: International Monetary Fund, 1997).
40. See *Trade and Development Report, 1997*, (op. cit., note 23).
41. This observation is based on comments about coordination problems in Pryor (op. cit., note 37).
42. The necessary perspective could develop partly on the basis of the principles of cooperation advocated in Robert Z. Lawrence, Albert Bressand and Takatoshi Ito, *A Vision for the World Economy* (Washington DC: Brookings Institution, 1996).

10. Corporate strategies and the environment*

Alan M. Rugman

1. INTRODUCTION

Today international firms must have in place a strategy to deal with environmental regulations. This requires that managers understand the political and legal process by which environmental regulations are drawn up and implemented, including the interactive lobbying between business, governments, bureaucracies, and environmental non-governmental organizations (ENGOs). In this chapter, building upon work in Rugman, Kirton and Soloway (1997), we examine the interactive roles of governments and firms, using insights from the relevant fields of economics, strategy, politics and law. Not all of these fields can be accorded equal treatment, instead the most relevant ideas will be used. A framework is proposed in which the manager is the focus of attention and emphasis is upon firm-level strategic decision making rather than government policy making.

In Section 2 we set the stage for this chapter by reviewing economic theory on the environment as a public good and how the multinational enterprises (MNEs) can act as an internalizer to overcome market imperfection in the environment. In Section 3 we examine the relationship between the strength of government-imposed environmental regulations and the firm's responsiveness to them. Initially, we use the resulting matrix (Figure 10.1) to position the key international organizations across these two dimensions, including the environmental provisions of the North American Free Trade Agreement (NAFTA). NAFTA is the first international trade agreement to explicitly incorporate environmental issues, and to establish a bureaucracy to

* Research assistance has been provided by Julie Soloway of the Centre of International Studies at the University of Toronto. She is the primary contributor of materials in Section 4 of this chapter. Financial assistance has been provided by the Social Sciences and Humanities Research Council of Canada. This chapter was drafted while Professor Rugman was at the Joseph L. Rotman School of Management, University of Toronto.

administer trade and environment interaction, primarily through the NAFTA Commission on Environmental Cooperation (CEC). NAFTA and the CEC can be seen as benchmarks for analysis of other international environmental organizations and agreements, which we discuss in Section 4.

In Section 5, we develop a matrix in which managers can determine the appropriate choice of strategy in response to globalization and environmental pressures. Here globalization pressures represent a shorthand way of capturing the basic economics-driven generic strategies of cost, differentiation and focus (Porter 1980). To these, we add a 'green' corporate strategy, under which firms can develop managerially-based skills in environmental awareness and environmental management systems (EMS). Such skills can yield competitive advantage over firms which ignore environmental issues. At one extreme a 'green alone' strategy, conceptually, can be good enough for a firm to outcompete other firms on the environmental dimension alone. However, in most cases firms will seek to develop a mix of conventional economics-based and new green competitive advantages. In Section 6 we discuss the argument that Mexico is a pollution haven.

As a special case of the corporate strategy matrix (Figure 10.2) we discuss in Section 7 the environmental argument of Michael Porter (1990) as refined by Porter and Van der Linde (1995). Porter argues that tight home government environmental regulations will force domestically-based firms to develop a 'green' strategy. In time, firms with a strong home base can use their environmentally-based skills to take products and services to new foreign markets, in which they will enjoy a competitive advantage over other firms which were not forced to become green. We find that Porter's argument is correct for triad-based firms, but not for firms from smaller countries. The latter firms rely on market access to triad economies and they need to respond to host country environmental regulations rather than home country ones.

2. ECONOMIC THEORY, MNEs AND ENVIRONMENTAL ISSUES

While the issues of trade and the environment are multidisciplinary, this chapter uses a corporate strategy approach rather than an economics or public policy approach. Thus we note but do not focus on economics-based issues of whether the environment is or is not a public good, the pricing of externalities, costs of pollution, and so on. Nor do we consider potentially broader public policy issues relating to the interaction of

MNEs with governments, except in the area of environmental regulations. We consider only tangentially (in Sections 6 and 7) how MNEs may potentially change location decisions based on weak or strong environmental regulations, as in the pollution-haven case and in the Porter case of strong domestic environmental regulations.

In order to place this research in context we do conduct (in Sections 3 and 4) a detailed review and synthesis of all major existing national and international environmental regulations, in order to examine their interaction with firm-level strategy. To facilitate this we develop a new conceptual framework to analyse government-level and firm-level interaction.

Hoekman and Kostecki (1995) argue that the world trading system (GATT–WTO) is unlikely to develop a set of global rules for environmental issues. This conclusion is based on a conceptual framework which relates forces favouring global norms to forces favouring diversity. They state that environmental issues fall into a quadrant of weak global norms and strong national diversity. Due to major differences across countries in their approach to environmental regulations, global standardization will not be possible. Perhaps minimum standards may be accepted and general principles developed, as occurred in NAFTA (Rugman, Kirton and Soloway 1997). Related work, by Lundan (1997), supports the basic premises of this chapter, namely that improvements in environmental standards will arise due to the strategies of MNEs, rather than to national policies or multilateral environmental regulations.

A basic issue to clarify is the notion that the environment is, in the terminology of economics, a 'public good'. By a public good is meant a good whose consumption by one party does not deny consumption by others. Examples would be the air, which everyone could breathe, or knowledge, to which everyone should have access. In a sense the environment can be viewed as a public good, but only if there are no externalities. In reality the environment is not a public good due to the existence of externalities, such as inadequate (or non-existent) pricing mechanisms which lead to overconsumption of the 'global commons'.

As is well known in transaction cost economics the mechanism to overcome such types of market failure is to allocate property rights, that is, ownership. If knowledge is a public good it will be underproduced, because firms and inventors cannot earn any return on a zero-priced good. Thus, ownership of knowledge (in the form of patents, copyrights, licences or other types of proprietary control) will overcome this externality. In an international dimension the MNE can be an internalizer whose organizational structure overcomes the externality of knowledge as a public good (Rugman 1981). Similarly, if consumption of the environment is excessive the demand can be reduced by allocation of private property rights. Thus the owner of natural resources will have a vested self-interest in conservation and long-term sustainability. In some political and economic systems the state may be able to exercise ownership of key aspects of the environment, but in most Western democracies the government is subject to the power of lobbies, resulting in a suboptimal administration of environmental regulations.

In this chapter it is not realistic to proceed with the assumption that the environment is a public good. Most of the evidence of the pollution of the global commons and the overuse of forests, other natural resources, the oceans, and so on, points towards a host of externalities and related market failures. As has been demonstrated elsewhere (Rugman 1981, 1996), in the face of natural market imperfections for knowledge an efficient response has been the development of MNEs as hierarchical organizations. Similarly, the environmental externalities can best be analysed by the use of predictions from transaction cost economics, for example that property rights in firms will help alleviate pollution costs and other environmental externalities. At the very least, the role of the MNE as a vehicle for the reduction of environmental market imperfections needs to be taken seriously in research.

This focus on the MNE as an internalizer of environmental market imperfections will clash with stakeholder theory. In stakeholder theory, the MNE needs to consider and weigh the relative views of customers, employees, society and other groups. Yet in a strict transaction cost economics approach the MNE is the driver of environmental efficiency, not the other stakeholders with their interests in equity and distribution. If environmental market failure is an issue of inefficiency, and the MNE as an internalizer is an efficient alternative to market failure, then the stakeholder focus on equity is not appropriate. Consequently the stakeholder approach is not pursued, and the efficiency aspects of corporate strategy are emphasized in this chapter.

3. ENVIRONMENTAL REGULATIONS AND CORPORATE STRATEGY

In Figure 10.1 we depict the relationship between corporate strategy and environmental regulations. On the vertical axis we place the firm's responsiveness to environmental regulations, either weak or strong. This axis builds on a previous discussion in Rugman (1995). On the horizontal axis we place the strength of environmental regulations imposed

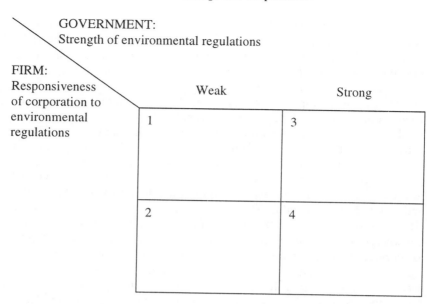

Figure 10.1   Positioning of international environmental organizations

by governments, either weak or strong. This axis incorporates ideas in Rugman and Verbeke (1994). Several insights can be gained into the trade and environment literature by the use of this matrix. We shall focus on two: first, an application to describe the type of international environmental agreements in place. This is done here and in Section 3. Second, a more specific application to corporate strategy. This is done in Sections 4 and 5.

In Figure 10.1, the major international environmental agreements can be classified as follows:

Quadrant 1:   OECD non-binding environmental regulations, policies and principles.

Quadrant 2:   International organizations with weak enforcement provisions, for example, UNCED's Rio Declaration of 1992.

Quadrant 3:   The environmental standards of the EU, and its 'eco-labels'. Multilateral Environmental Agreements (MEAs) with strong enforcement provisions, such as the Montreal Protocol.

Quadrant 4:   NAFTA and the CEC. GATT/WTO trade disciplines on environmental regulations.

The positioning of these international agreements requires further explanation. In the remainder of this section we shall highlight the key provisions in each agreement which determine placement in the matrix. In the next section we shall explore the legal and institutional details of these organizations in greater detail.

The environmental measures of the OECD are in quadrant 1 of Figure 10.1. The OECD cannot enact binding environmental regulations on its members, yet its recommendations about environmental policy are extremely influential with firms, who see the OECD as setting benchmarks for international business. For example, multinational enterprises (MNEs) have been highly responsive to the OECD's investment codes (Safarian 1993; Rugman and Gestrin 1997). Thus, these MNEs can be expected to respond relatively strongly to OECD environmental regulations, even though the latter are weaker than conventional government-imposed regulations.

International organizations with weak enforcement provisions are found in quadrant 2 of Figure 10.1, as firms will not adjust their strategy to respond to such regulation. For example, while the United Nations Conference on Environment and Development (UNCED) has promoted international environmental concerns, as evidenced by the attendance of over 100 heads of state at the Rio Summit's Earth Day in 1992, it cannot directly make or enforce laws.

NAFTA is in quadrant 4 of Figure 10.1, rather than in quadrant 1, since there is, as yet, no effective institutional mechanism to force compliance of companies with the new and relatively strong environmental provisions of NAFTA. If the CEC were to become an effective bureaucracy, with active dispute settlement procedures and active investigations to prevent trade-related environmental disputes (as its mandate permits), then NAFTA would move from quadrant 4 to quadrant 3. To date, there is no evidence to support the placement of NAFTA in quadrant 3, since the CEC is not seeking to investigate and mediate the 24 trade-related environmental disputes identified in Vogel and Rugman (1997).

In contrast to NAFTA, the EU has a stronger bureaucracy to enforce its environmental regulations, placing it in quadrant 3 of Figure 10.1. The EU 'eco-labels' are in quadrant 3 since these are enforced by the strong Brussels bureaucracy. The eco-labels can even be used as a barrier to entry against foreign firms (Rugman 1995; Vogel 1995). Similarly, MEAs such as the Montreal Protocol are in quadrant 3 as the signing governments take measures to force compliance by their domestic firms, through domestic legislation. Other MEAs with trade-related environmental measures (TREMs) which may be in quadrant 3 include the Basel Convention on Hazardous Wastes (1989) and the convention on the International Trade in Endangered Species (CITES) (1973).

4. LEGAL AND INSTITUTIONAL ASPECTS OF ENVIRONMENTAL REGULATIONS

The positioning of key international organizations in Figure 10.1 is strongly influenced by the precise legal nature of the environmental regulation under consideration and the institutional process by which it was made at the international and domestic levels. In this section we turn to a more detailed discussion of the legal nature of environmental regulations and related policies, as they are positioned in Figure 10.1, and how they will thereby affect trade and corporate strategy.

The European Union (EU)

The EU has strengthened its commitment to environmental regulation and enforcement with each successive change to the Treaty of Rome. Prior to 1987, there were no explicit legal provisions dealing with Community environmental concerns. There are now provisions which require the Commission to establish and enforce a high level of protection for the environment and for human health. The Maastricht Treaty established a clear environmental legal framework in Title XVI of the Treaty of Rome, signalling the need to combine free trade objectives with environmental protection (Richardson 1992). The European Court of Justice also plays a role in enforcing EU environmental law (Somsen 1996), placing the EU in quadrant 3 of Figure 10.1 Eco-labelling is administered in the EU (and in almost all developed countries) on a country-by-country basis. Germany has 'Die Groene Punkt' and the Blue Angel which are strong and effective indicators of the 'environmental soundness' of a product. Denmark has passed strong eco-labelling requirements as well. The EU has increased enforcement of its environmental agenda through the Single European Act and the 1992 amendments.

NAFTA

The NAFTA is the first multilateral trade agreement ever to incorporate sustainable development principles and objectives formally in both its preamble and its articles. Article 1114 of NAFTA expressly prohibits a party from voluntarily lowering its national environmental standards for the purpose of encouraging investment in polluting industries. Chapters seven and nine of NAFTA impose disciplines on the use of standards-related measures. Both of these chapters allow member countries to establish appropriate levels of environmental protection in accordance with transparency-oriented risk assessment.

An environmental standard that discriminates may be permitted if it meets the conditions set out in the environmental provisions of NAFTA. Parties to the NAFTA agreement have the right to adopt standards-related measures at the level of protection they deem appropriate, including measures which relate to the protection of the environment (broadly defined here to include human, animal and plant life and health). Parties further have the right to restrict trade in goods or services that do not comply with those measures (Article 904(1)). These provisions follow the Canada–United States Free Trade Agreement (FTA) and the work of the General Agreement on Tariffs and Trade (GATT) in the area of standards-related measures.

The side agreement to NAFTA, the North American Agreement on Environmental Cooperation, established an environmental institutional framework including the CEC and a council comprising the party's three environment ministers. The functions of the CEC include the evaluation of complaints by individuals and ENGOs about a party's failure to enforce its environmental laws. This provision has been used to challenge logging practices in the US national forests, a new cruise ship pier development in Cozumel, and the protection of migratory bird wetlands in Alberta. The CEC's functions include the consideration of issues pertaining to the compatibility of environmental regulations and standards as well as problems hindering resolution of environment-related trade disputes. The inability of the CEC and council to take action on relevant issues places NAFTA in quadrant 4 of Figure 10.1.

GATT/WTO

Article XX of the GATT provides exceptions from the application of the GATT provisions for acts designed to protect human, animal or plant life or health and the conservation of exhaustible natural resources. Article XX has been the subject of considerable jurisprudence. Like NAFTA, GATT imposes trade disciplines on the use of environmental measures. The World Trade Organization (WTO) established two additional agreements: an agreement on sanitary and phytosanitary barriers to trade (the SPS agreement) and an agreement on technical barriers to trade (the TBT agreement). Both of these agreements limit the way in which countries can set standards-related measures. While these represent strong environmental regulations, enforcement is weak and firms do not need to comply. The GATT/ WTO measures are thus in quadrant 4 of Figure 10.1. The WTO may play a bigger future role in this area. The GATT established a Committee on Trade and the Environment (CTE) in April 1995 to study trade and environmental measures, and to promote sustainable development (Makuch 1996).

OECD

The OECD is primarily a research organization but it also serves as a business secretariat. It first created a committee on the environment in 1970. The OECD makes recommendations which are binding for those states which accept them (Somsen 1996). The OECD is influential in the development of national and international environmental law, and is therefore in quadrant 1 of Figure 10.1. An example is the polluter pays principle, which was first elaborated by OECD and has subsequently became a key part of environmental policy at the EU. Additional fundamental principles first developed by OECD include those of consultation, the precautionary principle, non-discrimination and equal access to justice (Somsen 1996). Detailed standards which developed under the OECD include: the management of hazardous waste, transfrontier air pollution, beverage containers and recycling of paper. The OECD also established the International Energy Agency and the Nuclear Energy Agency. Further, the OECD and its member states participate in ongoing exchange, thereby influencing each other's policy. For example, in 1991, the Canadian government formed an Interdepartmental Committee on Trade and the Environment, involving seven departments, to help formulate its policies for the OECD. Additionally, Canada's OECD delegation maintains regular contact with interested ENGOs (Kirton 1992).

Multilateral Environmental Treaties (MEAs)

There are over 107 MEAs in existence today, but only about twenty of these have trade-restricting provisions. Three MEAs that contain or could promote trade-related environmental measures (TREMs) are:

Montreal Protocol on substances that deplete the ozone layer (1987). This agreement is designed to discourage free riders by penalizing non-parties by placing restrictions on their access to foreign markets. There are over 136 signatories representing 99 per cent of the world's population. All major producers of ozone-depleting substances are parties to the treaty.

Basel convention on the movement of hazardous wastes (1989). Noncompliance with prior informed consent provisions can result in a ban on the importation of hazardous waste.

Convention on the International Trade in Endangered Species (CITES) (1973). Prohibits trade in endangered species through the use of import and export permits.

Responsiveness at the firm level to environmental regulations is really a function of the political will behind an agreement and its provisions to enforce and monitor compliance. MEAs with strong enforcement provisions will then elicit the greatest response from corporations either through pressure from their national governments or for competitive reasons (market access). Therefore, effective TREMs can be found in quadrant 3 of Figure 10.1, while other MEAs without solid enforcement provisions can be found in quadrant 2 of Figure 10.1. The 1994 International Tropical Timber Agreement is an example of an MEA with weak enforcement provisions. Violations are referred to a council of parties to the agreement, although reviews usually do not lead to action due to the consensual procedures that are required before action can be taken (Koskenniemi 1996). The placement of MEAs in Figure 10.1 depends on enforcement. In some cases, where a secretariat is established, implementation and compliance can be monitored. For example, CITES establishes a secretariat which has the power to seek information and prepare reports on implementation of the convention and on any violation it has found. Parties to CITES can then recommend sanctions against the state (Burhenne 1996). Thus CITES, the Montreal Protocol and the Basel Convention are all in quadrant 3 of Figure 10.1.

The Montreal Protocol provides an example of the importance of domestic institutional structure for effective environmental regulation. International treaties need to be implemented through domestic legislation in order to become really effective. The Montreal Protocol has three parts: (i) it requires parties to significantly reduce consumption and production of chlorofluorocarbons (CFCs); (ii) it promotes technical cooperation; (iii) it imposes trade restrictions on non-parties. CFCs are man-made products and have a wide variety of industrial applications such as aerosol manufacturing, coolants, electronic solvents, synthetic foams, industrial cleaning agents and insulating materials. This will affect manufacturers of car seat cushions, refrigerators, air conditioners, microchips and hospital equipment (Renzulli 1991).

EU implementation
On 16 September 1987, the EC was among the 26 parties that signed the Montreal Protocol. The Council of the European Communities adopted the exact terms of the Montreal Protocol by enacting Regulation No. 3322/88 in October 1988. There have been subsequent revisions which strengthen the Montreal Protocol. In 1990, the EU and 92 other countries agreed to eliminate CFCs and to reduce production of other ozone depleting chemicals by the year 2000. The EU has implemented this legislation through a variety of measures. Germany requires its manufacturers to switch to environmentally safer substitutes more rapidly than in other jurisdictions. This may give German firms a competitive advantage over firms taking longer to adjust, by keeping them out of the German market (Renzulli 1991). In contrast, Spain is having trouble meeting the target set by the EU.

US implementation
The Montreal Protocol is implemented through the US Clean Air Act. Its provisions apply to any individual, corporate or government entity that produces, imports, or exports the controlled substances. These entities must file reports and records required for compliance determinations with the Administrator of the Environmental Protection Agency. On 6 February 1992, the US Senate passed a proposal to cease the production of ozone depleting chemicals by a vote of 96–0.

Canada's implementation
Under the Green Plan which controls ozone depleting substances, regulatory controls will be accelerated, support recovery and recycling of CFCs will be established, and Environment Canada will verify the effectiveness of the control effort. *The Code of Practice for Reducing CFC Emissions from Refrigeration and Air Conditioning Systems* is being widely distributed to Canadian industry due to a joint federal–provincial effort which focuses on these industries, where more than 50 per cent of all CFCs are used. By June 1991, the consumption of CFCs was 45 per cent lower than in 1986 (Raiczyck 1991).

5. CORPORATE STRATEGY WITH GLOBALIZATION AND ENVIRONMENTAL PRESSURES

The full force of corporate strategy cannot be captured in Figure 10.1 alone. A firm is driven by motives of survival, profitability and growth

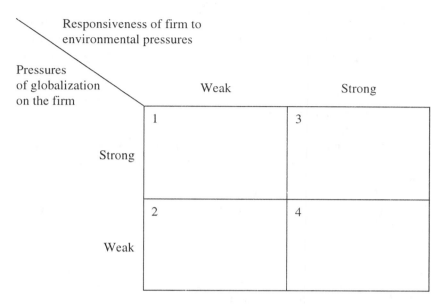

Figure 10.2   Corporate strategy with globalization and environmental pressures

so it needs to pay attention to a large set of economic drivers, as well as to environmental pressures. In order to build a more realistic picture of corporate strategy we need to relate the economic-driven pressures of globalization to environmental pressures, and deduce a series of possible strategies for firms to follow. This is done in Figure 10.2.

In Figure 10.2, on the vertical axis, the economics-driven issue of globalization is captured. From the viewpoint of a senior manager, corporate strategy needs to take into account these pressures of globalization, weak or strong. A strong degree of globalization pressure means the need to achieve economies of scale in order to be a cost leader and compete according to the first of the three generic strategies of Porter (1980). The others are to differentiate the produce or to find a global niche. The horizontal axis of Figure 10.2 is essentially the same as the vertical axis of Figure 10.1, namely the responsiveness of the firm to environmental pressures, weak or strong. It is necessary to move this environmentally-driven axis to the horizontal axis of Figure 10.2 in order to build upon the now conventional work on corporate strategy and globalization by Bartlett and Ghoshal (1989). Figure 10.2 is a relatively simple modification of their globalization–national responsiveness matrix and it has been explored previously by Rugman (1995), where applications were made to the Canadian forest product sectors.

Based on Figure 10.2, the four types of corporate strategies that can be developed are as follows:

Quadrant 1:   conventional globalization-driven three generic strategies of cost, differentiation and focus (Porter 1980, 1990) where environmental regulations are totally ignored.

Quadrant 2:   uncompetitive, large, domestic firms who are restructuring and exiting or domestic small and medium-sized firms which can ignore both globalization and environmental pressures.

Quadrant 3:   firms which conduct joint economic and environmental strategies. These firms are more than in compliance with environmental regulations; they anticipate environmental regulations and are first movers in turning them into competitive advantages, just as they do the globalization pressures.

Quadrant 4:   a 'green alone' firm, which can beat other firms with a pure environmental strategy, ignoring globalization pressures entirely. Here the firm is 'environmentally responsive' which is a similar concept to the potential advantage of being 'nationally responsive' in the framework of Bartlett and Ghoshal (1989). This is a type of resource-based managerial skill first identified by Penrose (1959) and it is consistent with the resource-based view of the firm (Rumelt 1984; Barney 1991; Conner 1991). To be successful in quadrant 4, the firm must anticipate environmental regulations such that it can beat the average competitor on its environmental skills alone. A similar managerial skill is required in quadrant 3. It is pretty obvious that relatively few firms have yet developed such skills, whereas they are all aware of the generic strategies.

ISO 14000

One significant firm-level response to the increase in international government regulation has been the development of ISO 14000. Flowing from the regulation of national governments and bodies like the OECD, this is a joint public–private sector initiative which seeks to rectify the increasing problems of disparate environmental standards. The International Organization for Standardization (ISO), with members in over 50 nations, is developing a set of international environmental management voluntary standards for business (ISO 14000) (Benson 1996). Firms which adopt ISO 14000 will be placed in either quadrant 3 or 4 of

Figure 10.2, as they move beyond mere compliance with environmental legislation towards a more pro-active management of corporate environmental assets and liabilities. To manage for environmental quality, many companies are now applying the same quality management techniques used by manufacturers in the 1980s to improve competitiveness.

Eco-labelling Requirements

Eco-labelling schemes identify for the consumer those products which are environmentally less harmful than other competing goods within the same product category, either because of their composition, the way in which they were made, or both (Staffin 1996). Eco-labels can be mandatory or voluntary and can occur at the national or international level. There are eco-labels for washing machines, light bulbs, dishwashers, packaging, refrigerators, paper, batteries, detergents and shoes. Once an eco-label is official, manufacturers may apply for it in the EU country where the product is manufactured, first marketed or imported. For firms an approved eco-labelled product has a competitive advantage when consumers are highly motivated to buy 'green' products, placing eco-labels in either quadrant 3 or 4 of Figure 10.2. Eco-labelling schemes usually favour domestic production (Staffin 1996) at the expense of imported products unless an MNE is nationally responsive to the host country eco-label, that is, in quadrant 4 of Figure 10.2.

6.   THE POLLUTION HAVEN CASE

Additional important issues of corporate strategy and environmental regulation can be explored using Figure 10.2. One of the most critical is the argument that countries with lax environmental standards (in quadrant 2) can attract firms away from countries with tight environmental standards (in quadrant 3). In the NAFTA context it has been alleged that Mexico is a 'pollution haven' compared to Canada and the United States. This is not the place to test this issue. However, the matrix is robust enough for us to capture the 'pollution haven' case in quadrant 2.

Alleged industries attracted to Mexico's border area are automotive accessories, electrical and electronics industries and metal products. It is alleged that there has been serious environmental damage along the border regions, and especially in the maquiladora manufacturing region. Industry was allegedly attracted to maquiladoras because of the 'hands-off attitude toward environmental protection and labour costs, and the fact that Mexico allows 100 per cent ownership of maquiladora plants' (Richardson 1992). While Mexico has strict environment laws 'on the book', enforcement remains a serious problem (Richardson 1992). An MNE normally operating in quadrant 3 in Canada or the United States would not move into quadrant 2 in order to operate in Mexico. Rather it would move to quadrant 1, where it can use a successful generic strategy. If it is in quadrant 1, the only one of these three generics of relevance is the low-cost strategy, not the brand/differentiation or niche strategy.

The one effort at a transectorally comprehensive study of the impact of NAFTA on the United States and Mexico was a study released by the US NGO Public Citizen in January 1996. It found that, based on interviews and media reports, NAFTA has increased the illegal dumping of industrial wastes, air pollution, hepatitis and birth defects along the US–Mexican border. The focus of concern was on increased infrastructural pressure due to growth in all industries, especially those which are pollution-intensive such as trucking and chemical/petrochemical production (Public Citizen 1996). These findings can be contrasted with a study commissioned by the CEC which has indicated that Mexico is not a pollution haven. MNEs have worldwide environmental mandates, often with suppliers, and use their best available environmental technology abroad, rather than out-of-date production processes (Kirton and Soloway 1996).

Two recent empirical studies tested the pollution haven hypothesis, and neither found evidence in support of it. Lucas et al. (1992) observed that when pollution-intensive industries have moved to developing countries, it is a function of industry expansion rather than displacement. Indeed, the paper finds that toxic intensity of output declines as incomes rise because the share of manufacturing in total output declines beyond a certain level of income. Similarly, Low and Yeats (1992) found that while developing countries have more dirty industry than developed countries, there is no evidence to support the claim that location decisions are based on environmental considerations. Thus, the evidence indicates that an MNE normally operating in quadrant 3 in Canada or the United States would not move into quadrant 2 in order to operate in Mexico.

The pollution haven argument is further weakened by the environmental policy adjustments made in Mexico, prior to its entry into NAFTA. International pressure and increased domestic activism led to the creation of the Mexican government's environmental institutions – SEDESOL, PROFEPA, and INE – in response to new domestic ENGO activity and citizen concerns as well as US Congressional allegations.

In 1992–93, the Mexican government launched a series of environmental inspections of foreign MNEs. SEDESOL inspectors closed one of Ford's plants for a week, as well as a Kimberly Clark plant. This action led Ford to establish an environmental quality office and, along with other companies, develop a global environmental plan. NAFTA thus helped produce an environmental consciousness, an environmental business ethic, and stringent environmental rules within MNEs in Mexico. NAFTA reinforced a trend begun in 1990 when Colgate Palmolive responded to multi-stakeholder pressures by starting to green itself (Kirton and Soloway 1996).

It remains an empirical question as to whether or not certain industries would actually relocate to Mexico even if there are lower environmental standards, given the high sunk costs of physical capital. Indeed, even if chemicals (and related manufacturing) are competing in quadrant 1 of Figure 10.2, the potential cost savings by relocating to Mexico into quadrant 2 are highly unlikely to be a significant factor in firm-level strategic decision making.

7. THE PORTER HYPOTHESIS AND THE RUGMAN REBUTTAL

Porter and Van der Linde (1995) argue that it is good policy for a government to pass strict environmental regulations. Then firms based in that country (usually the United States) will have to develop new core competencies in environmentally-sensitive manufacturing. Eventually, these firms can go abroad and use their strong home base as a staging ground to beat other less environmentally-sensitive firms in global markets. The Porter and Van der Linde hypothesis presumes that other countries will not 'compete' by inconveniently raising their own domestic environmental regulations too soon (before the US-based firms have geared up at home) and that the regional and multilateral organizations also follow along, rather than initiate new environmental regulations. Thus it is a matter of timing. If the US government is a first mover, it can spur US-based firms to be the first 'green' MNEs and their environmental credentials should help them beat out competitor firms on the world stage, once the world stage also becomes green.

In Figure 10.3 the Porter and Van der Linde (1995) propositions can be illustrated. Actually, the same point can be traced back to Porter (1990), where he first argued that stringent environmental standards and regulations could put pressure on firms to upgrade their competitive

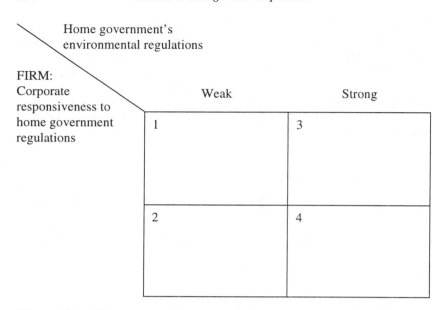

Figure 10.3   Home versus host government environmental regulations

advantage. If the home government imposes strong environmental regulations and enforces these tightly, then domestic firms are forced to comply. In time, the investments made by such home firms will upgrade their environmentally-related competitive advantages. Porter also states that home-based firms could then expect to go abroad and be able to beat foreign firms who have not yet been exposed to such tight environmental regulations. Two caveats are important. First, this only happens when the home government is clever enough to anticipate international trends in environmental regulations. Second, it only works for a very large, triad-based country (like the United States or the EU) whose economic influence on the world economy is immense; it will not work for smaller countries, as discussed below.

The Porter and Van der Linde hypothesis is placed in quadrant 3 of Figure 10.3. Domestic firms will be highly responsive to home government regulations. In contrast, in quadrant 4, small and medium-sized firms are unlikely to comply as they are primarily domestic in the scope of their operations, so they will not invest in order to do well in foreign markets, even when there are tight home government environmental regulations.

The work of Rugman (1995) is also shown in quadrant 4 of Figure 10.3. Even large MNEs is smaller countries will not benefit from tight environmental regulations, according to Rugman, since the relevant environmental regulations are those of their foreign customers. These firms, from smaller countries, need to monitor the environmental regulations of host countries, rather than those of the home country. Only rarely will a small country home government (like Canada) be able to anticipate international environmental trends for the benefit of home-based MNEs.

The problem with the Porter and Van der Linde hypothesis, from a Canadian perspective, is that it is difficult to think of any sector where it could be applied. Virtually all Canada's MNEs sell far more abroad than at home. The average ratio of foreign to total sales for Canada's largest 20 MNEs is over 70 per cent (Rugman 1990). Thus, if the Canadian government were to impose tight new environmental regulations, Canadian-based MNEs would have to invest and restructure for a market which takes a minority of their sales. These firms would prefer to adapt their manufacturing to suit the environmental regulations of their major customers abroad (especially when the big market for Canadian firms is the United States). In short, as far as Canadian competitiveness is concerned, the Porter and Van der Linde hypothesis is completely misleading. By forcing Canadian-based firms to take on board stronger, new environmental regulations, the Canadian government will actually reduce the international competitiveness of such firms as it changes their strategic focus from their major markets and makes them inward-looking instead of outward-looking FDI. These points were first developed in Rugman (1995) and explored within the context of the Canadian forest products sector and associated environmental regulations.

A final point is that while the Porter and Van der Linde hypothesis builds upon the Porter (1990) home-base diamond framework, the Rugman rebuttal builds upon the 'double diamond' framework (Rugman and D'Cruz 1993). In the context of environmental issues a double diamond approach suggests that MNEs from smaller countries will adapt to host country (triad) environmental regulations (or multilateral ones if they are ever created by groups like the OECD or WTO). In turn, these MNEs could then transmit the higher host country environmental standards back to their home country. The MNEs would be customer driven in this double diamond framework, rather than home country government policy driven.

8. CONCLUSIONS

In this chapter we have produced a new conceptual framework which integrates environmental regulations and corporate strategy. This is an alternative to the approach which starts with the environment as a public good. In Figure 10.1, we are able to position all relevant international environmental organizations within a matrix linking firm-level strategy and government-level regulations. In Figure 10.2 we are able to explore a fourth generic 'green' strategy option, along with the conventional strategies of cost, differentiation and focus. In Figure 10.3 we explored the Porter hypothesis and found that while it could work for firms with triad-sized home bases, it would not be relevant for smaller, open economies (such as Canada's) whose firms need access to a triad market. We found that this analysis of the dynamic tensions between trade and the environment can provide valuable insights for managers responsible for corporate strategy.

In contrast, this work offers no support for the viewpoint that environmental regulations can be developed by policy makers to provide global complementarities. There is no effective global institution to set worldwide environmental standards. There is little prospect of harmonization of standards. The WTO, if it goes anywhere on this issue, will only set minimum environmental standards and it can only hope that MNEs will build on these to raise standards in the future. The key actor on the stage of global environmental complementarity is the MNE, not the nation state. If environmental standards are harmonized and improved in any significant manner it will be due primarily to the corporate strategies of MNEs.

REFERENCES

Barney, Jay (1991), 'Firm resources and sustained competitive advantage', *Journal of Management*, **17** (1): 99–120.
Bartlett, Christopher and Sumantra Ghoshal (1989), *Managing Across Borders: The Transnational Solution*, Boston: Harvard Business School Press.
Benson, Christina (1996), 'The ISO 14000 International Standards: moving beyond environmental compliance', *North Carolina Journal of International Law and Commercial Regulation*, **22** (1): 307–64.
Burhenne, Wolfgang (ed.) (1996), 'Strengthening the application of interational environmental law', *Environmental Policy and Law*, **26** (4), 170–74.
Commission for Environmental Cooperation (1995), *NAFTA Environmental Effects, Potential NAFTA Effects: Claims and Arguments, 1991–1994*, Montreal: Commission for Environmental Cooperation.
Conner, Kathleen R. (1991), 'A historical comparison of resource-based theory

and five schools of thought within industrial economics', *Journal of Management*, **17** (1): 121–54.

Hoekman, Bernard M. and Michael M. Kostecki (1995), *The Political Economy of the World Trading System: From GATT to WTO*, Oxford: Oxford University Press.

Kirton, John (1992), 'Canada's contribution to a new trade–environment regime', *Trade, Environment and Competitiveness: Sustaining Canada's Prosperity*, Ottawa: National Round Table on the Environment and the Economy.

Kirton, John and Julie Soloway (1996), *Assessing NAFTA's Environmental Effects: Dimensions of a Framework and the NAFTA Regime*, NAFTA Effects Working Paper Series, Working Paper No. 1, Montreal: Commission for Environmental Cooperation.

Koskenniemi, Martti (1996), 'New institutions and procedures for implementation control and reaction', in Jacob Werksman (ed.), *Greening International Institutions*, London: Earthscan Publications Ltd, pp. 236–48.

Low, Patrick and Alexander Yeats (1992), 'Do "dirty" industries migrate?', in Patrick Low (ed.), *International Trade and the Environment*, World Bank Discussion Paper 159, Washington DC: The World Bank, pp. 89–103.

Lucas, Robert E.B., David Wheeler and Hemamala Hettige (1992), 'Economic development, environmental regulation and the international migration of toxic industrial pollution', in Patrick Low (ed.), *International Trade and the Environment*, World Bank Discussion Paper 159, Washington DC: The World Bank, pp. 67–88.

Lundan, Sàrianna (1997), 'The benefits and costs of market-driven signals to guide environmental investment: the case of the pulp and paper industry', paper presented at the Business Strategy and the Environment Conference, Leeds, UK, 18–19 September 1997.

Penrose, Edith (1959), *The Theory of the Growth of the Firm*, London: Basil Blackwell.

Porter, Michael E. (1980), *Competitive Strategy*, New York: The Free Press.

Porter, Michael E. (1990), *The Competitive Advantage of Nations*, New York: The Free Press.

Porter, Michael E. and Charles Van der Linde (1995), 'Toward a new conception of the environment–competitiveness relationship', *Journal of Economic Perspectives*, **9** (4): 97–118.

Public Citizen (1996), *NAFTA's Broken Promises: The Border Betrayed, NAFTA's Environmental Effects*, Washington DC: Public Citizen, January.

Raiczyck, Glenn B. (1991), 'Montreal Protocol on substances that deplete the ozone layer: conference calling for the accelerated phase-out of ozone depleting chemicals is planned for 1992', *Temple Journal of International and Comparative Law*, **5** (2): 363–78.

Renzulli, Jeffery J. (1991), 'The regulation of ozone depleting chemicals in the European Community', *Boston College International and Comparative Law Review*, **15** (2): 345–58.

Richardson, Sarah (1992), 'Overview on trade, environment and competitiveness', *Trade, Environment and Competitiveness: Sustaining Canada's Prosperity*, Ottawa: National Round Table on the Environment and the Economy.

Rugman, Alan M. (1981), *Inside the Multinationals: The Economics of Internal Market*, New York: Columbia University Press.

Rugman, Alan M. (1990), *Multinationals and the Canada–United States Free Trade Agreement*, Columbia, SC: University of South Carolina Press.

Rugman, Alan M. (ed.) (1994), *Foreign Investment and NAFTA*, Columbia, SC: University of South Carolina Press.

Rugman, Alan M. (1995), 'Environmental regulations and international competitiveness: strategies for Canada's west coast forest products industry', *The International Executive*, **37** (5): 451–65.

Rugman, Alan M. (1996), *The Theory of Multinational Enterprises: Volume Two of the Selected Scientific Papers of Alan M. Rugman*, Cheltenham: Edward Elgar.

Rugman, Alan M. and Joseph R. D'Cruz (1993), 'The "double diamond" model of international competitiveness: the Canadian experience', *Management International Review*, **33** (2): 17–39.

Rugman, Alan M. and Michael Gestrin (1997), 'New rules for multilateral investment', *The International Executive*, **39** (1): 21–34.

Rugman, Alan M. and Alain Verbeke (1994), 'Foreign direct investment and NAFTA: a conceptual framework', in Alan M. Rugman (ed.), *Foreign Investment and NAFTA*, Columbia, SC: University of South Carolina Press, pp. 80–104.

Rugman, Alan M., John Kirton and Julie A. Soloway (1997), 'NAFTA, environmental regulations and Canadian competitiveness', *Journal of World Trade*, **31** (4) August: 129–44.

Rumelt, Richard P. (1984), 'Towards a strategic theory of the firm', in Richard B. Lamb (ed.), *Competitive Strategic Management*, Englewood Cliffs, NJ: Prentice-Hall, pp. 556–70.

Safarian, A.E. (1993), *Multinational Enterprises and Public Policy*, Aldershot, UK: Edward Elgar.

Somsen, Han (1996), 'The European Union and the Organization for Economic Cooperation and Development', in Jacob Werksman (ed.), *Greening International Institutions*, London: Earthscan Publications Ltd., pp. 181–204.

Staffin, Elliot B. (1996), 'Trade barrier or trade boon? A critical evaluation of environmental labelling and its role in the "greening" of world trade', *Columbia Journal of Environmental Law*, **21** (2): 205–86.

Vogel, David (1995), *Trading Up: Consumer and Environmental Regulations in a Global Economy*, Cambridge, MA: Harvard University Press.

Vogel, David and Alan M. Rugman (1997), 'Environmentally-related trade disputes between the United States and Canada', *American Review of Canadian Studies*, **27** (2), October: 271–92.

11. Advanced political development and collective management

Gavin Boyd

INTRODUCTION

As previous chapters have indicated, the world economy is being restructured, through deepening integration, with limited degrees of spontaneous or negotiated order, under market discipline. National institutions and policies are recognized to be of decisive importance for growth as competition for world markets intensifies, but these institutions and policies continue to be shaped mainly by national cultures and by the dynamics of country-specific decision processes.[1] Corporate organizations and operations also reflect the enduring influence of national cultures, but a common trend is a weakening of home country ties, except in the cases of firms operating out of highly integrated national societies.[2]

The deepening integration is driven by expanding corporate activity, notably by more internationally competitive firms which operate with increasing freedom as they displace weaker enterprises and choose between the location advantages offered by host countries. The scope for choice is wide, and often widening, because of the commitments of many governments to trade and investment liberalization which are implemented with numerous resorts to investment bidding. The substantial degrees of economic openness facilitate an increasing internationalization of market efficiencies, but the deepening integration lacks the coordinated dynamic growth that could be possible in view of the available institutional resources and technological capabilities. Corporate strategies, for the most part, are implemented with emphasis on totally competitive rather than cooperative strategies: increasing international oligopoly power results, with rationalizations that cause extensive externalities, and with rises in entry barriers that limit the scope for innovative new firms. Macromanagement failures by governments, meanwhile, burden many economies with heavy debt, diverting investment from productive use.[3]

National administrations are challenged to promote increases in structural competitiveness, so as to secure more gains from the deepening integration. In the industrialized democracies what can be achieved by consulting with, guiding, supporting and regulating firms, and by improving infrastructures and administrative services, depends on evolving patterns of advanced political development. Degrees of such development are evident in most of the industrialized democracies, and distinguish them from states – among the newly industrializing countries – which have relatively efficient administrative structures, but which function with substantial elements of personal rule.

Structural competitiveness is improved or weakened in contexts of structural and policy interdependence. These assume larger dimensions as firms increase production and exchange linkages between national economies and as each administration's involvement in its economy is affected by the activities of other governments. For each state economic sovereignty is weakened, but can be strengthened through enlisting the cooperation of firms and of other states: endeavours to raise structural competitiveness can be collaborative at the international level, as well as transnationally. Achievement of the primary objective – to increase gains from foreign trade and transnational production – tends to depend, more and more, on what kind of cooperation can be undertaken with the corporations that are shaping structural interdependencies and with other governments whose policies in various ways assist or restrict those corporations.

In international systemic perspectives, focusing on the developmental problem of the world economy, advanced political development in the industrialized states, especially the major ones, has to take directions conducive to the structuring of comprehensive and integrative cooperation. As largely unguided deepening integration continues, the basic logic of social cooperation for growth, through the coordination of specializations, which is at the basis of rationales for structural policies, demands international application.[4]

ANALYSIS

Advanced political development can be understood in terms of capacities for highly interdependent macromanagement, or simply in terms of a market-type equilibrium, resulting from the trading of political services, with a spread of benefits that is sufficient to ensure continuity. The latter concept engages the attention of rational choice theorists who study institutional arrangements conducive to efficiency in the trading of political services.[5] The former concept is significant for political economy scholars with concerns about efficiencies and failures in the real economy and related government efficiencies and failures. With such concerns imperatives are seen for technocratic functions serving the common good, and exercised without political trading by assertive groups with narrowly focused rationality.[6] Institutional development is seen to require learning and socialization processes oriented towards the provision of wide ranges of public goods.[7]

Considerations about dedicated administrative services have been reflected in studies of public management reforms introduced by Western democracies. These studies have evidenced the concerns of governments to enhance growth and employment by improving business environments, so as to increase national gains as deepening integration continues. The public management reforms have been motivated by rivalries to raise levels of structural competitiveness, in response to intensifying competition between firms for world market shares.[8] The striving for improved structural competitiveness, however, generally demands more than public management reforms: progress in advanced political development becomes necessary, while the costs of any problems of governance become more serious with the continuing rises in structural interdependence and the increasing dimensions of cross-border market failure problems, notably the growth of international oligopoly power.

The most common problems of governance are political contests which drive fiscal expansion. Allocative laxity and overproductions of bureaucratic goods and services tend to impose increasingly heavy costs. Gains from deepening integration are affected firstly because of strong import drawing effects and larger diversions of investment away from productive use, and secondly because transnational enterprises benefit more, at the expense of these states, by serving their markets from foreign locations and driving into decline their domestic firms, which tend to be disadvantaged by greater tax exposure.[9] Vicious circles can result, in which the costs of problems of governance, in terms of growth and employment, make those problems more intractable, while the pressures to achieve higher levels of structural competitiveness become stronger.

Macromanagement achievements by states that have made further progress in advanced political development tend to activate virtuous circles in which consensus sustains allocative discipline and restrains bureaucratic expansion, while aiding the transnational operations of home country firms and retaining their loyalties. The more efficiently managed states benefit more from, and have relatively more control over, the evolution of internationalized market efficiencies and failures. The efficiencies tend to increase under the pressures of oligopolistic competition, in which transnational enterprises are in various ways aided by home and sometimes host governments. International oligopolistic market power, however, is typically used, with network partners, to force weaker firms into decline, rather than collaborate for their adjustment and growth, and to extract higher profits from the strong market positions which have been gained. Weaker firms, notably in the less efficiently managed states, and those at lower levels of industrialization, are less and less acceptable as subordinate partners.

Issues of systemic development in the global political economy are posed by the evolving configuration of relatively advantaged and relatively disadvantaged industrialized states and the changing international corporate strengths. The imbalances in gains from deepening integration include the directly structural aspects of oligopoly power and the effects of that power on labour markets.[10] There are international system-building imperatives which clearly have to be accepted by government leaders in industrialized states, especially on the basis of their extended accountabilities to foreign communities affected by their policies and by firms variously aided by those policies.

Expectations of an international market-driven equilibrium are not encouraged. Competitive pressures tend to force adoption of the most efficient management systems by contending firms, together with governmental quests for optimum structural policies, but the most competitive firms and the most effectively managed states tend to gain cumulative advantages. The recent history of market changes and structural changes in the world economy is a record of imbalances and of the emergence of a hierarchical pattern of dominance, with the European Union lagging behind the structural competitiveness of Japan and the USA.[11]

In the study of advanced political development and structural competitiveness, questions about the coordination of innovative entrepreneurship have to be considered. After infrastructure development and the provision of basic administrative services the most important macromanagement task is to promote the coordination of innovative entrepreneurial activities. This is necessary because, in the increasing complexities of deepening integration, problems of informational market failure are sources of uncertainties and risks that limit the scope for entrepreneurial initiatives. It is also necessary because oligopoly power, as it becomes more secure, obstructs the emergence of new firms with innovative potential.

Entrepreneurship has been neglected in economics, and, to the extent that it has been studied, coordination problems have been given little recognition.[12] The functional significance of concerted entrepreneurship, on the basis of relational intercorporate bonds, has been apparent in Japan, but this has been somewhat obscured by literature criticizing anticompetitive aspects of that country's industry groups. Pressures to raise structural competitiveness obligate administrative encouragement of productive rather than rent-seeking entrepreneurship and, to be fully productive, the entrepreneurial activity has to be cooperative, indeed, integratively cooperative, for the generation of efficiencies in networks, alliances and industry groups. This is necessary for highly innovative entrepreneurial activity, as that has to be planned and managed interactively, with collaborative adaptations to the widening breadth of advances in frontier technology and with much information sharing about potentials for evolving complementary strategies.[13]

Major innovations in frontier technology occur in uneven patterns and are often unpredictable; hence potentials for entrepreneurial use of these depend very much on patterns of trustful interactive management.[14] To the extent that broadly concerted innovative entrepreneurship results, with complementary specializations, it must be recognized as a public good. Problems of governance can hinder the realization of such a good by hindering the coordination of functionally-oriented decision processes at the administrative level, discouraging corporate trust in that level, failing to promote trustful information sharing, obstructing institutional learning, and generally obliging corporate managements to operate with maximum reliance on their own resources, rather than in collaboration with other firms. Transaction costs and risks, in such contexts, tend to be high.

In structural policy rivalry the intended country-specific public good of concerted innovative entrepreneurship is difficult to attain, and is insecure, because of the cross-border linkages that increase with deepening integration. Questions about macromanagement functions thus lead into questions about the evolution of the international political economy. The logic of coordinating entrepreneurial activity at that higher level has to be considered. Industrialized states have facilitated the internationalization of financial markets, and substantial liberalization of markets for goods and services, but have not formed structures for collective management of the resulting structural interdependencies, except in the European Union.

The experience of the European Union has shown that where states form an elementary system of regional integration the liberalized market activities result in imbalanced spreads of gains and larger and more rapid concentrations of corporate power, making further advances in collective management politically more difficult but economically more desirable.[15] Political designing for smoother progress in collective management might therefore emphasize the potentials for more balanced interdependent growth that could be envisaged through consultative partnering for the development of widening complementarities.

Collective management options are often considered in terms of choices between interventions in economic activity and collaborative liberalization. The main thrust of European collective management has been progressive intrazonal liberalization, motivated by hopes of raising efficiencies generated in intercorporate rivalries for shares of the internal market.[16] The demands on capabilities associated with advanced political development at the national level have been moderate, but subsequent adjustment problems have caused resorts to protectionist and industrial policy measures, within contexts set by collective decision processes in the Union.

The Union's experience has shown how intensifying rivalries for market shares focus policy processes in ways that divert attention from imperatives for progress in collective management, in response to rises in asymmetric structural interdependence. Advanced political development can thus assume directions opposed to imperatives for systemic development in the international political economy. This, however, need not happen if trade and investment liberalization, allowing more scope for market forces is accompanied by endeavours to promote complementary patterns of industrial capacity through the sponsorship of coordinated entrepreneurial planning.

STRUCTURAL COMPETITIVENESS

The increasing rivalries for international market shares evoke differing responses by governments endeavouring to raise levels of structural competitiveness. These responses mix industrial, foreign direct investment, competition and trade policies in the course of political–economic cycles, and are implemented with diverse forms of corporate cooperation, offset by patterns of corporate opposition and avoidance, and complicated by virtual shifts of structural power to cooperating and noncooperating firms. The contexts are conditions of relative economic openness and foreign penetration, determined by the policy mixes, by bargaining over questions of market access, and by the entry barriers and opportunities associated with the operations of national and foreign firms.

The increasing pressures to raise structural competitiveness tend to obligate efforts to improve the effectiveness of each policy mix, and to provide shelter for vulnerable sectors. The functional significance of the measures adopted, and the potentials for improvement, vary with the culture, structures, and dynamics of each national political economy. Qualities of the culture are evidenced in degrees of community formation, the vitality of civic associations, the social organization of trust, and the integration or fragmentation of the intercorporate system. Value orientations in the culture tend to be expressed in the development and operation of institutions: these structures have differing capacities for policy making that is consensual or conflicted, reactive or forward looking, and biased by political exchange concerns or functional in the common interest.

In strongly individualistic societies the scope for measures to raise structural competitiveness is limited because of the difficulties of aggregating preferences on a stable basis and because corporate trust in administrative competence and integrity is generally low, while individualistic entrepreneurship, which can be dynamic, is typically very self-reliant. In societies which emphasize community welfare, policy mixes tend to engage more comprehensively with problems of structural competitiveness, on a basis of broad consensus and established patterns of administrative–corporate cooperation. In these political economies allocative discipline tends to keep down the costs of government, industrial policy dominates the microeconomic policy mix, political–economic cycles are under more collaborative control and less subject to governmental or corporate manipulation.

Policies for structural competitiveness tend to be liberal in strongly individualistic political economies, facilitating autonomous entrepreneurial development by providing highly developed infrastructures and efficient administrative services, while using regulatory measures to activate competition. Corporate tax levels are kept low, and industrial relations policies favour managerial interest in labour market flexibility. The functional significance of all the liberal measures, however, can be affected by pluralistic stagnation, biases favouring key support groups, allocative patronage, and rising costs of government.

The liberal orientation entails reliance on agglomeration trends induced by market-friendly location advantages, including dynamic centres of innovation aided by technology policies.[17] The technology attraction becomes more significant as advances in frontier innovations continue, but government and corporate investments in liberal policy contexts tend to be lower than those in more community-oriented states at similar levels of industrialization. Their more integrated political economies can finance larger investments in new technology, on the basis of longer-term government planning and corporate planning.

Gains in structural competitiveness by the more integrated political economies are less vulnerable to the destabilizing effects of volatility in world financial markets. The domestic markets for corporate control are restricted by systems of corporate governance which maintain stable cross-holdings and which constitute virtual applications of internalization logic at the intercorporate level.[18] The currency is substantially protected from speculative attack because of informal restraints on portfolio inflows, and the national loyalties of home country investors, which sustain limitations on the internationalization of the domestic financial markets.

In quests for improved structural competitiveness, economies of scale and scope, and resources for high-cost investments in new technology, assume increasing importance: hence the dimensions of effective foreign market access become more significant, and bargaining leverage to expand such access tends to be used increasingly in trade and investment relations. Large industrialized democracies can thus be advantaged in regional contexts, especially where no system of collective management has emerged, and strengths gained in such contexts can sustain more extensive engagement, to maximize global market shares.[19]

The principal regional contexts offering wider effective market access are East Asia, North America, and the European Union. In East Asia the highly integrated Japanese political economy has an important zone of effective market access, on a basis of bilateral interactions with newly industrializing states, and asymmetries in this pattern enable the home economy to maintain its role as the centre of an integrated regional production system. In North America an elementary system of regional economic integration has given the pluralistic US political economy a less extensive zone of effective market access, although with the advantages of greater bargaining strengths in relations with its partners. The regionally acquired economic power is thus less significant for US global involvement, in which the main external region of engagement is Europe.[20]

In the European Union, the only advanced system of regional economic integration, Germany's central role is more dependent on structural competitiveness than on capacities for market-opening leverage because of the constraints of highly interdependent policy making within the structure of collective management. The effective market access has been derived mainly from those structures, but is challenged very powerfully by US corporate involvement in the Single Market. Economic strength gained in Europe is of modest significance for Germany's involvement in the rest of the world economy, where the principal contenders for market shares are US and Japanese firms.[21] Germany's regional gains in structural competitiveness have been limited by slack growth in its Union partners, attributable to their problems of governance and long delays in regional market integration. The pattern of advanced political development has been subjected to strain because of the extraordinary costs of national unification.[22]

SYSTEMIC CONTRASTS

As macromanagement systems the major political economies contribute to the evolution of institutions and policies for economic cooperation. There is a pattern of causal relationships, with the USA and the European Union dominating interactions that shape global institutions and their activities. Japan's foreign economic diplomacy has a rather restricted reach, but is associated with vigorous corporate involvement in structural change, notably in North America as well as East Asia. Germany has a distinctive role, in terms of the quality of structurally competitive macromanagement combined with constructive participation in the European system of collective management.

German macromanagement is broadly consensual and functional. Intercorporate cooperation and administrative corporate cooperation, in a setting of extensive civic collaboration and of partnership between the differing levels of government, with spontaneous restraints on political competition, maintains a highly functional form of macromanagement. Policy communities operate with a tradition of knowledge-intensive application to administrative efficiency, and government performance is under constant review by an independent Council of Economic Experts, at the apex of a large assortment of advisory organizations. The resulting informal accountability and learning processes sustain elite networks with broad agreement on imperatives to maintain a system of organized capitalism in a social market economy.[23]

The pattern of corporatist collaboration, however, is under strain, primarily because of debt burdens and welfare costs associated with the rehabilitation of the former East German economy. Intercorporate solidarity has been weakened as large firms have made wage pacts with strong unions which have been costly for small and medium-sized enterprises, which have been leaving major business associations. Large firms, moreover, have begun shifting operations to foreign locations, including lower-cost areas, in Europe and elsewhere.[24]

Prospects for improved growth depend very much on the utilization of the Single Market's opportunities by other Union members, which have been severely affected by the deflationary effects of high German interest rates. Germany's structural interdependencies are regionally concentrated, as roughly 70 per cent of its exports and imports are European. The regional concentration is being increased, mainly through trade, but foreign direct investment outflows, which are modest, have been going mainly to the USA, where the direct investment position is about one-third of the Japanese and the British totals.[25] There are marked asymmetries in the Union pattern of interdependencies, due to the weaker competitiveness of most of the regional partners, and their higher levels of domestic market penetration. The share of foreign (US, other European, and Japanese) affiliates in German manufacturing output was only 13.2 per cent in 1990 (a decline of 2.5 per cent from 1980), compared with 28.4 per cent in France (an increase of 1.8 per cent from 1980) and with 25.1 per cent in Britain (a rise of 5.8 per cent from 1981). The exposure of the German market to imports of manufactures from all sources was about 27 per cent in 1990, that is about 3 per cent lower than that in Britain and France.[26]

Within Europe the main competitive challenge is the American corporate presence. Sales by the nonbank affiliates of US firms in Europe totalled $897 439 million in 1994, while German exports to the rest of Europe that year were $225 781 million. US rivalry, together with growing Japanese penetration of the Union market, is adding to the incentives for German firms to expand trade and production outside Europe, especially in the USA and the high-growth areas of East Asia. Such expansion is relatively slow, because of a high technology lag behind the USA and Japan, the growth limitations of the European region, and the domestic strengths of US and Japanese firms.

Germany's policy interdependencies mainly reflect the regional concentration of its structural interdependencies, but they are higher than those of the USA and Japan. The complex regional policy interdependence extends to the Atlantic and global levels where Germany interacts with the USA and Japan on international monetary issues. Within the Union the most demanding task is to work for renewed regional growth, and this necessitates choices between emphasis on expanding German direct investment in other members and on collaborating with them for the development of a common structural policy. More active manufacturing presences in higher-growth areas outside Europe will be necessary for global competition against US and Japanese firms, it must be stressed, and this requirement overshadows the intra-Union options. Of these the structural policy choice, while clearly in the regional interest, is discouraged by the difficulties of achieving regional consensus and by the prospect of bearing a large proportion of the likely costs.

The regional focus of German policy tends to increase with Union enlargement, because of the multiplication of issues and bargaining processes. As the number of participating governments increases a leadership role that has been assumed with France has to be exercised with wider coalition building. This is especially complex because of the involvement of German state governments and business groups in consultative interactions with the European Commission, and with subnational authorities and commercial associations in other Union members.[27]

Japan's macromanagement system operates with fewer and more manageable policy interdependencies, but with more authoritative and less accountable technocratic functions, in synergistic interaction with a more integrated intercorporate system. The technocratic functions have become mainly advisory, with shifts away from the direct subsidizing of firms and from regulatory methods which had been sources of inefficiencies. The changes were made in recent years in response to corporate demands and to pressures from the USA for liberalization of the internal market. The intercorporate system operates with much spontaneous organization, and with a spirit of intense competition that is nevertheless solidarity based, ensuring extensive information sharing and risk sharing, notably within industry groups.[28]

The intercorporate system is the principal source of inputs into the policy process, and especially into the work of the two major structures dominating that process – the Ministry of International Trade and Industry, and the Ministry of Finance. By comparison with Germany the legislature has a weaker role, the political parties are at lower levels of institutional development, civic associations are less active and there is no independent high status review institute to assess administrative performance. There is strong allocative discipline, however, and the concerting of entrepreneurial activities, with technocratic advising, is more dynamic than that achieved in the looser German system of organized capitalism. This entrepreneurship, moreover, is more vigorously outward oriented, in line with a tradition of collective response to acute resource deficiencies.

Japan's structural interdependencies, expanding with export-led growth and more recently with large-scale foreign production, are spread much more widely than Germany's, and have greater asymmetries, due to low penetration of the internal market by imports and incoming direct investment. The range of external commerce includes substantial market shares in North America and East Asia, and considerable involvement in the European Union, where imports from Japan are about one-quarter of the volume of Germany's exports to other member states. It has been necessary to develop economic links mainly outside the immediate environment, which until fairly recently has been mostly backward and unfriendly. Substantial gains in structural competitiveness have been made principally through penetration of the US market.

The economic links with industrializing East Asian states are now about as large as those with the USA, and are growing fast, with favourable bargaining asymmetries, and these partner countries are becoming more closely related to the Japanese economy than to each other.[29] Low levels of solidarity in the Association of Southeast Asian Nations prevent its members from relating effectively to Japan on common interests. Indonesia, the largest member of that association, is the main regional destination of Japanese direct investment, and sends roughly one-quarter of its exports to Japan. In managing economic links with the association's members, and with South Korea and Taiwan, Japan has wide scope for initiative, not only because of the bilateral character of the relationships, but also because of extensive informal ties between Japanese industry groups active in the area and their home government.

The growth of connections with industrializing East Asian states is not significantly affected by Japan's involvement in the mainly consultative functions of the Asia-Pacific Economic Cooperation forum (APEC). In this association the principal exchanges are with the USA, and its efforts to strengthen political ties with East Asian members have to contend with the structurally more active Japanese involvement. US attempts to enlist support from these states for a regional trade liberalization drive that would be directed mainly against Japan have not held out incentives that would be sufficient to reduce the priorities which most of those states have to give to cooperation with the expanding Japanese presence.[30]

The demands of managing the current pattern of policy interdependencies are not changing the rather closed character of the Japanese macromanagement system. Economic nationalism, roused in strained relations with the USA, has tended to maintain the degree of closure. This has been advantageous for consensus building, despite some recognition of the benefits of external pressure for the introduction of deregulatory measures to improve the home economy's efficiency. Domestically, a degree of economic liberalization has been accompanied by an ambitious technology programme which, with very active corporate participation, promises wider and more competitive applications of research frontier advances. The intended technological trajectory could help to sustain the home economy as the main centre of advanced manufacturing while ensuring technological leads for Japanese firms that would help to limit penetration of that economy by foreign enterprises.[31]

The USA's macromanagement system, less integrated than Japan's and Germany's, operates with problems of governance and with a political tradition that restricts administrative corporate cooperation and intercorporate collaboration. Popular distrust of concentrations of political and economic power are at the basis of this tradition and it has been criticized as a hindrance to the evolution of a system of corporate governance more suited for structural competitiveness. The problems of governance are difficulties of functional representation, institutional development, and administrative performance. High pressure representations of constituency interests cause intensive contests for continuous popular approval by contenders for office. These contenders are heavily reliant on resources secured individually, due to the organizational weaknesses of civic associations, political parties, and business groups. These weaknesses tend to prevent consensus formation, and thus necessitate much trading of favours in a divided authority structure which can become dysfunctional.[32] There are rivalries between the executive and the legislature for control of the bureaucracy, in which contradictions tend to be built in by awkward compromises between rival legislative groups.[33]

A dynamic pattern of highly individualistic corporate activity has evolved, relating distantly and somewhat distrustfully to the administration. The system of corporate governance has been shaped to a large extent by a restrictive competition policy legislated while the national configuration of competitive managerial capitalism was being formed. Vertical and horizontal forms of cooperation are severely discouraged, financial institutions cannot participate substantially in the ownership and operation of manufacturing firms, cross-holdings between such firms are prevented, and the shifting preferences of widely dispersed shareholders are the main sources of pressures for performance.[34] These pressures, operating through an active market for corporate control, result in much emphasis by managements on short-term profit seeking, and contribute to the preservation of strongly hierarchical forms of corporate organization. Antitrust enforcement is not effective against tacit collusion, but the uncertainties and restraints of enforcement practices, which encourage litigation, give incentives to firms to undertake operations in less constricting foreign business environments. These incentives operate in conjunction with those motivating the establishment of a presence in each major external market, and the acquisition of tax advantages associated with foreign operations.[35]

Structural policy initiatives are allowed little scope by the political tradition and accordingly macromanagement depends very much on fiscal, monetary and trade measures. As allocative compromises tend to force unsustainable deficit financing, monetary policy has had to have deflationary effects, which slow growth, while the import-drawing effects of fiscal deficits exert downward pressures on the currency.

Substantial trade deficits encourage interest group demands for shelter, which is available mainly through a system of administered protection.[36] Pressures from such groups meanwhile motivate trade policy activism, to widen access to foreign markets. The economy remains substantially open, partly because of the interests of US exporters in opposing policies that would provoke foreign discrimination against their products. The degree of openness is a source of vulnerabilities, partly because of the USA's deep involvement in world financial markets, and the danger of a 'domestic' financial crisis, due to high-volume speculation. The US system of financial regulation could have difficulty in coping with such a crisis, and its costs could be borne disproportionately by national firms that have not undertaken extensive foreign operations.[37]

Increasing vulnerabilities, as deepening integration continues, have entailed risks and costs for US domestic sectors, as in most other industrialized states, relating especially to externalities associated with restructuring by international firms, and to disruptions caused by competing imports. US compensatory, protective and support measures have had to deal with welfare problems smaller than those in the European Union, but the financing of such measures has been burdensome because capital has been more footloose than in Europe. Pressures to reduce the federal administration's heavy deficits, moreover, have become strong.[38]

Because of the strong pluralism of the American macromanagement system and its institutional weaknesses, the quality of professional economic advice to the executive and to policy communities is potentially very significant. The Council of Economic Advisors appointed by each President, however, does not have the independent and accumulated expertise of the German Council of Economic Experts, and the economics profession in the USA has been evolving as a more detached discipline than its counterpart in Europe, with an emphasis on abstract modelling.[39] The advice offered generally represents mainstream thinking in the profession, emphasizing the efficiency of market forces. On problems in the operation of these forces the professional preference is to change incentive patterns, but this is typically opposed by noneconomists, especially those with legal training, who prefer reliance on regulatory methods. The Council is under pressure to engage with vast numbers of microeconomic issues, and this allows little time for consideration of macroeconomic policy questions. Dealing with the microeconomic issues requires intensive interaction with senior officials who expect their active short-term political concerns to be reciprocated, and who can often be reluctant to accept appeals to economic rationality.[40]

INTERNATIONAL SYSTEMIC CHANGE

Because of the size of the US economy and the scale of its involvement in the world trading, production and financial systems, its policies and the activities of its firms have far-reaching international effects. These, however, are less coordinated than those resulting from Japan's macro-management and corporate operations. There is less administrative control over the deepening integration experienced by the US economy, and as US firms expand their global activities their scope for independent strategic choices tends to widen more than is possible for Japanese enterprises.

Continuity in the outward thrust of US corporate activity has market and structural effects principally in Europe, where the large direct investment position is expanding substantially. The scale of this involvement, and of related US trade, increasingly complicates issues of structural policy cooperation in the European Union, and larger questions of Atlantic structural and trade policy cooperation. The development of a coordinated Union structural policy tends to become more difficult, while for the Union the costs and vulnerabilities of the present openness in Atlantic economic relations tend to obligate compensatory outlays and resorts to protection.

The high volume of US corporate activity in Europe is conducive to intensive networking and alliance formation, and to collaborative political action for the representation of interests to the European Commission. Very large US firms are advantaged because of the resources with which they can support such lobbying, and they operate mainly in rivalry with the European Round Table of Industrialists, which has close informal links with the European Commission. US firms, however, benefit from the efforts of several member states, especially Britain, to attract foreign direct investment. Union governments implement their own foreign direct investment policies, in competition against each other, and attempts by the European Commission to regulate such policies, through its competence on trade policy, have had little effect on the investment bidding.[41]

Outside Europe the main area of US corporate activity is East Asia, where contributions are made to a vast process of structural change in rivalry with Japanese enterprises engaged in higher-volume trade and direct investment. The US presence has been expanding less than that of the Japanese firms, whose activities constitute an integrated pattern, backed by home government policies. As an integrated Japanese–East Asian production system is being established, in complex partnering with technologically rather advanced sectors in South Korea and Taiwan, and technologically less advanced sectors in Southeast Asia and China, the technological trajectories of South Korea, Taiwan, and the Southeast Asian states are strongly influenced by ties with Japanese corporations, and these firms are tending to assume more significance in the investment development paths of those states. Intensive efforts are being made by the South Korean and Taiwan governments and their firms to develop advanced technological capabilities, for less dependent partnering with Japanese enterprises. For these efforts the broadening of opportunities for technology transfers through the attraction of US high technology investments is necessary, but tends to be made difficult by the faster growth of incoming Japanese direct investment. Weak technological capabilities in the Southeast Asian states severely limit their potentials to absorb transfers from foreign firms, and they attract Japanese investment mainly into assembly-type manufacturing. US direct investment is attracted for similar operations. Substantial inflows are also received from South Korea and Taiwan, mostly for less sophisticated assembly-type production.[42]

Industrialization in the Chinese Communist regime, assisted by Japanese, US, European, South Korean and Taiwanese direct investment, is changing the regional context, with longer-term implications for Japan and the USA. The incoming investment is mainly for assembly-type manufacturing like that in Southeast Asia, and potentials for transfers that would aid substantial technological upgrading are limited by the regime's relatively low capacities for absorption, and by the caution of the foreign managements. Improvement of the regime's technological capabilities tends to be hindered by the effects of political controls and bureaucratic deficiencies on the activities of research institutes and enterprises, especially those in the state sector.[43]

Continued industrialization with gradually rising technological levels is in prospect, but subject to political stability. The principal danger is rivalry between Communist Party leaders identified with its organizational structure and those in the higher levels of the army's command system. The social base of the party has been weakened by the deradicalizing effects of current economic policies, while the army's capacity to maintain internal security has become formidable because of its size and modernization, which is continuing with very substantial government financing and some transfers of dual-purpose technology from Japan and the USA. The ruling elite has long been factionalized, but endeavours to maintain effective central authority while restricting interaction within the secondary elite and relating to its members individually. Because of strong emphasis on asserting central power there are serious coordination problems similar to those caused by heavily centralized authority in the former Soviet Union.[44]

In the rest of the third world, Latin America ranks next after industrializing East Asia as an area of deepening integration, but with a US presence much stronger than Japan's. Mexico has drawn the main concentration of US direct investment, and this has contributed to diversified industrialization, reducing the ratio of energy sales in total exports and raising that of medium technology manufactures to roughly 60 per cent. Dependence on trade with the USA is very high, and contrasts with Brazil's external commerce, which is at approximately the same level but is primarily with Europe and secondarily with Asia. Mexico is gradually making an export-led recovery from a severe 1994 financial crisis which had caused stagnation throughout the region. Growth is now hindered by the servicing of heavy external debt – 69 per cent of GDP at the end of 1995 – and is vulnerable to slowdowns in the US economy.[45]

Acute problems of governance have been pervasive in Latin America, as forms of personal rule with strong neopatrimonial features have operated in contexts with weak civic associations, fragmented intercorporate systems, and low levels of institutional development. There have been serious deficiencies in technocratic capabilities, which have been reflected in weak technological capacities and in the persistence of high levels of technological dependence and investment dependence. In all these respects there have been similarities with Indonesia and Thailand, with developmental failures that have precluded advances towards the levels of administrative performance in South Korea and Taiwan.[46]

The consequences of problems of governance, in terms of external dependence, have been distinctive in part because of the smaller scale of Japanese regional involvement. Japan's trade with and direct investment in the area have been at low levels, competing only in minor respects with the USA's extensive involvement. The demonstration effect of Japanese macromanagement has been much weaker than in

East Asia, US corporate involvement has not been significantly challenged by Japanese competition, and the ranges of options for Latin American firms and governments developing external links have accordingly been narrower than those for firms and governments in industrializing East Asia.[47]

REGIONAL COLLECTIVE MANAGEMENT

Structural change in the major areas of deepening integration is continuing mainly because of extensive transnational corporate operations that are expanding with little policy-level guidance, except in the Japanese case. Overall, the autonomy of leading transnational enterprises is being strengthened as they exploit location advantages in numerous host countries. Policy issues arise because of imbalances in the spread of gains from the growth associated with deepening integration, and because the capacities of national administrations to reduce those imbalances, through structure and trade measures, are weakening as transnational corporate activities expand.[48]

Complementarities between government interests in regional economic cooperation and related corporate interests have been evident in the European, North American, Pacific and Latin American contexts. Reductions of administrative barriers to trade and investment flows have been seen to promise higher shared growth as firms gain wider scope for operations in the settings of increased economic openness. The terms on which such openness develops, however, are outcomes of policy-level bargaining processes and of rivalries between firms with differing degrees of competitiveness. The growth and employment effects tend to cause the perspectives of governments to diverge, while indicating requirements for collaborative management of the rising structural links between their economies. Corporate preferences, however, may not favour the development of such management, because of the collective regulatory potential which may result. Over time, corporate regional expansion tends to merge into globalized strategies that are seen to require very independent decision making.

European Union structures for collective management have evolved with slow policy-level learning about the logic of regional market integration and about imperatives for structural policy cooperation to cope with losses in world market shares. Regional corporate groups benefiting from market integration are challenged to implement highly self-reliant strategies for global operations in rivalry with generally stronger US and Japanese firms. The regional intercorporate pattern is fragmented, regionalized civic groups and political party groups are weak, and member governments favour national firms competing within and outside the Union. Intra-Union and extra-Union networks and alliances are formed instrumentally, rather than integratively, on the basis of complementary technological capabilities and market strengths.[49] The German political economy, at the centre of the regional pattern, provides a high degree of leadership at the policy level but can contribute little to the development of effective cross-border aggregating and consensus-forming associations within the Union.

Problems of governance in most of the member countries have hindered effective macromanagement at the national and Union levels, and have been made more difficult by the heavy costs of protecting vulnerable sectors and communities against the effects of intraregional liberalization and deepening integration in the world economy. Because of the mobility of capital the costs have tended to fall more on labour, while intra-Union rivalries have hindered collective adjustment. At the same time the scope for regulatory responses has been limited, at the national and Union levels, because of the advances made towards the formation of the Single Market and the difficulties of forming consensus on a policy for more control over the region's integration into the world economy. Intensified interest representation at the national and Union levels, activated by the growth and employment problems, has meanwhile strained the capacities of governance institutions at each level.[50]

Advanced political development in Germany has had positive significance for the evolution of an effective Union system of collective management, although the policy orientation emphasizes the efficiencies of market forces, signalling expectations of consolidating the dominant position that has been gained in the regional market. Anticipations of further collaboration with France for Union leadership are factors in the German regional policy, and any serious strains in the relationship could provoke currents of German nationalism opposed to increases in policy interdependence within the Union.

Political evolution in France has had less positive significance for the development of the Union system of collective management, mainly because high welfare costs and slack growth in recent years have dramatized the nation's smaller sharing in regional commerce while tending to widen an ideological gap between the conservative and socialist groups. The corresponding political cleavage in Germany is smaller, and remains smaller because of the tradition of cooperation between the country's institutionally more developed major political parties. French policy processes are considerably more conflicted, with effective participation restricted to the higher levels, where the mobilization of general support for major options depends very much on the projection of leadership qualities. France's investment development path and technological trajectory have less positive implications for structural competitiveness than Germany's and, therefore, for the growth of domestic consensus in support of stronger regional collective management.[51]

Political evolution in Britain has taken directions favouring restraint on Union advances to higher levels of economic cooperation. Progress towards such levels has accordingly been difficult for the Union, because of its emphasis on consensus, but the British preference has forced fuller and more persuasive affirmations of integration logic in Union deliberations, notably through European Commission initiatives, including the sponsorship of research studies and of dialogues with major corporate groups. Associated with the British preference, in recent years, have been concerns about the costs and vulnerabilities experienced in the operation of the Single Market and its involvement in global processes of deepening integration. These costs have been similar to those in France, with burdens also falling heavier on labour than on mobile capital, but a liberal tradition has hindered the development of administrative corporate cooperation.[52]

Britain's economic policy processes have been strongly influenced by the representation of financial rather than manufacturing interests: institutions and policies have been less oriented towards the funding of industry than in Germany or France. Britain's exports of manufactures to the European Union lag behind France's but constitute roughly 50 per cent of Britain's worldwide sales and are more than four times greater than those to the USA. Overall British dependence on the Union market is somewhat below the German level and rather more below France's. Within Europe Germany is the main trading partner, receiving exports which have been growing considerably faster than those to the USA, and which are tending to overtake the latter.[53] The structural interdependencies with the Union are tending to become larger as British industrial interests focus more on Europe, and accordingly a policy shift towards association with Germany and France in leadership for more advanced regional integration could be considered advisable.

German cooperation with France in Union leadership is expressed in sustained exchanges, on the basis of technocratic concerns with the operation of the Single Market, which influence Union policy communities. The most important result thus far has been the consensus for establishing a monetary union, to facilitate commerce in the internal market and enforce collective fiscal discipline, while eliminating the foreign exchange risks of separate currencies. The formation of such a union, however, will accelerate a concentration trend, through the displacement of weaker firms, which began with the completion of the internal market. Disparities in the intrazonal spread of gains are thus likely to become more pronounced, notably between the more industrialized northern members and the less industrialized southern members. Meanwhile agglomerations of industrial activity will probably develop at a shrinking number of major centres, unless there is concerted planning.[54]

Interdependent political development is an uneven Union trend. With the evolution of the present system of collective management all members have experienced a regionalization of their policy processes with multilevel effects, but with differences in orientations towards, and capacities for, engagement in the building of stronger regional institutions.

Germany has maintained a high degree of internal system autonomy, combining this with leadership for monetary union and, indirectly, for fiscal cooperation, together with market-oriented rather than structurally-oriented microeconomic cooperation, in effect contributing to foreign direct investment policy competition within the Union. In the rivalry to attract such investment Germany has remained rather apart, with less effective openness than Britain and France, a more self-reliant investment development path, higher structural competitiveness, and more control over deepening integration processes. A higher technological trajectory has been associated with the degree of structural competitiveness. All this has been possible because of greater integration in the national–political economy, facilitating cooperation between manufacturing firms, the financial sector, unions, and the administration, for long-term objectives.[55]

France's more hierarchical and less integrated political economy has experienced less multilevel Europeanization of its policy processes, although with a constructive orientation towards regional macroeconomic policy cooperation, aligned with Germany's. There has been more high-level discretion in responsiveness to the interests of other Union partners, but high-level direction of the political economy has weakened. There has been a major shift away from a tradition of strong central direction of industry, to allow much private sector autonomy. This has happened without the formation of active consultative links with firms, especially because managements have been intent on asserting their freedom, in line with longstanding distrustful and adversarial attitudes to central authority, while administrative traditions have not favoured conversion to consultative methods in relations with managements. The new liberalism has opened the way for a less self-reliant investment development path, which has evolved with a technological trajectory below Germany's. The costs of vulnerabilities in deepening integration have become very high, obligating heavy tax burdens, while slowing growth.[56]

Britain's political economy, with a liberal tradition less open to Europeanization of its policy processes, has evolved with ambivalent participation in the regional drive for monetary union. There has been self-reliant striving for structural competitiveness, but with emphasis on attracting foreign direct investment by offering a very market-friendly environment. The investment development path has become more rather than less dependent, in conditions of structural policy inaction that have reflected a history of distant administrative relationships with a fragmented intercorporate system. The technological trajectory has been at about the same level as that in France. Raising this level by promoting higher investments in new technology is difficult because of the costs and vulnerabilities in deepening integration, which slow growth and give more impetus to capital mobility than in France.[57]

FREE TRADE AREAS

The only system of regional economic integration that to a degree balances the global role of the European Union is the North America Free Trade Area. It has been formed at an elementary level of regional cooperation without commitments to initiate processes of collective management, and its strongly hierarchical configuration, resulting from the dominant position of the United States, has major implications for its evolution. The pattern of advanced political development in the USA largely determines possibilities for policy-level changes in the area. The very extensive scope for corporate autonomy in the USA meanwhile enables its firms to be very active in shaping structural change within Canada and Mexico.

Market integration in North America, as in Europe, has accelerated restructuring. Stronger firms have strengthened their positions at the expense of weaker ones. Adjustment possibilities have been limited because of the fragmentation of intercorporate systems in the USA and Canada, and the more serious fragmentation of the underdeveloped intercorporate system in Mexico. The US investment development path in this regional context has become more asymmetrical, and those of Canada and Mexico have become more dependent, while the US technological trajectory has moved higher relative to those of its two regional partners. Changes in relative bargaining strengths have resulted from these opposed trends and from the disruption of the Mexican economy after its 1994 financial crisis.[58]

US policy has a traditionally strong emphasis on maintaining independence on foreign economic relations, and a high priority current objective is to increase gains from access to western hemisphere markets that will compensate for difficulties in penetrating European and East Asian markets. Entries to those markets are seen to be restricted by the policies of uncooperative governments and firms. US trade with the western hemisphere is roughly balanced, but with Canada and Mexico there are deficits, each about 30 per cent of the US deficit with Japan. The deficits are accounted for partly by US manufacturing in Canada and Mexico for export to the USA, and are offset by the sales of US firms producing in those countries for the host economies.

For Mexico and Canada the regional free trade arrangement provides secure access to the large US market, although with the risks associated with weaker structural competitiveness and inferior bargaining power on issues regarding the evolution of the arrangement. The USA has been in a position to secure side payments.[59] The disparities in bargaining strength are likely to become greater as US firms become more active in the structural changes that have been facilitated by trade liberalization. Yet, despite the absence of commitments to form an arrangement for collaborative decision making, there may well be growing interest, in each member government, in the exploration of ways of coordinating fiscal and monetary policies. This process could begin between Canada and the USA, and could be given some impetus by monetary union in Europe, as European banks will then have excess dollar reserves.

The logic of macroeconomic cooperation could be accepted without recognizing a rationale for regional community formation: preferences for integration mainly through arm's-length free trade could be maintained, especially in the USA, because of confidence that its bargaining strength would be further increased as structural changes continued. The poor record of macromanagement in Mexico will probably strengthen the influence of concerns with comparative advantage in US policy communities. A focus on exploiting these advantages within the North American context has tended to have a strong influence on the perspectives of those communities.[60]

The formation of the North American Free Trade Area has posed several challenges for Mexico's Latin American neighbours. Many of these are involved in subregional market integration schemes of uncertain viability. The largest, with the most significant volume of intrazonal commerce, is Mercosur, in which Brazil, the core member, is associated with Argentina, Uruguay and Paraguay. Intrazonal exports account for about 20 per cent of the group's total commerce. Brazilian policy has shown strong preferences for subregional rather than regional trade liberalization, and has exhibited anxieties about the vulnerabilities which its manufacturing sectors would experience in a free trade arrangement with the USA. Priority is given to developing economic ties with the European Union, as its imports from Brazil are roughly double those from the USA. Brazil's exports to the USA have been stagnating for the past half decade, while those to the rest of the western hemisphere and to Asia have been growing rapidly, and are now about twice those to the United States. Rapid growth in commerce with Argentina has been part of this pattern, and this state's exports to the USA have also been stagnating: they are now below those to Asia, less than half those to Europe, and even less than those to the rest of the western hemisphere, as commerce with these areas has been growing rapidly.[61]

Over time, the incentives for Mercosur countries to fully liberalize intrazonal trade and absorb new members are becoming stronger, as are those to further develop economic ties with Europe and Asia. In the longer term, a stronger Mercosur, with more substantial European and Asian trade connections, could have significant bargaining assets for interactions with the USA on proposals for the expansion of the North America Free Trade Area. In mid-1996, Mercosur reached free trade understandings with Chile and Bolivia which were expected to be followed by agreements with other Latin American countries.

Pacific free trade, to which members of the Asia Pacific Economic Cooperation forum are committed in principle, is a project for which the United States is the principal advocate, but progress towards it would require overcoming problems more difficult than those in the western hemisphere. The principal negotiations would have to be conducted with Japan and industrializing East Asian states. There would be little scope for bilateral dealings like those which are possible in the western hemisphere, and the advantages of favourable asymmetries in bargaining strengths would be much smaller. Free trade with the Chinese regime would have to be deferred until its economy had been much more extensively liberalized, and that would be an uncertain prospect. Freer trade with Japan would be a more important objective, but would be extremely difficult to negotiate, because of the US interest in committing the Japanese administration to a competition policy that would reduce solidarity in that country's industry groups.

The difficulties to be reckoned with by the USA as the leading promoter of Pacific trade liberalization are tending to increase. Japan's trade and production links with industrializing East Asian states are being strengthened, and with them it prefers informal unilateral liberalization measures, in discretionary reciprocation. The increasing importance of Japanese investor confidence for the stability of the American economy, moreover, is also shifting the balance of bargaining strengths in that bilateral relationship. Japan and the industrializing East Asian states could benefit greatly from Pacific trade liberalization, depending on the terms that would result from the regional bargaining. The continuing improvement of Japan's bargaining strengths, however, makes delays advantageous, partly because substantive negotiations on regional trade issues could lead to the formation of a coalition of industrializing East Asian states: the benefits of bilateral dealings with each of them could thus be reduced. In this process, moreover, their political links with the USA might well be strengthened.

Investment competition is more active in the Pacific than in Latin America, shaping investment development paths and technological trajectories. The most dynamic competitors are Japanese firms extending their integrated East Asian production and marketing system and linking it with their activities in North America. Investment competition by US firms is less coordinated, and less guided by long-term planning. Advances in applied technology by the Japanese firms tend to be faster because of their larger allocations for research and development and their greater sharing of innovative achievements within their industry groups. Networks and alliances with American and European firms are being formed, for more discriminating technology sharing and development, but the Japanese corporate presence retains its distinctive identity and its close association with its home government.[62]

A hierarchical pattern of investment interdependence and technological capacities is being formed, with many complex features because of production specializations induced by Japanese strategies in industrializing East Asian states and the limited scope for the development of technological capabilities in those states. American corporate involvement penetrates this pattern, offering alternative sources of support for technological development, but influenced by the modest capabilities of the industrializing East Asian states to absorb new technology. This corporate involvement, although increasing, has been declining relative to that of the Japanese firms. In North America, however, Japanese investment competition, contending with the very large resources of US firms, has to rely more on intercorporate solidarity, as an industry group-specific advantage, and has to manage more equal technological relationships that demand significantly reciprocal sharing. Superior

American basic research capabilities are important factors in those relationships.[63]

US–Japanese technology-based networks and alliances are becoming more significant than such links with European enterprises, because of the technological lag in Europe. The US–Japanese corporate linkages are especially important in high technology sectors, notably computers and communication systems, electrical machinery and propulsion systems. Advances in these sectors by US and Japanese firms tend to increase Europe's technological lag. For the acquisition of resources to support large investments in new technology, however, US firms are tending to become more dependent on their operations in Europe. Links with European firms for research-intensive production, although affected by their technological lags, are important ways of supplementing the benefits of technology cooperation with Japanese enterprises.[64] In the development of technology-based collaborative projects with European firms, moreover, US corporations are advantaged, compared with their Japanese rivals, because of the greater size of their presence in Europe and the cultural affinities which facilitate its expansion.

The triad pattern of investment development paths and technological trajectories, dominated by US firms, is being influenced at the policy level mainly by forms of cooperation between Europe and the USA. These are conducive to relatively balanced structural interdependencies, compared with those in the Pacific, and because of affinities that aid understanding they can become more active. The European interest, however, is in macroeconomic cooperation, in so far as this can contribute to stable demand expansion in the USA, rather than greater trade and investment cooperation, as moderate protection of the internal market can assist exploitation of its potential by Union firms.

TRANSREGIONAL AND GLOBAL COOPERATION

Atlantic macroeconomic cooperation has been mainly restricted to episodes of monetary collaboration between the USA and Germany, with pressures by each government on its central bank for expansionary shifts in domestic monetary policy that were opposed by the Bundesbank and the Federal Reserve. Fiscal policy cooperation has not been politically feasible, and the foreign exchange problems resulting from the import-drawing effects of US fiscal deficits have been engaged through what appear to have been informally coordinated interventions. These have slowed the decline of the dollar and have limited speculative exploitation of its volatility.

With the establishment of a monetary union the European Central Bank will relate to the Federal Reserve in place of the Bundesbank on the basis of Union bargaining strength, but undoubtedly with pressures from member governments for some monetary loosening. Such pressures could well be supplemented by the US administration, but the Union would have become less vulnerable to fluctuations in the dollar's exchange rates, which its Central Bank would probably not be committed to help stabilize. The USA, meanwhile, would have to cope with a general reduction of the dollar's international role, and in particular with a reduced European need for dollar reserves. The US interest in securing informal exchange rate cooperation from the European Central Bank would almost certainly be quite active, but the size of the European monetary policy community would tend to prevent informal coordinated interventions like those which seem to have been possible through rapport between the Federal Reserve and the Bundesbank.[65]

The changes in Atlantic monetary relations would affect monetary cooperation between the USA and Japan. The European Central Bank could be expected to have a strong interest in monetary cooperation with Japan, and the Japanese would be freer to reciprocate, as the USA would be less able to assert its preferences in ways that have been feasible thus far because of the absence of close ties between the German and Japanese administrations. Reduced Japanese monetary cooperation with the USA could thus be in prospect.

For exchange rate stability and price stability, monetary policy cooperation is becoming increasingly necessary between the USA, Germany and Japan, and will become even more necessary when Germany's role is replaced by the European Central Bank. Monetary policy sovereignty, however, is being reduced, especially for the USA, by the vast growth of international financial markets, in which greatly expanded operations by securities firms, outside the reach of monetary policy, have reduced the significance of traditional banking, while drawing banks into those operations through activities outside the scope of central bank controls. The international securities markets function with unresolved regulatory problems which allow much exploitation of their volatility. These problems, however, are less serious for the less liberalized financial markets of Germany and Japan than they are for the more open financial markets.[66]

German, French, and other European concerns about stability in financial markets may cause the European Central Bank to assume or press for supervisory and regulatory functions in order to bring securities firms in the Union under strong control. The effectiveness of the Bank's dealings with the European banking system will be increasingly reduced if the Union's nonbank financial institutions are not subjected to a virtual expansion of central bank authority. In addition to being exercised for a strengthening of supervisory and regulatory functions, this authority may have to be used to engineer drastic change in the Union's securities markets, to ensure greater service of the real economy, with improved risk management, substantially reduced speculation, and much less diversion of investment into such speculation.[67]

For the USA, enhancing the effectiveness of monetary policy for price stability and exchange rate stability is becoming more urgent, because of high levels of exposure to volatility in international financial markets, the destabilizing dangers of large fiscal and trade deficits, and the fragility of the financial sector. Strengthening supervision and regulation of the securities firms is more imperative than it has become in Europe, as there is a more serious danger of a financial crisis. The strong pluralism of the USA's political processes, however, makes the necessary institutional changes very difficult. Altering the structures of the securities markets would be highly desirable, but would be even more difficult than instituting substantially improved supervisory and regulatory functions.[68] Instability in financial markets has posed risks for firms serving foreign markets primarily through exports, but has been a less serious problem for enterprises producing at several foreign locations.[69]

Trade policy cooperation, principally between the USA and the European Union, has been a low-level form of collective management within the World Trade Organization as the global bargaining forum for trade liberalization. As a forum the World Trade Organization operates with institutionalized collaborative assessments of member states' trade policies, and with a disputes settlement mechanism. Deals bargained in conflict with the organization's basic principle of trade liberalization, however – for example, obliging one party to accept export restraints – can be disguised, and can encourage further use of leverage by states with strong bargaining power.

The terms on which trade is liberalized under World Trade Organization auspices are typically set by bargaining processes in which leverage is used to extract concessions on market access. These processes are dominated by the USA and the European Union, as rivals with shared and competing interests. Their leverage is potent, because of the size of their markets and the absence of effective coalitions in the rest of the world, due to Japan's lack of political allies, the political fragmentation of the industrializing and less-developed states, and the weaknesses of ties between the transitional political economies.[70]

The market and structural changes associated with trade liberalization include disruptions of industries exposed to competition by foreign sectors which may not be more efficient but which may have larger resources. While the disruptions may be caused by foreign firms unsupported by their governments, moreover, they may also be caused by such firms acting with diverse forms of aid from their home administrations. The uncertainties to be reckoned with therefore justify caution, especially by states with weaker bargaining strength, but also for others, and all the more so because, *with the vast expansion of transnational production*, disruptive imports may originate in states whose trade policies have been relatively cooperative. The independence with which transnational corporations expand their activities poses increasing uncertainties about the practical effects of trade liberalization arrangements. Guarding against these is of course a reason for care regarding market entry concessions that may be gained through leverage in trade negotiations.

The costs of actual and anticipated vulnerabilities, in contexts of trade liberalization, but experienced increasingly with the rising flows of foreign direct investment, tend to activate compensatory and sheltering measures.[71] The vicious circles associated with the financing of such measures encourage policy-level attention to tasks of enhancing structural competitiveness rather than participating in trade negotiations. For the structural endeavours the uncertainties that have to be reckoned with regarding the strategies of transnational enterprises assume increasing significance, and imperatives to influence, guide, and restrict or counter those strategies, for the benefit of national firms, are likely to become stronger, especially in states coping with weaknesses in bargaining leverage and in structural competitiveness.

Substantial competition policy cooperation would be a highly important international public good, but clearly would be more feasible at the regional rather than the global level. A competition-oriented approach to trade negotiations can be advocated in view of the extent to which markets are being served through transnational production, with high-volume intrafirm trade, with gains for multinational enterprises and more diffuse country-specific benefits.[72] Yet adoption of this approach, requiring nondiscrimination against foreign firms in direct investment policy, would be politically difficult because of the pressures obligating efforts to raise structural competitiveness. There would be some prospect of resolving the difficulty on an intraregional basis if a substantial common structure policy were being implemented, but that has not yet been feasible in the European Union.

Experiences of vulnerabilities in liberalized trade and in openness to foreign direct investment influence policies on the liberalization of trade in services, as the terms on which it may be negotiated have implications for the international marketing of goods and for the operation of transnational production networks. The General Agreement on Trade in Services, negotiated as part of the Uruguay Round, is a soft framework understanding, expressing the preferences of the European Union and several developing countries rather than those of the USA, which had advocated generally binding obligations to liberalize.[73] The differences in preferences across the Atlantic partly reflect European concerns to facilitate the regionalization of Union financial, communication and transportation services, for greater efficiencies in the Single Market, under a common regulatory structure.

BUILDING COMPLEMENTARITIES

Vast problems of systemic development are evident, and they raise urgent questions about managing the interdependencies between governments and firms, between governments, and between firms. The interdependencies that have most significance for the resolution of internationalized market failure problems, and in particular for the provision of international public goods, are those between governments and firms. Constructive engagement with issues in government–corporate relations can have positive significance for the resolution of problems of government failure, in as much as corporate inputs into policy making can be conducive to functional partnering and to responsible fiscal and monetary measures.

Potentials for learning in consultative exchanges between administrations and firms have to be explored, to enhance possibilities for interdependent entrepreneurial discovery and interdependent technocratic discovery. For this purpose the concept of *entrepreneurial discovery*,[74] can be oriented more towards collaborative investment and production decisions, and not simply towards trading activities. This, moreover, can be done with recognition that high levels of coordinated entrepreneurial innovation have to develop through trustful and wide-ranging managerial exchanges, facilitated with technocratic skills developed through multigroup coordination endeavours.

Literature on entrepreneurial innovation has rather neglected its significance regarding high-cost long-term investment outlays and the development of broadly complementary strategies extending beyond those in networks and alliances. The large uncertainties concerning the possibly complementary, diverging, and competitive strategies of other firms, as well as market trends, technology trends, and policy changes, tend to obligate caution, delays, and provision for drastic adjustment if not reversal of likely decisions.[75] Possibilities for collaborative reduction of these uncertainties have received insufficient attention, because of assumptions about the persistence of totally competitive intercorporate relationships. Meanwhile possibilities for structural policy learning have been neglected, partly because of general awareness of motivational problems at the political and bureaucratic levels. These include some identified in economic analyses of what has been seen as self-interested official behaviour, in complex contexts of political contracting, with moral hazards and processes of organizational manipulation.[76]

The literature on consulting services helps to illuminate entrepreneurial discovery problems but indicates that these services typically do not contribute to interactive learning between the managements of different firms or to the exploration of corporate–government learning potentials. Consulting services are provided for individual firms, generally not on a group basis, and rarely on a multigroup basis. The consulting literature, moreover, gives little attention to technocratic learning through exchanges identifying potential compatibilities between entrepreneurial planning and technocratic planning in technology, infrastructure, foreign direct investment, and trade policy areas. Much of the literature has focused on ways of promoting X efficiencies within organizations through normative integration and the encouragement of working-level autonomy, but this has been done with surprisingly little recognition of the efficiencies generated in Japanese firms.[77] Yet it is clearly possible to cultivate dedicated technocratic skills for consultative learning with managements, oriented towards extensive entrepreneurial coordination. Such skills could be considered analogous to the tacit technological skills which develop in firms, and to the entrepreneurial capabilities which managements develop in synergistic partnering with those tacit technological skills.[78]

With deepening integration, entrepreneurial innovation becomes increasingly interdependent, especially in higher technology sectors. It is interdependent not only because of emerging frontier technologies but also because of variously shared potentials which future technologies are likely to help combine; in addition it is interdependent in that investment and production planning by each firm has to take into account whatever is known or conjectured about the planning of many other firms. Surveillance of the broad trends and probabilities within and across sectors can be seen to require a technocratic function, in the public interest and for the benefit of firms, in view of the potential concerting of entrepreneurship with public goods implications.

The logic of technocratic–corporate consultative interaction has a potential application in relations between industrialized states, for the promotion of more balanced complementarities and higher growth. Promoting such complementarities may be possible through techno-cratic collaboration between those states for the sponsorship of conferences with firms. Leadership for endeavours of this kind could be provided by the USA, Germany and Japan. The cooperation could become a *structural complementarities initiative*, focusing not on issues of market access through trade and direct investment but on the constructive task of facilitating integrative entrepreneurial collabor-ation, on the basis of which *structural impediments* would become susceptible to spontaneous adjustment. The rationale for this consulta-tive initiative could be presented in terms of efficiencies generated through concerted entrepreneurship on a multigroup basis, with explicit recognition of the value of the Japanese model of technocratic–corporate partnering.[79]

The consultative partnering could become a 'soft' form of micro collective management, based to a large extent on the functional logic of the Japanese model. The logic of the Japanese model has to be recognized because of the way in which it focuses technocratic expertise on the public good of concerted entrepreneurship in line with sectoral potentials, for high growth, with cooperative competition, in a context of trust and informal accountability. Recognition of this model can help understanding that the public goods issues raised by transnational corporate activities demand government attention, and that if inter-ventionist methods are to be avoided solutions have to be found through the educative processes of consultative interaction.

The feasibility of triad administrative–corporate consultative inter-action demands very careful consideration, but with some understanding that prospects for productive outcomes would depend on very intensive governmental and corporate interactions between Germany and Japan, to ensure communication flows as dense as those between the USA and Japan, and the USA and Germany. The change would have significant implications for American learning at the governmental and corporate levels. It would also have important implications for a transformation of German involvement into European Union participation in the triad conferencing, as a structural policy capability developed with the forma-tion of a more advanced system of collective management in Europe.

The consultations could develop through sequences of high technology conferences attended by representatives of corporate groups and by industry and trade department officials. A focus on high technology sectors would be appropriate because of the diffuse effects of advances in those sectors on mature and low technology industries. The European Commission could play an important role in sponsoring these conferences, because of accumulated expertise gained by many members of its staff in consultations with Union firms and business groups. The Organization for Economic Cooperation and Development could assist in the sponsoring, especially on the basis of its public management research projects, which have studied consultative methods of implementing structural and trade policies.[80] An independent role could be assumed through participation in the technocratic presentations at the conferences, and through assessments of their results that would contribute to their continuing interactions. This involvement could give some impetus to the development of more active links between triad structural policy communities – links which could be expected to multiply through the dynamics of the conferencing.

The principal benefits of the consultative interactions would be patterns of coordinated entrepreneurial activities, conducive to higher and more stable shared growth, with more balanced triad complementarities. Associated with these patterns would be supporting systems of technocratic expertise, operating with intensive cross-border exchanges. Extensive processes of structural change could thus become more orderly, with improved capacities for adjustment to strains. Issues of macroeconomic policy cooperation could then be approached with more confidence, under less pressure for burden sharing, and hopefully with increased goodwill generated through the structural conferencing. Meanwhile the difficulties of regulating international financial markets could be made more manageable, partly through collaborative reductions in the scope for regulatory arbitrage, and partly through inducing extensive corporate cross-holdings that would give more stability to the market-based systems of corporate governance.[81]

NOTES

1. See Suzanne Berger and Ronald Dore (eds), *National Diversity and Global Capitalism* (Ithaca: Cornell University Press, 1996); observations on institutions and policies in Mancur Olson, 'Distinguished lecture on economics in government', *Journal of Economic Perspectives*, **10** (2) Spring 1996: 3–24; and Peter Nunnenkamp, Erich Gundlach and Jamuna P. Argarwal, *Globalisation of Production and Markets* (Tubingen: J.C.B. Mohr, 1994).
2. See Louis W. Pauly and Simon Reich, 'National structures and multinational cor-

porate behavior: enduring differences in the age of globalization', *International Organization*, **51** (1) Winter 1997: 1–30.

3. See *Globalisation of Production and Markets*, John Hagedoorn (ed.), *Technical Change and the World Economy* (Aldershot: Edward Elgar, 1995); and Bruno Dallago, 'Investment, systemic efficiency, and distribution', *Kyklos*, **49** (4) 1996: 615–42.

4. This conclusion extends the logic of cooperation for innovation in Christian De Bresson et al., *Economic Interdependence and Innovative Activity* (Cheltenham: Edward Elgar, 1996).

5. On the dynamics of agency-type democracies see Randall L. Calvert, 'The rational choice theory of social institutions: cooperation, coordination, and communication', in Jeffrey S. Banks and Eric A. Hanushek (eds), *Modern Political Economy* (New York: Cambridge University Press, 1995) 216–68; and Anthony King, 'The vulnerable American politician', *British Journal of Political Science*, **27** (1) January 1997: 1–22.

6. On the problems caused by these groups see Mancur Olson, 'The varieties of Eurosclerosis: the rise and decline of nations since 1982', in Nicholas Crafts and Gianni Toniolo (eds), *Economic Growth in Europe since 1945* (Cambridge University Press, 1996) 73–94.

7. The normative basis for this perspective can be seen in Amartya Sen, 'Moral codes and economic success', in Samual Brittan and Alan Hamlin (eds), *Market Capitalism and Moral Values* (Aldershot: Edward Elgar, 1995) 23–34, and in Rabindra N. Kanungo and Manuel Mendonca, *Ethical Dimensions of Leadership* (Thousand Oaks: SAGE, 1996).

8. See *Governance in Transition: Public Management Reforms Governance in OECD, Countries* (Paris: OECD, 1995).

9. On the fiscal deficits see *Managing Structural Deficit Reduction* (Paris: OECD, 1996, Public Management Occasional Paper 11). On the costs of shelter related to vulnerabilities caused by market penetration, and the burdens for labour rather than for capital, see Dani Rodrik, *Trade, Social Insurance and the Limits to Globalization* (Cambridge: National Bureau of Economic Research Working Paper 5905, January 1997).

10. Deepening integration is altering the context in which employment problems have to be considered, as international corporate restructuring after large acquisitions of world market power is typically followed by staff reductions and shifts of some operations to low-cost areas. Welfare costs associated with the restructuring are factors in the sheltering allocations studied by Rodrik (op. cit., note 9).

11. See Gavin Boyd and Alan M. Rugman (eds), *Euro-Pacific Investment and Trade* (Aldershot: Edward Elgar, 1997).

12. See comments on entrepreneurship in Mark Casson, *Entrepreneurship and Business Culture* (Aldershot: Edward Elgar, 1995) chapter 5.

13. These observations are based on DeBresson (op. cit., note 4), and Peter Howitt (ed.), *The Implications of Knowledge-Based Growth for Micro-Economic Policies* (Calgary: University of Calgary Press, 1996).

14. See DeBresson (op. cit., note 4).

15. See *Economic Growth in Europe since 1945* (op. cit., note 6).

16. See Kees Koedijk and Jeroen Kremers, 'Market opening, regulation and growth in Europe', *Economic Policy*, **23**, October 1996: 445–67.

17. On agglomeration trends see Anthony J. Venables, 'Localization of industry and trade performance', *Oxford Review of Economic Policy*, **12** (3) Autumn 1996: 52–60.

18. See discussion of Japanese corporate governance in W. Carl Kester, 'American and Japanese corporate governance: convergence or best practice?', in *National Diversity and Global Capitalism* (op. cit., note 1), 107–37.

19. On the extraction of concessions by large states in regional contexts see Carlo Perroni and John Whalley, *The New Regionalism: Trade Liberalization or Insurance?* (Cambridge: National Bureau of Economic Research Working Paper 4626, January 1994).

20. See 'US direct investment abroad: detail for historical-cost position and related capital and income flows, 1995', *Survey of Current Business*, **76** (9) September 1996: 98–128.

21. See *Direction of Trade Statistics Yearbook*, 1996 (Washington DC: International Monetary Fund).

22. See *Economic Growth in Europe since 1945* (op. cit., note 6).

23. See Collin Randlesome, *The Business Culture in Germany* (Oxford: Butterworth-Heinemar, 1994) and *OECD Economic Surveys, Germany, 1996* (Paris: OECD).

24. See Stephen J. Silvia, 'German unification and emerging divisions within German employers' associations: cause of catalyst?', *Comparative Politics*, **29** (2) January 1997: 187–208.

25. See 'Foreign direct investment in the United States: detail for historical-cost position and related capital and income flows, 1995', *Survey of Current Business*, **76** (9) September 1996: 69–97.

26. See *The Performance of Foreign Affiliates in OECD Countries* (Paris: OECD, 1994) chapter 2.

27. See symposium on 'The European Union and a changing European order', *Journal of Common Market Studies*, **34** (1) March 1996.

28. See Kester (op. cit., note 18); Masahiko Aoki and Ronald Dore (eds), *The Japanese Firm* (Oxford: Oxford University Press, 1994); and Michael L. Gerlach, *Alliance Capitalism* (Berkeley: University of California Press, 1992).

29. See Walter Hatch and Kozo Yamamura, *Asia in Japan's Embrace* (Cambridge: Cambridge University Press, 1996); and Rob Steven, *Japan and the New World Order* (New York: St Martin's Press, 1996).

30. See Michael G. Plummer, 'US policy coherence and ASEAN economic development', in Kiichiro Fukasaku, Michael Plummer and Joseph Tan (eds), *OECD and ASEAN Economies* (Paris: OECD, 1995) 141–62.

31. See Yasunori Baba and Tokio Suzuki, 'Japan's evolving strategies for science and technology: toward the 21st century', and Shoichi Yamashita, 'Japan's role as a regional technological integrator and the black box phenomenon in the process of technological transfer', in Denis Fred Simon (ed.), *The Emerging Technological Trajectory of the Pacific Rim* (Armonk: M.E. Sharpe, 1995) 275–92 and 338–56; Thomas S. Arrison et al. (eds), *Japan's Growing Technological Capability* (Washington DC: National Academy Press, 1992); and Martin Fransman, 'Is national technology policy obsolete in a globalised world? The Japanese response', *Cambridge Journal of Economics*, **19** (1) February 1995: 95–120.

32. See King (op. cit., note 5); Frederic L. Pryor, *Economic Evolution and Structure: The Impact of Complexity on the US Economic System* (New York: Cambridge University Press) 19; Kester (op. cit., note 18); and *OECD Economic Surveys, United States, 1995–6* (Paris: OECD) pt 4.

33. See Thomas H. Hammond and Jack H. Knott, 'Who controls the bureaucracy? Presidential power, congressional dominance, legal constraints, and bureaucratic autonomy in a model of multi-institutional policy-making', *Journal of Law, Economics, and Organization*, **12** (1) April 1996: 119–66.

34. See Kester (op. cit., note 18).

35. On antitrust policy see *Antitrust and Market Access* (Paris: OECD, 1996) 165–88. The tax advantages of foreign operations are reviewed in Martin Feldstein, James R. Hines and R. Glenn Hubbard (eds), *Taxing Multinational Corporations* (Chicago: University of Chicago Press, 1995).

36. See Anne O. Krueger, *American Trade Policy* (Washington DC: AEI Press, 1995).

37. On the dangers of a financial crisis see Frederic S. Mishkin, 'Preventing financial crises: an international perspective', *Manchester School Papers in Money, Macroeconomics and Finance*, **LXII**, Supplement, 1994: 1–40.

38. See comments on fiscal deficits in *OECD Economic Surveys, United States* (op. cit., note 32) p. 7.

39. See comments in *Kyklos*, **48** (2) 1995 – Special Issue: Is there a European Economics?

40. See Charles Schultze, 'The CEA: an inside voice for mainstream economics', *Journal of Economic Perspectives*, **10** (3) Summer 1996: 23–40; and Martin Feldstein, 'The Council of Economic Advisers and economic advising in the United States', *Economic Journal*, **102** (414) September 1992: 1223–34.

41. The European Commission has some influence on direct investment flows through its implementation of competition policy. See Lee McGowan and Stephen Wilks, 'The first supranational policy in the European Union: competition policy,' *European Journal of Political Research*, **28** (2) September 1995: 141–69. See also *Formal and Informal Investment Barriers in the G7 Countries: The Country Chapters* (Ottawa: Industry Canada, 1994), Occasional Paper 1, vol. 1, Appendix 1.

42. See Akira Kohsaka, 'Interdependence through capital flows in Pacific Asia and the role of Japan', in Takatoshi Ito and Anne O. Krueger (eds), *Financial Deregulation and Integration in East Asia* (Chicago: Chicago University Press, 1996) 107–40; Yamashita (op. cit., note 31); Hatch and Yamamura (op. cit., note 29); and Steven (op. cit., note 29).

43. See Zhou Yuan, 'Reform and restructuring of China's science and technology System', in Simon (op. cit., note 31), 213–38; *China in the 21st Century* (Paris: OECD, 1996) and Brian Hook (ed.), *The Individual and the State in China* (Oxford: Oxford University Press, 1996).

44. See references to central power in Yuan (op. cit., note 43); and *China in the 21st Century* (op. cit., note 43). On the army's role see David Shambaugh in Hook (op. cit., note 43), 104–48.

45. See *OECD Economic Surveys: Mexico, 1997* (Paris: OECD) and references to Mexico in *Economic Survey of Latin America and the Caribbean, 1995–6* (Santiago: UN Economic Commission for Latin America and the Caribbean).

46. On problems of political development in Latin America see Scott Mainwaring and Timothy R. Scully (eds), *Building Democratic Institutions: Party Systems in Latin America* (Stanford: Stanford University Press, 1995).

47. See references to Japanese involvement in Latin America in Steven (op. cit., note 29).

48. The imbalances in high technology trade are reviewed in Paulo Guerrieri and Carlo Milana, 'Changes and trends in world trade in high technology products', *Cambridge Journal of Economics*, **19** (1) February 1995: 225–42.

49. There is a preference for acquisitions rather than alliances: see Neil M. Kay, Harvie Ramsay and Jean-Francois Hennart, 'Industrial collaboration and the European internal market', *Journal of Common Market Studies*, **34** (3) September 1996: 465–76.

50. On the problems in France see Andrea Boltho, 'Has France converged on Germany? Policies and institutions since 1958', in Berger and Dore (op. cit., note 1), 89–106.

51. See Elie Cohen 'France: national champions in search of a mission', in Jack Hayward (ed.), *Industrial Enterprise and European Integration* (Oxford: Oxford University Press, 1995) 23–47.

52. See Stephen Woolcock, 'Competition among forms of corporate governance in the European Community: the case of Britain', in Berger and Dore (op. cit., note 1), 179–96.

53. See *Direction of Trade Satistics Yearbook* (op. cit., note 21).

54. See Venables (op. cit., note 17).

55. See Randlesome (op. cit., note 23), and Josef Esser, 'Germany: challenges to the old policy style', in Hayward (op. cit., note 51), 48–75.

56. See *OECD Economic Surveys: France, 1994* (Paris: OECD).

57. See David Coates (ed.), *Industrial Policy in Britain* (London: Macmillan, 1996).

58. On investment development paths see John H. Dunning and Rajneesh Narula (eds), *Foreign Direct Investment and Governments* (London: Routledge, 1996) chapters 1 and 3. On Mexico see *OECD Survey* (op. cit., note 45), and on Canada see *OECD Economic Survey 1995* and *1996*.

59. See Perroni and Whalley (op. cit., note 19).

60. See Graciela Chichilnisky, 'Strategies for trade liberalization in the Americas', in

Trade Liberalization in the Western Hemisphere (Washington DC: InterAmerican Development Bank and Economic Commission for Latin America and the Caribbean, 1995) 165–88; and Patricia Gray Rich, 'Latin America and present US Trade policy', *The World Economy*, **20** (1) January 1997; 87–102.

61. See *Direction of Trade Statistics Yearbook* (op. cit., note 21).
62. See Kohsaka (op. cit., note 42), and Hatch and Yamamura (op. cit., note 29).
63. See Jean L. Johnson, John B. Cullen, Tomoaki Sakano and Hideyuki Takenouchi, 'Setting the stage for trust and strategic interaction in Japanese–US cooperative alliances,' *Journal of International Business Studies*, **27** (5) Special Issue, 1996: 981–1004; and *Japan's Growing Technological Capability* (op. cit., note 31).
64. See Guerrieri and Milana (op. cit., note 48).
65. See C. Randall Henning, 'Europe's monetary union and the United States', *Foreign Policy*, **102**, Spring 1996: 83–104.
66. See Alexandre Lamfalussy, 'Central Banking in Transition', in Forrest Capie, Charles Goodhart, Stanley Fischer and Norbert Schnadt (eds), *The Future of Central Banking* (Cambridge: Cambridge University Press, 1994) 330–341; and Tommaso Padoa Schioppa, 'Adapting central banking to a changing environment', in Tomas J.T. Balino and Carlo Cottarelli (eds), *Frameworks for Monetary Stability: Policy Issue and Country Experiences* (Washington DC: International Monetary Fund, 1994) 529–55.
67. On the policy problems for all industrialized states see Philip G. Cerny, 'International finance and the erosion of state policy capacity', in Philip Gummett (ed.), *Globalization and Public Policy* (Cheltenham: Edward Elgar, 1996) 83–104; and *Policy Sciences*, **27** (4) 1994 – symposium on international capital mobility. See also Geoffrey R.D. Underhill, 'Keeping governments out of politics: transnational securities markets, regulatory cooperation and political legitimacy', *Review of International Studies*, **21** (3) July 1995: 251–78 – especially references to Europe.
68. See *Journal of Law, Economics and Organization*, **6**, Special Issue, 1990 – symposium on US institutions; and Ronald C. Moe, 'Traditional organizational principles and the managerial presidency: from phoenix to ashes', *Public Administration Review*, **50** (2) March/April 1990: 129–40.
69. See comments about large international firms in Underhill (op. cit., note 67).
70. For assessments of the World Trade Organization see Bernard Hoekman and Michel Kostecki, *The Political Economy of the World Trading System* (New York: Oxford University Press, 1995); and John H. Jackson, 'The World Trade Organization: watershed innovation or cautious small step forward?', *The World Economy – Global Trade Policy 1995* (Special Issue). See also David Henderson, 'The world trading system', in John Llewellyn and Stephen J. Potter (eds), *Economic Policies for the 1990s* (Oxford: Blackwell, 1991) 293–324.
71. See Americo Beviglia Zampetti and Pierre Sauve, 'Onwards to Singapore: the international contestability of markets and the new trade agenda', *The World Economy*, **19** (3) May 1996: 333–44.
72. See Rodrik (op. cit., note 9).
73. See Bernard Hoekman, 'General Agreement on Trade in Services', in *The New World Trading System: Readings* (Paris: OECD, 1994) 177–88.
74. See Israel M. Kirzner, 'Entrepreneurial discovery and the competitive market process: an Austrian approach', *Journal of Economic Literature*, **35** (1) March 1997: 60–85.
75. On the influence of uncertainties on direct investment decisions see Pietra Rivoli and Eugene Salorio, 'Foreign direct investment and investment under uncertainty', *Journal of International Business Studies*, **27** (2) 2nd Quarter 1996: 335–58.
76. On problems of structural policy learning in the USA see Roger G. Noll, 'Structural policies in the United States,' in Samuel Kernell (ed.), *Parallel Politics: Economic Policymaking in the United States and Japan* (Washington DC: Brookings Institution, 1991) 230–80.
77. See Harry Scarbrough (ed.), *The Management of Expertise* (New York: St Martin's Press, 1996).

78. See DeBresson (op. cit., note 4).
79. See Gerlach (op. cit., note 28).
80. See *Building Policy Coherence: Tools and Tensions* (Paris: OECD, 1996, Occasional Paper 12).
81. See rationale for shifting to a system fostering long-term high-trust relations in Andrew P. Dickerson, Heather D. Gibson and Euclid Tsakalotos, 'Short termism and underinvestment: the influence of financial systems', *Manchester School Papers in Money, Macroeconomics and Finance*, **63** (4) December 1995: 351–67.

Index